Best Left as Indians

W9-AAF-853

McGill-Queen's Studies in Ethnic History
Donald Harman Akenson, Editor

Best Left as Indians

Native-White Relations in the Yukon Territory, 1840–1973

KEN S. COATES

McGill-Queen's University Press
Montreal & Kingston • London • Buffalo

© McGill-Queen's University Press 1991
ISBN 0-7735-0780-9 (cloth)
ISBN 0-7735-1100-8 (paper)

Legal deposit fourth quarter 1991
Bibliothèque nationale du Québec

First paperback edition 1993

Printed in Canada on acid-free paper

This book has been published
with the help of a grant from
the Social Science Federation of Canada,
using funds provided by
the Social Sciences and Humanities
Research Council of Canada.

Canadian Cataloguing in Publication Data

Coates, Kenneth, 1956–
  Best Left as Indians: native-white relations in the
  Yukon Territory, 1840–1973

  (McGill-Queen's studies in ethnic history; 11)
  Includes bibliographical references and an index.
  ISBN 0-7735-0780-9 (bound)
  ISBN 0-7735-1100-8 (pbk.)

  1. Indians of North America – Yukon Territory –
  History. 2. Yukon Territory – Race Relations.
  I. Title. II. Series.

  E78.Y8C63 1991   971.9'100497   C91-090376-X

Typeset in Palatino 10/12 by Caractéra inc.,
Quebec City.

To Cathy, with love

Contents

Tables

Acknowledgments

No academic works alone. The book that finally emerges from the word-processor inevitably owes a tremendous debt to a complex network of librarians, archivists, colleagues, friends, anonymous reviewers, editors, and family members. The present study is no exception; if anything, I think I owe far greater debts, intellectual and personal, than is the norm.

This book is much changed from the PHD thesis accepted by the University of British Columbia in 1984. That I have had the opportunity to expand and improve on the original work is because of the generosity of Brandon University and, particularly, the University of Victoria. A leave fellowship provided by the Social Sciences and Humanities Research Council of Canada provided the time necessary to pull the final threads together. All of this support is greatly appreciated.

At a much earlier time, I was blessed with excellent teachers and advisors. Dr David Breen, Department of History, University of British Columbia, supervised my doctoral research. His assistance and guidance were exemplary; a student could not have hoped for a better combination of encouragement, professional insight, and editorial advice. Other members of the UBC faculty, especially Dr Allan Tully, Dr Robert McDonald, and Dr A.J. Ray, made numerous contributions to my work. I owe a particular debt to Dr Doug Sprague, Department of History, University of Manitoba, whose methodological innovation and passion for history provided a vital spark to my professional career.

I have been aided, in ways too numerous to count, by many archivists and librarians. Helpful staff of the National Archives of Canada (particularly the northernists on staff, Terry Cook and Doug Whyte), the Manitoba Provincial Archives, the Hudson's Bay Company Archives, UBC Special Collections (especially George Brandak, a great friend of historians and researchers), and the General Synod Archives of the Anglican Church of Canada cheerfully guided me through complex finding aids and massive collections. I must extend special thanks to the staff at the Yukon Archives, a remarkable research facility operating under the direction of M. McTiernan. The staff at this fine institution have been unfailingly helpful and have dealt with many demands – some of them unreasonable – on their time and expertise; the archives is a cultural hearth for northern studies and deserves great recognition for its contribution to the north.

I have also benefited over the years from the wonderful community of scholars working in northern studies. My good friend and writing partner, Dr Bill Morrison, has listened to more tirades and sermons on aspects of northern history than any normal person would tolerate; my work over the past seven years has benefited enormously from his friendship, encouragement, and ability to spell. Conversations, typically at conference gatherings, with such excellent and helpful scholars as Dr Claus Naske, Dr Tom Morehouse, Dr Julie Cruikshank, Shelagh Grant, and Aron Senkpiel, dean of arts and science at Yukon College, have provided much inspiration and insight, and I am thankful for their willingness to share their ideas.

Five years ago, in the summer of 1986, I accepted a job with the Department of History at the University of Victoria. Moving from Brandon University, I assumed that my appointment to a larger university would carry certain professional benefits. I did not then have any more than an inkling of what I would gain from the change of venue. My colleagues at the University of Victoria have created a truly remarkable scholastic atmosphere, one that may be without parallel in Canada. The department is marked by a uniform commitment to research and teaching, and an atmosphere of collegiality that we all value very highly. I have benefited, particularly, from the professional advice and friendship of Drs Peter Baskerville, Eric Sager, Ian McPherson, and Tom Saunders, whose gentle chiding and constant encouragement have contributed significantly to my development as an historian. Many thanks also to June Bull for typing the manuscript.

McGill-Queen's University Press has also treated me with particular kindness. I shall always remember the first time I met Dr Don Akenson. He was visiting the University of Victoria as a Lansdowne lecturer and, taking his assigned role very seriously, met with several of the junior faculty to discuss our future publishing plans. His initial gentle encouragement was followed a few days later by a short but blunt letter. The message, in what may be typical Akenson style, was short and to the point. Arguing (correctly by the way) that I was spending too much time on "popular" writing, he gently advised me that I was, to put his words in a somewhat more polite fashion, wasting my career on transitory pursuits. It was a rude, but necessary, awakening for a fairly young academic, and one I have greatly appreciated. That this work is finally seeing the light of day owes a great deal to Dr Akenson's willingness to risk insulting me (he did not) in the interests of getting me on track. I hope that this book justifies the faith that he expressed in me several years ago.

This is the second book of mine that Dr Curtis Fahey has handled as editor, and I remain most impressed with the sharpness of his editorial eye and his dedication to his task. What you are reading is a great deal different from the manuscript I initially submitted. It is, I can assure you, much better. That this is so is owing largely to Curtis Fahey's dedication and fine historical sense; his skills as an editor are perfectly complemented by his academic abilities. For all the help he gave me, I am very grateful.

Finally, that this book has been completed at all is the result of the persistence and loyalty of my wife, Cathy Coates. She has provided a stimulating home environment for me and our three children, Bradley, Mark, and Laura, and has tolerated my preoccupation with the Canadian north and Native issues with greater compassion and good humour than I have a right to expect. The debt goes deeper than this. It was at her urging that I turned my attention to the redrafting necessary to transform a thesis into a book. It is because of her support and encouragement that I found the time and the energy to complete the work. Cathy has been my source of inspiration for many years; I trust that this book repays, in a modest way, the dedication and love that has sustained me throughout my academic career.

Preface

The Yukon Territory has an unusual place in the North American historical consciousness. The region is the site of the Klondike gold rush, one of the few events in Canadian history that is known around the world. It also sits astride the route of that massive exercise in Canadian-American relations, the Alaska Highway, and, in recent years, has been the focal point for intense debates over controversial pipeline proposals, constitutional reforms, and Native land claims. Because of all of this, the territory and its residents have, from time to time, captured the southern public's attention and imagination. The Yukon has not, however, been able to escape from the limitations of an episodic history. The drama of a few spectacular events, particularly the Klondike gold rush, has come to symbolize the region's entire past and, through the government's careful cultivation of the tourist trade, has provided a foundation for the Yukon's present.

Although the images projected by the gold rush, the building of the Alaska Highway, and the dramatic politicization of Canada's Native people are attractive, they obscure the underlying continuity of the territory's historical experience between 1840 and 1990 – the time from the arrival of European fur traders to the present. Beginning in the 1840s, when the first Europeans arrived, Natives and non-Natives have co-existed, not always easily, in the Yukon River basin. Territorial society rested on the sporadic exploitation of abundant resources,[1] and suffered from the consequent dislocations of a boom-and-bust economy.[2]

The Native population has been the principal constant in Yukon history. Prospectors entered the region by the thousands, but most left soon after, their pockets bare. Many whites who identified themselves as "Yukoners," or carried the proud appellation "Sourdough,"[3] actually passed much of the year in the south, working the river boats or the gold dredges during the summer months but leaving for warmer climes before winter set in.[4] Even the government – the federal parent of the colonial territorial child – was not a constant element in the north's history. The official presence was one of sudden growth and decline, notable throughout for the government's pessimistic assessment of the prospects for sustainable economic development.[5] While miners, missionaries, and government officials arrived and departed with alarming rapidity, the Indians remained behind, almost the only permanent inhabitants. Although they felt the disruptions and shared some of the opportunities attending the Klondike gold rush and subsequent booms, the Natives retained their attachment to both the region and a hunting-gathering way of life.

A study of Indian contact with the ever-changing Euro-Canadian presence provides a useful means of charting the broad transformations of northern society. What emerges is a clear portrait of the persistence of the non-Natives' racial (and often racist) attitudes, the fluctuating official and southern perceptions of the north, the continued viability of the fur trade, the existence of distinct economic sectors within the regional order, and the comparative stability of Native society. The Yukon example also provides a starting-point for an examination of historic patterns of Native-white interaction in the middle north – that enormous band of land between the agricultural lands of the south and the tundra plains of the north. There has been surprisingly little study of this important region and theme. The tiny corps of northern historians tends not to have adopted the regional focus that now dominates much of Canadian scholarship, opting instead for an Ottawa-based perspective on the region.[6] Similarly, few historians have systematically examined the process of Native-white contact in the region, particularly for the period after 1870.[7] The interests of northern Canadian historians lie elsewhere, primarily with the agents of southern Canada involved in the lengthy process of opening the Canadian north.[8]

Some scholars have made preliminary moves away from the nineteenth century and have begun to trace aspects of Native-white contact in the twentieth century. Charles Bishop's ethnographic *The Northern Ojibway and the Fur Trade*, A.J. Ray's recent work on the post-1870 Hudson's Bay Company (HBC) and Hugh Brody's *Maps and Dreams* provide provocative analyses of economic and social relations under the changing pressures of the post-Confederation period.[9] In the main, however, historians continue to avoid the twentieth century and the middle north in favour of topics concerning earlier eras or southern locales.[10] There is thus a strong need for historical studies of all chronological periods and the various regions of Canada. As

Bruce Trigger argues: "I am convinced that it is worthwhile to trace the history of specific native groups from pre-historic times to the present. Such studies are not only interesting as ends in themselves to native and Euro-Canadian readers, but also provide building blocks from which a detailed picture of native history can be constructed on a national and continental scale."[11]

Anthropologists and ethnographers are at the forefront in providing these "building blocks" in the Canadian north. Many of the Native groups, areas and periods that historians have largely ignored have been studied intensively by scholars from these disciplines. In the 1930s ethnographers, anthropologists, and archaeologists began undertaking numerous studies of the aboriginal inhabitants of the upper Yukon River valley. Cornelius Osgood, Anne Acheson Welsh, Catherine McClellan, John Honigman, Dominique Legros, Julie Cruikshank, and others have drawn on field study, Native oral tradition, and limited documentary research to create sensitive and sensible portraits of indigenous cultures in the Yukon.[12] Yet, although often exemplary works within their disciplines, anthropological and ethnographic studies focus primarily on questions of Native culture and society, offering little systematic analysis of Native-white contact. The Yukon Natives have, therefore, been studied intensively, but narrowly. This work serves as an important foundation for an historical investigation of post-contact developments. The transference of concepts across various disciplines is not easy, however, despite the impressive efforts made by ethnohistorians to bridge the intellectual barriers.[13]

Historians have long had difficulty merging the insights of their methodology and discipline with those of anthropology and ethnography. For scholars working on the middle north, the limited contact between the disciplines is due, at least in part, to a different sense of change over time. Much of the anthropological and ethnographic work on this region, including the encyclopaedic compendium of recent research in the *Handbook of North American Indians*,[14] adopts an ahistorical framework. The period of contact in the north is broken between "contact-stable," covering the fur-trade period, and "post-1945 government intervention." This view of a stable fur-trade economy over two centuries ignores the reorganization of the industry following the termination of the HBC's monopoly, subsequent competition for Indian trade, changes in Native technology, and the emergence of a twentieth-century fur trade that was significantly different from its nineteenth-century predecessor. It also obscures the impact of northern adventurers, scientists, prospectors, missionaries, and government agents, all active throughout the middle north long before 1945. For the Yukon Territory, the disruptions caused by the Klondike gold rush and the building of the Alaska Highway negate any description of the region as culturally or economically stable.

A recent study by J.C. Yerbury suggests that anthropological interpretations of the pre-contact state of Native society – the foundation upon which the discipline has built descriptions of subsequent Native society – may be seriously flawed by an unwillingness to examine properly the historical record. In criticizing the "illusion of cultural-historical continuity," Yerbury offers a challenge to those who argue for social and cultural stability through the pre-1945 period.[15] On a more general level, Charles Bishop and A.J. Ray have offered a different chronology of the contact period for the central sub-Arctic, one more properly reflective of the changing pattern of social relationships in that region.[16] While the Bishop-Ray chronology does not fit the historic experience of the Yukon Territory, their implicit contention that a more evolutionary sense of history should inform the investigation of Native-non-Native contact does.

There are other difficulties – disciplinary bias, reliance on different forms of evidence,[17] the comparative role of theory in the two fields of study – that have led historians and anthropologists down separate paths. This divergence is unfortunate because, as the work of ethnohistorians in other regions has demonstrated, the melding of disciplinary perspectives can be most rewarding. But the ethnohistorian is a particular breed, comfortable in the formalism of historical methodology and the theory of anthropology. Most historians, the present author included, place themselves more squarely in the historical tradition, examining questions left vulnerable to the written record (albeit broadly defined to encompass the full range of documentary and quantifiable materials).

Robin Fisher's introductory comments to his path-breaking study of Indian-European relations in British Columbia are worth considering in some detail:

One of my purposes is to establish the role of the Indians in the history of British Columbia, but this volume is not an Indian history. It is a history of the contact of two cultures, of Indian-European relations. Though some historians have tried to put the Indian at 'the centre of his own history,' they have generally proceeded to write descriptions of Indian and European relations. Since the historian relies largely on written, and therefore European, sources, which inevitably impose limits on his appreciation of the Indian side of the story, it is perhaps more valid to deal with Indian-European relations rather than with so-called Indian history. These sources obviously contain distortions resulting from ignorance and prejudice, but they still reveal much about what the Indians were doing and, sometimes, about what they were thinking.[18]

   While Fisher's main point is accepted – historians should stick to what they are trained to do – more recent work has convincingly illustrated the need for a more thorough understanding of the nature of Indian society. Wilcomb Washburn argued that ethnohistory allowed scholars to view Indians "in the round," as complete figures instead of the one-dimensional stereotypes often described in the European documents.[19] Calvin Martin summarized his defence of ethnohistory: "Ethnohistory offers a belated means of resolving the dilemma of the bifurcated Indian – the Indian of anthropology and the Indian of history. In reconciling the two we are presented with an individual who makes sense in his own social and cultural context, operating on a different epistemological and phenomenological track from that of the white man. Ethnohistorians have crossed the frontier, theoretically and figuratively, to confront the Indian who confronted us – this time on *his* terms."[20]

   The point is simple, but essential. There are numerous areas of Native life and culture, including spirituality, social organization, and attitudes toward the environment, that seldom appear in the written record. These aspects can be ignored, in full recognition of their importance and the limitations of historical methodology to address them, and the historian can turn to the more traditional topics of government policy, educational initiatives, and white images of the Indians. But many ethnohistorians and social historians of Native-white relations are drawn to the very topics ignored in conventional historical accounts, such as the impact of Christianity on Native spirituality or Native responses to the economic opportunities of the fur trade. None of these topics can be examined solely through traditional historical sources.[21]

   The choice is between ignoring the issues, relying on a sparse documentary record, or enhancing one's sense of the historic experience available from written sources through anthropological and ethnographic reconstructions of contact cultures.[22] The latter route has been taken here. This work is not an exercise in ethnohistory. It is rather a study primarily of Native-white relations, with an emphasis on the non-Native forces at work in the Yukon Territory. No attempt will be made, as Colin Yerbury and Kerry Abel have recently done, to use historical methodology to assess the ramifications of European expansion on Native social organization and internal mechanisms of control. The questions I address relate to points of contact between an advancing European culture and an indigenous population. The Natives encountered must, however, be placed within the context of their culture and with full recognition of the fact that their values and attitudes shaped the contact experience. Implicit, also, is the argument that Native people were not passive in the face of a non-Native onslaught. Instead, they were (and are) capable of recognizing their self-interest and responding to many of the forces of change.[23]

The manner in which scholars approach the study of Native-non-Native relations is conditioned, perhaps only subconsciously, by the image they hold of the contact cultures. Traditionally, the ethnocentricism of non-Native scholars led to a deprecation of indigenous cultures and an overly impressive portrait of European participants.[24] More recent scholarship, much of it instigated by Marshall Sahlins's seminal *Stone Age Economics*,[25] points to the considerable achievements of harvesting peoples; indeed, Sahlins himself described them as "the original affluent society." Within the context of their own cultures and the constraints of their expectations, Sahlins argued, harvesters satisfied their biological and material needs. To the Natives, the flexibility, leisure, and mobility afforded by reliance on natural resources served as an agreeable focus for economic and social behaviour. Europeans, conversely, viewed this manner of living with disdain, considering it inferior in all aspects to the systematic work habits of the early industrial age. Although contemporary and scholarly observers for many years deemed aboriginal methods impractical – allowing for nothing more than subsistence and survival – the Natives clearly favoured the harvesting way of life.[26]

Much of what constituted the Native lifestyle flowed from their commitment to a harvesting existence. Their relationship to their physical world, in which the environment was viewed as a partner in life rather than a threat,[27] conditioned both social organization and aboriginal belief systems. The availability of natural resources set population limits, determined habitation patterns, and influenced social structures.[28] The ability of an aboriginal population to hunt, trap, and fish in the post-contact period – to continue the economic pursuits which gave coherence to their pre-contact culture – is therefore a central concern in assessing the extent of, and motivation for, Native adaptation to an encroaching European society. As the experience of the Indians of the Yukon and the Natives of northeastern British Columbia, described by Hugh Brody, demonstrates, this environmental accommodation is not an "aboriginal artifact" but rather a positive, ongoing adaptation to economic realities.[29]

The Indians' commitment to a harvesting way of life did not blind them to the many advantages of European culture. The Natives easily

accepted technological innovations, from the metal axe to the out-
board motor. Once gained, these tools were not readily surrendered.
The acquisition of such material possessions required a reconciliation
to the capitalist market-place of the fur traders, miners, and developers, and therefore entailed certain costs. Considerable tension
existed between the cultural attraction of a harvesting existence and
the material needs which necessitated involvement in a foreign economic order. Michael Asch has argued that the Mackenzie valley
Indians created a "mixed economy" in response to these tensions.
Although the Natives continued, by preference, as hunters, they also
participated in the white-dominated economy – from the fur trade
to hard-rock mining – in order to satisfy new material needs.[30] The
situation in the Yukon seemingly fits Asch's description. The Yukon
Indians did not remain solely as hunters and gatherers, nor did they
simply meld into the advancing Canadian economic frontier.

There are several plausible explanations for this behaviour. The
Indians may have been reacting as economic conditions dictated.
Combining harvesting and participation in the transportation and
mining sector may have been the only possible response for people
permanently resident in the economically vulnerable territory. At the
same time, there seems to have been a strong element of cultural
preference. It appears that the Natives preferred the flexibility and
mobility inherent in a hunting and gathering existence over the rigidity of the industrial work place. The third alternative, equally plausible, is that non-Native workers and employers made little room for
Native people in the industrial work place. The Natives' continued
participation in the harvesting economy – both for subsistence and
commerce – reflected their accommodation to an externally imposed
order and their willingness to perpetuate a favoured way of life.

Considerations rooted in an acceptance of anthropological descriptions of pre-contact Indian cultures provide a foundation for assessments of subsequent Native activities in the Yukon, but since this is
not solely a study of Indian history, it is also important to consider
the background of the advancing European culture. The white population approached the north within a framework etched by contemporary perceptions of the land and the indigenous population. The
fur traders arrived in the upper Yukon River basin in the 1840s, long
after the fur trade to the southeast had set standards of economic
and social conduct. Gold miners first entered the region in the 1870s,
carrying with them a very different outlook on resources and aboriginal people. By the 1890s the full assortment of frontier types was
present – fur traders, missionaries, government agents, prospectors,
miners, developers, and settlers. They were drawn north by the

promise of wealth, either in the form of untouched fur reserves or promising mineral deposits. Few, however, viewed the Yukon River valley as a permanent home. They carried the standard southern assessment of the far north as a cruel, forbidding land, and of its inhabitants as primitive and living on the margins of bare subsistence.[31] Only a handful saw beyond the stereotypes that conditioned much of the non-Native reaction to the people and the land.

Transients dominated non-Native society in the Yukon, limiting the prospect for extended personal contact between the races, and ensuring that stereotypic images would dominate Native-white relations. The pursuit of money dominated white frontier societies, particularly those, like the Yukon, that can be characterized as sojourner, or transient, societies.[32] The preoccupation with quick returns provided the psychological foundation for a boom-and-bust economy, and for a lack of concern with the environment and the aboriginal inhabitants. Most whites came north determined to leave soon and rich. An overwhelming majority achieved the first goal; only a few accomplished the second. The capitalistic and acquisitive values held by these northern migrants, their short-term interest in the region, and their unease about, if not fear of, the environment went a long way toward determining their response to the indigenous population.

Tremendous cultural and intellectual space existed between aboriginal and white concepts of economic behaviour, social control, and religion. The meeting of the races was, first and foremost, a confrontation of cultures and world views, often incompatible, seldom mutually understood. Natives and whites often came to the same conclusions – they agreed, for example, on the need to keep the Indians as harvesters of game – but they did so for very different reasons. Contact between the races in North America has been marked by fundamental misunderstanding, mutual or one-sided, unintentional or malevolent. The case of the Yukon Territory is no different.

Best Left as Indians

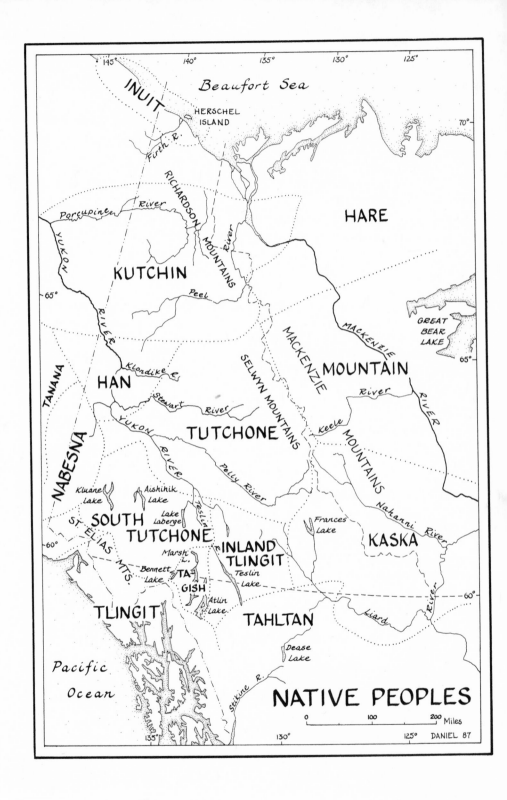

NATIVE PEOPLES

DANIEL 87

Introduction:
The Background

The ancestors of the Natives of the Yukon River basin reached North America across the Bering Strait land bridge, a fact long recognized by the Natives but only recently by scholars.[1] One government official, visiting the Copper (Tanana) Indians near Kluane Lake in 1908, said: "They have a tradition that they came from a distant country lying to the North. Their idea is that the Tribe migrated from Northern Asia, walking over. Many of their ordinary words such as those for fire and water are the same as in the dialects of Northern China."[2] Scholars eventually reached much the same conclusion, but remain divided about the timing of this migration; some archaeologists claim that early sites indicate habitation dating some 27,000 years BC. The general consensus is that the Yukon basin was first occupied around 11,000 years BC.[3] Between that time and the arrival of the HBC fur traders in the 1840s, the Natives occupied and utilized the ecologically diverse region now called the Yukon. Through the millennia, they adapted to the local environment, and divided into separate, but similar, cultures. This evolution, cut off from the technological and cultural transformation of Europe and other continents, created the aboriginal societies extant when the fur traders arrived to place the Yukon basin on the maps of the world.

Native societies represented a sophisticated and comprehensive adaptation to the regional environment. Non-Natives would later describe the northwest in simplistic images, pointing to the apparent barrenness and harsh climate of the region as impediments to "civilization." They misunderstood the richness and complexity of the Yukon basin, whose ecological zones became home to distinct Native cultures. The current Yukon Territory, given institutional form in 1898, is dominated by a large central plateau, flanked on the east by the Mackenzie mountains and on the southwest by the formidable

St Elias range. It is carved by rivers, principally those of the Yukon River network. The Yukon and its tributaries – the Porcupine, White, Stewart, Pelly, and Teslin – drain much of the region. Several areas fall outside the central river system. In the southeast, the Frances River watershed is part of the massive Mackenzie River drainage basin; to the extreme southwest, the Alsek River flows directly into the Pacific Ocean. The Peel River bisects the territory in the north, draining to the east and joining the Mackenzie River shortly before the latter empties into the Arctic Ocean. These waterways are frozen much of the year, a reflection of the winter grip of a sub-Arctic climate that has only seventy frost-free days annually. Much of the Yukon is heavily forested, although the temperature and limited precipitation stunts tree growth. Animal life is diverse and relatively abundant, with moose, caribou, mountain sheep, goat, bear, and a variety of fur-bearers to be found. There are annual salmon runs along the Yukon and Alsek rivers, and whitefish, grayling, lake trout, and several other species of fish inhabit the Yukon's many rivers and lakes. The Yukon does not contain an inexhaustible bounty of harvestable resources, but neither is it the barren wasteland that many early non-Native visitors described.[4]

It is still difficult to portray the nature of Native life in the Yukon River valley before the arrival of the HBC. Few adequate or insightful contemporary commentaries are available. Although they were intimately involved with the Natives, fur traders and missionaries seldom recorded details of Native society and customs. Fur traders A.H. Murray, Strachan Jones, and William Hardisty and missionaries W.W. Kirkby, V.C. Sim, and T.H. Canham provided comparatively useful portraits, but all focused on the Porcupine River-Fort Youcon area.[5] Subsequent descriptions by explorers, travellers, miners, and police officers belong to a separate period – that of the pre-Klondike mining era – and are of less use in assessing aboriginal life in the mid-nineteenth century.

Ethnographic and anthropological reconstruction provide additional tools for defining the contours of Native society. Cornelius Osgood, who worked among the Han and Kutchin in the 1930s, and John Honigman, who studied the Kaska in the following decade, offer detailed summaries based on extensive interviews with Natives. More recently, Catherine McClellan, Julie Cruikshank, Anne Acheson Welsh, Dominique Legros, and others have reconstructed patterns of Native existence and thought before the arrival of Europeans. In conjunction with more general literature on Athapaskan societies, their works allow for a preliminary description of Native society.[6]

Six principal Native groups – the Kutchin, Han, Kaska, Tagish, Tutchone (North and South), and Teslin (or Inland Tlingit) inhabited what is now the Yukon Territory. With the exception of the last group, tied linguistically and culturally to the coastal Tlingit, all were Athapaskans. The Yukon Natives, as a result, conformed in many ways to the larger cultural patterns of the hunters of the sub-Arctic forest. The Natives did not, of course, inhabit areas that fit the artificially imposed boundaries of the Yukon Territory. Kutchin bands, for example, ranged from the lower Mackenzie River to east-central Alaska. Similarly, the Han Indians straddled the 141st meridian (eventually to become the Canada/Alaska border) along the Yukon River. Moreover, ethnographic divisions, which have important linguistic, cultural, and social dimensions, were not formalized through political organization or tribal consciousness. The anthropologist James VanStone suggests that the Athapaskan cultures represented "a cultural continuum carried on by a series of interlocking groups whose individual lifeways differed only in minor details from those of their most immediate neighbours."[7] Those "minor" differences were important, however, for they typically reflected cultural adaptation to specific regional environmental conditions. Although there is sociocultural justification for describing Yukon Natives as a single unit, such a definition must be qualified with an understanding of the importance of regional variation.

VanStone describes the Yukon basin Athapaskans as following a central-based wandering pattern. Cultural groups gathered on a regular basis, usually during the spring or summer fishery. When harvesting ended and when demand for food exceeded the local supply, the Natives dispersed into smaller units, usually extended family groups. The region's limited resources forced continued mobility through much of the year, ensuring that more compact and permanent settlements did not develop.

The Yukon basin Indians hunted a variety of animals and birds, caught several species of fish, and collected different kinds of plants in the course of their seasonal movements, the particular mix depending on the regional availability of resources. Yukon Natives fished in the summer, drying and storing much of the catch for later use. Fall hunts were particularly important, as the rivers remained open and permitted transportation of meat. Hunting continued through the winter months, although severe climate, limited game, and reduced mobility occasionally brought hardship to the unlucky or the ill prepared.

The Natives stayed largely in the river valleys and travelled to the high country only in pursuit of specific game. The seasonal migrations of animals and fish, particularly of the caribou and salmon, determined patterns of mobility. Equally, moose and smaller game could not be killed indefinitely from one site, forcing regular camp movements. Although Yukon Natives operated out of a selected central base – a seasonally occupied camp on a lake shore or river bank – they travelled extensively in pursuit of game. Regional variations in climate, geography, and the availability of game also forced significant adaptations. The Kutchin of the Peel-Porcupine river area hunted the large caribou herds, using circular enclosures called surrounds to trap the migrating animals.[8] Along the Yukon River, the Han built fish traps or used gill nets to collect salmon.[9] Natives in the Alsek River-Dezadeash Lake district similarly relied heavily on salmon stocks, although local conditions meant that different methods were used.[10] In all areas, Natives hunted moose and caribou, supplementing their food supplies with small game, stream and lake fishing, and berry picking.

The extensive mobility required by such hunting, fishing, and gathering determined the nature of aboriginal social organization. A band system evolved, based on the annual summer gatherings, but even these groups had limited structural significance. Leadership remained vaguely defined, varying according to the tasks involved and the skills of the men in the group. Often one man functioned as the trading chief while another led the band during hunting expeditions. Women did not enjoy formal rank within the bands, although the societies were matriarchal in structure. Their lack of formal power, however, belied their importance within the bands, where they served as educators, gatherers, and story-tellers.

Shamans, or medicine men, exerted considerable power through their ability to understand and manipulate the spiritual world, but religious beliefs lacked rigidity or regional consistency. In contrast to the codified structures European missionaries would shortly offer, the Natives held imprecise, individualistic interpretations of the spiritual world, dominated by the knowledge that spirits suffused the natural surroundings, forest, and fauna. There was no systematic or shared assessment of the significance and power of those spirits; in other words, there was little that non-Natives would see as religious beliefs. This spirituality was highly functional, forming an integral part of the Natives' relationship with the animal world and influencing the pursuit of sustenance.[11]

The essence of Athapaskan society in the Yukon basin was a consistent ability to adapt to human circumstances (including war, migration, and territorial expansion) and ecological change. Social organization, religious beliefs, hunting practices, and habitation patterns were consistent only in their ultimate flexibility. The substantial differences between the different cultural groups reflected not only environmental diversity, but also the impact of a harsh, often unforgiving, northern setting. The scattered nature of animal resources, annual freeze-ups of rivers, and the limited regenerative capacity of flora and fauna exacted their toll. The environment similarly required that the people function primarily in the smallest viable social unit – the extended family – which again restricted the possibilities for a more extensive social structure.

This family-oriented, mobile, subsistence lifestyle formed the basis of Native society in the Yukon River basin before the arrival of the HBC explorers. The state of aboriginal society at the point of contact represented the culmination of generations of change, adaptation, and cultural growth. Important regional variations in hunting and fishing patterns, seasonal movements, and language and tribal identification represented comparatively minor deviations from the common threads tying together Native existence in the region. The environmental relationship – a delicate, occasionally unreliable balance between people and resources – defined the contours of Native social behaviour. Native adaptation following the arrival of Euro-Canadians started from the Indians' pre-contact condition. Despite the comments to the contrary of fur traders and missionaries, the Natives' lifestyle was not a desperate struggle for subsistence. Instead, hunting and gathering provided a way of life which the Natives regarded as comparatively "affluent." Consequently, reactions to social and economic change attending non-Native expansion, originated in the Natives' belief in the efficacy of their lifestyle and their commitment to maintaining a hunting-gathering existence as a preferred form of economic activity.

One other major question – that of aboriginal population – remains to be addressed. Determining the extent of aboriginal population is made highly difficult by the absence of evidence and by the mobility of northern Native society. Providing such an assessment is, however, vital, because the meeting of races across North America was far more than a clash of values and customs. It was, at a more basic level, a confrontation of immunological systems, as the non-Natives brought diseases and infections that devastated the Native population.

As a hunting-gathering people in an area typically regarded as harsh and forbidding, the sub-Arctic Natives have usually been described as being few in number, widely dispersed, and living on the fringes of subsistence. This view, however, has been tendered without a proper assessment of the likely pre-contact population.[12] On this score, two major considerations complicate any calculations of the extent of aboriginal population. First, indirect contact and thus the potential spread of disease began long before Robert Campbell and John Bell breached the eastern and southern mountain barriers.

Russian, Spanish, and English traders first navigated the waters of the Pacific northwest in the middle to late eighteenth century. North-West Company (NWC) and HBC traders were similarly active in the nearby Mackenzie River drainage basin in the late eighteenth century, and the Russian American Fur Company began trading on the lower Yukon River in the 1830s. The Natives of the upper Yukon River basin participated in the expanding fur trade through intertribal exchange and, in certain circumstances, through direct contact with distant trading posts.[13] Before the first non-Native commentators reached the area, diseases had already been visited upon the Natives, hampering any specific determination of the aboriginal population based on historical sources.

Compounding this difficulty is the absence of useful contemporary enumerations for the pre-mining period. The few census lists extant are highly localized, referring to specific bands or narrowly defined regions. The only significant data relate to the northern Kutchin Indians. Estimates by fur traders, missionaries, and ethnographers have allowed Shepherd Krech III to study demographic change in this region and to determine the likely extent of the pre-contact Kutchin population.[14] Similar records do not exist for the rest of the region, a reflection of the limited travel by non-Natives before the gold-mining period.[15] As a result, a systematic reconstruction along the lines adopted by Krech for the Kutchin is not possible.

While statistical precision cannot be achieved, recent research on proto-historical Native populations allows for a speculative excursion into the field. Until recently, scholars deemed the Canadian north capable of supporting only a sparse, non-agricultural population. James Mooney's *The Aboriginal Population of America North of Mexico* (1928), long the standard work on the topic, suggested a Yukon valley population of around 4,000.[16] A.L. Kroeber attempted greater precision, arguing that the barren northland supported a population density of less than one person per 100 square kilometres, a figure which converts to a pre-contact Yukon population of approximately 4,700.[17] Ethnographer C. Osgood lent credence to the low estimate when he suggested in 1936 that the initial Kutchin population (covering about one-third of the territory but extending far beyond the Yukon's boundaries) had been close to 1,200.[18]

The Mooney-Kroeber estimates, which posited a total Native population in North America of about one million before the arrival of Europeans, faced few challenges before the 1960s. The first indications of the need for a reassessment emerged from scholars studying Mexico, particularly W. Borah and S. Cook.[19] Henry Dobyns brought their insights to a consideration of North American aboriginal population when he suggested that there may have been ten million Natives north of Mexico – ten times Mooney's estimate.[20] Dobyns's article sparked new interest in the topic, leading to a spate of work on Native demography. The historiographical re-evaluation filtered through to the Canadian north. Shepherd Krech III examined the northern Yukon-lower Mackenzie River Kutchin relative to Dobyns's analysis. He concluded that the aboriginal population of the Kutchin stood at approximately 5,400, double Mooney's and Kroeber's estimates and about one-third the total calculated through an application of Dobyns's depopulation ratio.[21]

Krech's work considers two approaches to estimating Native populations: a calculation based on population density utilizing available documentary evidence, and a determination of depopulation as suggested by Dobyns. An extrapolation from the data in Krech's detailed study – and it is important to note that he makes no claim for his work beyond the Kutchin Indians – leads to the conclusion that the pre-contact Yukon population likely stood at between 7,000 and 9,000. The population was unevenly distributed, with larger concentrations in the resource-rich Southern Lakes, Alsek-Kluane, central Yukon and Porcupine River districts. This number of Natives, which is on the order of three times the first federal estimate of 1895, appears consistent with population loss among other North American Native groups and with the evidence Krech marshalled in analyzing the Kutchin.

To validate further the proto-historical population, it is essential to account for the population decline from 7,000 to 9,000 to the federal estimate of 2,600 in 1895.[22] (The latter figure, more a guess than an enumeration, was likely too high.) Limited evidence dictates that the period to 1900 be examined through documentary sources. Further, estimates of the impact of disease before the arrival of the fur traders in the 1840s remain speculative, and are based on extrapolation from conditions in adjacent territories. It seems clear, nevertheless, that a major depopulation occurred before the turn of the century. The study of the demographic consequences of contact has attracted considerable interest of late.[23] Few scholars of Canadian Native people have contributed to this debate;[24] Robin Fisher, in his detailed study of Native-white relations in British Columbia, argues that the demographic consequences of contact have been overestimated.[25] Fisher is, however, outside the historiographical mainstream on this topic; most scholars agree that the arrival of Europeans had a severe impact on aboriginal peoples.

The precipitous decline originated in the virulence of "virgin soil epidemics." According to Alfred Crosby, the term refers to those epi-

Table 1
Yukon Native Population Ratios

Author	Ratio	Nadir Population	Estimated Pre-Contact
Dobyns (1966)	20/1	1,500	30,000
Krech (1978)[2]	6/1	1,500	9,000

[1] Approximate Yukon Native population in 1930 from DIA, *Annual Report, 1929*. Several Yukon Indian groups were included in BC population statistics.
[2] Research relates only to the Kutchin Indians. Ratio is applied to the total Yukon.

Table 2
Pre-contact Population Density

Source	per 100 sq. km	Total Yukon[1] Pre-Contact
Kroeber (1939)	.87	4,700
Krech (1978)[2]	1.70	9,100
DIA (1895)	.48	2,600

[1] Area of Yukon equals 536,324 sq. km.
[2] Estimate relates to Kutchin only

demics "in which the population has had no previous contact with the diseases that strike and are therefore immunologically almost defenseless."[26] From recorded experiences throughout North America, such epidemics killed thousands of Native people. As Crosby succinctly puts it, "the evidence is that when isolation ceases, decimation begins."[27] There is no reason to suspect that the Natives of the Yukon were any less vulnerable, although some might argue that the isolation of the Upper Yukon River valley protected the inhabitants from the spread of deadly illnesses.

In considering the possibility of shelter through isolation, it must be remembered that interregional exchange characterized pre-contact life in the area. These trading networks, the use of which expanded as Europeans advanced, served as conduits for epidemic disease. Given the rapid diffusion of disease along communication corridors, an occurrence A.J. Ray has demonstrated for the Canadian plains,[28] illnesses introduced to the Pacific northwest, lower Yukon, or Mackenzie River drainage soon spread to the Yukon basin. From 1835 to 1839, for example, a smallpox epidemic swept through the Alaskan interior and the Lynn Canal region.[29] It is difficult to believe that the disease did not reach into the upper Yukon basin. Suggestive evidence of such early illnesses comes from Anglican missionary T.H.

Canham, who was active in the Porcupine River district in the 1880s. In a thoughtful commentary on the life of Native people, drawn from extensive discussions with them, Canham attributed a "great diminution during the past century in the number of native inhabitants" to "the ravages of smallpox communicated from the southern Indians soon after the date of earliest explorations."[30] The appearance of smallpox, consistently the most deadly of all virgin-soil epidemics, at an early date suggests a significant population loss before the arrival of non-Natives.[31]

There is more substantial evidence of a major depopulation among Yukon Indians. HBC traders and Church Missionary Society (CMS) clergymen offered several firsthand accounts of the continuing devastation caused by European diseases. Shortly after reaching Fort Youcon in 1847, Alexander H. Murray noted "the great mortality amongst their women last summer," although he did not attribute their deaths to a specific cause.[32] Four years later, Robert Campbell and the Fort Youcon traders described an epidemic "carrying off" a large number of Indians. Campbell, travelling along the Yukon River in the summer of 1851, estimated that as many as one-third of the Natives died from an illness he believed to be the mumps.[33] Minor outbreaks, often with numerous fatalities, were so frequent that HBC traders seemingly became inured to the sight of sick Natives.[34]

A scarlet-fever epidemic which hit the area in 1865 was among the most severe, and the most extensively documented, outbreaks. HBC boat crews from Fort Simpson carried the disease into the Yukon.[35] The company permitted the supply vessels to continue, despite the possibility that they would infect the Natives, in order to supply Fort Youcon and maintain the trade. The disease did indeed spread rapidly. Natives at the posts became ill and, as they had in the past, carried the fever to distant bands.[36] The illness spread up and down stream, the path of the epidemic tracing the Native trading networks emanating out of Fort Youcon. James McDougall at Fort Youcon estimated that half of the post Indians died and that he knew of at least 170 Natives who had perished. The trader at Lapierre's House similarly noted that almost half the local band, 34 in all, succumbed within a matter of days.[37]

That epidemics had such a severe impact reflects both the Natives' immunological weaknesses and their inability to deal effectively with such afflictions. Faced with an inexplicable illness, the Natives relied on their shamans to explain and counter them. Diseases were typically blamed on sorcerers, and non-Natives came under the net of accusations. An elderly woman died shortly after Fort Youcon was established in 1847. Some blamed the traders for the disease, but the men decided that "her death was caused by another nation further down the river, near to the sea, and all of the party except three old men have started to have revenge for the death of said woman."[38] When several men died following an attack on the HBC's post at Fort Selkirk in 1852, the Natives blamed Campbell's "bad medicine" and threatened to attack Fort Youcon.[39] Insufficient knowledge also limited the Native response to the outbreaks. Instead of isolating or quarantining those affected, the Indians typically fled the scene of infection, which resulted in a wider spread of the disease and a further weakening of those already stricken.

The Natives' inability to treat the sick also influenced the severity of the illnesses. Ravaged by disease, the Natives often sank into lethargy and despair. Efforts at hunting and fishing dropped off, and fewer and fewer attempts were made to minister to the sick; as Reverend Canham noted, they "soon lose heart in time of sickness."[40] Fur traders and missionaries often misunderstood the Natives' confusion and attributed their malaise and inactivity to "stupidity" and "laziness." It was suggested that the Indians could have escaped the force of the epidemics had they acted with more dispatch in caring for themselves.[41] The apparent resignation of the Natives in the face of fatal illnesses is a further indication of their devastating impact.

The appearance of epidemics and a high initial death rate do not, of necessity, point to an on-going depopulation. Robin Fisher argues that unless mortality is "age-selective," with particular impact on women of child-bearing age, the Native population could quickly stabilize after an epidemic.[42] Although Fisher appears to have decidedly understated the impact of disease on the west coast,[43] his argument is worth considering. Contrary to Fisher's portrayal of British Columbia, evidence in the Yukon suggests that adults were seriously affected by disease. On separate occasions HBC traders noted that various illnesses caused "great mortality amongst their women"[44] and the death of "several of the most influential men"[45] and that the 1865 scarlet-fever scourge had "carried off nearly half of them, and amongst those many of our best provision hunters."[46] Similarly, when the Tlingit (Chilcat) returned to the coast after ransacking Fort Selkirk, several of their number died.[47] High mortality among adults likely characterized the general impact of epidemics. Hunters and traders maintained extensive contacts with different Native groups and non-Natives and consequently faced the greatest exposure to disease. Far from being immune to the devastation, the adults of child-bearing age appear to have suffered as much as other members of the Yukon Native population.

Depopulation, then, started long before non-Natives made direct contact with the Yukon Indians and accelerated with the arrival of traders, missionaries, and miners. Although the individual outbreaks did not match the severity of the 1865 scarlet-fever epidemic, the number and variety of diseases had a great cumulative impact. Measles, influenza (la grippe), dysentery, and a host of unspecified maladies assaulted the Natives.[48] Imprecise reporting and the fact that most Yukon Indians remained beyond the purview of non-Native commentators make it difficult to make a specific measurement, but the effects of depopulation were evident throughout the region. Bishop W.C. Bompas noted that 39 individuals died in the Dawson-Fort Selkirk region between 1895 and 1898. In the same period the group of less than 200 Natives recorded 12 live births.[49] When the documented severity of virgin-soil epidemics throughout the world and the appearance of small-pox, scarlet fever, mumps, measles, and influenza between 1840 and 1890 is taken into account, the suggested depopulation ratio of 2:3, although shocking in its scale, appears consistent with both evidence and logic.

Until the turn of the century, Yukon Natives encountered substantial population loss, with obvious economic and social consequences. Natives, their numbers reduced by up to two-thirds, were deprived of considerable flexibility in their dealings with non-Natives. Seasonal cycles and work patterns had been disrupted by what Crosby called the "pulverizing experience" of successive epidemics.[50] The non-Natives' "bad medicine" widened the gap between Native and white, adding to the Natives' suspicion of the intruders and convincing many traders, missionaries, and miners that the widely held image of the diseased and demoralized Indians reflected Yukon realities.

Disease is a matter of first, not secondary, importance in the field of Native-European relations. As has been shown, epidemic illnesses both preceded and accompanied non-Native expansion into the northwest. It is difficult to judge the cumulative impact of the depopulation that followed. Dozens of elders died, sometimes before they could pass on their knowledge and hence parts of their culture to the next generation. Such deaths also upset patterns of leadership, inheritance, and cultural identification in the Native bands, as groups disintegrated or combined following the ravages of disease. The documentary record, sadly, is relatively silent on the social consequences of disease, as most non-Natives wrongly assumed that such ill health had always characterized Native society.

All analysis of Native-European contact in the Yukon basin must begin with a sensitivity toward the depopulation and cultural loss that accompanied epidemic disease. The forces of depopulation did more than kill many Native people; the ravages of the new illnesses called into question the Indians' confidence in their spirituality and shamen, lessened the Natives' ability to fend for themselves, and destroyed many elements of aboriginal culture in the Yukon River basin. As fur traders arrived in the district, to be followed shortly by missionaries, miners, government agents, and hundreds of others, they encountered an aboriginal society already shaken to its foundations.

The general pattern of post-contact Yukon history is easily described. As noted, direct contact with Europeans began in the 1840s, when traders from the HBC and the Russian American Fur Company reached the upper Yukon River basin. The fur trade remained the chief point of interaction between Natives and non-Natives until an expanding gold-mining sector reached the region in the 1880s. The miners' discoveries were slim at first, sufficient to encourage continued exploration but not rich enough to stimulate great interest. The Indians remained numerically dominant in the area, although growing enthusiasm for gold prospects had relegated their concerns to the background.

The discovery of gold on Rabbit Creek in August 1896 touched off the world-famous Klondike gold rush. For a few short years, the Yukon attracted thousands of stampeders anxious to capitalize on the fabled riches of the far northwest. The lives of Yukon Indians were severely disrupted by this massive invasion; many responded by moving away from the gold-fields. As the gold ran out, and as capital-intensive dredging operations replaced the prospectors, the territory's non-Native population declined precipitously, once again raising the profile of the aboriginal people.

The comparative isolation of the Yukon Territory was again sharply broken in 1942, when military concerns about Japanese designs on Alaska convinced American authorities to build a network of highways, pipelines, and airfields in the Canadian northwest and Alaska. The resulting "invasion" disrupted life in the construction corridors and served as a harbinger of the "modern" north. The post-war changes, only a few of which were related to the military construction projects, were indeed sweeping. The federal government, having long ignored its northern responsibilities, assumed a new activist role. As mineral exploration and development increased, Yukon Indians found themselves rejected by the dominant non-Native society and forced off the lands that had sustained their ancestors for generations.

By the 1960s Yukon Indian society faced innumerable challenges – from an assimilationist education system to an often racist non-Native population, and from an industrial economy that had no place for aboriginal skills to a government bureaucracy that had little time for Indian customs and traditions. In an atmosphere of considerable distrust and tension, the Yukon Indians began to pressure for a settlement of their outstanding aboriginal land rights. This movement culminated in the publication of *Together Today for Our Children Tomorrow*, the land claim of the Yukon Native Brotherhood (YNB), in 1973. The formalization of the land-claim process, which dragged on for seventeen years before a final resolution in 1990, set Native-non-Native relations in the Yukon Territory on a new path, for the Indians had made it clear that they intended to play a major role in determining the future of their homeland.

This brief summary notwithstanding, the history of Native-white relations in the Yukon Territory is not easily divided into chronological sections. I have opted, therefore, for a rather different approach. This book is divided into four sections, each of which examines a specific theme in the contact history of the Yukon. The first three sections, which focus on economic relations, the nature of social contact, and the interaction of church, state, and Native people, consider the sweep of historical events from first contact to 1950. This structure permits a chronological division of Yukon history into segments that make sense to a particular theme, rather than forcing a more artificial structure on the overall investigation. The final section examines the diverse and rapidly changing nature of Native-white relations in the post-war era, culminating with the signing of an agreement in principle on the Council of Yukon Indians' land claims in April 1990.

Relations between the indigenous people in the Yukon and the non-Native immigrants have been anything but simple or one-dimensional. Natives and whites met in numerous places, from the fur-trade post to the church and from residential schools to police courts. They met in the towns and in the bush, as friends and as rivals. They greeted each other with pleasure and openness on occasion, and with fear and distrust at other times. These relations had a significant impact on both parties. Equally, they went a long way towards determining the pattern of economic, social, and cultural life in the Yukon Territory.

Economic Relations

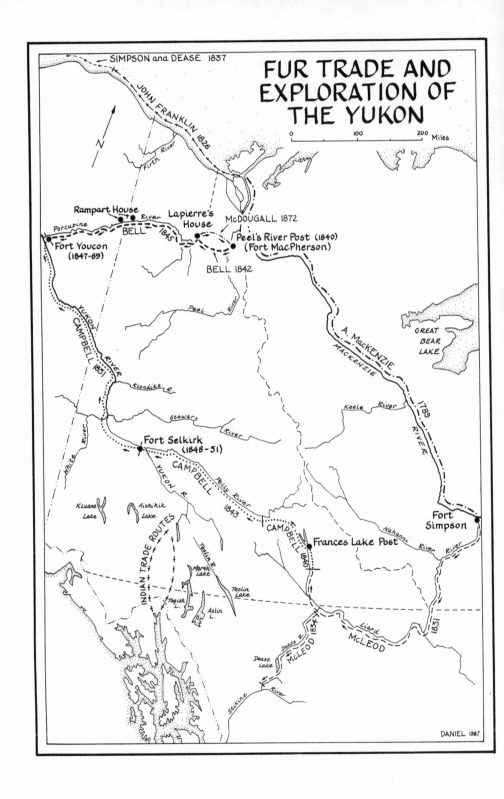

FUR TRADE AND
EXPLORATION OF
THE YUKON

SIMPSON and DEASE 1837

JOHN FRANKLIN 1826

Firth River

N

0   100   200   Miles

Rampart House

Porcupine   Bell   River

Lapierre's
House

McDOUGALL 1872

BELL   1845

Fort Youcon
(1847-69)

Peel's River Post (1840)
(Fort MacPherson)

BELL 1842

YUKON   CAMPBELL 1851   RIVER

Peel   River

A. MacKENZIE

GREAT
BEAR
LAKE

MACKENZIE

Klondike R.

Keele   River

1789   RIVER

White   River

Stewart   River

Fort Selkirk
(1848~51)

CAMPBELL   1843

Pelly River

YUKON R.

Fort
Simpson

Kluane
Lake

Aishihik
Lake

CAMPBELL 1840

Frances Lake Post

Nahanni   River   River

INDIAN   TRADE   ROUTES

Teslin R.

Marsh
Lake

Teslin
Lake

Tagish
L.

Atlin
L.

1831

McLEOD

Liard   River

Dease R.

McLEOD 1854

Dease
Lake

Stikine   River

DANIEL 1987

Economic Relations

The historical assessment of Native-European contact in Canada has been dominated by consideration of its economic implications. A vibrant and on-going debate over the role of Native people in the fur trade[1] is central to this historiography, but studies of Indian involvement in the British Columbia economy[2] and the economic lives of the Dakota[3] and Plains Cree[4] have broadened the analysis to take into account the years of settlement and industrialization. The emphasis on economic activities is crucial to an understanding of the Natives' changing role in Canadian society. Native involvement in the fur trade, mining, farming, and industry illustrates a great deal about their options and goals as well as their attitudes towards the advance of European society.

This literature, particularly the very strong material for the fur-trade era, illustrates the Native peoples' perceptive understanding of the structure and purpose of the European economy. It also highlights their attempts to combine a desire to preserve aboriginal traditions with a growing reliance on manufactured items and with the need to respond to dramatic social and ecological changes. In most instances, of course, Native people ran out of options. In agricultural areas, the imperatives of settlement forced the Natives off the land, led to the destruction of wildlife and undermined hunting, trapping, and nomadism. Historians used to see the clash between the harvesting lifestyle and the agricultural frontier as one between the "savage" and the "civilized" worlds. Now there is greater recognition of the complexity of this confrontation, and of changing aboriginal expectations. Historians have also charted the ability of Natives to adapt to new economic regimes and the unwillingness of many non-Natives to accept Indians as partners in growth and change.

In most areas of Canada there is little opportunity to assess the nature of Native choice. In settled regions, agricultural development has effectively eliminated the harvesting option; Native people have either adapted quickly to the new economic order or have come to rely on reserve-based welfare programs. Similarly, in more heavily industrialized areas, pressures on the land and resources have altered the Natives' attachment to the land. On the other hand, in much of the land north of the settlement belt, the imperatives of the agricultural, industrial, or resource-based economies arrived much later, usually after the Second World War. Natives in these areas had no choice but to continue harvesting, trading surplus furs to the HBC or its rivals in exchange for needed manufactured goods.[5]

The Yukon fit between these extremes, particularly after the arrival of gold miners in the 1870s and 1880s. Although agricultural development remained miniscule, and tied to local consumption, exploitation of the region's mineral resources ushered in a very different economic order. Mining placed few demands on the surrounding land; much of the Yukon remained untouched until the mining boom of the 1950s and 1960s. At the same time, harvesting was economically and socially viable in the territory until after the Second World War, offering Native people an alternative to incorporation into the mining/industrial economy. The Yukon, then, presents an unusual opportunity to assess the range of Native choices and the factors that limited or restricted those choices.

The following three chapters examine aspects of Native economic activity in the Yukon Territory before 1950. The first chapter considers the Natives' response to the fur trade and argues that circumstances in the Yukon paralleled patterns of relations elsewhere in Canada. The second chapter considers the Indians' reaction to the advance of gold miners in the late nineteenth century and early twentieth century. Consideration is also given to the efforts of non-Native people, for economic and social reasons, to restrict the activities of Natives within the emerging mining sector. The final chapter examines the economic role of Native people in the twentieth century, when a vibrant fur trade and a small but important mining sector competed for Native talents and time. This period provides the best chance to examine the degree of Native commitment to harvesting and the limits on their participation in non-traditional sectors of the Yukon economy.

CHAPTER ONE

Economic Relations in the Fur-trade Era

The aboriginal inhabitants of the upper Yukon River valley felt the impact of the expanding European fur trade long before the arrival of the first white men.[1] The traders of the Russian American Fur Company did not extend their operations beyond the Pacific coast and the lower reaches of the Yukon River, but exchange between Native groups ensured that Russian trade goods passed into the interior. After the HBC expanded to the northwest following the 1821 merger with its long-time rival, the NWC explorers working along the Liard and Mackenzie rivers found numerous signs of the extensive reach of the Russian trade.

When John McLeod explored the upper Liard River basin in 1831, he found that many Natives possessed Russian goods.[2] Hundreds of miles to the north, along the Porcupine River, John Bell similarly encountered substantial evidence that indirect Russian trade had penetrated well within British territory.[3] Even the Inuit along the Arctic coast were able to secure coveted manufactured goods through intermediary groups.[4]

Regular native trade within and between regions pre-dated the arrival of European traders. The distribution of indigenous resources was such that most groups possessed an abundance of particular commodities, but lacked other useful supplies. Native groups traded their local surplus for goods not readily available and developed institutional arrangements to facilitate exchange. As both John Franklin and Thomas Simpson observed on the Arctic coast, formal trading partnerships existed between Kutchin and Inuit traders. Hostilities often erupted between these groups, but the formal partnership system allowed trade to continue even in times of conflict. Similar arrangements conditioned exchange between the Tlingit Indians of the Pacific coast and their inland trading partners, although military imbalances favouring the coastal Natives ensured that the trade was not equal. Groups in the interior, closer to each other in culture and language, did not require the same measure of formality, but institutional structures were created to expedite trade. These Native trading networks and institutions, formed in the pre-contact period, assumed even greater importance when European traders appeared.[5]

Europeans moved slowly onto the outer fringes of the Natives' trading networks in the Yukon basin. The Russians established posts along the lower Yukon and Pacific coast; the NWC and, after 1821, the HBC established themselves on the Mackenzie River and in the Liard River basin. The institutional arrangements created to exchange indigenous commodities were quickly adapted to aid the dispersal of the new European goods. Not all the earlier trading networks survived. The cost and availability of European wares now determined the structure of Native exchange. Access to a dependable supply of European manufactures allowed the Tlingit Indians to expand their inland trade and domination. Acting through Han and Tutchone intermediaries, the Tlingits soon drew much of the upper Yukon basin into their trading sphere.

Such pre-eminence was conditional upon the ability of Native trading partners to locate a better supply of European goods. As the foreign traders expanded their operations, the Native exchange system changed in response. The arrival of NWC and HBC traders in the lower Mackenzie early in the nineteenth century provided the eastern bands of Kutchin Indians with a secure source of supply. These bands, in turn, established themselves as middlemen between the western Kutchin and the Han Indians, a reversal of earlier trade networks.[6] Pre-contact institutions remained in place, and intertribal trade retained its importance after the arrival of European traders. Specific trading patterns, however, proved to be highly variable, as Native groups reoriented their activities to exploit new opportunities.

Native trading systems proved influential as the HBC expanded into the Yukon River basin. Following the discovery of the Colville River by Thomas Simpson and Peter Warren Dease in 1837,[7] the firm undertook a two-pronged exploration of the region west of the Mackenzie River. In both instances, the Natives' desire to protect their trading interests impeded the progress of the fur-trade explorers. The Indians realized the importance of maintaining a monopoly over both a source of supply and a trading district. They were able to use their position to limit, at least temporarily, expansion of the HBC because of the availability of alternative supplies of European manufacturers through the Tlingit Indians or from Natives trading along the lower Yukon River.

The expansion to the northwest came at a critical juncture in the HBC's long history. The market for beaver pelts, the mainstay of the HBC's trade, dipped precipitously in the 1830s, as the beaver hat lost out to the inexpensive silk hat. The company's warehouse in London filled with unsaleable beaver skins, which had to be sold off at great discounts. To counter this serious loss of markets, the HBC began promoting luxury furs – mink, fox, and especially marten – in an attempt to create new demand and sustain its corporate empire. Company officers were extremely pleased to discover that the Yukon basin contained one of North America's richest marten regions. If the firm needed any inducement to expand to the northwest, it was provided by the changing character of the European fur markets.[8]

The company's first westward thrust centred on Peel's River Post (later Fort McPherson), opened in 1840 by John Bell following an unsuccessful attempt to cross the Richardson mountains.[9] The Peel River Indians found themselves in an enviable middleman position, and were determined to slow Bell's attempts to push further west. HBC Governor George Simpson ordered Bell to continue his quest, but he received little help from the Natives. They frequently misrepresented the difficulty of the terrain and the problems of transmontane transport. Similarly, individual Natives agreed to guide the company's men, only to abandon them long before they reached their objective.[10] On at least two occasions, Indians from west of the Richardson mountains visited Peel's River, and offered seductive descriptions of the prospects for trade in their home area.[11] Encouraged by such reports and prodded by Governor Simpson, Bell finally crossed the mountain barrier in 1842, but was abandoned by his guide once again.[12] Bell solved his problem in 1845 when, acting on Simpson's advice, he hired Native tripmen who knew nothing of the area being explored, and whose personal interests did not conflict with the purposes of exploration. Bell finally reached the "Youcon" River, believed at the time to be the Colville.[13] The Peel River Kutchin ultimately failed to hold the HBC in the Mackenzie River basin. Their active interference had, however, postponed the firm's expansion into the Yukon River watershed for more than five years.

Bell's discovery changed but did not destroy Native trading patterns. In 1846 Lapierre's House, a small outpost, was built on the west side of the Richardson mountains. The following year Alexander Hunter Murray led a contingent to the junction of the Porcupine and Youcon rivers, where they erected Fort Youcon.[14] The eastern Kutchin lost a valuable trading position, but bands around the new post assumed the role of middlemen. Trade prospered from the beginning, with the Natives often bringing in more furs to exchange than the

HBC could buy.[15] The Kutchin in the Fort Youcon area, formerly dependent on other Natives for supplies of European manufactures, now possessed their own source. Many of the post Indians stopped or limited their trapping activities and assumed a new position as fur traders and provision hunters. The company's expansion had, in sum, merely leap-frogged one link in the native trading network, displacing one band but offering new commercial power to another.[16]

The existence of flourishing Native trading systems similarly interfered with the HBC's planned expansion from the south. This second phase, led by Robert Campbell, was to push north along the Liard River and, if possible, cross into the watershed of the Colville. Campbell moved northwest in short, tentative steps, first establishing trading posts on Frances Lake and the upper Pelly River in 1839–40. Although initially encountering little difficulty, he also attracted very few furs. As he extended his operations towards the Yukon River, however, Campbell found himself facing the formidable interior trading system of the Tlingit (Chilcat) Indians.[17] When he attempted to explore further in 1843, his Native tripmen stopped prematurely, ostensibly for fear of "savage" Indians downstream.[18] Campbell had encountered the same reluctance which characterized Bell's Indian guides to the north. He finally succeeded in opening a post at the junction of the Lewes (Yukon) and Pelly rivers in 1848, his progress delayed by years of procrastination and hardship. Once established, however, Campbell was to find that his troubles were far from over.

Tlingit traders had long controlled the trade of the southern interior, travelling inland regularly to meet their Athapaskan partners. The establishment of Fort Selkirk challenged that decades-old domination. The Tlingit Indians continued their annual excursions, sending thirty men inland in 1849 and outbiding the company's traders for the local Natives' furs.[19] Campbell tried to retaliate in kind, but transportation and supply problems, as well as the firm's unwillingness to lower prices to a competitive level, undermined his effort. During his five-year tenure at Fort Selkirk, he did not record a single yearly profit.[20]

The attempted expansion to Fort Selkirk suffered an ignominious end. Chilcat traders, returning from an extensive inland trading journey, reached the post on 21 August 1852. Campbell had only two men with him, the rest having been dispatched on provisioning and trading duties. He stood by, powerless, as the coastal Indians ransacked the place.[21] Campbell must bear some of the responsibility for the episode, but the attack is indicative of a much broader conflict. Bell's expansion to the Yukon River had overturned trading relationships of relatively short duration. Campbell, on the other hand, had interfered with a more established and more economically viable network.

Campbell had recognized the vulnerability of his position shortly after he arrived at Fort Selkirk. The Chilcats' knowledge of the terrain and the customs and language of the interior natives, Campbell argued, allowed the coastal Indians to maintain their supremacy.[22] In addition, the company's men faced other problems which only increased the Tlingits' advantages. The HBC relied on the Liard River as a supply route. This turbulent, unforgiving waterway offered difficult access to the northwest, interfering with company efforts to keep Fort Selkirk adequately supplied. Campbell was also ordered to adhere to the Mackenzie River district pricing structure, despite the fact that the Chilcats offered much better terms.[23] The coastal Natives participated in the competitive maritime trade, and as a result could offer regular supplies, comparable quantity, and substantially lower prices. This, on top of their longstanding military and economic domination of the interior bands, enabled the Chilcats to beat back the HBC's challenge. These economic considerations, even more than the longevity of the trading networks, ensured the Chilcats' continuing supremacy.[24] Fort Selkirk and its predecessors, Pelly Banks and Frances Lake, never proved profitable. Following the destruction of Fort Selkirk in 1852, and despite Robert Campbell's passionate appeals for a chance to vindicate his former management, the HBC abandoned further efforts to revive the southern Yukon fur trade, and concentrated instead on the more promising Fort Youcon operation.[25]

The company officers in the Yukon River basin soon discovered serious limits on their ability to dominate the fur trade. The Native traders were as determined as their white counterparts to have the exchange serve their own interests. The HBC men, used to the benefits of uncontested monopoly trade, were poorly prepared for the exacting conditions demanded by the Indians in this new region.

There were several signs that the company traders seriously misunderstood the nature of exchange in this region. In the first days at Fort Youcon, the post's outfit was too small and there was a severe shortage of those items, especially guns and beads, in greatest demand. The traders tried to override this problem by taking advantage of their knowledge of Native trading institutions. The traders believed that, if they forged an alliance with a band's trading chief, they would, in turn, be able to dictate terms of trade to the entire group.[26] In times of shortage, the company officers traded such highly valued goods as guns and beads only with these "principal men."

This was a mistake; the HBC employees had overestimated the personal status of the trading chiefs. The Native bands selected the trading chief to represent their interests at the trading post, but arrangements thus concluded were not binding on band members. On several occasions, the HBC officers granted preferential treatment to a chief, only to find that the remaining Indians took their furs elsewhere.[27]

This was not the only time that HBC traders misjudged their ability to control the fur trade, nor the only one when their earlier experience in areas where the firm enjoyed a solid monopoly served them poorly. Standard company policy dictated that items in short supply, such as guns and beads, be offered only in exchange for high-value furs, especially prime beaver and marten. Traders at Fort Youcon attempted to abandon this policy, primarily because their annual outfits did not contain enough of the goods in greatest demand. The Natives, however, had come to regard the relationship between prime furs and highly valued items as a "standard of trade" and they refused to offer their better quality skins unless guns or beads were provided in exchange.[28] William Hardisty, chief factor in charge of the Mackenzie River district, faced similar resistance when he attempted in 1865 to stop granting supplies on credit to the Indians. Company traders attempted to implement the change throughout the district, but the effort failed at Fort Youcon. Extant Fort Youcon account books indicate that in 1869 the traders granted more than 1,000 "Made Beaver" in debt.[29] Much like other Natives active in the fur trade, the Indians at Fort Youcon resisted attempts to impose unfavourable conditions on their exchange.

The Natives' ability to influence the direction and substance of trade in the Yukon River basin rested in large part on their willingness to exploit competition between European trading firms. The Indians clearly understood the Europeans' motives for trading furs and quickly realized the implications of competition for trading conditions. The first sign of the Indians' ability to use competitive trade to their advantage appeared in 1847, when Alexander Murray arrived to construct Fort Youcon. At that juncture, the only alternative to the HBC was a small, irregularly maintained Russian American Fur Company outpost at Nulato, some seven hundred miles downstream from the British establishment. The Indians at Fort Youcon eagerly reported that the Russians were planning to expand upstream, claiming they had reached Murray's location the previous year and were scheduled to return.[30] Murray knew only too well that his post stood well inside Russian territory, in contravention of a trade agreement with the Russian American Fur Company. He feared that direct competition with the HBC's Russian rivals would cause a diplomatic incident and undermine the potential profits of the Yukon River trade.[31] He was not, however, prepared to lose trade and he promptly told the Natives of "the manner in which they were cheated by the Russians."[32]

Perhaps sensing Murray's concern, the Natives continued to provide the Fort Youcon chief trader with information on the Russians. They claimed at various times that the competitors had armed their boat with a cannon, had offered generous gifts and better prices, and were spreading rumours about the HBC.[33] The stories appear not to have been true, although recent research suggests that the Russians were in fact planning to explore further upstream.[34] The Natives were eager to exploit the HBC's officers' fear of Russian expansion, although the company balked at suggestions that the regional tariff be adjusted to take competitive circumstances into account.

The response to the prospect of a Russian encroachment was not always in the Indians' favour. Special efforts were made to respond to certain Native requests, especially demands for specific trade goods. The Fort Youcon traders requested that the company's Pacific division collect certain coastal shells, highly valued in the Yukon, and forward them to Fort Youcon.[35] Attempts to secure a modification of the tariff, or pricing structure, were less successful. The high costs of transportation, company officials contended, could be met only if the tariff remained unaltered. The Peel River Indians posed a further complication. They traded in the Mackenzie River valley, where the HBC enjoyed an unchallenged monopoly. These Indians were, none the less, well informed of conditions to the west of their homelands. They threatened to resort *en masse* to Fort Youcon if rates of exchange were improved too much beyond the Peel River tariff. Faced with the possible desertion, and the attending cost of having to carry additional furs back across the Richardson mountains, Mackenzie district officials resisted requests from the Fort Youcon traders for a more competitive tariff.[36]

The Indians' repeated warnings of an impending Russian advance eventually backfired. The HBC finally received tangible evidence of Russian competition when a servant of the Russian American Fur Company arrived at Fort Youcon.[37] Employees along the chain of command believed the arrival signalled an impending Russian expansion, a threat that seemed all the more real given the Natives' oft-repeated descriptions of Russian plans. The response was uncharacteristically aggressive. Strachan Jones, a Fort Youcon trader, initially travelled some six hundred miles down river, hoping to induce Natives on the lower Yukon to visit the HBC post for trade.[38] When that did not work, the company decided to risk expanding further into Russian territory.

Annual trading boats were sent downstream each year, adding greatly to company profits but cutting the Fort Youcon Indians out of their jealously guarded middleman trade.[39]

The Natives' ability to influence the fur trade did not rest entirely on the existence, real or imagined, of competition. There were a variety of other ways of encouraging the HBC to meet the Indians' needs. The vulnerability of Fort Youcon – an isolated island of fewer than twenty men in the midst of several thousand Natives of dubious loyalty – weighed heavily on the firm's men, especially Alexander Murray. The Natives spoke openly of their plans to attack the post unless the company offered more favourable conditions of trade. The Chilcat attack on Fort Selkirk, coupled with the HBC's refusal to retaliate, increased the belligerence of Indians throughout the upper Yukon basin.[40] Company traders tried to calm the Natives by reminding them of the economic value of Fort Youcon, and the dislocation that would result if the post closed. The officers were satisfied that the effort worked, although it is unlikely that the Indians in the interior had ever seriously considered attacking the fort.[41]

The Natives frequently threatened to withhold their furs unless the company provided the right trade goods, and they occasionally followed through on these threats. Robert Campbell was convinced that the Indians around Fort Selkirk had formed a "combination" to protest the terms of trade. They unanimously refused to bring either furs or meat to the post.[42] Such boycotts did, on occasion, force a modification of the company outfit, but district policy placed limits on the officers' flexibility. The Natives' refusal to trade with Strachan Jones in 1864 convinced the company to reassign him.[43]

The Indians dealt effectively with the intrusion of European capitalism into the Yukon River valley. In the first quarter century of direct Native-white trade, the Indians, through intertribal trading networks, artificially enhanced competition, intimidation, and trading boycotts, overcame the HBC's apparent monopoly and secured more favourable trading conditions.

The American purchase of Alaska from Russia in 1867 altered the economic equilibrium established in the period of initial contact. Yankee traders moved into the lower Yukon River valley shortly after the purchase. Two years later, with the aid of a sympathetic national government, the traders reached Fort Youcon. Captain Raymond of the US Navy was dispatched in 1869 to investigate reports of HBC incursions onto American soil. His subsequent discovery that the post was indeed on United States soil – an open secret within the HBC for years – led to the forced removal of the company's establishment to British (soon to be Canadian) territory. Even more, the arrival of the American traders led to a rapid restructuring of the regional economy.[44]

The reorganization started with the retreat of the HBC. The Fort Youcon establishment was removed to Rampart House along the Porcupine River in 1869. The post burned down the same year and the officers and men moved upstream to Lapierre's House. A second Rampart House was opened a short distance upstream from the first in 1871, used primarily to prevent the advance of competitive traders into the lucrative Mackenzie River trade.[45] The post remained there until 1890, when another American surveyor, J. Turner, discovered that the company's post was still on American soil. Rampart House was moved again, this time to a site slightly east of the Canada–United States border.[46]

The actions of American traders were no less erratic. Independent traders as well as several small companies and larger firms vied for what all believed to be a profitable trade. Posts opened and closed regularly, and new companies formed as competitors merged in an attempt to counter the high cost of doing business in the isolated district. By 1874 the Alaska Commercial Company dominated the exchange, running a steamboat along the Yukon River to supply an expanding string of posts.[47] The Alaska Commercial Company's domination did not eliminate competition, since small independent traders stayed in business. But the comparative stability of the pre-1869 trade was gone, replaced by a more fluid, irregular framework.

The Natives, especially those directly attached to Fort Youcon, resented the Americans. They pledged their allegiance to the HBC and initially refused to trade furs and provisions with the interlopers. Many Fort Youcon Indians followed the company traders during their poorly planned retreat up the Porcupine River.[48] The animosity proved short-lived, and was limited to those Indians eliminated from their profitable, if declining, middleman position by the arrival of the Americans. The HBC believed that continued Native support rested on the quality of their goods and the fairness of their trade. But some in the company felt, on reflection, that the Indians' loyalty was due largely to the presence of James McDougall, a highly respected Fort Youcon trader. When McDougall left the area, most of the Natives abandoned the HBC post. Earlier protestations of lasting loyalty proved unreliable. As the economic advantages of the American trade became more apparent, the Indians dropped their allegiance to the British trading firm.[49]

The HBC attempted to meet the American challenge, but ultimately with little success. Traders granted more credit to reliable Natives – those likely to continue trading at Rampart House. Also, since 1847

the firm had hired Natives as tripmen, hunters, fishermen, and interpreters. The availability of such positions enhanced the prestige and
income of the "home guard" Indians around Fort Youcon. After its
retreat up the Porcupine River, the company offered longer-term
employment (three to six months) in an attempt to strengthen its
influence over important Indians and skilled trappers.[50] These
attempts to secure the Indians' allegiance proved of little benefit.
Native traders continued to trade at Rampart House, often travelling
hundreds of miles to do so. The attraction, however, was not the HBC
or its meagre attempts at generosity. Instead, the available supply of
such high-quality items as blankets and tobacco ensured that a small
portion of the Yukon trade would continue to find its way to Rampart
House.[51]

The complacency and inaction of the HBC stood in stark contrast
to the aggressive strategy of the Yankee traders. The Americans
adopted the standard tactics of fur-trade competition, granting generous gratuities, lowering prices, travelling to visit distant bands in
their camps, and incorporating HBC trade goods into their outfits.[52]
When such methods proved only partially successful, the Americans
tried other techniques. Several independents hired Native runners to
travel to distant tribes to solicit trade, a practice often used to good
effect by the HBC elsewhere.[53] Although the first American traders to
ascend the river did not carry alcohol,[54] their competitors soon did.
In addition, the largest American firm, the Alaska Commercial Company, set up Indians as free traders near Rampart House, providing
them with a generous complement of goods and encouraging their
partners to offer credit and better prices to attract more furs.[55]

The rivalry between the HBC and the American traders consistently
worked to the economic benefit of the Indians. The Yankee expansion
offered alternative trading sites, additional casual employment, a
wider range of merchandise, and a more advantageous pricing policy.
It also meant less travel for the Natives. To them, traditional loyalties
were dispensable as they readily altered their trading patterns to
secure the best possible conditions. Some maintained their ties with
the HBC for economic reasons. The pricing structure at Rampart
House was less favourable than along the Yukon River, but readily
available credit and the possibility of employment offered sufficient
attraction to keep some Natives with the HBC.[56] The firm's hold on
this dwindling segment of the trade was never very secure, however,
and even its supposedly loyal Natives abandoned it at times for the
Americans.

The HBC's problems, and therefore the Natives' opportunities, were
compounded further by the expansion of commercial whaling oper-

ations to Herschel Island in the late 1880s. The Arctic mariners quickly discovered that the fur trade offered quick and lucrative returns, and ignored the conventions of the interior exchange in order to secure substantial short-term profits. The whalers traded alcohol and Winchester repeating rifles, although both were banned for trade to the Indians by the Canadian government.[57] The raucous drinking binges and wild parties associated with the arrival of the whaling fleet proved to be an attractive alternative to the sedate exchange of the interior. John Firth, the HBC trader at Rampart House, watched helplessly as the remnants of the firm's once flourishing Yukon basin trade were siphoned off to Herschel Island.

The Native people had responded enthusiastically to the reorganization which followed the arrival of the Yankee traders. But an even greater challenge loomed on the horizon. Not all the new arrivals were fur traders. The vanguard of the aggressively expansive North American mining frontier reached the Yukon River valley in the 1870s. American companies continued to trade with the Indians, but they placed more emphasis on serving the expanding mining sector. By the early 1890s the fur trade had surrendered its pre-eminence, and a new social and economic order had emerged. Unlike the fur trade, the mining economy did not have an important role for the Native people. It was uncertain how the Indians would adapt to the challenges of the mining frontier and whether the new arrivals would welcome Native participation in their economy.

CHAPTER TWO

Indians and the Mining Frontier

The arrival of miners in the Yukon River valley quickly altered both its economic base and the Natives' place in the regional order. Yet the fur trade did not stop. Neither the withdrawal of the HBC from Fort Youcon nor the steady advance of the gold-mining frontier slowed the trade in furs. There would, however, no longer be a single cash economy as in the past. Instead, the region's marketable wealth came from two sectors – mining and fur trading – with only tenuous links between the two. The Natives' role in this evolving economic order would be determined by the comparative viability of the fur trade and the need for labour in the gold-fields. A variety of factors, including manpower requirements in the diggings, demand for country provisions,[1] racially inspired limitations on the use of Indian labourers, and the Natives' own economic priorities, determined the extent of their involvement in the mining economy.

The first reports of sizeable gold deposits in the region surfaced years before professional miners reached the Yukon valley. HBC officers and Anglican clergymen later claimed to have known that paying quantities of gold could be found in several tributaries of the Yukon River. The fur traders, anxious to maintain the area as a fur preserve, and the missionaries, fearful that their Native charges were not yet prepared for close contact with miners, kept the information to themselves.[2] The effort was doomed to eventual failure as the gold frontier edged slowly northward, reaching British Columbia in the 1850s and touching off a minor rush to the Cassiar district in 1872. Within a decade, prospectors had reached the upper Yukon basin.

The early work rested largely on faith, as preliminary diggings along the Yukon River and its tributaries proved unsatisfactory. Still, traders Leroy McQuesten, Arthur Harper, and Alfred Mayo continued to "grubstake" the prospectors, providing necessary supplies in return for a share in future discoveries. These men, like the larger Alaska Commercial Company (which eventually absorbed the smaller operations), balanced their mining investment with participation in the still lucrative northern fur trade.

The situation changed drastically in 1885 with the discovery of what appeared to be a major strike on the Stewart River. Faced with the sudden prospect of a mining boom, the commercial traders shifted their business, closing down several fur-trading posts and moving closer to the gold diggings. The Stewart River discovery was soon played out, but before disenchantment could again set in, Henry Madison and Howard Franklin struck gold on the Fortymile River. Another mini-rush ensured in 1886, when miners and traders in the north stampeded to this rich new field and the community of Fortymile appeared. Seven years later another discovery was made on Birch Creek on the American side of the border. Traders, including Leroy McQuesten, again followed the miners, and another town, Circle City, sprang up on the banks of the Yukon River.[3]

The establishment of Fortymile and Circle City added a measure of stability to the regional mining economy, but did not settle the restless prospectors. The mining population fluctuated widely, as disenchanted or financially ruined prospectors departed and were replaced by those optimistic enough to believe that riches could still be found. The mining community remained volatile, prepared to abandon the diggings at the slightest hint of a new discovery. While those with paying claims near Fortymile or along Birch Creek stayed put, others pressed on. The miners scoured the tributaries, forming partnerships with others who shared their faith in a particular stream, and disbanding their arrangements when they faced disagreements over the best place to try next.[4] Initial returns were slender – one estimate sets the average return at Fortymile at about $800 per year – but most miners were optimistic that a major strike loomed in the not too distant future.[5]

There appeared, at first glance, to be hardly any place for the Natives in this new economic order. Indians seldom staked claims, apparently seeing little attraction in the hard and dirty work undertaken with no guarantee of a profitable return. Those few who followed the miners into the gold-fields usually sold their claims within a short time. The limited opportunities which existed for Natives were as labourers for the non-Native miners. The prospectors generally worked alone however, because the mining technology restricted the need for additional labour. Unlike quartz or hard-rock mining, which required labour- and machine-intensive operations, placer mining remained small-scale, powered by hand and the manipulation of natural water supplies.

Northern conditions demanded specific adaptations to longstanding placer techniques. The first miners worked sand-bars in the rivers, gathering the loose gravel and washing it for signs of gold. Most of the Yukon basin gold remained embedded in the permafrost, however, forcing the miners to develop new methods of extracting the mineral. The innovations came out of the Fortymile field, where gold was discovered on the bedrock below the creek bed. Work was slowed by the frozen ground, and impatient miners had to wait for the summer sun to thaw the surface soil. The breakthrough came in 1887, when it was discovered that fires built on the soil melted the permafrost, allowing the gold-bearing dirt to be extracted. Miners could now accumulate the potentially rich gravel until spring, when it could be washed through a sluice box.[6] The mining technology ensured that operations remained highly seasonal and mainly small in size, operated by individuals or partnerships. Additional labour was occasionally required during spring run-off, when the gold-bearing dirt had to be washed while water levels remained high.

Although non-Natives dominated the gold-fields, there was some room for Native participation. The Indians welcomed the new economic order, because it often paid better than the fur trade. Moreover, the isolated location of the mining field ensured that few casual, non-Native labourers were available, and so employers turned, albeit reluctantly, to Native workers. Retailers and wholesalers supplying the mining towns often required short-term assistance unloading sternwheelers. Much like seasonal and temporary chores during the fur trade, packers' jobs fell largely to the Indians. The mines in the Fortymile and Circle City regions were a considerable distance from the town site. Miners either carried their own supplies or, as many chose to do, hired a Native packer to do the work.[7]

Yet, while casual work could be found, wages were not particularly high. Packers, seldom challenged by non-Natives, received up to $.30 a pound for carrying goods as far as 85 miles from Fortymile to the creeks. Winter rates fell to approximately one-third of the summer fee, largely because the use of dog teams made the work more efficient.[8] Wage rates in the mines reflected the differential treatment of non-Native and Native workers. Most labourers earned between $6 and $10 a day, a standard maintained by the labourers' refusal, expressed through an informal combination, to accept lower rates.[9] Native workers received less; a healthy, well-regarded Indian male might earn from $4 to $8 each working day (Bishop Bompas estimated the wages as £3.00 for non-Native and £2.00 for Native workers).[10] There were, in addition, several racially motivated attempts to exclude the Indians from the lucrative mine work.[11] To the suggestions that the Natives should demand fair treatment, Bishop Bompas commented: "In regard to the exclusion of the Indians from the mines, I do not think it would be wise to advise the Indians to insist on their strict rights in this respect and thus imperil the good feeling at present existing between Whites and Indians."[12] The limited demand for Native workers, coupled with restrictive attitudes toward them, prevented the Indians from controlling their labour more assertively, as they had done in the fur trade. In the short term, however, the comparatively high wages and demand for Native labour masked the structural changes in the use of Indian workers.

Mining offered other opportunities for Indians. The demand for foodstuffs increased dramatically over the fur-trade era. Salmon was needed for dog food; moose, caribou, and other game were required to supplement the miners' supplies. The mines were located close to the migratory trails of northern caribou herds, and moose were readily available in the river valleys, allowing the Indians to find enough game for their needs and those of the non-Native population.[13] As Bishop Bompas noted in 1895, the Indians "become rich by trading meat and fish with the miners, and working for them."[14] Natives living close to the mines tended to work as packers, mine labourers, and traders, leaving the provisioning trade to Indians a short distance away.

The economic effects of gold mining spread throughout the upper Yukon basin, although the primary changes centred on the Fortymile creeks. Many of the prospectors entering the district crossed the Chilkoot Pass, a small mountain divide connecting Lynn Canal and the headwaters of the Yukon River. The coastal Tlingit (Chilcat) Indians and, to a lesser degree, the inland Tagish bands transported supplies through the mountains. Prospectors and travellers complained of usurious charges, but the Chilcats protected their monopoly of the pass jealously and most travellers paid, albeit reluctantly.[15] The prospectors' willingness to risk the occasionally treacherous waters of the Yukon River in hastily built scows and rafts thwarted an extension of this shipping work into river travel. As well, Alaska Commercial company stern-wheelers plying the waters of the Yukon River from American territory well up into Canada brought in the bulk of provisions required by the miners. Natives did find some work along the river as guides, pilots, and packers, but most prospectors lacked the money to hire them on a long-term basis.[16]

Only occasionally did the Indians participate directly in the mining activity. Some did stake claims on newly opened creeks, but usually sold them at a substantial profit to other miners.[17] Flushed by the prospect of fabulous wealth, the prospectors often paid huge sums to secure a toe-hold on promising properties. Following the Rabbit (Bonanza) Creek discovery and before many realized the extent of the gold-field, miners bought Indian cabins located nearby, paying from $100 to $200 for each of the small structures. With hindsight and the intervention of Church of England missionary William Bompas, the Natives appealed for an extra payment in keeping with the rapid inflation in the area. In this instance, the Natives would have done well to hold onto their buildings.[18]

In August 1896 Tagish Charlie, Skookum Jim, and George Carmack discovered gold on Bonanza Creek. Carmack soon convinced others of the magnitude of their strike. Fortymile and other mining camps emptied as almost everyone in the area headed to grab a share of the new "Eldorado." Many of the Natives followed the migration to the new community at Dawson and re-established themselves in their now accepted role as provision hunters and casual labourers. The Klondike gold rush which followed reshaped the economic and social fabric in a way few envisaged. It was a major find to be sure, but those on the scene foresaw room for only a few thousand extra miners on the creeks. In the short term, before news of the strike reached the outside world in 1897, the Yukon economy continued largely as before, with the Natives secure in their role as a supplementary labour force to the mining community.

The early gold-mining frontier had brought surprisingly little change to the economic strategies of the Yukon Indians. Mining activity, which centred on the Stewart River and Fortymile region, directly affected less than one-fifth of the area. Most Indians stayed with hunting, gathering, and the fur trade. For those Natives drawn toward the mines, however, the potential for change was great. A cash economy based on wage labour and retail stores operated on a large scale for the first time. The comparative stability of the HBC trade was gone. The American, or free-trade, period had served as something of an intermediary stage between these apparent extremes, but it had not functioned independently long enough to serve as a real transition. With higher wages and more competition for their work, those Natives close to the diggings and personally disposed to participate in the mining economy found within it a means of satisfying their still limited material needs.

The Natives' economic position through the fur trade and the pre-gold rush mining interlude remained surprisingly consistent. The Fort Youcon Natives, for example, participated in both. While the HBC was in place, they worked as traders, fishermen, provision hunters, and part-time labourers. The onset of mining did not alter their economic activities in a major way. Wages and material rewards increased, but the Indians remained as provisioners and a short-term labour force engaged primarily in transportation and packing. These Indians also continued in the fur trade, particularly as middlemen, and they traded with distant bands denied access to the mining centres.[19] In brief, they retained a role similar to that held during the HBC era, a position which allowed them to earn sufficient cash (or barter potential) to purchase their material requirements from non-Native traders while interfering in only a limited way with their hunting and fishing cycles.[20]

The part-time and seasonal activities undertaken for both the fur traders and miners largely conformed to the annual cycles followed by the Indians. That the Natives could provide for their own subsistence, provision an expanding non-Native population, and occasionally work in mine-related ventures underscores the comparative affluence of the Natives' way of life. From an economic standpoint, mining activity did little to change the central basis of the Indians' lifestyle or their seasonal dependance upon the products of field and stream. The expanded opportunities for short-term employment did make it easier, however, to satisfy a small but growing appetite for the retailers' wares. The Natives purchased luxuries, including alcohol, more readily than before, and items such as guns, knives, and other iron goods which had been integrated into the Indians' material culture could be acquired with less effort. The combination of seasonal wage labour and a continued fur trade offered a new level of affluence for those Natives able to participate in mining.

If the arrival of the miners did not immediately alter Indian economic behaviour, it did introduce the structures of an industrial economy to the Yukon River basin. The fur trade with its racial accommodation and interdependence remained, but the old order was relegated to the background. Mining now dominated non-Native interest. Gold, not fur, was king and its requirements were to determine the contours of regional economic development over the following decades. Since the Indians were potential labourers, the dynamics of the labour market held the key to the level of Native integration in the mining economy. Their ability and desire to work, the availability of non-Native workers, the seasonal fluctuations in economic activity, the nature of work performed, and the employers' willingness to hire Natives worked together to form the framework of the mining labour market. This market, a highly informal and fluid construct, was of limited importance in the pre-gold rush years, but the system laid the basis for the Indians' participation in the new economic order.

The Yukon mines offered little regular work on the creeks for anyone without a claim. Employment prospects came primarily from the main support industries, transportation and provisioning. Labour demand was highly seasonal, requiring large numbers of workers in the summer months but few during the remainder of the year. Skilled workers were seldom required. Technicians were occasionally needed on the river boats, and the trading posts required clerks, but most jobs needed only a strong back and a solid constitution.

On the supply side of the equation, potential employers drew from a small, irregular pool of non-Native labourers or a larger, stable number of Indian men. A few non-Natives came north each year, drawn by reports of high wages. Given the cost of reaching the west-central Yukon, this cadre of workers remained small. A second, and larger, group of labourers included those miners yet to strike pay dirt or temporarily out of supplies. Short of funds but unwilling to abandon the quest for gold, these miners offered their services in hopes of raising money for yet another foray onto the creeks.[21] While more numerous than the first group, this second body of men was a small and unstable work-force, its size dependant upon the failure of prospectors already in the region. While the men were the first to be employed, especially for work in the diggings, it could not be counted on as a steady pool of seasonal labour.

By default, this left the Indians. Self-supporting through fishing, hunting, and fur trading, close at hand because of the fortuitous juxtaposition of the gold-fields and the home territories of the Kutchin and the Han, willing to accept menial work to help satisfy their material desires, the Natives were ideally situated to serve the labour needs of the embryonic Yukon mining industry.

The structure of the local labour market, in which the Indians served as a casual, seasonal work-force,[22] accounted for the Natives' successful and remunerative adaptation to the mining frontier. The service sector sought unskilled labourers and not skilled technicians, and, as long as the available pool of non-Native manpower remained small and variable, the Indians were assured of a significant economic role in the mines. Restricted access to external markets also ensured a steady need for the fish, meat, and fur harvested by the Indians when they were not working in the mining sector.

The fur trade had offered the Yukon Indians a profitable entrée into the white economy, but small-scale mining activity before the Klondike gold rush provided an even more advantageous economic situation for those Natives positioned to participate.[23] Their status was precarious, based as it was on the small number of much preferred non-Native labourers and the limited technology of placer-gold

extraction.[24] Still, the Natives had achieved a successful accommodation to a small-scale, localized mining community; whether this
balance would withstand an onslaught of miners and growing
sophistication in mining technology remained to be seen. The miners
had made no attempt to draw the Indians into the centre of the new
economic sector. The now dominant non-Native community accepted
the Natives' role as provisioners and seasonal labourers, but did not
encourage racial integration of the mines. It had, in effect, established
a racial class system, which ensured a constant supply of labour. The
Natives seldom challenged the exclusiveness of the placer diggings,
simply because the opportunity to combine harvesting pursuits and
occasional wage labour served their cultural and economic interests.

The onset of the Klondike gold rush quickly changed the dynamics. The story of the gold rush is familiar; only the bare outlines need
be sketched here.[25] News of the Klondike discovery reached the outside world in the summer of 1897, when miners carrying thousands
of dollars worth of gold disembarked from steamers in Seattle and
San Francisco. Depression-ridden North America responded overnight. Thousands of men and a scattering of women – some bonafide
miners, most starry-eyed dreamers and camp-followers – quit their
jobs, left their families, and struck out for the Klondike. A few thousand made it to the Yukon that same year, but the majority arranged
their affairs so as to arrive in the gold-fields the following summer.
Estimates of the size of this human wave vary, but as many as 50,000
arrived in 1898 alone. Most of the would-be miners were quickly
disabused of their expectations. The prime gold-bearing land had all
been staked before news even reached the outside. Disgruntled and
demoralized, thousands left soon after arriving in Dawson City, a
centre which had sprung up on the flats at the mouth of the Klondike
river and which proudly described itself as the largest Canadian city
west of Winnipeg. While the mining and urban population quickly
dropped from the heady heights of 1898–99, the federal census of
1901 still recorded over 27,000 people in the territory.[26] Gold discoveries at Nome, Alaska, and Atlin, British Columbia, in 1898 encouraged miners to leave for richer fields. But the Yukon continued to
exert its magnetic appeal. Each year, would-be prospectors shrugged
off the endless tales of hardship and broken dreams and decided to
try their luck in the district. By 1905, however, the gold rush had
dwindled to a trickle. Aided by a sympathetic federal government,
large gold concessionaires bought up the creek beds, gained control
of water rights, and brought in big dredges and hydraulic operations.
The technology allowed the companies to strip the river bottoms and
hillsides of their wealth more quickly and efficiently than the small-

scale, independent placer miners had done.[27]

As an economic and social event, the gold rush lasted less than a decade, giving way to the more systematic and highly capitalized exploitation of the Yukon's mineral resources. Yet its short duration obscures its significance, for in short order the Klondike gold rush overturned the demographic, racial, and economic balance of the Yukon river valley. Before 1896 Natives had outnumbered others by approximately four to one; the 1901 census, taken two years after the height of the rush, revealed a population of eight non-Natives for every Indian.[28] In these circumstances the tenuous prosperity of Indians involved in the mining economy was at risk. Just as important, amidst the aggressive, individualistic frenzy of the gold rush, the need for an accommodation with the Indians evaporated. Any prior consideration of the Natives' interest was consumed by the lust for gold.

Whereas the effects of the initial mining development had remained localized, Indians throughout the region were drawn into the gold rush. Prospectors used several corridors to reach Dawson, although most crossed by way of the Chilkoot or White Pass. Other routes, including the Dalton Trail in the southwest corner of the district, and a variety of branch routes connecting the self-proclaimed gateway to the Klondike, Edmonton, and the gold-fields, similarly provided access to Dawson.[29] Indians along each of these routes were drawn, often in a tangential and temporary fashion, into the gold-rush. The Bennett Lake corridor, however, remained the principal focus.

The mining activity itself centred on the tributaries of the Klondike river, and while Indians throughout the district felt the magnetic pull of the gold-fields, the economic forces were strongest in the area immediately surrounding the mines. A significant number of Natives moved closer to Dawson City, hoping to take advantage of perceived economic opportunities. Although decimated by disease, the Han Indians remained in the area, as did a number of former inhabitants of the Fortymile district who followed the miners' migration upstream. Natives from as far away as Fort McPherson on the Peel river and along the Porcupine River in the northern Yukon came to Dawson.[30] Although most of the Yukon Indians remained far away from the gold-fields, the ripple effect of this dramatic economic reorganization reached throughout the territory.

The most noticeable characteristic of the Yukon Indians during the Klondike period was their comparative anonymity. In earlier times, the Natives had maintained a high profile and contemporaries had frequently commented on their activities. During the gold rush, they received less attention. The records illustrate that the gold rush was an overwhelmingly non-Native phenomenon, with the Native people swiftly relegated to a peripheral position. The stampede produced a prodigious volume of diaries, autobiographies, and travelogues, but the Indians, where they appear, do so only on the margins. The authors, and one suspects the readers, of these tracts had little interest in what many perceived to be the dying remnants of yet another group of Indians. The prospectors' relentless pursuit of gold, and the hardships they encountered, monopolized the attention of southern audiences. Government agents and even most clergy viewed the care and protection of the non-Native population as their principal responsibility, and as a result comments on the Indians appear irregularly in their records.[31] But despite limited contemporary comment, the Natives played a role in the development of the gold-fields, and their experience represented an important phase in their adaptation to the changing Yukon economy.

At the beginning of the gold rush, the Natives attempted to retain the functions they had performed at the Fortymile camps. A number of them worked as labourers, guides, or wood-cutters, always on a short-term basis.[32] In addition, the miners' need for meat escalated. In the first months of the rush, therefore, demand for Native labour exceeded all previous experience, and high wages predominated.[33]

As prospectors prepared to cross over the mountain passes and into the Yukon basin, Indians resident near the routes found ready and remunerative employment as packers. At the foot of the Chilkoot Pass, Tlingit Indians offered to pack goods up the steep trails. Their prices had risen in step with demand, jumping from 1 cent per pound in 1896 to from 5 to 7 cents in 1897. The continued onslaught of stampeders in 1898 and 1899 did not, however, bring greater rewards. Expanded use of pack trains and tramways and eventually the opening of the White Pass and Yukon Route Railway, connecting tidewater and Whitehorse, undercut the Indians' packing enterprise.[34] Similar opportunities existed on a small scale in the far north, along the mountain passes between the Mackenzie and Yukon river basins. The Kutchin found well-paid employment packing supplies across the Stony Creek Pass, which joined the Peel and Porcupine rivers, and providing provisions for poorly prepared miners encamped along that route and the Peel-Wind river path to the Klondike. The rush through the northern Yukon lasted only two years, and never attracted a non-Native entrepreneur to compete with Indian labour.[35]

For many Yukon Indians, the gold rush initially brought greater prosperity than had the fur trade or early mining frontier. The expansion of mining activity and the scale of the invasion ensured that the economic benefits were dispersed more widely than previously. Such returns proved transitory, however, for they rested on a scarcity of non-Native labour and lack of alternatives to Indian manpower. The arrival of thousands of miners, few of whom staked paying claims, and the expansion of roads and rail lines between Dawson City and the creeks eliminated much of the need for local Indian labour.[36] The non-Native invasion undercut many Native occupations and severely restricted Native participation in the emerging economy.

Provisioning, an important aspect of the Native economy since the first days of the fur trade, proved to be the only sector to provide consistent returns. Natives throughout the region participated in the provisioning of thousands of miners, government officials (especially policemen), and the few emerging settlements (Whitehorse, Dawson, Carcross, and Selkirk being the most notable). Nevertheless, while the markets increased, there were significant limits on the Natives' ability to develop the full potential of the provisioning trade. To prevent widespread starvation, the Canadian government decreed that each person entering the territory bring 1,000 pounds of foodstuffs, an estimated one-year supply.[37] This strictly enforced edict obviously lessened demand for indigenous products. That many of those entering the district left soon after their arrival in Dawson compounded the impact of the supply regulations. These disgruntled sojourners sold their outfits in the mining camps, using the proceeds to raise funds for their return trip. The miners could not bring in fresh meat and fish, but many did hunt, thereby further restricting the market for animal carcasses and increasing pressure on local game resources. At times, the miners also competed with non-Native fishermen for access to the Yukon River salmon run.[38] Additional improvements in transportation, particularly the opening of a year-round rail link between Whitehorse and coast, ensured a reliable supply of foodstuffs from the south and a further reduction in demand for supplies from the Indians.

Other avenues of employment existed, but few offered regular incomes. Women earned money manufacturing clothing for sale to the miners. A market existed for such Native products as snowshoes and sleds, but the Indians' inability and unwillingness to produce large quantities restricted the market.[39] Similarly, in the first days of the rush, there seemed to be an insatiable demand for dogs, and those Indians willing to part with their animals earned sizeable sums. But since these same dogs were essential to their hunting activities, the Natives seldom surrendered their teams. Several non-Native entrepreneurs capitalized on the demand for dogs by heading to the northern reaches of the territory – the Porcupine River country and the Arctic slope – where they purchased dogs from Indians and Inuit. They then drove the animals back to Dawson and sold them for a handsome profit.[40]

The limited availability of government relief also altered economic conditions and options. Prodded by Bishop Bompas and other members of the CMS to provide better care for the Natives,[41] the federal government directed the North-West Mounted Police (NWMP) to provide emergency supplies for destitute Indians. But only those Natives with access to the police posts scattered along the Bennett-Dawson corridor could benefit. Moreover, general prosperity together with strict government regulations ensured that few asked for the parsimonious allotments. Some of the ill and aged relied on government relief. Others, on rare occasions, found government support to be a useful counterbalance to the occasional insecurity of the hunting and gathering economy, especially in those areas feeling the impact of combined Native and non-Native hunting.[42]

While most Yukon Indians continued to hunt for sustenance and market and trap furs for trade, others participated more actively in the mining economy. Several found semi-skilled employment. Some worked as deck-hands on the steamboats plying the waters of the Yukon, others as woodcutters supplying cordwood for the same vessels.[43] Several Native groups, such as the Peel River Kutchin, migrated towards Dawson City, where they found seasonal and temporary employment. Richard Slobodin, who interviewed some of these "Dawson Boys," wrote: "Summer activities, however, opened up a new life. Fourteen major summer occupations for this period have been recorded, of which ten were quite novel to these people. They included deckhand on steamboats, scow pilot, carpenter, motorboat mechanic, pool-hall handyman, licensed trader, and, for women, laundress and mining camp cook."[44]

While a variety of employment prospects existed, most of them similar to work done during the fur-trade and early mining periods, they continued to be seasonal in nature. The Natives left their summer positions each fall and returned to their hunting camps and traplines. The Indians' accommodation to the new economic ventures occurred, importantly, within the contours of their hunting-gathering patterns. As anthropologist Alice Kehoe wrote of the impact of the gold rush: "Dene, eager for cash or novelty, flocked to these towns, men selling fish and meat or working as labourers on the steamboats, at the river docks, and in the towns, women working as laundresses if their husbands brought them along. The majority of Dene men made excursions for wage labour in the pattern of hunting and trapping, leaving the wives and children in camp."[45] Her description conforms closely to Asch's characterization of the "mixed economy," with the Indians accommodating varied, but transitory, sources of income into regular seasonal cycles.[46]

A small number of Yukon Indians, including the codiscoverers of the Klondike gold-fields, Skookum Jim and Tagish Charlie, prospected for gold and other minerals. It is extremely difficult to gauge the level of this activity. Several commentators observed that Native people staked paying claims only to have them, in Bishop Bompas's words, "bargained away from him by the cleverer white."[47] Considerable attention focused on the efforts of Skookum Jim and Tagish Charlie, who, with another Native, Jim Boss, searched for another bonanza. They were not able to repeat the Klondike strike.[48]

Already wealthy from their initial discovery, Skookum Jim and Tagish Charlie had the option of stepping outside the hunting and trapping order. There is considerable evidence that the two men struggled with the demands associated with their wealth and their unexpected position between their people and the materialism of non-Native society. Tagish Charlie did not enjoy the financial rewards from his claim for long. Crossing the railway bridge in Carcross in 1908, he fell into the frigid waters and drowned. Skookum Jim, as Morris Zaslow has written, "tired of trying to keep up with the whites, eventually withdrew to Carcross and the safety of the church-dominated environment where he, too, died, in 1916."[49]

Others demonstrated greater entrepreneurial skill. Chief Jim Boss, variously a miner, trader, and road-house operator, adapted easily to the demands and values of the commercial frontier. His case, which was exceptional, indicates that there was no single Native response to the changes in the Yukon economy. Location, timing, and personality all played important roles in determining the response of individual Indians to the prospects and limitations presented by the expansion of mining.

One of the most significant implications of the Klondike gold rush lay in the extension of non-Native economic interests throughout the territory. Before 1896 non-Native activity extended little beyond the west-central Yukon and the Porcupine River. Many Natives consequently had little or no contact with non-Natives. The gold rush broke down the old barriers, usually established by other Indian bands, that had prevented such groups from visiting the non-Native settlements. The Copper Indians in the White River district had been prevented by the Han from contacting Fortymile and by the Tlingit from reaching the Haines area. When the first NWMP patrols had reached the White River district, the officers noted the Indians' reliance on outdated firearms, a lack of many supplies, and the Indians' general "backwardness" as compared to other Yukon Natives.[50] The isolation of the Copper, Kaska, and eastern Tutchone bands gradually dissolved as prospectors and traders expanded their operations. For these Natives, new economic opportunities included little more than provisioning and fur trading, but improved accessibility to non-Native traders made the acquisition of material goods far easier.

As before, the economic prospects of the Yukon Natives depended on their own interests and the structure of the territorial labour market.[51] The relationship between the miners' needs and the available supply of able-bodied workers went a long way toward determining the number and type of positions available. The economy retained much of its seasonal character, expanding in the summer, contracting dramatically as winter approached. As the placer-mining process passed from individual miners to the gold concessions, and as the regional transportation system improved, the need for skilled workers escalated. Lacking the requisite technical skills and without the industrial work ethic demanded by most employers, the Natives vied for a declining number of unskilled positions. Even here, they faced increasing competition from the large number of non-Natives who continued to enter the Yukon Territory after the initial bloom of the gold rush faded. Unable to find paying gold claims, these men often offered their services to others, taking up work along the rail line, in Whitehorse, on the steamboats, in Dawson, or on the creeks. The size of this labour pool forced wage rates down, despite uniformly high prices. Additionally, the Native workers found few openings in the mining or service sectors.[52] They were regarded as a labour source of last resort by most employers, because of non-Native perceptions of the Indians' unwillingness to work. Indians were increasingly limited to pursuits deemed, by Natives and non-Natives alike, fitted to their Native status. All in all, their decision to participate only marginally in the mining economy made sense, for they probably earned as much from hunting and trapping as they could through temporary employment in the mining camps. The Indians consequently remained what they had been before 1896 – fur trappers, casual labourers, and meat harvesters – although they faced increasing competition from the non-Natives in these areas as well.

The forces of the market-place had uneven effects. Supply and demand served, ironically, to bar Indian women from prostitution. In other gold-rush and frontier settings, Native women (usually under the control of Native or non-Native men) earned a considerable amount of money as prostitutes.[53] Given the substantial sexual imbalance of the incoming population, many government agents and missionaries feared that Native prostitution was inevitable. Little such activity occurred, however, less even than in the early days at Fortymile when Indian women frequently visited the miners' cabins. The tremendous publicity surrounding the gold rush ensured that white women with an inclination to satisfy the miners' sexual needs quickly found their way north and began to "mine the miners."[54] The availability of non-Native prostitutes meant that Indian women found little place in this financially rewarding, if socially undesirable, profession.

On balance, the cumulative legacy of the Klondike gold rush for the Native population was decidedly less positive than that of earlier mining developments. Previously profitable Native involvement in mining activity, based on a scarcity of non-Native labour, gave way as the massive flood of would-be prospectors filled most available jobs and even spilled over into the Indian sphere. The Yukon Indians no longer occupied the centre of the territorial labour pool. Left on the periphery, they continued to hunt and sold their surplus to the miners and camp followers. As time passed, however, there was increasing competition for fur and meat resources, reducing Native returns from this source. The fur trade continued to offer respectable returns,[55] but for Indians near Dawson City, fur resources dwindled rapidly. At the opposite end, the emergence of Native capitalists, individuals motivated by the search for profit and personal gain, indicated the full range of the Indian response to the new economic realities. In the final analysis, the gold rush revealed the nature of the Natives' precarious link to the mining economy. Non-Native society did not encourage the integration of Natives and non-Natives. The Indians served for a time as a casual labour pool, but generally remained outside the mainstream of the new economic order. The Natives accepted this state of affairs with equanimity, for with only a few exceptions most of them willingly and ably maintained their valued hunting and gathering pursuits. There were, however, some problems. Some Indian groups, notably the Han, faced a major depletion of game in their area, and Natives throughout the territory now had to deal with regular incursions by non-Native prospectors and hunters. The isolation of earlier periods was gone. All Yukon Indians would now have to deal with the demands and opportunities of the new economy.

The economic order presaged by the Stewart and Fortymile River gold camps did not come to pass. In its stead, the Yukon economy began to separate into two sectors, one based on the extraction and transportation of mineral resources, the other on fur trapping and the pursuit of game. Points of contact were few. By the end of the Klondike gold rush, the Yukon economy had been set on a new course. The rush had further entrenched the two-sector structure of the territorial economy.

CHAPTER THREE

Yukon Indians in the Post-1900 Economy

The Klondike gold rush pushed the Yukon Indians to the periphery of the regional economy. The returns from gold-fields soon slowed, and many miners left the region as quickly as they had arrived. The future course of the territorial economy lay uncharted, no obvious successor emerged to replace the rich placer fields. Yet the magnitude and intensity of the upheaval experienced from 1896 to 1905 would remain unmatched until the Second World War, when American soldiers and construction workers invaded the region and recast the territorial economy. Though short-lived, the Klondike gold rush had reshaped the territorial order.

Initially, the Klondike gold rush simply replaced the region's dependence on the fur trade with a reliance on gold. The economy evolved and diversified in the following years, contracting in scale but expanding in variety. The continued exploitation of the Klondike gold-fields, a revived search for new deposits, the opening of several new mines, and a myriad of related transportation and supply activities formed the central core of the Yukon economy. Government attention, public expectations, and investment capital focused almost exclusively on the prospects for mineral development. The hunting and trapping sector, operating away from the Whitehorse-Dawson corridor, had markedly different characteristics. Based on a resurgent fur market and a growing interest in big-game hunting, and reaching into virtually every corner of the Yukon, this segment attracted little outside interest. The Indians had a role in both sectors. Their participation in the mining economy was tangential and seasonal; in the fur and hunting trades, it was permanent and central. Significantly, they provided the principal bridge between the two sectors.

Mining remained the main focus for the Yukon economy. The slow death of the gold rush, as much a social as an economic phenomenon, sapped the territory of much of its vitality, but mining activity continued and even diversified. The gold-fields near Dawson City remained in production, albeit under markedly different circumstances. The prospector's tools became obsolete, replaced by mammoth dredges which scoured the gravel of the river beds once again, seeking the fine gold dust and small nuggets that had eluded the inefficient sluicing operations of the early placer miners. Simultaneously the prospector/placer miner – the central figure of Yukon legend – was effectively shut out as the creeks fell under the control of large mining corporations. The arrival of the concessionaires, assisted by a federal government committed to helping its Liberal friends and encouraging the rapid exploitation of what they viewed as a marginal resource base, initially generated much animosity. As returns from individual holdings declined, however, most prospectors realized that their era had passed, and they moved on. There was nothing romantic or attractive in the mammoth dredges; nothing that could match the aura surrounding the human toil and suffering of the Klondike rush. But they were efficient. The highly mechanized industry continued to find gold, although in decreasing quantities. Further rationalization of the industry became essential, leading to the formation in 1929 of the Yukon Consolidated Gold Corporation, a consortium of the three largest dredging firms. This new corporation, aided by stable gold prices, continued operations through the 1930s and provided much of the territory's gold production.[1]

A few determined miners, dogged by a relentless lust for gold and an irrepressible optimism, continued the search for a new Eldorado. They turned away from Dawson and environs and scoured the territory from the southern border to the Arctic coast, pushing with limited success into a number of previously undeveloped areas. Promising reports filtered in from around the region, as one prospector after another staked a discovery claim on yet another creek. But only a few sites, such as the Livingstone Creek area in the central Yukon and the gold and silver deposits in the Kluane Lake district, attracted more than a cursory glance.

The most promising mineral activity came not from gold, but from other ores detected in the search for placer deposits. Copper mines opened near Whitehorse at the turn of the century, although high transportation costs limited the profitability of such enterprises. Prospectors identified a major silver-lead deposit in the Mayo area around 1906, but the discovery lay undeveloped for another decade. Once exploited, the Keno mines provided a crucial economic boost for the Yukon. By the 1920s, several mines and a concentrating mill were in operation. The opening of the Mayo-Keno area required extensive changes in the transportation infrastructure, including an upgrading of rail capacity and the deployment of new, shallow-draught steamers along the Yukon and Stewart rivers.[2]

This restructured and diversified mining economy held only a peripheral role for the Indians. It needed heavily capitalized and mechanized operations as well as skilled labourers to operate the equipment. The demand for workers, while more specialized, was also more limited and stable; the externally controlled mining corporations ensured that the required workers were on site. Industrial work in the Yukon retained its seasonal dimensions, particularly in the transportation sector, although hard-rock mining around Mayo continued year-round. Improved communication and transportation links to the outside, principally the Vancouver market, allowed employers to meet most of their labour needs without resorting to Indian workers.

Some Natives did find employment in this sector. Native people continued to prospect, hoping for a repeat of the strike that brought wealth and fame to Tagish Charlie and Skookum Jim. Paddy Duncan, later imprisoned for murder, discovered gold on Squaw Creek and made a considerable amount of money, which did not last for long.[3] In 1924 two Natives, Sam Smith and Big Lake Jim, struck gold near Little Atlin. They told their Native friends before informing non-Natives in the area, resulting in Native domination of the initial staking rush.[4] This particular rush, like so many others, proved illusory, but it did demonstrate Native interest in prospecting. A small number of Indians actually worked in the mines,[5] especially at the small copper properties near Whitehorse. But few managers, most of whom carried decidedly negative stereotypes of Indian labour with them from the south, willingly substituted Native workers for the readily available and skilled, albeit more expensive, white workers.[6] A.E. Green, the inspector of Indian schools for British Columbia, wrote of the Natives after a tour of the Yukon: "Only a small number of these Indians know how to do any ordinary work, and even if they did, there is not work to be had anywhere near where they live."[7] Not many Indians challenged the racial economic barriers barring them from work in the white man's world. It was just as well, for there were few openings.[8]

If the Indians could not, or would not, meld into the expanding industrial order, they none the less would make a fair return supplying the mines and in related transportation activities.[9] In 1916, for example, eight Native longshoremen worked out of Whitehorse.[10] Several others worked each year as deck-hands on the river boats and as section-hands for the White Pass and Yukon Route Railway. No figures are available on the numbers securing such positions, but it is likely that the total seldom exceeded a few dozen. Any estimate is further clouded by a Department of Indian Affairs official's observation that a group of Fraser River Natives from southern British Columbia came to the Yukon each summer to find work on the vessels. The Yukon River steamship fleet consumed vast quantities of wood each year, and a profitable market developed along the river banks. For those living close to the river, woodcutting provided a good source of income and was easily incorporated into seasonal harvesting cycles. By the mid-1920s, small steamers plied most of the navigable streams, extending the opportunity throughout the district. As in other such profitable ventures, the Indians soon found their predominance challenged by white woodcutters.[11] Supplying the steamers, however, remained a major source of income for the Indians, particularly those who lived along the heavily travelled Yukon River route.[12]

Provision hunting for the mines and settlements proved even more remunerative while also serving to draw the Indians closer to the white communities. In the three principal centres, Dawson, Whitehorse, and Mayo, the demand for wild game remained steady. Beef and pork were hard to obtain, and local residents turned to less familiar, but less expensive, indigenous supplies. Many whites hunted for themselves, but others relied on Native and white provision hunters.[13] For the Indians, the attraction of this activity lay in the comparatively high financial return and the fact that it drew on, rather than displaced, seasonal patterns and Native skills.

There are few statistical indications of the size of the provision market. One recent estimate of the demand in Dawson City in 1904, when the population was approximately 9,000, suggests that residents required some 600 moose and 2,300 caribou annually to supplement available meat stocks.[14] While a good portion would have been provided by residents themselves, particularly in the Dawson area where the Fortymile caribou herd annually passed within a few miles of the town, provision hunters still had a significant role. The market proved variable, however, dependent upon the consumption habits of the local population, the price and availability of alternative meats, competition from white hunters, and the availability of game near the towns. In addition to the town markets, Indians in outlying districts sold meat to fur traders and policemen. The traders, in a manner reminiscent of the similar trade in the HBC era, relied heavily on foodstuffs purchased from the Natives. It was only in this small, isolated market that the Indians enjoyed even a modicum of security and freedom from white competition.[15]

Government records provide scant evidence on the contours and profitability of the Yukon provision trade. A list of game licences issued in 1921 illustrates the extent of white competition in the supposedly Indian field. Of the fifty-three licences recorded, only seven went to Natives (all from the Mayo area).[16] This in no way indicates the comparative participation of whites and Indians, for Natives only occasionally took out the licences formally required for the trade. It does, however, illustrate that a sizeable number of white hunters engaged in this enterprise. Statements of game purchased by Waechter Brothers of Dawson City in 1925 and 1927 reveal further aspects of the competition and returns from the sale of meat. In both years, Native hunters far outstripped whites, both in the number offering produce for sale and the quantity of meat sold. Prices ranged from 10 cents to 22 cents per pound, with payment dependent upon the type of meat and the manner in which it was dressed. For several Indians, the transactions proved quite lucrative. B. Silas and J. Johns earned $236 and $565 respectively for meat sold in 1927. It is possible that these men also sold to other retailers or, as is more likely, directly to consumers.[17]

Native hunters faced some difficulties selling their produce because urban purchasers allegedly favoured the meat offered by white hunters. George Jeckell, controller for the Yukon, pointed out in 1944: "In past years the white population was small and the amount of game sold to the white population by the Indians was insignificant, and this was particularly due to the fact that white people in general do not care to purchase game from Indians because the game they take is not slaughtered carefully and not kept clean and wholesome."[18] This stereotype of the "dirty Indian" was characteristic of white attitudes toward the Indians of the Yukon. In this instance, white perceptions of Native customs and harvesting practices likely carried significant economic costs.

Provisioning was a double-edged sword for the Indians, offering a welcome if inconsistent source of funds while simultaneously adding to the pressure on available game stocks. Whether harvested by Natives or whites (and the latter demonstrated little interest in the long-term stability of the trade), game supplies adjacent to major centres were seriously depleted. The market continued into the 1940s, ending only when heightened concern for wildlife conservation convinced the territorial government to join other Canadian jurisdictions in banning the harvesting of wild game for retail sale.[19]

For many Natives, the provision trade and the similarly structured woodcutting enterprise provided the only significant points of contact with the industrial and town economies. Through a combination of Indian preference for harvesting and white-imposed restrictions on Native workers, the Indians found themselves relegated to the economic periphery. The tasks thus left open to them, woodcutting and market hunting, did not require a repudiation of their nomadic and cyclical patterns. Instead, as Michael Asch argues, they became key elements in the "mixed economy." The Indians sought some accommodation with the cash economy (beyond the fur trade) to pay for required or desired trade goods. Short-term participation did not indicate that the Indians wished to abandon their harvesting mode of production in favour of an industrial pattern. Ironically, both Natives and whites found the Indians' position on the fringes of the industrial economy to be acceptable, although each approached the economic contact with very different motives and perceptions.

The moderate level of industrial activity, subject to periodic fluctuations caused by declining resources or falling prices, remained in place for over thirty-five years, recalling the comparative stability of the pre-Klondike mining era and highlighting the episodic nature of that dramatic event. The onset of the Second World War, and particularly the construction of the Alaska Highway and Canol Pipeline, quickly altered the nature of the regional economy and for a short, intense period, not unlike the Klondike era, upset the relatively stable, if modest, territorial economy.

Northern promoters had, for years, lauded the potential benefits of a highway to Alaska. Early in 1942, facing the apparent threat of a Japanese invasion, the American government decided to act. Thousands of men, accompanied by tons of equipment and supplies, descended on the Yukon. More than thirty thousand men eventually worked on the highway, pipeline airfields, and related projects. By October 1943, a military road passable in winter had been opened, and work began on upgrading the highway.[20] This massive infusion of capital and people, and the construction of a transportation route through the previously inaccessible southern Yukon, had significant implications for the territorial economy.[21]

While most of the work-force consisted of labourers imported from southern Canada and the United States, local residents found some opportunities. A number of Natives joined the new enterprise, hiring on as guides for survey crews, as labourers and, in a few instances, as equipment operators. Money was also to be made selling meat and fish to the construction camps.[22] Employment prospects for Indian women were more limited, but some living near construction camps found work taking in laundry, sewing, and house cleaning. The government attempted to encourage the demand for Native handicrafts,[23] sponsoring a program to encourage Indian women to make souvenirs and clothing for the soldiers and construction workers. But the Natives' lack of interest, and the realization that many young women did not have the required skills, ultimately forced the abandonment of the project.[24]

During the construction phase there were jobs to be had, and many Indians took advantage of the short-term opportunities. A shortage of white workers in the Dawson area in 1942 forced the Yukon Consolidated Gold Corporation to take the unheard of step of hiring Indians as labourers. It did so with trepidation, unsure that the Natives would adapt well to the industrial work routine. The company's fears were realized when the Indians left their jobs in time for the fall hunting.[25] Such conflicts of economic interest, reflecting the Natives' desire to mix industrial labour and harvesting, were not unusual during the building of the highway.

Government officials, interestingly, did not support the integration of Native people into the construction work-force. C.K. LeCapelain, Canadian liaison officer, observed: "Technically, I believe, the Indians are free agents and should be permitted the same opportunities of obtaining lucrative employment as white people and of associating with them. In practise this will be to their detriment if the majority of them die of disease within a few years. Consequently, I think every endeavour should be made to influence or persuade them to continue their ancestral and normal nomadic life of hunting and trapping and to avoid close association with white people."[26]

The new activities, while rivalling the fabled gold rush in scale and drama, did not signal an immediate or lasting alteration of Native economic behaviour nor of white attitudes towards Indian workers. The type of employment available to the Indians – unskilled and temporary – resembled the positions Natives had held in the mining and transportation sector in the previous half century. As before the ready availability of skilled, non-Native labour ensured that project organizers would view the Indians only as a casual labour pool. Called upon when required, working largely when industrial labour meshed with harvesting activities, the Indians found only a minor role in Alaska Highway construction.

Between 1900 and 1950 the Yukon Indians' accommodation to the work habits of the industrial sector remained limited. This was largely because the second sector of the territorial economy was still viable. Despite extensive mining activity in the Yukon, the Indians retained an option shared by few other Native groups in North America – that of maintaining a hunting-trapping lifestyle into the second half of the twentieth century. The white population was small, dropping to 2,700 in the 1920s and 1930s, and was seasonal and concentrated in Dawson, Mayo-Keno, and Whitehorse. There was, consequently, little competition for the land and resources of the territory. Whites sought minerals, removing only an insignificant portion of land from general use. For much of the territory, the pursuit of game remained the most important economic activity.

Given their skills and habits, the Yukon Indians continued to favour hunting and trapping. They were seldom completely alone. Their activities intertwined with those of white fur traders and their prosperity was determined as much by the volatile fur markets of North America and Europe as by harvesting conditions in the Yukon. In addition, Native harvesting procedures were subject to fluctuating pressure from non-Natives drawn to trapping by potentially high returns. A fur trade markedly different from its nineteenth-century ancestor served as the mainstay of this sector of the Yukon economy, but fishing and big-game hunting also attracted Native attention. These latter pursuits, small in scale and economic impact, will be examined first.

Fishing, which formed a crucial part of the aboriginal seasonal cycle, seldom enjoyed much success as a commercial venture. Natives around the territory, but particularly along the Yukon River and in the Alsek River drainage, harvested salmon during annual runs.[27] They caught other species of fish as well, particularly whitefish and lake trout, when available and when required. These also provided an adequate supply of food to feed the dogs so crucial to northern Indian life. Most fishing, therefore, served primarily to satisfy personal needs, with only occasional surpluses offered for sale. The government permitted the Indians free access to the fishery, stepping in whenever non-Native catches threatened Native harvests.[28] Canadian officials could, however, do little to prevent the massive over-fishing of salmon by Americans on the lower Yukon, and all but ignored the environmental impact of placer mining on fishing streams and rivers. Some Natives attempted to sell their catch, particularly in Dawson City, but these were only small ventures. In one instance, a Moosehide Indian named Silas enjoyed short-lived success marketing his fish to a Dawson restaurant. The profitable operation ceased when a non-Native fisherman protested against the unlicensed activity. The investigating officer noted that previous fish sales in town had been unchallenged, but, faced with the fisherman's complaints, he had no option but to prevent the Natives from selling their catch.[29] The Yukon River fishery remained modest, serving little more than personal needs, as indicated by the Indians' reluctance to take out the licences required to market their harvests legally.[30]

While the Yukon River fishery provided few prospects, conditions in the Alsek drainage were more favourable. Larger fish runs in the southwest and limited non-Native activity ensured that the harvesting of salmon remained a vital part of the Natives' food production. Because of the limited market, fishing satisfied subsistence needs and little more. Still, access to the rich resources, particularly at Klukshu, was jealously guarded; loud protests followed any infringement of fishing territories or attempted government interference in the harvest. The opportunity for Natives to participate in the Haines, Alaska, salmon fishery was of greater significance. While it remained impossible to market Yukon-caught fish, Natives in the southwest exported their labour to take advantage of the high wages on the coast. For generations, Yukon Indians had made annual treks to the Pacific coast for trade and social events. They easily adapted this cycle to incorporate a short stint in the fishery, where high fish prices (8 cents per dog salmon and 30 cents for each Coho and Sockeye in 1918) ensured a profitable return. Yet, in this instance as well, commercial fishing was a casual rather than regular occupation, resorted to only when a specific need or desire dictated.[31] On a territory-wide basis, fishing had a limited market function, serving more as a source of food than income.[32]

While only technological improvements and a small cash market separated the fishery from aboriginal practices, big-game guiding represented a major departure from the Natives' lifestyle. The occupation emerged early in the twentieth century, increasing slowly in scale as the Yukon came to be recognized as a world-class preserve of trophy sheep, moose, and caribou. Throughout this period, however, it remained small and geographically restricted. Most of the activity focused on the southern territory, particularly the Carcross and Kluane districts, but the Mayo-Pelly region also attracted some hunters. Fewer than twenty hunters per year entered the territory in pursuit of trophies. While the hunters paid sizeable sums for the privilege of hunting on the last frontier, the overall impact of the industry was limited.[33]

Although most of the chief guides were white, the most famous Yukon guide was Johnny Johns, an enfranchised Indian from the Carcross area. The Yukon Territorial Game Ordinance of 1923, however, barred Natives from serving as chief guides, limiting them to inferior positions as assistant guides and camp helpers.[34] The government later eased that provision, giving the controller of the Yukon discretionary power to decide if the Indian requesting approval could meet the anticipated responsibilities. The government had a second reason for this discriminatory regulation: "In a

Territory so much on the frontier as the Yukon is it has been considered inadvisable to issue Chief Guide Licenses to Indians indiscriminately as under the Yukon Ordinance a Chief Guide is in fact a Game Guardian."[35]

There is little doubt that the government, supported by other guides, worked to keep the Indians out of this potentially profitable enterprise. In one case in 1941, a Native, Billy Hall, applied for a licence to guide a party into the Little Atlin region. The government sent a police officer to investigate Hall's personal and financial status. The policeman's report offered a positive character reference, but questioned Hall's ability to supply the necessary equipment. Commissioner Jeckell refused the application.[36]

Such discriminatory action stemmed from a belief that Indians could not adequately serve the hunters and would thereby harm the region's image in the industry, an argument which appears badly strained by the fact that Johnny Johns became one of the most highly respected and famous hunting guides in North America. There was also a fear that allowing too many guides into the industry would hurt the returns of those already in business; most guides, in fact, also worked as trappers or traders. While the non-Native big-game guides' arguments were clearly self-serving and exclusionist, they were successful in limiting the Indians' role in the industry.

The few jobs available from the guiding operators were eagerly sought after by Natives. In the late 1920s an assistant guide could earn as much as $10 a day.[37] But few Natives, particularly those in the southern Yukon, had access to these employment opportunities. Those who did, according to Eugene Jacquot, a chief guide at Burwash Landing, could earn between $300 and $500 over the course of a summer in the 1940s.[38] While guiding enjoyed a high profile, it did not represent a major economic departure before 1950; there were only 3 licensed chief guides in the territory in 1941.[39] Like most of the other opportunities available to the Indians, guiding called on talents deemed to be particularly "Native," primarily the ability to hunt and track game.[40]

The fur trade stood in stark contrast to fishing and big-game guiding. The industry had long since lost its high profile in Canada, but the northern fur trade remained surprisingly vital, even expansive. If not the most remunerative activity in the Yukon (mining led the fur trade in gross receipts), the fur trade was more geographically dispersed. Natives in all corners of the territory participated directly, with trading posts located near most major centres of Native population. In 1921, for example, the Yukon government issued licences for twenty-seven separate establishments, operated by eighteen different companies or individuals. The only area not served directly

Table 3
Fur Returns by District, Selected Years ($)

Year	Whitehorse[1]	Dawson	Central[2]	North
1920	104,951	79,634	48,488	125,643
1922	100,556	33,806	18,273	55,223
1924	129,690	41,217	53,005	70,901
1939	143,109	82,958	23,073	69,563
1943	170,025	67,998	45,982	90,056

Source   YTA, YRG1, series 4, vol. 17, file 336A, Regional Breakdown of Number of Pelts, Maltby to Mackenzie, 31 August 1920; ibid., Maltby to Telford, 28 November 1922; ibid., vol. 18, file 336B, Maltby to Reid, 7 January 1925; YRG1, series 3, vol. 10, file 12–19B, Statement re: Fur Production, Trapping Season 1938–1939; ibid., file 12–20c, Statement re: Support Tax Collected for Year Ending March 31, 1943, in Different Districts. The dollar values in the table were calculated by multiplying the number of pelts collected in the different districts (as noted in the above sources) by the average value of pelts of each species marketed in Canada. The latter value was derived from *Canada Year Book, 1919–1944*.
[1] Includes Liard district, 1939, 1943.
[2] Includes Selkirk-Carmacks and Upper Stewart districts.

that year – and it was a major exception – was the Old Crow-Porcupine district. Nine years later, when the fur trade neared its zenith, the industry expanded to forty-six posts operated by thirty different traders. A Yukon-based company, Taylor and Drury, ran eleven of the posts. The number of establishments varied from year to year, according to changing world prices for furs, climatic conditions, and the profitability of individual establishments. In most years, Natives throughout the Yukon could select from several posts within a reasonable travelling distance. In the volatile markets of the 1910s, 1920s, and 1930s, Native traders readily capitalized on the competitive opportunities. It was not uncommon, for example, for trappers from Old Crow to travel to Herschel Island to trade.[41]

The eagerness with which traders entered the market indicates the general profitability of the fur trade. From 1920 to 1950, traders annually exported an average of $304,060 worth of pelts from the territory.[42] Prices fluctuated widely, reflecting the capriciousness of the international fur markets. Totals of over $600,000 were attained in 1927–28, 1944–45, and 1945–46. At the opposite end, the market bottomed at $78,000 in 1920, with a secondary benchmark of $123,000 in 1933. As with most commodity markets, the fur trade moved in cycles, peaking in the 1924–25, dropping noticeably for a five-year period, and then regaining its previous form for most of the 1940s.

The market for individual species went through similar cycles. Yukon trappers lived in a region which supported a variety of fur-bearing animals in harvestable quantities, the most important of

Table 4
Yukon Fur Returns, 1919–50

Year	Number of Pelts	Value Of Pelts ($)
1919–20	55,354	323,467
1920–21	16,125	78,189
1921–22	69,796	203,402
1922–23	46,198	199,522
1923–24	50,070	347,079
1924–25	36,616	309,549
1925–26	35.767	320,803
1926–27	25,991	382,261
1927–28	64,375	610,348
1928–29	35,736	484,919
1929–30	108,632	295,492
1930–31	61,832	145,224
1931–32	57,679	132,268
1932–33	52,282	146,055
1933–34	43,803	122,999
1934–35	41,309	230,074
1935–36	42,768	276,946
1936–37	50,308	347,558
1937–38	67,655	295,857
1938–39	77,475	267,721
1939–40	80,617	288,292
1940–41	70,953	373,399
1941–42	66,700	398,132
1942–43	52,897	338,035
1943–44	78,005	467,188
1944–45	87,292	669,495
1945–46	107,252	677,495
1946–47	58,777	373,176
1947–48	131,227	230,117
1948–49	151,969	143,810
1949–50	153,574	199,086

Source   Rae, *The Political Economy of the Canadian North*, 386–7.

which were marten, beaver (when not protected by government edict), lynx, muskrat, and several types of fox. But even this variety did not insulate the territorial market from the vagaries of international demand. Muskrat prices, for example, ranged from a low of only 53 cents in 1931–32 to over $3 a pelt in 1946. Among the higher priced furs, the silver fox was particularly vulnerable to changing demand, with the national market price dropping from a 1919 figure of $246 to slightly over $12 thirty years later. Seldom gradual, and difficult to forecast, these fluctuations originated largely in the changing trends of high fashion. In the troubled fur markets of 1947–50, prices fell between 60 and 75 per cent in three years.

Table 5
Fur Prices, ($), Five Year Averages, 1920–49

Year	Beaver	Lynx	S. Fox	Marten	Mink	Muskrat	W.Fox
1920–24	17.8	21.4	152.9	24.5	9.8	1.6	38.1
1925–29	23.9	31.7	94.4	24.7	15.1	1.5	41.5
1930–34	13.1	23.9	44.2	14.6	9.2	.7	23.0
1935–39	11.4	30.6	27.7	22.1	11.1	1.1	13.8
1940–44	26.2	42.9	23.8	38.5	12.1	2.0	22.8
1944–49	33.9	27.2	18.4	36.0	20.2	2.4	38.5

Source   Dominion Bureau of Statistics. *Canada Year Book, 1920–50.*

Since the prices noted here represent final and average market values, they indicate only in a general way the amount of money actually paid for furs in the Yukon River basin. High costs for transportation, labour, and supplies, combined with the Yukon businessmen's eagerness to protect themselves from an ever-changing market, ensured that the Natives received only a fraction of the final market value of the pelts. At the same time, the Yukon's extreme winter climate meant that the territory's trappers delivered a prime product, usually receiving the highest return at auction. Unfortunately, no traders' records which would allow for an analysis of fur prices exist.[43] Several observations, however, can be ventured. Anglican missionary Charles Johnson noted from Carcross in 1920 that two local traders had bought 300 muskrats from trapper Johnny Johns for $1,000 and that the price subsequently rose to $5 a pelt. The national price for muskrat pelts that year averaged only half of the latter sum.[44] Estimates made by Corporal Thornthwaite of the RCMP of the value of furs traded in the Porcupine River area in 1928 seem closer to the mark. Cross fox that he listed at $40 sold nationally for an average of $75; lynx estimated at $30 per skin brought the wholesaler around $47.[45] Similarly, muskrats bought near Old Crow in 1930 for 20–25 cents each sold in southern markets for around 84 cents.[46] N.A.D. Armstrong, a non-Native hunter/prospector, priced his fur packet at Fort Selkirk in 1925 and received the following quotations:

5 Marten-Brown	@ $8.00	$40.00
2 Marten-Dark Brown	@ 10.00	20.00
1 Marten-Fall	@ 2.50	2.50
2 Marten-Brown (Poor)	@ 1.50	3.00
5 Mink	@ 4.00	20.00
17 Ermine	@ .35	5.95
10 Ermine	@ .25	2.50

1 Otter	@ 8.00	8.00
7 Wolverine	@ 7.00	49.00
6 Wolves	@ 7.00	42.00
6 Beaver	@ 6.00	36.00
11 Beaver	@ 3.00	33.00

Total $261.95

The Fort Selkirk prices appear to be approximately one-third of the national market price (average for 1925–29) period.[47]

Estimating the prices received by Yukon Indians is a futile task because of the lack of systematic evidence and, more importantly, because most trade operated on a barter and credit system. Traders manipulated prices simply by increasing the cost of their trade goods, thereby reducing the real value of the trappers' returns; the latter, for their part, received much less than the price of the furs at auction, for traders, shippers, and auctioneers all extracted their cut. Still, even though the various middlemen took a substantial share of the financial return from the trade, evidence suggests that the fur industry offered a reliable source of income for successful trappers, Native and non-Native. A non-Native trapper, Jack Pringle, reportedly harvested between $2,500 and $3,000 in pelts in the winter of 1917, close to the norm for the people around Dalton Post.[48] That same year, however, another non-Native trapper, Fred Watt, trapped only seven lynx, leaving him and his family destitute.[49] One 1930 survey of the Champagne district reported that the trappers, Native and non-Native alike, earned between $1,000 and $2,000 per year.[50]

Variable returns and the high cost of outfitting for a winter's trapping led to extensive use of credit, called "jawbone," in the Yukon. The granting of credit – payment in advance of delivery of pelts – had been a feature of the Yukon trade from the early days of the HBC. As traders fanned throughout the territory after the gold rush, they found that the Indians expected to receive trade goods on account.[51] The system had as many variants as it had practitioners, with terms changing according to market conditions and the nature of local competition. Traders spared little effort in their attempts to tie individual trappers, especially those of recognized skill, to their trading post. Competition raged, particularly in the halcyon days of the 1920s and 1930s. In 1928, for example, six traders vied for the Porcupine River trade, with two establishments at Rampart House, three at Old Crow, and a final one at LaPierre's House. The returns that year, estimated to be in excess of $133,000, justified the vigorous battle.[52] Under such circumstances, traders granted credit to any competent trapper, expecting right of first refusal to his catch. The competition had the related impact of forcing prices up (and commodity prices down).

The Natives were well versed in competitive trade and sought the best market for their furs. If a local trader offered acceptable prices and extended credit, he could likely count on a sizeable portion of the local trade.[53] At the same time, and as in the nineteenth century, Natives willingly travelled considerable distances to other trading posts if the traders in their home areas were believed to be offering low prices for furs. This eagerness to exploit competitive trade escalated with the introduction of the motor-powered boat in the 1920s, thus making traders more aware of the need to respond quickly to changes in market conditions.[54]

Though far from compliant pawns in the fur trade, the Natives were vulnerable to price changes and the withdrawal of credit. The Indians became accustomed to a yearly cycle which included the securing of supplies on credit in the fall and the repayment of debt in the winter or spring. Any sudden or unexpected alteration in the availability of credit, either for market or punitive reasons, would upset the trappers' plans and prospects. Rampart House trader Dan Cadzow, an ardent Anglican who saw his role as extending far beyond the trading post, used the withholding of credit to encourage Natives to act "responsibly," according to his definition of the market.[55] But altering the pattern of credit disbursement typically lacked such philosophical overtones. In 1914 C.C. Brett of Teslin noted that "the Indians will be in need of relief about Xmas. Taylor and Drury have cut off their credit entirely, as they conduct business to suit themselves and as Mr Drury told me that 'they weren't running a benevolent society for the Indians.'"[56] As Adrian Tanner demonstrated in his study of twentieth-century trading practices, the granting of credit varied markedly from monopoly to competitive situations, with the latter of obvious benefit to the Indians.[57] Improvements in transportation technology, high prices, and a consistently large number of independent traders ensured that from the 1920s Natives found credit readily available in their district or within a reasonable distance.

The contours of the fur trade remained intact through the period from 1900 to 1950. Prices varied according to year and the quality of the furs, but available credit and competition ensured a reasonable return to the fur trappers. The pursuit of fur-bearing animals provided a respectable, and at time lucrative, income but not without major variations which caused short-term and localized distress. Natural cycles in the availability of game remained an integral part of the Natives' hunting-trapping economy and had to be accommodated. Price fluctuations and changes in market demand proved a greater source of instability, but longstanding experience in the fur trade, credit disbursements, and the traders' and trappers' faith in the resilience of the industry carried both through lean years. Government regulations proved more difficult to accommodate, principally because they generally emerged outside the context of the fur trade.

Most government intervention in the fur trade came in the form of export taxes targeted at the marketing end of the industry. In the 1920s and 1930s, however, growing concern about the depletion of resources led the Yukon government to impose a series of trapping restrictions. The regulation of the taking of game had noticeable repercussions on the fur-trade economy. The seasonal cycles of the Indians and their non-Native counterparts involved the regular trapping of various species. Government efforts to prevent the taking of a particular fur-bearing animal disrupted routines and schedules while also interfering with the trappers' ability to repay accumulated debts. Similarly, traders faced the unwelcome prospect of being unable to supply an eager market. There were several major trapping closures before 1950, including beaver (1916–24, 1928–31, 1946–49), marten (1924–26),[58] and a series of seasonal closures on other species.[59] While granting short-term concessions, such as allowing traders to export furs caught before the new regulations had been explained to trappers, the government enforced the legislation with considerable rigidity. Trappers typically accepted the various restrictions without prolonged argument, switching their traps to other game where possible. Eventually the government eased the transition somewhat by imposing only seasonal closures, with the period set aside for harvesting often coinciding with prime trapping times. Beaver, for instance, are of greatest value in mid-winter, when the pelt is at its thickest. When the total closure on beaver was lifted in 1924, the government imposed a shortened season stretching from 1 January to 15 May.[60] Since most trapping of beaver for market occurred in the winter months, this particular restriction was not onerous.[61]

A series of government regulations barring non-Yukon Indians from hunting within the territory had a more direct impact. The various game laws were not explicitly intended to exclude the Natives. Rather, poor planning and limited knowledge led to the inadvertent closure of traditional hunting territories. The Yukon Game Ordinance of 1927 required a payment of $100 from all persons not resident in the territory in return for a grant of hunting privileges.[62] The new regulations severely affected Natives hunting in the Porcupine River area. Alaskan Natives had long entered the district to trade and avoid export taxes,[63] and Indians from Fort McPherson continued to hunt in the Peel River basin and on the western slopes of the Richardson mountains. Federal government officials, particularly O.S. Finnie, urged the territorial government to remove the restrictions on Natives from the Northwest Territories.[64] Citing allegations of over-hunting by the Fort McPherson Indians, the Yukon government initially refused to comply. They finally capitulated and, on 3 September 1929, revised the Territorial Game Ordinance.[65] No similar provisions were forthcoming for the Alaskan Natives, who likewise had a traditional claim to harvesting east of the Canada/Alaska boundary. The Indians of Old Crow, however, supported the government's decision to keep the Alaskan Indians out, because they posed a direct threat to the viability of the local fur trade.[66] To the south, the Yukon-British Columbia border region posed problems, as Natives routinely ignored the boundary. In this instance, an amicable relationship between Yukon Indian Agent John Hawksley and his counterpart in the Stikine district of British Columbia, Harper Reed, limited the effect of hunting and trapping regulations. Both agreed, however, that the Indians had to observe all provincial and territorial regulations.[67]

While territorial regulations governing harvesting were not tied exclusively to the fur trade, they had the effect of controlling, and occasionally restricting, the options of Native harvesters. Until the 1940s, the government pursued a relatively open policy, permitting all residents, Native and non-Native, and approved non-residents to compete for available fur-bearing animals.

The first appeals to regulate individual access to wildlife came from Native trappers. Joe Squam, an Indian chief from Teslin, requested in 1932 that an area he described as "my hunting and trapping ground" be permanently reserved for his personal use.[68] The government rejected his appeal for fear, as Controller G. Jeckell phrased it, that "such actions would greatly hamper the exploration and development of the mineral resources of the territory."[69] While authorities ignored this suggestion for the designation of traplines, increasing tensions between Native and non-Native trappers in the 1940s brought the issue to the fore once more. In British Columbia, trapline registration started in 1926, and was generally conceded to have been effective in protecting Native access to game.[70] In 1947 the Yukon government opened discussion on a similar system, believing that it would protect Natives from non-Native encroachment. The proposal had originated with Indian Agent R.J. Meek, newly arrived from British Columbia, and was supported by a nascent conservation movement within the territory.[71] Meek suggested that traplines be granted first to Indians, then to half-breeds and "old-timers," and lastly to non-Native trappers drawn into the business in the 1940s.[72] With widespread support for the program, including Meek's assurance that the Natives wanted it, the Yukon government instituted trapline registration in 1950.

When unveiled, the registration program contained an unwelcome surprise. Yukon Game Commissioner Thomas Kjar imposed a $10 annual fee per trapline. With fur prices at an abnormally low level, many feared that the Natives would be unable to make the payment. Again, Indian Agent Meek petitioned on behalf of the Natives, arguing that the payment was excessive, that British Columbia imposed no such fees on Native trappers, and that low fur prices rendered trapping uneconomical.[73] Although Meek's appeal garnered support within the federal bureaucracy[74] and among the Native population,[75] it failed to change the territorial government's mind. Registration proceeded in the fall of 1950 with the $10 charge intact.

The registration program came into effect just as fur prices entered a prolonged downward slide and as a limited, but growing, number of alternative employment prospects became available. There were other problems. Government agents encountered serious difficulties getting the Natives to identify their personal trapping areas; many disputes arose as some trappers seized the moment to expand their traplines. Even more important, the Euro-Canadian insistence on male ownership and inheritance ran counter to the Natives' matrilineal social structure and threatened the stability of social relations in many Native camps.[76] Over the long term, the registration program contributed to a steady decline in the fur trade and aided a transfer of control of traplines from Natives to non-Natives.

Competition between trappers began long before 1950 and added to the already precarious nature of the trapping industry.[77] Natives frequently complained of non-Native incursions onto their trapping grounds, and they vigorously opposed the territorial government's decision to allow non-Natives, but not Indians, to use poison to kill wolves. Typically less committed to trapping as a full-time occupation, non-Natives entered the field as prices rose and dropped out at the first sign of major decline. The suggestion that Native and non-Native trappers co-existed harmoniously is not supported by available evidence,[78] although it is equally incorrect to suggest that the traplines became a focus for interracial violence. Government agents and police officers frequently commented on interracial tensions, typically pointing out that the non-Native participants exhibited little respect for Native rights and endangered game stocks with their exploitative

habits.[79] Non-Native trappers occasionally expressed similar senti-
ments about the Indians, blaming them for any decrease in returns
from trapping.[80] Archival records reveal no instances of violence over
trapping activities, but relations in the woods were far from tranquil.

The Indians outlasted most of their competitors because the non-
Natives could not overcome the market fluctuations in the fur trade.
Throughout the first half of the century, and excepting those few
who accepted a more complete accommodation with the mining
economy, the Yukon Indians followed a pattern of subsistence hunting, gathering, and fishing. Those who worked as woodcutters, game
guides, or day labourers did so only seasonally, devoting much of
their time to the pursuit of game.[81] The Natives were not indifferent
to the fur trade. They developed a taste for – even a dependence
upon – the products of the trading post, but neither were they irrevocably wedded to it. Low prices or insufficient demand forced the
Natives to postpone trapping ventures until markets recovered or
they developed an acute need for particular goods.[82] In extreme cases,
Natives abandoned the trade for one or two seasons, usually because
of a decrease in local food supplies. The Natives could and, on occasion did, survive without the fur trade. This flexibility and the ability
to survive the vagaries of the market-place through a reliance on
subsistence hunting (which, in turn, was based on the fact that the
Natives did not seek to acquire material wealth) assured the Indians
of a pre-eminent role in the Yukon fur trade.

The twentieth-century fur trade stood in stark contrast to the comparative stability of the HBC era. Even after the arrival of American
traders along the Yukon River after 1869, the trade had focused on
a few HBC and Alaska Commercial Company posts. Competition was
vigorous, but controlled, with both firms looking to the long-term
interests of the industry. After the turn of the century, and particularly in the 1920s, conditions changed. Although Taylor and Drury
maintained a commanding presence, the trade included numerous
independents. Price fluctuations, government regulations, competition from non-Native trappers, frequent alterations in trading patterns, improvements in harvesting techniques, and differential credit
systems added to the complexity of the fur trade.

These changes affected the Natives most strongly. As before, competition worked to their short-term benefit, forcing up prices for furs,
lowering commodity costs, and encouraging more flexible credit
arrangements. The expansion in the number and distribution of posts
doubtless aided Native trappers, and allowed for the manipulation of
competition. New credit arrangements encouraged Natives to transfer their allegiance as market forces dictated, and the introduction of

a monied trade (if only in Taylor and Drury Company tokens) represented a significant shift from the comparatively inflexible trade of the HBC period. Technological innovations, especially motorized boats, added to the ease of trapping and enabled a more rapid exploitation of resources. That trapping, by Natives and non-Natives, was occasionally excessive is illustrated by the territorial government's decision to regulate harvests.

The revitalization and expansion of the fur trade clearly benefitted the Yukon trappers, particularly those well placed and conditioned to respond to the new opportunities. Far from being forced into the fur trade through exclusion from the industrial sector, Natives instead chose the industry for its flexibility, its compatability with the seasonal and cultural patterns of their way of life, and its comparatively profitable returns.

The Natives' reaction to poor trapping conditions reveals that the harvesting of fish and game remained the foundation of participation in the fur trade. The pursuit of fur-bearers became feasible only when required amounts of food had been set aside. Whenever meat supplies fell low, the Indians lacked the resources to pursue smaller game. Until they solved this fundamental problem, trapping operations remained in abeyance. There are a number of recorded instances, particularly in the Old Crow area,[83] where poor meat harvests forced indefinite postponement of trapping.[84] Trader Dan Cadzow reported from Rampart House in 1917, a year when fish and meat supplies fell perilously low: "there is quite a little fox and martin[sic] but no lynx but the trapping is at a standstill."[85] The interdependence of hunting and trapping worked both ways, keeping the Natives in the bush when markets declined but, conversely, limiting trapping activities when food shortages loomed.

The hunting-trapping economy relied on a ready and consistent supply of ungulates and fur-bearing animals. Throughout the twentieth century, however, some observers charged that overhunting by Natives and non-Natives had depleted animal resources. There is no doubt that the influx of gold seekers during the Klondike rush put abnormal pressure on game stocks, particularly in the Whitehorse-Dawson corridor,[86] but the territory-wide impact is less clear. Allegations surfaced in the Kluane-Burwash area in 1911 and again in 1920 that Indians, upset over non-Native incursions, wantonly destroyed game in an attempt to drive out the miners. The Natives' apparent disrespect for the authority of the police sent to investigate the dispute served, in the minds of some, to confirm the reported destruction.[87] But not everyone was so quick to accuse the Natives of over-hunting.[88] In an official report on the preservation of game in the Yukon, police Superintendent R.E. Tucker noted, "Some time ago the Indians did slaughter game ruthlessly, but now the export of hides is forbidden there is no object to killing more than they require for food." Tucker, whose experience in the territory dated from 1896, also commented that big game was more plentiful in 1920 than twenty years earlier.[89] The question of over-hunting is difficult to resolve adequately, although it is important to indicate that subsequent surveys of the Yukon turned up few signs of unwarranted destruction of game. When confirmed depletion occurred, authorities generally attributed the decline to wolves.[90] Police constable McCormick offered a widely accepted assessment of Native hunting: "The Indians are careful about killing game, having had lots of experience of being on short rations, indeed almost starving some years."[91]

The construction of the Alaska Highway, discussed earlier in relation to the industrial sector of the territorial economy, also affected hunting and gathering. The major impact came from hunting along the newly opened corridor. Civilian and military personnel working on the highway received special hunting permits, granting them the same rights as territorial residents. Allegations subsequently surfaced that Americans killed animals solely for sport and that great wastage of game occurred.[92] The comments, although exaggerated, convinced the government to prohibit the discharge of firearms within one mile of the highway. The Natives in the Burwash-Kluane Lake region were hurt more directly by the 1942 decision to set aside much of the land between the highway and the Alaska boundary as a game sanctuary.[93] The government declared the Kluane Game Sanctuary, later a national park, off-limits to all hunting and trapping, barring local Natives from a well-used and well-stocked hunting ground. Appeals on the Indians' behalf by Indian Agent Meek and local Catholic missionary E. Morrisset[94] convinced the government to make limited muskrat-trapping concessions within the park.[95]

The opening of the Alaska Highway did not dramatically alter occupational patterns. The Natives of the southern Yukon, the area most affected by construction, remained primarily hunters and trappers, participating in the industrial sector in a limited and impermanent fashion. An Anglican missionary at Champagne in the summer of 1949 offered a succinct summary of the local employment situation: "The white population is occupied exclusively in connection with the maintenance of the Alaska Highway ... Many of the Indians are similarly occupied, though spasmodically, in more menial capacities. Hunting and trapping in winter, and fishing in summer, are the principal interests of the Indians generally, the young men being employed by the various Highway authorities occasionally. Few of the Indians accept, or are suited for, regular employment."[96]

The Natives of the Yukon adjusted their economic patterns on a seasonal and occasionally annual basis to take advantage of new opportunities. They had done so in the early fur trade, during the initial expansion of mining, and through the gold rush. Occupational flexibility continued up to 1940. Native work during the construction of the Alaska Highway, consisting mainly of guiding and labouring, fit this pattern. When these opportunities ended, as most did after the initial construction phase, the Natives returned to their traplines and hunting grounds. Even the more regular opportunities, such as highway maintenance, fit into a seasonal cycle which centred on the pursuit of game but accommodated season-specific employment in the industrial sector.[97]

There is little usable statistical data on the level of Native participation in the harvesting and industrial sectors. Census data is sporadic and inconclusive. There was, for instance, no systematic recording of the number of Native people pursuing harvesting activities. One set of documents, registrations of Native births, provides some imprecise indications of Native economic patterns. The registrations of Native births began in the 1930s, but became systematic only after the introduction of the mothers' allowance in 1944.[98] As part of the registration process, the recording agent (usually the territorial Indian agent) noted the father's occupation. A sample of 30 per cent of registration entries indicates that the majority of Indian males continued to consider themselves hunters and trappers, even after the construction of the Alaska Highway. Two weaknesses in the data base suggest that these figures understate the importance of harvesting in the economic life of Yukon Indians. Because of Indian Agent Meek's interest in encouraging industrial employment, it is likely that he and other recording agents over-emphasized non-traditional economic activities. Many of those reported as being employed in industrial occupations likely continued to hunt and trap as well. Similarly, the absence of truly systematic reporting meant that inaccessible areas, where trapping and hunting predominated, were unrepresented in the sample. The following table none the less illustrates the continued importance of hunting and trapping, while also providing a rough indication of the increased involvement of Natives in industrial forms of labour. While by no means conclusive, the data suggests the continued importance of hunting and gathering to the Yukon Indians into the 1950s.

While the Natives continually opted for harvesting, a decision conditioned by non-Native economic exclusionist policies and Native preference, it is incorrect to suggest that the pre-1950 period saw few

Table 6
Father's Occupation as Listed at Time of Registration of Native Birth, 1930–50

Occupation	1930–35	1936–41	1942–50
Trapper	40 (87%)	63 (85%)	113 (75%)
Labourer	4 (9%)	6 (8%)	14 (9%)
Section Hand	–	–	4 (3%)
Woodcutter	–	2 (3%)	12 (8%)
Not Given/Dead	2 (4%)	3 (4%)	7 (5%)
Total	46 (100%)	74 (100%)	150 (100%)

Source   Government of Yukon, Dept. of Statistics, Birth Registry.

changes in the economic lives of Yukon Native people. The advance of non-Natives brought many new uncertainties: competition for game, American over-fishing on the lower Yukon River, temporary employment in the industrial sector, and continued improvements in the technology of transportation and hunting. At the same time, the hunting-gathering economy offered numerous prospects. Some sectors, such as the fur trade, were reasonably lucrative. Subsistence hunting also allowed for the continuation of the Natives' preferred practices and customs. While occasional hardship remained part of the Indians' accepted lot, those Natives opting for the pursuit of game usually made a decent living.

The Natives' lack of interest in the aggressive, acquisitive materialism of the industrial world ensured that few accepted the discipline and control of the non-Native work place. The fur trade and provision hunting, both of which fit the skills, cycles, and traditions of the Natives' subsistence lifestyle, provided for their limited material needs. Although on the margins of the larger Yukon society, particularly as viewed from the non-Native, industrial perspective, the Natives generally accepted the cultural and material advantages of their mixed economy. Despite significant economic change in the Yukon, the Indians avoided gradual or rapid integration into the industrial order, preferring a tangential and peripheral accommodation which permitted a continuation of harvesting practices. Within the framework and constraints of their economic outlook, which the non-Natives found difficult to comprehend, the hunting-trapping economy offered the Natives a realistic, even appealing alternative to the uncertainties of wage labour. From the expansion of mining in the 1880s through the construction of the Alaska Highway in the 1940s, the enticements of the industrial economy could not overcome the special appeal of a way of life which meant so much to the Natives and so little to the other residents of the Yukon Territory.

The Nature of Social Contact

The Nature of Social Contact

The meeting of Native and non-Native people in the Canadian north involved far more than economic accommodation. It also brought together individuals with very different cultural values and expectations. The social relationship that developed was never completely separate from economic concerns, nor was it totally removed from the efforts of church and state to administer the aboriginal people. The values, attitudes, and patterns that emerged out of the fur trade and that continued through the first half of the twentieth century reveal a great deal about non-Native aspirations for the Yukon Territory and Native efforts to reach a social accommodation with the incoming non-Native people.

Canadian historians have neglected the evolution of northern society. A preoccupation with explorers, government scientists, and Euro-Canadian mining activities has diverted attention from this important field of inquiry. The prevailing notion of the Yukon as a temporary society has resulted in detailed studies of social conditions during, and immediately after, the Klondike gold rush,[1] but there has been little study of previous or subsequent patterns of interaction. This over-emphasis on the gold-rush period has obscured both long-term changes in the territory and the evolution of Native-white social contact.

As noted, the central threads running through the social history of the Yukon are the permanence of the Native people and the transiency of the non-Natives. The territorial population has fluctuated widely over time, reflecting the cyclical nature of the northern economy. The Natives vastly outnumbered non-Natives during the fur-trade period, despite a major population decline following the introduction of new diseases. The arrival of thousands of gold seekers during the Klondike rush upset the comparative equilibrium of the

Table 7
Yukon Population, 1901–71

Year	Total Yukon	Native	% Native
1901	27,219	3,322	12.2
1911	8,512	1,489	17.5
1921	4,157	1,390	33.4
1931	4,230	1,638	38.7
1941	4,914	1,508	30.7
1951	9,096	1,563	17.2
1961	14,628	2,207	15.1
1971	18,385	2,580	14.0

Source   Canada Census, 1901–71.

Table 8
Sex Ratios, Yukon Population, 1901–51

Year	Males per 100 Females
1901	572
1911	325
1921	211
1931	202
1941	179
1951	150

Source   Canada Census, 1901–51.

early mining frontier. By 1900 non-Natives far outnumbered the dwindling Native population, but their numbers declined thereafter as the gold economy withered.[2] The Natives regained their numerical importance, constituting nearly 40 per cent of the population in 1931; in real numbers, however, their population remained stagnant. The non-Native population grew rapidly after 1940, as wartime construction projects drew thousands into the territory.

The demographic imbalance, including early Native dominance and subsequent non-Native numerical superiority, strongly influenced the evolution of the regional society. So, too, did the striking sexual imbalance in the territory. The much higher number of males led to increased contact between Native women and non-Native men. Attitudes concerning the desirability of Native-white social contact proved as important as the shortage of non-Native women in determining the nature of relations. Beginning with the fur trade, racist attitudes towards aboriginal social and moral behaviour limited social contact. The region's dual economic nature was reflected in social patterns. The fur trade provided a relatively integrated setting, while non-Native exclusionist policies ensured that towns and mining camps remained largely segregated. The degree of social interaction illustrated most graphically the distance between Native and non-Native in the Yukon. Indians were relegated to reserves on the edge of town, restricted from access to hospitals and schools, and scorned as drunks, loafers, and carriers of disease. Such attitudes highlighted the Natives' marginalization and illustrated a central theme in the social history of the Canadian north. Contemporary northern communities, consisting of separate Native reserves and carefully protected Euro-Canadian subdivisions, are creations of the past, demonstrating the legacy of segregationist attitudes from the gold rush to the present.

The following two chapters explore different aspects of social contact in the Yukon, examining such themes as male-female relationships, prejudice and discrimination, and the continued ill-effects of imported European illness on the indigenous population. The first chapter considers Native-white social relations from the expansion of the fur trade through the Klondike gold rush. Direct contact predominately involved non-Native men and Native women, although the images and resulting patterns of discrimination directed towards Indians ultimately affected the Native population of the entire territory. In the second chapter in this section, the examination of social contact is carried through to 1950. The pattern of relations established in the pre-gold rush fur trade continued in some areas in the territory well into the twentieth century. But, as this chapter demonstrates, the increasingly urban, industrial, and middle-class nature of non-Native society in the Yukon placed additional restrictions on relations between Indians and whites.

CHAPTER FOUR

Native-White
Social Relations:
From the Fur Trade
to the Gold Rush

Work by Sylvia Van Kirk and Jennifer Brown has done much to document the nature of social interaction in the fur-trade era. For the purposes of this study, Van Kirk's analysis of changing marital patterns is of particular relevance. Focusing primarily on the Red River settlement and southern districts, Van Kirk argues that by the 1840s fur traders were choosing white women over Métis and Natives and long-term relationships with Native women were no longer accepted practice for HBC employees.[1] The new era was seemingly signalled in the Yukon with the opening of Fort Youcon in 1847. The fort's first commanding officer, Alexander Hunter Murray, brought his non-Native wife with him to the north.[2]

Van Kirk's thesis fits the Red River context, but not the pattern of social contact in the Yukon basin. Although HBC records offer little insight into personal relations between fur traders and Natives in the Yukon, some conclusions can be drawn. First of all, it is indeed true that by the 1840s the HBC's upper echelons were discouraging its officers from forming lasting liaisons with "inferior" Natives; Robert Campbell, for example, was warned by Governor George Simpson not to complicate his life by taking a Native wife while in the far northwest.[3] Yet, despite official disapproval, relationships with Native and mixed-blood women continued after the HBC expanded into the Yukon River valley. Several officers seem to have had temporary liaisons with Native women, although their correspondence and journal entries are understandably mute on this subject. Upper-level disapproval had even less effect on the company's lower ranks. Engaged servants and minor officials, especially those who acknowledged their limited prospects for career advancement, made no effort to hide their relationships with aboriginal women. Scattered comments by travellers in the area suggest that these liaisons were common-

place. Antoine Houle, the Métis interpreter at Fort Youcon, fre-
quented Indian camps and allegedly supported several wives.[4] John
Firth, who eventually became postmaster at Rampart House, married
a Fort McPherson Loucheux (Kutchin) Indian.[5] W. Dall, who visited
Fort Youcon in 1867, felt that the HBC actively encouraged such relationships. He reported that "every effort is made, to make these men
[company servants] marry Indian wives; thus forcing them to remain
in the country by burdening them with females whom they are
ashamed to take back to civilization and cannot desert."[6]

Dall's comments must be approached with caution. An American
unfamiliar with company-servant relations, he found the labour system at Fort Youcon archaic, almost feudal, in its oppression of the
workers. Nevertheless, the observation suggests that interracial relationships of this kind were common. Further confirmation is provided by Robert Kennicott, a scientist attached to the Smithsonian
Institution, who passed the winter of 1861 at LaPierre's House. He
thought little of the traders' choice of wives, pointing out that they
"were by no means fair to look upon, one was fat and the other forty,
[sic] age sixty, for that matter." He noted that post officer James Flett
and at least one other employee had Native wives.[7]

Marriage and baptismal records from Rampart House in the early
1890s provide still further evidence of interracial relationships.
Between 1890 and 1892 the Anglican missionary recorded six births
to Native mothers and HBC fathers; one of the engaged servants was
a Native, the others were mixed-bloods or Europeans. In only one
instance in this period, involving a Native HBC employee and a local
Native woman, were a company worker and the Native married.[8] Nor
were interracial marriages limited to the traders. In 1896 Bishop Bompas arranged the marriage of missionary Benjamin Totty to a local
Native woman. Although the Bishop expressed some displeasure
with the relationship, he did sound one positive note: "The influence
of a country-born wife is generally in favour of retaining a
Miss.[ionary] in this country, whereas an English wife has been often
a cause of his leaving it." The church's attitude to these marriages
mirrored that of the HBC – official disapproval of mixed marriages,
but acceptance of the same for members of the lower ranks.[9]

There is no indication of what happened to Indian wives of fur
traders when their husbands left the district. They probably stayed
behind if the trader departed for a distant post or Red River. Similarly,
there is no evidence to suggest how the Native women re-entered
Indian society, although it is likely that the pattern of easy and rapid
reintegration common elsewhere held true for the Yukon. Finally,
there is little documentation to indicate why Native women accepted

non-Native traders as mates, beyond the likelihood that they did so for personal gain and to solidify trading relations between the company and the band.[10]

The picture of social relations in the fur-trade era, then, is incomplete. Native men came into contact with white society almost exclusively through their economic activities, while traders drew an indeterminate number of Native women to fur-trade posts as short-term sexual partners.[11] Since some of those taking wives, such as John Firth, remained in the north and the number of women involved was small, the social dislocations were limited. At the same time, the lack of social approval ensured that the liaisons remained largely within the HBC's lower ranks and that the sanction for such activities was unwritten. To the élite fur traders, missionaries, and travellers, marriage to an Indian had become unacceptable. Characterized as "lazy," "aggressive," "turbulent" and, in Bompas's phrase, "the lowest of all people," the Natives clearly stood apart from the non-Natives.[12] As Bompas's comment suggests, the non-Natives' perception of Indians was partly inspired by the evolution-based theories of cultural superiority then current in western intellectual circles.[13] Their negative stereotype of the Yukon Indians, devoid of any conception of the "noble savage," subsequently provided the intellectual basis for attempts at social segregation.

Such concerns remained, for the moment, the preserve of the established classes. For the miners who followed the fur traders, considerations of racial character and the snobbish disapproval of interracial sex were meaningless. A common image of the early Yukon mining frontier was of a rapacious group of prospectors who, when not scouring the creeks for gold, eagerly debauched the local Natives.[14] There is a great deal of missionary hyperbole in this image, for the clergymen of the CMS were anxious to detect signs of the degeneration of the Indian in the face of advancing white civilization. Unfortunately, these same missionaries are the primary source of information on relations between Natives and non-Natives.

Sexual contact no doubt increased markedly in the early mining period, and these relationships differed strikingly from those of the earlier fur-trade era, mainly because of the larger number of white men and the fact that most miners did not have the fur traders' understanding of Native life. In the virtual absence of non-Native women in the area, Native females provided the only readily available heterosexual outlet. As the Reverend R. Bowen commented on the border region mining camps, "The white prospectors ... had been thoughtless enough to lure the Indian squaws into their home[s] and into the dance hall. The results of such action was seen in the number of half-breed children."[15] Yet, while sexual relations became the major point of contact between Natives and non-Natives, the frequency and significance of such encounters is less clear. Mixed-blood children appeared as a logical consequence of miscegenation, but a distinctive cross-cultural social group did not emerge. The missionaries saw these children as deserving of special consideration and attempted to draw them out of the Native world and place them under the wing of the resident clergy.[16] For the most part, however, the offspring of these liaisons remained with the Indians; there would be no institutionalization of "half-breed" status as happened on the Canadian prairies and in the Mackenzie valley. Unlike those areas, where a sizeable Métis population with a distinctive identity emerged, Yukon valley mixed-bloods remained members of Native society, barred by colour and lifestyle from a permanent place in the non-Native community.[17]

Missionary correspondence is replete with accounts of Native women lured unwittingly into miners' tents, of Indian men selling young daughters to avaricious prospectors, and of the widespread use of alcohol. Liquor figured prominently in the missionaries' rhetoric, typically being described as an irresistible lure for Native women or as a reliable method for placating Native men.[18] Similar themes appear in accounts of indigenous-white contact at Herschel Island, off the Yukon's northern coast. As indicated earlier, American whalers entered the area in 1890 and quickly established an extensive land-based fur trade that attracted many Indians from the Porcupine River district. The trading ceremonies were elaborate social events. According to various accounts, often embellished, Inuit women climbed on board the sailing vessels and into the arms of eager sailors, and the consumption of a seemingly endless supply of liquor ensured a constant state of inebriation. These coastal trading events stood in stark contrast to the sedate exchange of the interior, and drew many inland Indians to Herschel Island.[19] NWMP Inspector Charles Constantine, based several hundred miles to south, reported: "The liquor is sold or traded to the native for furs, walrus, ivorybone and their young girls who are purchased by the officers for their own foul purposes."[20] Along the Yukon River and at Herschel Island, there appears to be significant evidence to support claims about the debauching of the Natives.

The Indians recognized the opportunities, both social and economic, in the development of the mining camps. Tired of crossing the Yukon River at Fortymile, the Natives decided to build a dance hall on Mission Island and thereby attract the monies to their village. As the walls were going up, Bishop Bompas interceded. With the help of the NWMP, Bompas convinced the miners that they were not legally allowed on the island and persuaded the Natives to stop construction. Capitalizing further on the situation, the bishop purchased the partially built structure from the Indians, had the walls dismantled, and used the materials for a new church.[21]

The establishment of the interracial drinking party stands as one of the principal legacies of the pre-gold rush mining era. Natives spent most of their time away from the mining camps; when they visited them, the brief, intense celebrations became an important occasion for social contact. From the non-Native perspective – and this holds for miners, missionaries, and policemen – the Natives' behaviour at these parties confirmed the nineteenth-century North American image of the drunken and morally lax Indian.[22] The women's lack of "civilized" morals (an interpretation which conveniently ignored the non-Native males' role in such liaisons) and the men's inability to control the effects of liquor became the dominant features of the non-Native stereotype of Yukon Indians. For the Natives, however, these parties represented only brief flings, a welcome change from the routine of the bush and a component of the regular trading excursions.

Non-Native commentators, particularly CMS missionaries, decried the widespread availability of alcohol and feared the consequences of continued consumption. Their statements, relecting the widespread belief in the debilitating effects of alcohol, were prompted as much by self-interested anxiety about uncontrollable, inebriated Natives as by concern for the welfare of the Indians. Accepting the common images and fears, the Canadian government established a police presence in the area in 1894 and imposed an interdiction on Native drinking which was not lifted until 1960. When NWMP Inspector Charles Constantine first visited the region, he carried explicit instructions to address the problem of Native consumption of alcohol.

Police officers were pessimisitic about their chances of effecting a noticeable change in social relations; Constantine reported that "we cannot expect that a mining country will become polished and in a high state of civilization in the course of a few months ... [this has to be] done gradually more persuasively at first than by forcing it."[23] Nevertheless, the NWMP placed particular emphasis on restricting Indian access to alcohol. Much of the force's early effort concentrated on non-Native suppliers, with fines of $100 or more imposed on anyone caught selling or providing liquor to Natives.[24]

Laws aimed at controlling the use of liquor among Natives ended up shaping the structure of Indian drinking. Barred from legitimate supplies, Natives seeking alcohol turned instead to making homebrew or purchasing liquor from bootleggers. The illicit trade was particularly important, starting in the early mining period and following the miners and traders throughout the territory. Legal prohibitions also forced the Natives to consume their liquor in their camps or, as was common before the gold rush, in the miners' cabins. Ironically, the law brought Natives and non-Natives together in the presence of alcohol, precisely what the regulations were designed to prevent.[25]

While commentaries on Natives in this period are full of discussions of Indian drinking, the context and significance of that consumption is difficult to assess. Alcohol-use among Natives has drawn much attention, but has produced no consensus among anthropologists and historians. Donald Horton's argument that liquor reduced anxiety dominated the early academic debate. He suggested that alcohol served as a powerful disinhibitor which relaxed aggressive and sexual tensions to a tolerable level.[26] Numerous scholars, including I. and J. Honigman working among the Kaska, applied Horton's analysis to a variety of "primitive" groups, offering slight modifications of the central thesis.[27]

Horton's interpretation has not withstood subsequent testing.[28] Many, particularly those focusing on contemporary situations, emphasize "socio-economic deprivation" as the prime determinant of Native drinking.[29] Others argue that the Natives' insatiable demand for alcohol originated in liquor's ability to enhance dreams.[30] Alternate explanations suggest that drunkenness served as a substitute for institutionalized social interaction with non-Natives or, as Nancy Lurie says, an assertion of Indianness.[31] The various theories share a common inflexibility and assume a uniform Indian response to alcohol.

More useful, especially in allowing for historically based differences in drinking patterns, is the approach adopted in R. Edgerton and C. MacAndrews's *Drunken Comportment*. Arguing that there is no uniform physiological response to alcohol, they suggest that drinking behaviour has to be learned. In Native societies, which had few models for intoxicated behaviour, the patterns came from non-Natives.[32] Edgerton and MacAndrews, supported by a contemporary study of Indian drinking,[33] claim that social scientists typically attribute all deviant behaviour to post-contact consequences of alcohol-consumption, missing the obvious point that violent, aberrant actions were a part of Native life before the arrival of non-Natives.

The Yukon offers a useful case study of the Edgerton-MacAndrews approach. Natives greeted the introduction of alcohol enthusiastically. The demand, however, had finite limits, and there was little violence associated with drinking. Their "Hootch" parties remained peaceable, with few beatings, little destructiveness and no alcohol-related murders before the twentieth century. None the less, the police and missionaries refused to accept the recreational and peaceful use of alcohol among Natives, living in constant anticipation of drunken violence. That Natives failed to act as expected reflected the social context within which drinking took place.

The crucial initial exposure to alcohol came, for most Yukon Natives, in the form of "spree drinking." Miners returning from their diggings, often carrying the gleanings of a winter's work, and the whalers anchored off Herschel Island engaged in sporadic and raucous celebrations. The men, even before the arrival of the police, were not particularly violent, although the whalers were much more so than the miners. Despite the missionaries' remonstrances, Natives enthusiastically joined in the parties, but their behaviour seldom included violence or wild debauchery. Instead, liquor was typically consumed in small groups, in a party atmosphere, with the emphasis on what a Native woman from Teslin referred to as a "hi-you" time.[34]

Alcohol-consumption during the pre-gold rush period was, for Natives and non-Natives alike, recreational. The Natives integrated alcohol into their potlatches and other celebrations, and alcohol became closely tied to sexual relations between Native women and non-Native men. Liaisons of the "one-night stand" variety often developed out of the interracial drinking party; gaining access to Native women was, in fact, one of the major motivations for non-Natives to join in the parties. Some Indians saw the link between drinking and sexual relations as a standard social response to the use of alcohol.

This period also saw the emergence in the Yukon of a slightly different European type, typically (and derogatorily) referred to as a "squaw man." Commonly used throughout Canada and the United States, the pejorative term described those non-Natives who lived with Indians.[35] These individuals went further than simply taking a Native wife, although that alone was a socially questionable choice by the North American standards of the 1880s. "Squaw men" also chose to live in the hunting-trapping manner. But these men did not completely separate themselves from non-Native society, often retaining a materialistic outlook and pursuing personal profit through the fur trade or prospecting. With few exceptions, like long-time trader Arthur Harper, "squaw men" did not fulfill the role of "patrons" or intermediaries between the two cultures. "Squaw men" were effectively marginalized, only tangentially connected to non-Native society.[36] Non-Native miners, who saw little wrong with a short-term romance with a Native woman, heaped scorn on men who "descended" to live with the Indians. Natives had less difficulty accepting these men, allowing them into their camps, recognizing their marriages with Native women, and encouraging their participation in the harvesting economy.

Many of the "squaw men" stayed with their "wives" only a short time, often abandoning their families to pursue a life in the south. The children from such relationships typically, but not always, remained with their Native mothers. In the Fortymile area, the Anglican mission was pressured to take in the children. The Reverend R.J. Bowen reported one Indians' opinion of the process: "Indian boy, Indian want him, white boy, white man want him, – half breed no Indian, no white man, Indian no want him, white man no want him. I guess half breed Indian and a half."[37]

Natives and non-Natives did not reach a social accommodation in the pre-gold rush period. Alcohol and sex had, after the trading post, become the primary point of contact between the races. Those men who approached Native society more closely were generally scorned by other non-Natives in the area. Missionaries and police clearly exaggerated the level of exploitation and debauchery, but non-Natives did approach social relations with the Natives out of short-term self-interest. As late as 1896, however, most of the Indians of the Yukon had had only minimal contact with non-Natives. The only major settlements were in the borderlands area – Fortymile and Circle City; the rest of the territory was left to the Natives.

The demographic balance changed radically with the start of the Klondike gold rush in 1896. At first, the rush was localized. Prospectors from throughout the Yukon basin hurried to the Klondike region, where they staked claims on creeks about to become famous the world over: Eldorado and Bonanza. The following year, when news of the northern discovery reached the south, tens of thousands of would-be prospectors scurried to the northwest. In short order, the invasion swamped the Natives. As had happened in British Columbia during its gold rush in the 1850s,[38] the existing pattern of social relations quickly disappeared, swept aside in the hysteria and chaos of the stampede. Large-scale mining frontiers have seldom been kind to indigenous populations, as prospectors scour new ground, compete with Natives for limited game resources, and seek out Native women. The Klondike gold rush stands as something of an anomaly within this pattern. Despite the magnitude of the population shift, the narrow geographic focus of the gold rush limited interracial contact. With few exceptions, Natives stayed outside the new and growing settlements, placed by choice, prejudice, and regulations on the margins of territorial society.[39]

The pattern of racial exclusionism emerged, in large part, through the efforts of Anglican missionaries and the NWMP. Bishop Bompas's main task involved separating Natives and non-Natives. To the controversial bishop, the rationale was obvious: "To abandon them [the Indians] now that the place is overrun by miners would involve their destruction by more than a relapse to heathenism, namely in their being swallowed up in the miners' temptations to drink, gambling and immorality."[40] Anxious to protect the Natives from their "weaknesses," Bompas urged the Indians in the Dawson area to remain on the Moosehide reserve, downstream from the mining centre. The police seconded Bompas's efforts, particularly as regards alcohol. The presence of a sizeable police force added substance to earlier proscriptions; the NWMP spared little effort in pursuing people accused of distributing liquor to the Indians.[41]

Despite these efforts, alcohol remained the principal point of contact. The Natives' willingness to pay high prices for liquor ensured a consistent supply. Euro-Canadians, for their part, readily agreed that avaricious non-Natives led the Natives, known for their "insatiable" demand for intoxicants, towards inebriation and corruption. Since many non-Natives saw public drunkenness as a sign of demoralization, the general public readily accepted Bompas' conclusion that "their habits are deteriorating through too much contact with the whites."[42] But contrary to these assessments, the liquor parties hardly reflected Native lifestyle and customs. Occasional, often seasonal, events, such parties illustrated not that the Indians had sunk into depravity but that they remained socially distinct.

Social distance reflected two factors: that most Indians in the Yukon lived far away from the gold-fields, and that non-Natives gathered in a few settlements. The subsequent separation often reflected Indian choice. The NWMP officer at McQuesten observed in 1900 that many Natives left the area when non-Natives moved in.[43] Moosehide residents, living in the shadow of Dawson City, tended to stay in place, maintaining only irregular contact with the town. The high incidence of disease in the Moosehide community also restricted attempts by local Indians to enter Dawson's social sphere. Perceived economic opportunities attracted other Natives to the mining communities – including a group of men who migrated from Fort McPherson to Dawson City – but there is little evidence that they shared widely in the social activities of the gold-rush town.[44]

The miners' sexual needs created a certain demand for Native women. Government officials and police permitted prostitution, under certain guidelines, in recognition of the sexual imbalance in the territory (more than five to one in favour of the men as late as

1901) and the likelihood of unrest if the trade were banned. But as already noted, Native prostitution remained limited during the gold rush, mainly because of the ready availability of non-Native prostitutes. In several studies of prostitution in Dawson City, Native women are not mentioned.[45] With a ready supply of professionals on hand, miners resorted less often to the socially undesirable Native women.

For all of its grandeur and magnitude, the Klondike gold rush did not significantly alter patterns of social relations. The process of marginalization remained more one of disregard than of callous action by non-Natives. While the Natives stayed close by, performing minor but valuable seasonal functions, integration into the larger society did not follow. Liquor parties moved from the mining centres and dance halls to the Indian camps, for social and legal proscriptions had eliminated the public sanction for such activities. Native women no longer attracted as much attention as sexual partners. Instead, as widely held North American stereotypes of Indians as "drunken," "dirty," and "diseased" took firmer root, even temporary cohabitation with a Native caused intense social disapproval from the non-Native community.

The fact that Native people do not figure prominently in the vast literature on the Klondike gold rush is evidence of their social marginality. The stampede attracted a great deal of media attention; in an era of yellow journalism, writers earned sizeable sums feeding an insatiable southern demand for information on the northland.[46] Living in the Yukon, but not part of the now-dominant non-Native society, the Natives were described more often as part of the physical environment than of the elaborate social milieu.[47] It is significant that the only major published pieces dealing exclusively with the Natives – two short articles by well-regarded journalist Tappen Adney – described moose-hunting techniques among the northern Natives.[48] Much the same is true in the realm of popular literature, which focuses overwhelmingly on non-Natives in pursuit of gold. Jack London does mention Native people in a few of his short stories, and Robert Service wrote a poem entitled "The Squawman,"[49] all of which highlight the social marginalization of aboriginal people. The gold rush had developed around and among the Indians, but the new society seldom incorporated them in anything more than a marginal way. The limited accommodation that occurred resulted from economic considerations; the nature of those ties ensured that social integration did not follow.

CHAPTER FIVE

Native-White Social Relations: After the Gold Rush

The outmigration of non-Natives following the gold rush gave the Indians renewed numerical importance. The years from 1900 to the construction of the Alaska Highway did not, however, see significant alterations in existing patterns of social integration. Instead, the institutionalization of rigid exclusion of Natives from the dominant society characterized this forty-year period. The separateness of the races originated in the dualistic character of the regional economy and was supported by strong racist attitudes. The trapping business, which drew Natives and non-Natives together, stood in sharp contrast to the exclusive mining economy. The majority of the non-Natives, cloistered in protected residential environments or working in the white-dominated mining industry, remained socially segregated.

A more complete integration of Natives and non-Natives occurred away from the Dawson-Whitehorse corridor. In those instances where non-Natives worked and lived among the Indians and where economic prosperity hinged on interdependence between trappers and traders, harmonious relations existed. As the Reverend C.C. Brett observed regarding the Teslin area in 1914: "The whites generally speaking, are rather exceptional here. I heard the trader say that during his eight years here, he has not heard a native woman complain of a white saying anything to insult them. I don't wish to infer that the whites there pretend to be saints, but they are a pretty good crowd of men on the whole."[1] Although the Teslin Natives resented the occasional derogatory reference to themselves as "Siwashes," they appeared well satisfied with the nature of interracial relations.[2] In the back-country districts, such as Teslin, relations extended beyond trade and friendship. "Squaw men" were particularly prevalent, taking Native wives and often living permanently in the area. Dan Cadzow, a trader at Rampart House after the turn of the century, is perhaps the most prominent example; he took a Native wife soon after his arrival and remained a prominent figure in the Porcupine River region for years. Cadzow was unique in that he shunned the Native way, building a handsome house which he furnished with the best he could buy from southern retailers.[3] He and other "squaw men," such as Poole Field at Ross River, Eugene Jacquot at Burwash, and Del Vangorder at Ross River made a serious commitment to their Native partners and the territory.

Marriages did not always follow. The non-Native men, whether prospectors, trappers, or traders, often sought short-term liaisons, particularly during the 1920s and 1930s when the profitability of the northern fur trade brought a number of new operators into the business. The contention by Grafton Burke, physician at Hudson Stuck Memorial Hospital at Fort Yukon, that "traders in these isolated places vie with each other as to who can 'swell the population'" is overstated. Nevertheless, it demonstrates that many traders did not share the dedication of Cadzow and others.[4]

The general population continued to disdain, or at least question, the "squaw man." N.A.D. Armstrong's reaction to the marriage of his friend Coward to a "dusky bride" named Alice is not untypical. "What a pity," he confided to his diary, "that a fine specimen of a man should have fallen so low as to marry a full-blooded squaw – such is life."[5] NWMP Assistant Commissioner Z. Wood's comment on "Squaw men" is no less striking. Referring to the Whitehorse area, he wrote, "These men purchase liquor and retail it to the Indian, and we have also reason to believe they allow their squaws to cohabit with other white men and Indians."[6] Another police officer claimed that the Native women had been taken according to Indian custom, in which the man paid $50 to $100 to the parents and took the woman as his wife.[7]

Those who opted for an Indian bride faced ostracism from the "better" elements of non-Native society. Laura Berton described the case of one young man, the son of a Dawson civil servant, who had married a mixed-blood woman while his parents were "outside":

She was a pretty little thing, bright and neat, and I think could have made him a good wife, but the parents were so shocked they would neither see nor speak with him. This attitude drove him from the town and back into the bush, where his life was spent among the Indians, hunting and cutting wood for a living. Now here he was, standing by the river with his dark, wiry children clustered about him, the fish wheel in the background turning slowly with the current, the salmon smoking under the trees. In all intents and purposes he was a native.[8]

Occasionally, those who married a Native used their knowledge of the non-Native world to the benefit of their Native friends and family – Eugene Jacquot, for example, often petitioned on behalf of the Burwash Indians – but such men were exceptional because non-Natives seldom permitted the "squaw men" to play the role of intermediaries.[9] A number of the other "squaw men" did the opposite, using their connections with the non-Native community to take advantage of the Natives. Many of the bootleggers, for example, were "squaw men" who were able to capitalize on their close connections with the suppliers and customers of this lucrative industry.[10] (There was a question as to whether or not the Native women in such relationships had become wives of the non-Native men, thus losing status under the Indian Act and gaining the right to drink legally. The government argued – but did not enforce the point – that marriages conducted under Native rites were legally binding.[11])

The disdain for the "squaw men" was especially evident during attempts to provide school facilities in Dawson and Whitehorse for mixed-blood children. Although public schools were available in both centres, as late as 1947 it was noted that "it is not denied that these children (Native and mixed blood) are not welcome there."[12] Mission schools were created specifically for mixed-blood children, Natives already being served through Anglican day schools and the Carcross Indian Residential School. The Anglican Church built St Paul's Hostel in Dawson in 1920, and in 1946 the Reverend E. Lee opened a similar facility in Whitehorse. In both cases, the general public opposed the schools, although few accepted the alternative of allowing the children in the territorial establishments.[13] The opening of the schools did not stop public anger. Instead, the fact that the federal government provided financial assistance only added to the hostility.[14] Opposition to the founding of the Dawson hostel revealed general hostility to the "squaw men." As the *Mayo-Keno Bulletin* editorialized in September 1925: "Why should the people's money be used to house, feed and clothe the somewhat prolific progeny of able bodied men who have mated with native women ... Does the Federal Government realize that the result of its misplaced generosity is to encourage a certain class known as 'squawmen' to shift their parental responsibilities on the shoulders of an unwilling public."[15]

While the prevalence of Native-white liaisons cannot be questioned, there is no accurate means of assessing their number and longevity. Police Superintendent Snyder wrote of the situation around Whitehorse in 1909: "There are in this district a number of white men who are living with Indian women ... While some of these men profess to regard these women as their wives, I do not think any of them seriously intend to live with them for life – as otherwise there is nothing to prevent their being married to them in the usual manner legally."[16] Three years later Bishop Stringer noted that there were only "about half a dozen" non-Native men in the Yukon living permanently with Native women and interested in educating their children.[17] Given the far reach of the Anglican church and the missionaries' familiarity with local conditions, his estimate is likely close to the mark. It is impossible to be more precise because mixed marriages and those involving mixed-bloods were ignored in censuses and marriage registers.[18] The impermanent nature of most of these relationships would distort any statistics thus garnered. It should also be noted that the legality of informally constituted marriages, usually ratified only according to Indian custom, was an important issue. Any woman so marrying lost her legal Indian status, as did her children.[19]

Non-Native men who chose to live within the Native communities, usually as traders, exercised considerable authority among the local population. Dan Cadzow and Poole Field were the dominant personalities in the Rampart House and Ross River areas respectively. So too was Eugene Jacquot. As one witness observed: "Jacquot has been a sort of little king in that country until the Highway came along. He was the only intelligent, aggressive white settler about there. He runs the trading post and its establishment resulted in the Indians who lived not around Burwash Landing but at the north side of Kluane Lake before he came, building a village around him. He has a strong hold over the Indians and their ideas of white men, right and wrong, etc. are largely a reflection of Jacquot's influence."[20]

The frequency of informal and often transitory liaisons between non-Native men and Native women highlights the strong demographic pressures within non-Native society. Because of its northern location and economic instability, the Yukon remained a frontier society. Few long-term settlers came north; the work-force was sustained instead by a continuous circulation of transient workers. Because women were at a premium, these non-Native males lacked outlets for their romantic and sexual desires within the non-Native community, except through transactions with prostitutes, a small number of whom were Native women.[21] Given the continuing imbalance in favour of males, it is not surprising that some men sought out Native women. Originating more in lust and loneliness than romance, and contracted by men with little intention of remaining long in the north, these liaisons were typically short-lived, sexually oriented, and often related to drinking.

Native-non-Native liaisons carried a significant social cost. Pushed aside by Euro-Canadian competitors, many Native males found themselves unable to attract suitable partners until they were comparatively old. Bishop Stringer, speaking of a young woman named Sarah, wrote in 1915: "The great difficulty here is that the girls trained in the school seem to turn their thoughts more to the white man than to Indians. On the other hand, the white man on account of their superiority in appearance, dress, etc. pay them more attention than is good for them with the result that their heads become turned, and they seem to look forward to marrying white men. There would be no objection to this if suitable men would marry them, but so often it is some low down rascal who shows attention to them".[22]

Anglican church records of marriages involving Native people point to a fundamental transition in patterns of union between 1900 and 1950. Females consistently married younger than men, with the gap widening over time. Between 1925 and 1950 the average age differential between Native partners was twelve years, almost three times that of the preceding quarter-century. Other evidence substantiates this observation. Native birth registrations recorded the ages of fathers and mothers, and so permit a second survey of the age differences of partners. Again, the gap increased over time, although the change was less dramatic than that suggested by church materials. An analysis of the 1941 census points in the same direction. (It is difficult, however, to know just what constituted "married" according to the Yukon census-takers. It is likely that those living common-law, particularly if they had had children, were recorded as married). Over 40 per cent of women between the ages of 15 and 24 were married, compared to less than 13 per cent of the males in that age category. In the 25–44 cohort, fewer than 6 per cent of the females remained unmarried, while the percentage of males yet to marry remained three times as high. The cumulative evidence suggests that females readily found partners, Native or non-Native, at around twenty years of age, but Native males on average could not find a mate until they reached 29 years.[23]

While competition limited the Native males' ability to locate a wife, the impermanence of most relationships frequently hurt the females. Native women often found themselves pregnant by a non-Native who left the district before a claim could be made on his financial resources. Further, short-term liaisons, usually brief encounters following drinking parties, reinforced notions of Indian women as promiscuous and immoral. On the whole, interracial sexual relations re-emphasized the marginality of Yukon Natives, pointing once again

Table 9
Average Age at First Recorded Marriage, Anglican Church Records, 1900–50

Place	1900–24		1925–50	
	Females	Males	Females	Males
Ft. Selkirk	25.9 (29)	27.5 (33)	22.2 (13)	28.3 (14)
Rampart H.	17.9 (15)	22.0 (13)	18.0 (27)	36.5 (25)
Moosehide	20.5 (44)	25.6 (44)	–	–
Total Yukon	22.1 (95)	26.2 (95)	19.7 (51)	32.1 (51)
(Number in parenthesis indicates number of cases)				

Source Parish Records, Anglican Church, Diocese of Yukon.

Table 10
Ages of Fathers and Mothers, First Recorded Birth, 1930–50

Years	Males	Females
1930–34	23.7	21.3
1935–39	27.5	18.9
1940–44	28.3	20.7
1945–50	28.6	20.6

Source Birth Registrations, Vital Statistics Branch, Government of Yukon.

to the Natives' casual utility and the non-Natives' continuing refusal to welcome the Indians into their communities.

Anglican church records of interracial marriages suggest that such liaisons maintained a special character. Husbands averaged sixteen years older than their Native wives, most of whom married under twenty years of age. Most of the men were well established traders or trappers who had decided to remain permanently in the territory. Sanctioned alliances were still the exception; short-term relationships retained their prominence. In those areas removed from the mines and the Yukon River transportation system, especially the Kluane, Teslin, Pelly River, and Porcupine River districts, mixed marriages, formalized or not, of short or lengthy duration, were a fixture of the social fabric.

Two distinct social environments existed in the Yukon Territory, one encompassing the scattered fur-trading population, the other oriented around Dawson, Whitehorse, and the mining camps. In the former, the Natives predominated. The only non-Natives there were a few police officers, fur traders, missionaries, and trappers. Numerically, the Natives far outnumbered the whites. In the isolated Old Crow district in 1928, there were fewer than 25 whites in the midst of over 200 Natives. When the fur trade declined in the late 1940s, the number

Table 11
Conjugal Condition, Yukon Indians, 1941

	15–24		25–44		45–65	
	Males	Females	Males	Females	Males	Females
Total	142	137	167	173	144	137
Single	123	74	30	10	9	1
Married	18	58	126	149	114	86
Other[1]	1	5	11	14	21	50

Source   Canada Census, 1941.
[1] "Other" refers to separated, divorced, or widowed

Table 12
Age at Marriage, Native-White Marriages, Anglican Church Records, 1906–28

Age at Marriage	Husbands (White)	Wives (Native)
Less than 20	0	5
20–29	1	8
30–39	9	2
40–49	2	1
50+	4	0
Average Age	40.4	24.4

Source   Parish Records, Anglican Church, Diocese of Yukon.

of Europeans dropped to less than ten.[24] Under such conditions, and in a manner reminiscent of relations during the HBC era, Natives and non-Natives reached a mutually acceptable social relationship.

The reverse was true in the more densely populated Whitehorse-Dawson corridor, where the towns and mining remained non-Native enclaves. Non-Natives exerted considerable effort to ensure that the settlements retained their Euro-Canadian character. Aided by the government and the missionaries, the non-Natives attempted to keep the Indians out of town. Accomplishing this task was seldom easy. The availability of occasional work enhanced the attractiveness of the towns to Natives, as did abundant liquor supplies, eager bootleggers, medical facilities, and government officers. The number of Natives residing near and in the cities fluctuated according to the opportunity of wage labour. Similarly, the availability of government relief for indigents and health care for the infirm attracted the ill and the aged to Whitehorse and Dawson. Non-Natives reacted strongly when Natives tried to settle in the towns, urging government to maintain the tradition of social segregation.[25]

Government officials, including Indian Agent John Hawksley and various police officers, shared the residents' concerns. Investigating possible sites for an Indian residential school in 1910, school inspector T. Bragg echoed the widely held view that the Natives ought to be kept out of town: "immoral influences are generally found in white communities and such social conditions generally exist as will afford bad examples to Indian children and put temptation in their way ... it is safer to keep them away from places where liquor is sold and where Indians are known to procure it and from places where Indian girls are known to be living in amoral relations with white men."[26] From the government's paternalistic perspective, the towns were complex social environments from which the "childlike" Natives had to be protected. The decision to impose racial segregation resulted from two very different pressures: an official desire to shield the Natives from debauchery, and pressure from the non-Native residents to keep the Indians out of their towns.

The government adopted several approaches to prevent or regulate Native incursions into non-Native residential spaces. The physical segregation of the races was the most popular. The government established special Native reserves outside the towns. Given the fact that many of the Indians lived near the towns on a seasonal basis, the government opted to isolate them close to, but separate from, the urban centres. This maneuver worked both ways, keeping the Natives out of town and limiting non-Native access to the Native camps.[27] In all the major population centres – Dawson City (Moosehide reserve), Mayo, Fort Selkirk, Carmacks, Carcross, and Whitehorse – the government established small reservations designed to settle the Indians away from the non-Natives.

In most instances, the establishment of Native reserves followed non-Native protests. In Whitehorse, the construction of series of small Native huts among the non-Native homes resulted in a public furor and a decision to establish a reserve. John Hawksley commented on the Carmacks reserve: "Last year the white residents complained to me of the Indians camping within the limits of the village of Carmacks. Action was at once taken, authority was obtained from the Department of Indian Affairs (DIA) for surveying a reserve."[28] Practical considerations underlay the town of Mayo's insistence that the Indians be removed: "Some rich silver mines have been discovered and there is considerable activity in the vicinity ... It is thought that owing to the above the town will develop and the land which the Indians now occupy will be needed."[29] There was obviously more than the need for land behind the subsequent decision to relocate the Natives two miles downstream from Mayo – and on the opposite side of the river. The Indians were systematically, although not forcibly, removed and placed under the protection of a government reserve.[30]

Creating a residential reserve solved few problems, because the Natives seldom remained with its confines. There was no treaty with the government, and the tiny reserves served as only seasonal homes. The authorities had no legitimate means of forcing the Indians to stay out of town,[31] but were determined to keep them separate. In response to a letter from resident W.A. Puckett complaining about Natives moving into Whitehorse, the Indian agent replied, "I have no power to prevent it though I consider it a very unwise proceeding to allow them to do so."[32] In the absence of legal means, government officials found other tactics. As Superintendent Moodie reported in 1913, "They are kept out of town as much as possible, but it is only by bluff."[33] Lack of legal authority to block Native access proved to be little impediment. Indian Agent Hawksley regularly imposed curfews on the Indians, demanding that they vacate the towns each night (around 5 p.m. in winter and 7 p.m. in the summer).[34] He took a different tack for the Moosehide Indians, empowering the local band council to punish residents who broke curfew, were seen drinking in public, or were too friendly with non-Natives.[35] The Natives often resisted the regulations and Hawksley occasionally despaired over his inability to prevent the Indians from mixing with the non-Natives.[36] With the assistance of the police, however, the Indian agent expanded his curfew regulations in 1929, establishing a nightly limit of 8 p.m. (the end of the Dawson picture show), after which time all Natives had to leave town. The initiative remained in force even though known to be *ultra vires*.[37] By 1933 Hawksley allowed Natives to reside in Dawson only with a special temporary permit granted for employment purposes.[38] In 1947 Indian Agent R.J. Meek adopted similar tactics to keep the Natives on their reserve and away from Dawson.[39] Coupled with the establishment of residential reserves, these impediments ensured the Indians' continued physical and social segregation.

Of course, the mere existence of these regulations is evidence that Natives continued to enter the towns regularly, many seeking to stay there. The few enfranchised Indians could not be barred from the towns, and several managed to secure regular employment. As well, Natives were welcomed into towns for celebrations, such as the annual Discovery Day festival held in Dawson each August.[40] Preventing Native ministers of the Anglican Church from residing in the towns posed particularly sensitive problems. Mrs Robert McDonald, Native wife of the respected northern missionary, remained in Dawson after her husband's death, supported by church and government pensions. Similarly, Anglican synod meetings and other ecclesiastical gatherings often brought such Native missionaries as Julius Kendi and his wife into the towns for short periods; and Dawsonites found it hard to complain when the Women's Auxiliary of the Moosehide church opened a stall at the St Paul's annual sale.[41] While non-Natives accepted these selected exceptions, tolerance was not acceptance.[42] Even those accepted temporarily within the urban societies were there on sufferance.

That the non-Natives wished to avoid close contact is further demonstrated in the debate over Native involvement with schools and hospitals. Institutions which might have provided a meeting ground became instead the most visible symbols of racial segregation. The Anglican clergy encouraged the development of separate school systems. With a number of Natives and mixed-bloods residing near each town, however, integration with the territorial public school system seemed desirable. Any such attempted integration was sternly resisted; as late as 1949 Teslin offered the only integrated school in the Yukon.[43] Indian Agent R.J. Meek reported that year: "The Yukon School Ordinance does not discriminate against Indians, but the several times Indian children were placed in Territorial Schools it ended as a fiasco. A case as recent as 1947 happened at Mayo. Neither the administration nor the teachers would discourage admitting Indians to Territorial Schools, it is always a few parents who raise a violent objection."[44]

Further evidence of discrimination can be seen in the treatment offered to the Natives by the territorial medical fraternity. As with schooling, Natives encountered two standards of health care, one for themselves and one for the non-Native population. In most centres, the people consistently demanded the segregation of hospitals and refused to share wards with Native patients.[45] The Mayo hospital, funded by the Treadgold Mining Company, refused to admit Natives to its general wards. Instead, Indians received treatment in a tent to the rear of the main structure.[46] Protests by government officials led to a successful request to the federal government for a grant to build an extra room, reserved for Native patients, onto the hospital.[47] The solution solved the medical problem, but the continued segregation reinforced the social distance between the races in the community. In Whitehorse, similarly, there was a general hospital and, for a time, a small building "fitted for infirm and Tubercular Indian patients."[48] The medical professionals apparently shared discriminatory attitudes, although they continued to serve their Native patients. In 1939 several doctors refused to treat Natives at the same rates charged to the non-Natives. The DIA argued that it was "not prepared to admit that sick Indians are less desirable patients than white people,"[49] but the prevailing feeling in the district outweighed the department's opposition. As Yukon Controller G.A. Jeckell wrote concerning hospitalization practices, "They [white residents] most decidedly object in maternity cases to have their wives and infants share a maternity ward with an Indian mother and infant and the management of St. Mary's Hospital at Dawson is compelled to defer to this opinion."[50] Discrimination did not abate significantly over time. During a 1947 tuberculosis survey in Whitehorse, non-Native residents opposed the request that they share hospital gowns with "diseased" Indians. Alternatives were hastily found.[51] Medical care, like the schools and even the towns, became a bastion of segregation, providing graphic evidence of the gulf that still separated Natives and non-Natives in the Yukon.

The image of the Indians in the public mind derived from, and provided a justification for, these policies of social segregation. The Natives' assertive role in the HBC trade had contributed to a widely held view of the Indians as aggressive and self-interested,[52] but that perception died with the coming of the gold-rush stampede. Most of the new arrivals saw little utility in the Native way of life, and disdained Indian customs and standards. The emergent images reflected actual circumstances, while also illustrating a general twentieth-century depreciation of the vitality of Indian society.[53] The words "dirty" and "diseased" were frequently used in connection with the Natives, an indication of the impact of epidemics and disapproval of Native standards of cleanliness.[54] True, several commentators expressed hope for the "improvement" of Natives, provided they could be kept from alcohol and "undesirable" non-Natives.[55] But in general, a less positive appraisal prevailed. The Natives' peripheral economic and social position, the effects of disease, and the frequent appearance of inebriated Natives near population centres helped to give rise to the stereotype of the drunken and shiftless Indian. Based on incomplete knowledge and antipathy for Native culture, this stereotype contributed significantly towards the process of social segregation. Acting through the government, the non-Natives remained determined to keep the races apart. Indians had their world – in the bush – and the interests of both non-Natives and Natives would be best served if the latter remained among the trees and animals. The towns and mining camps, on the other hand, were to remain non-Native preserves.

Evidence on the success of government and non-Natives in keeping the races apart is contradictory and incomplete. If we assume that

Table 13
Native Rural/Urban Population, 1901–50

Year	Rural	Urban
1901	3,322	–
1911	1,152	337
1921	1,382	8
1931	1,469	158
1941	1,362	276
1951	1,320	230[1]

Source   Canada Census, 1901–51.
[1] Whitehorse only

Natives living on residential reserves were incorporated into urban totals, an assumption that appears safe for Whitehorse but questionable for Dawson City, few Indians lived permanently in the towns. In 1931, for instance, the national census listed 158 Indians as living in towns in the Yukon. Two years later, however, Indian Agent Hawksley noted that no Indians lived in Dawson, none in Mayo, and only four families comprising less than twenty people in Whitehorse. To complicate matters further, individuals often camped or occupied cabins near the towns on a seasonal basis, while spending most of their time in the bush. Census data, therefore, appear to overstate the number of Indians living permanently in town. Comments by other observers suggest that few Natives remained in the towns, that most visited on a seasonal basis, and that, when they did live in the towns, they resided on segregated reserves.

On the whole, the limited data suggests that the process of social isolation succeeded. In Dawson in particular, non-Native efforts to keep Indians on the Moosehide reserve seem to have worked. The figures for Whitehorse suggest otherwise, although population statistics do not separately list those on the reserve near town, where most Natives lived. Those Natives who insisted upon living near the towns, most of whom did so only on a seasonal basis, found themselves on the physical and social margins. Natives approached the non-Native settlements in larger numbers after the Second World War, but problems persisted. When a sizeable number of Natives moved inside Dawson City limits in the late 1940s, the Indian Agent noted that "with the incidence of tuberculosis at its present level, they constitute a menace to the settlement at large."[56] With some success, he urged the Natives to leave the "bad houses" in Dawson for better quarters in Moosehide.[57]

The construction of the Alaska Highway, begun in 1942, altered existing demographic and racial patterns in a manner reminiscent of the Klondike gold rush. Countless opportunities for Native-white interaction and new demands on the Natives worked against existing racial barriers. Despite the social restructuring attending the arrival of thousands of construction workers, however, attitudes and policies did not change significantly. With a number of jobs available along the highway route, the Native population shifted temporarily towards the development corridor, especially Whitehorse. That reorientation was neither uniform nor permanent.[58] Instead of a radically different social order, the Natives faced an elaboration and intensification of past experiences. The magnitude of social contact increased markedly, especially in previously isolated districts. There had been few non-Natives in the southwest corner of the territory before 1942; the coming of the highway brought several thousand workers through the area, if only briefly. Again, however, patterns of contact did not deviate significantly from past practices.

Alcohol and the interracial party continued as the principal medium of social interaction; as before, liquor was used to gain sexual favours from Native women. The social and recreational functions of liquor-consumption still dominated Indian drinking; there were only a few signs of the drinking problems that would characterize many Yukon Native communities in the post-Second World War period. The police stepped up enforcement procedures, particularly in the southern Yukon, leading to a substantial increase in arrests for alcohol-consumption. This dramatic rise led several commentators to argue that the construction of the Alaska Highway resulted in a qualitative change in Native drinking patterns.[59] But, as with most such social problems, recorded breaches of the law actually indicate as much about the zeal and size of the police and prevailing public attitudes as they do about actual occurrences. Evidence from the Whitehorse Police Court supports this contention. The increase in average yearly convictions from seventeen in 1940–44 to over fifty-three in the next five years implies a marked, but hardly alarming, rise in alcohol-consumption. The police had, however, relocated their headquarters from Dawson to Whitehorse in 1943–44, significantly increasing the size of the local constabulary. The increase in convictions for alcohol offences – and we should remember that Natives were in violation of the law for merely possessing or consuming alcohol – is thus attributable largely to the new pattern of law enforcement. This is not to suggest that there was not more drinking. Some individuals clearly had drinking problems (several were graduates of the Carcross Residential School) and appeared before the police court with some regularity. Further, the large number of soldiers and construction workers in the northwest ensured a steady supply of liquor

Table 14
Native Alcohol-related Convictions[1] and Police Manpower, Southern Yukon, 1940–49

Year	Convictions	Police Force
1940	3	4
1941	9	4
1942	28	4
1943	27	15
1944	34	25
1945	51	25
1946	75	30
1947	82	27
1948	61	21
1949 (to July)	32	22

Source   NA, RG18, RCMP Records, Whitehorse Police Court Register; RCMP *Annual Reports*, 1940–50.
[1] Supplying and Possession of Liquor Breaches of Indian Act, Drunkenness.

into the Native camps. Yet, for the most part, Native drinking adhered to the familiar pattern of interracial parties and spree or potlatch drinking.

Native-white sexual relations also increased, and venereal disease became virtually epidemic among young Native women. Non-Native prostitutes again followed the construction workers north, lessening demand for Native women, except in isolated districts where Native females, even young girls, attracted considerable attention.[60] The incidence of sexual contact stands in stark contrast to the continuing pattern of racial segregation. But it was the overabundance of single men, free from the moral bonds of settled society, and not a shift in attitudes towards the Indians, that accounted for much of the interest. This pattern of resorting to women outside "acceptable" society is not uncommon and stands as one of the more constant features of frontier societies. Sex and liquor continued to provide the meeting ground for the races in the Yukon.

The coming of the Alaska Highway increased the frequency of interracial contact, but did not alter the basic relationship between the races. Improvements over the pre-1942 period were minor indeed. In 1950 large numbers of American and Canadian troops were stationed for a time in Whitehorse as part of "Operation Sweetbriar." Native and mixed-blood girls in Whitehorse were in particular demand; while the troops were in town, the girls of the Whitehorse Indian School were escorted by a staff member during trips to downtown Whitehorse.[61] There were a few signs of change. Indian Agent R.J. Meek observed in 1948: "The Indians of Whitehorse seem to be slowly breaking down certain barriers of prejudice which was [sic] unfortunately very prevalent in the past. At the ceremony in celebration of Scout Week, Indian boys were invited to participate."[62] Such victories, however, had little impact; only a limited number of Yukon Natives moved toward complete integration. Changing employment habits and the willingness of some parents to educate their children, particularly evident among the Natives around Whitehorse and Carcross, suggested that some Indians had abandoned the old ways. But until 1950 that group was a small minority, not representative of the larger Native population which preferred the pursuit of game over the pursuit of material wealth.

In the 1950s, as government programs such as family allowance, old age pensions, and increased welfare assistance expanded and as falling fur prices undermined the viability of the hunting-trapping way of life, the old patterns of social relations persisted. Combined forces drew the Indians into the towns, but public attitudes remained the same. Indeed, segregation policies, in place since the gold rush, took on new meaning as the Natives moved closer to Whitehorse, Dawson, and other towns through the 1950s and 1960s. Solidly entrenched and seldom before challenged, the exclusionist barriers proved difficult to break down.

White settlement patterns, social barriers, and racial images contributed to the isolation of Native from non-Native culture; they did not insulate Natives from the ravages of European diseases. In chapter one we traced the demographic consequences of epidemic disease in the nineteenth century, and described the catastrophic depopulation of the Yukon River basin in the years before the Klondike gold rush. Medical and demographic conditions changed significantly after the turn of the century, but health problems continued to be a major source of conflict and crisis.

Early reports by missionaries and police officers informed the Canadian government of the continuing devastation caused by newly introduced diseases. In the post-gold rush era, federal authorities moved rapidly when they learned of an outbreak of disease to isolate affected individuals and groups through official quarantines. Such measures sought to limit the spread of the disease among the Native population and, equally, to prevent the Indians' illnesses from being transmitted to the non-Native settlements. Decisive action seemed to work; a 1918 order to quarantine in Skagway all persons entering the Yukon Territory kept the infamous Spanish influenza epidemic of that year out of the territory and doubtless saved many lives.[63]

Systematic attempts to control and treat diseases had the desired effect, and death rates fell far below the estimated figures for the pre-

Table 15
Recorded Native Births, Deaths, and Natural Increase, 1931–50

Year	Births	Deaths	Natural Increase
1931	15	24	(9)[1]
1932	15	25	(10)
1933	29	20	9
1934	24	18	6
1935	26	33	(7)
1936	17	37	(20)
1937	35	29	6
1938	34	25	9
1939	34	28	6
1940	32	20	12
1941	35	26	9
1942	45	64	(19)
1943	37	52	(15)
1944	57	48	9
1945	36	35	1
1946	50	35	15
1947	77	28	49
1948	81	42	39
1949	65	35	30
1950	67	32	35

Source   Canada, *Vital Statistics, 1930–50.*

[1] Parentheses signify net decline in population.

Klondike era. Haphazard recording of Native vital statistics between 1900 and 1930 hampers a consideration of death rates in this period, as does the fact that many Indian people remained outside the reporting network. By the 1930s, recording and coverage had improved, although there is no question that numerous births and deaths continued to be unrecorded. Recorded deaths from 1930 to 1950, however, illustrate the impact of improved medical assistance, since death rates remained comparatively low. In the period before 1942, the effects of quarantines and medical help, combined with increasing Native immunity to some of the diseases, limited the annual number of recorded deaths to between eighteen and thirty-seven.

The Natives' continuing vulnerability to imported diseases was apparent from time to time between 1900 and 1930, as new illnesses swept through a community or region and caused several deaths. An outbreak of diphtheria in Moosehide in 1907 claimed four lives, including three under the age of eight years, before a quarantine was established. Once a physician arrived, eight people were hospitalized and three of those died.[64] A serious disease swept through Rampart House in 1917. To quote one resident: "Since I wrote to you last Amos has lost another daughter (Mary) and Bruce lost an infant child also, and at present Billy Joe No. 2 a young son of Mrs. Charlie Wolverine is expected to die soon. He is about 12 years of age and one of Jacobs brightest pupils ... There has been 17 deaths since last New Years (1916)."[65] The second major invasion of the northwest, during the building of the Alaska Highway and Canol Pipeline between 1942 and 1945, highlighted the Indians' lack of immunity. During the construction phase, hundreds of Natives who had previously experienced little direct contact with non-Natives encountered thousands of soldiers and project workers. The Canadian liaison officer on the project wrote,

There is no question but what the impact of all the construction activities in the Southern Yukon and its consequent influx of white people is having a very harmful effect upon the natives, and its noticeable that the degree of this harm is in direct proportion to the closeness of the association that the natives have with the whites. The new era is here to stay and is and will continue to present many problems to the administration. One of these problems is how to soften the blow upon the natives and ameliorate conditions so as to prevent their complete devastation.[66]

This description was on the mark, as the 64 recorded deaths in 1942 represented a twenty-year high. The impact of the highway on Native health was particularly evident at Teslin that same year. Dr John Marchand of the Public Roads Administration recorded successive epidemics of measles, German measles, dysentery, catarrhal jaundice, whooping cough, mumps, tonsillitis, and meningitis.[67] In 1943, 128 of the 135 Native people in Teslin suffered from measles, a sign of the pervasiveness of the illness.[68] Few areas faced such sustained pressure,[69] but no bands in the southern Yukon completely avoided the devastation.

On a territory-wide scale, Native population change between 1900 and 1950 consisted of marginal losses and gains. The high estimates of Native population before 1911, while suggestive of earlier habitation levels, were not based on sound data and are of little utility. There is also insufficient corroborating evidence to suggest that the pre-Klondike population loss continued to 1911 on the scale suggested by published population figures. From 1911 to 1951 Yukon Natives maintained a rough equilibrium, with regular enumerations ranging between 1,300 and 1,600 people. But recorded Native births and calculations of natural increase for the period 1945–50 point to the beginning of a new era. A slow population increase through the 1940s coincided with an increased incidence of short-term liaisons between construction workers and Native women. The resulting surge in births over deaths foreshadowed a large increase in the Yukon Native population. Trends established in the late 1940s, which mirrored a nation-wide increase in aboriginal population,[70] continued over subsequent decades. The territorial Native population, which stood at 1,583 in 1951, rose to 2,207 ten years later and to 2,580 by 1971.[71] The Yukon Indians did not regain the population levels postulated for the pre-contact period, but they have rebounded from the demographic crisis of the late nineteenth century and the stagnation of the first half of this century.

The demographic stability evident by the 1940s reflected a combination of a birth rate close to the national average of 50 births per 1,000 people each year and a comparatively high death rate. The age-sex structure of the Native population provides further evidence of the internal demography of Yukon Indian society. All in all, the demographic structure of the Native communities in the territory looks very much like that of other pre-industrial populations. There is evidence of high natality, severe infant and child mortality, and a steady erosion of population through the life cycle. The population structure also held the prospect of rapid increase. Medical care targeted at infants and youths, combined with more adequate protection from disease, promised improved prospects for survival for children, a decrease in population wastage through the child-bearing years, and a concomitant increase in the number of Indians. Federal government health programs for Native people, beginning in the late 1940s, achieved such results; a 65 per cent increase in population between 1931 and 1971 indicates that a substantial demographic reconstruction occurred.

While this general profile suggests the demographic framework within which the Yukon Indians lived and died, a consideration of the causes of death and the impact of endemic disease is necessary to complete the picture. An analysis of the causes of recorded Native deaths illustrates both the irregular impact of epidemics and the ongoing struggle with tuberculosis. During the twentieth century this single ailment accounted for between 25 and 50 per cent of all recorded deaths. Tuberculosis was, by all accounts, endemic throughout the territory, and was firmly rooted in the social and economic conditions facing Native people.[72]

Tuberculosis is primarily a disease of poverty, spawned in malnutrition, overcrowding, and poor hygiene; it is also the most widespread of all infectious diseases.[73] While there has been considerable debate as to whether or not tuberculosis was indigenous to North America, there is no doubt that the arrival of non-Natives dramatically

Table 16
Causes of Death among Yukon Native People, Selected Diseases, 1900–49

Years	Tuberculosis[1]	Pneumonia	Old Age	Infant Death	Heart	Influenza	Meningitis	Whooping Cough	Measles	Total Deaths
1900–04	39(25%)	11	6	2	–	–	–	–	4	157
1905–09	24(27%)	3	2	2	3	–	–	–	–	90
1910–14	44(38%)	3	2	–	4	–	3	–	–	117
1915–19	47(32%)	1	4	5	3	13	1	3	1	146
1920–24	34(25%)	5	4	–	–	13	1	–	–	98
1925–29	23(33%)	10	3	–	3	1	1	1	–	69
1930–34	53(46%)	6	9	1	5	1	2	–	–	115
1935–39	88(58%)	9	12	2	2	9	–	–	–	152
1940–44	68(35%)	22	13	6	4	7	5	4	14	194
1945–49	74(40%)	18	8	7	7	5	–	4	–	184

Source   Canada, *Vital Statistics, 1939–50,* and Death Register, Vital Statistics Branch, Government of Yukon.

[1] For much of the period before 1930, tuberculosis was alternatively listed as consumption.

increased the incidence of the disease.[74] Across the continent, tuberculosis became one of the greatest killers of aboriginal people and poor non-Natives. The Indian mode of life increased their vulnerability as regular trading excursions brought them into contact with tuberculin Natives and non-Natives, and their cramped living quarters proved to be excellent breeding grounds for the disease.

Yukon Natives faced the same problems with tuberculosis as did other North American aboriginal peoples.[75] Non-Natives agreed that tuberculosis stemmed from the Natives' living conditions, but held out little hope that the problems caused by cramped quarters, poor hygiene, and inadequate nourishment could be rectified.[76] L.A. Pare, assistant surgeon for the NWMP, offered a graphic description of Natives:

They are a squalid, pitiable looking lot of people. Those who do not exhibit advanced symptoms of disease show signs of the existence of germs. They are particularly unclean in their habits and almost entirely destitute. I declare I have not seen in the different tents I have had occasion to enter, a decent pair of blankets; they have but small flimsy things, and in most cases a mere heap of rags. It is a fact as incontrovertible, as it is deplorable, that disease, actual want and destitution prevail among the majority of them.[77]

Police officers, medical doctors, and particularly the Anglican missionaries did what they could to prevent the spread of the disease. Natives received basic education in the pathology of tuberculosis and were encouraged to improve sanitary practices. Following a visit to

Fortymile in 1915, Indian Agent John Hawksley noted with pride that earlier appeals to ventilate cabins, change bed-linens regularly, and move outhouses away from homes had been successful.[78] Such triumphs often proved highly localized and transitory. Nevertheless, government and church officials in the territory remained committed to the nation-wide campaign to wipe out the "white plague."[79]

Although hundreds of Yukon Native people suffered from tuberculosis, the extent of the infection remained unknown until the late 1940s.[80] Between 1947 and 1949 the Canadian government conducted several x-ray surveys throughout the territory. The goal was to identify those with the disease and to insist upon hospitalization for the severely afflicted.[81] The government sent Natives with the disease, especially children, to the newly opened tuberculosis ward at the Whitehorse General Hospital or to the Charles Camsell Hospital in Edmonton for specialized care. The surveys offered few surprises. Work in the central Yukon revealed that 52 individuals had some sign of a tuberculin condition; 311 showed no evidence of tuberculosis.[82] Other tests indicated that close to 25 per cent of the Natives suffered from advanced tuberculosis. A July 1949 survey, for instance, demonstrated an infection rate of 143 out of 605 Natives tested.[83] While the confirmed rate of secondary tuberculosis simply illustrated the extent of the disease, the surveys marked the beginning of a concerted effort to deal with the problem. For over half a century, tuberculosis had been the major cause of death among Yukon Natives, striking children and adolescents with particular virulence. In the late 1940s authorities took tentative steps towards fighting, if not immediately eliminating, the disease.[84]

One medical expert observed that tuberculosis "flourishes wherever there is poverty, malnourishment, poor living conditions, and a lack of medical care."[85] Available commentaries on Native housing and sanitation practices conform to medical descriptions of conditions under which tuberculosis thrives. In the semi-permanent camps and on residential reserves, Natives inhabited small, crowded houses, often poorly ventilated, handled human and cooking wastes improperly, were often dirty, and ate food which fluctuated between the standard fare of the northern harvester and the processed food products of the south. Continued mobility, particularly through fur-trading ventures, aided the transmission of tuberculosis and other diseases, ensuring that isolated, and previously unaffected, bands would face exposure to the illness.

Beside the obvious demographic implications, tuberculosis had considerable social and economic consequences. Tuberculosis attacks the respiratory system with particular virulence, leading to a shortage

Table 17
Deaths of Yukon Native People, by Age, 1900–46
(% of Total Native Deaths)

Years	Less than 1	1–19	20–49	50 +
1900–04	8.5	45.8	27.7	17.0
1905–09	16.5	36.5	36.6	10.6
1910–14	19.6	38.2	27.5	14.7
1915–19	12.6	42.2	26.7	20.0
1920–24	2.1	45.3	30.5	22.1
1925–29	14.7	44.1	23.5	17.6
1930–34	12.2	53.0	16.5	18.3
1935–39	19.2	41.1	19.9	19.9
1940–44	21.2	37.0	23.8	18.0
1945–49	25.8	31.9	25.3	18.7

Source   Canada, *Vital Statistics, 1930–50,* and Death Register, Vital Statistics Branch, Government
of Yukon.

Table 18
Average and Median Age at Death, by Sex, 1900–49

Year	Average Age at Death			Median Age at Death	
	Male	Female	All	Male	Female
1900–04	21.9	25.6	23.6	18	20
1905–09	22.3	20.4	21.3	20	15
1910–14	19.4	23.5	21.2	18	17
1915–19	22.2	25.8	23.6	17	19
1920–24	25.2	31.4	28.2	16	25
1925–29	25.6	19.6	23.4	16	12
1930–34	25.0	19.1	22.8	12	11
1935–39	23.7	25.9	24.7	12	15
1940–44	21.4	22.8	22.1	11	19
1945–49	23.4	24.2	24.0	14	17

Source   Canada, *Vital Statistics, 1930–50,* and Death Register, Vital Statistics Branch, Government
of Yukon.

of breath, a significant drop in stamina, and general physical debility.
Given the Natives' subsistence activities and the need for extended
physical exertion, these symptoms struck at the heart of the aboriginal way of life. The Indians' hunting pursuits placed a premium on
travel by foot and boat, demanded extensive if not regular physical
activity, and required considerable health and strength. Along with
respiratory ailments such as pneumonia and bronchitis, also common
among the Indians in the post-contact period, tuberculosis attacked
precisely those qualities necessary for survival in the northern envi-

ronment. On a regional basis, the cumulative impact was significant. Many Natives reduced their physical activity, a serious problem in a harvesting society. Others, particularly in the 1940s and after, left for distant hospitals, never to return. Beyond this, the widespread stereotype of the malingering Native, based on routine observations of men and women seemingly incapable of physical exertion, raises the possibility that many of these "lazy" Indians suffered from tuberculosis or another similarly debilitating disease. Any discussion of the non-medical consequences of tuberculosis must remain speculative, however, as the documentary record offers few insights into the effects of the disease on work patterns and activity levels. This limitation notwithstanding, there is little question that the illness had a widespread social and economic impact which mirrored its demographic implications. Tuberculosis killed dozens of Yukon Natives; it also contributed significantly to the gradual decay of the harvesting lifestyle.

The arrival of non-Natives in the Yukon River valley had demographic results which both conditioned and reflected social relations. The introduction of new diseases in the early years had contributed to a major decrease in population and obviously influenced relations between Natives and non-Natives. The Indian characterizations of diseases as the non-Natives' "bad medicine" increased social and economic tensions. Conversely, the sight of many sick Natives, apparently incapable of caring for themselves, confirmed non-Native stereotypes of aboriginal people as disease-ridden.

After the gold rush, the impact of disease on Yukon Indian limited their ability to respond positively to new opportunities and threatened their precarious position within the Yukon economy. At the same time, the regular appearance of disease among the Natives and the perception of non-Natives that such illnesses threatened their communities added support to government and public efforts to segregate the Natives.[86]

Church, State, and the Native People in the Yukon Territory

Church, State, and the Native People in the Yukon Territory

As the previous chapters have documented, a combination of economic and social forces relegated Yukon Natives to the margins of territorial society. These processes, reflecting broadly based non-Native attitudes and aboriginal values, generally lacked sharp focus or direction. They were, in Ralph Linton's phrase, examples of non-directed cultural change. But there were additional forces at work in the territory which, in contrast, sought deliberately to alter the shape and substance of indigenous life. The church and the national government approached the Native people with purpose and intent. Missionaries and government officials attempted, with varying degrees of success, to recast aboriginal values and customs. They did so, almost uniformly, from the conviction that the Native people had to be kept apart from non-Native residents of the Yukon until an undefined time when they were ready for more complete integration. The effort did not work as planned, reflecting the unwillingness of central organizers to support northern programs with money and the Natives' resistance to many of the proposed changes.

Existing literature on church and state in the north strays little from a south-centred perspective.[1] Priority is given to the creation of, and justification for, national or ecclesiastical policies, and often to the role of dominant personalities in the development of such initiatives.[2] To the degree that the experience of clergy and federal officials is considered, it is typically examined in the context of their personal lives rather than as an essential part of their relationship with the local residents.[3]

The national or institutional perspective is, of course, essential to an understanding of the motivation, priorities, and programs of both church and state. It is equally important that this perspective be balanced with a view from the field and with an understanding of the problems and decisions arising when the agents of social change met face to face with the subjects of cultural imperialism. The following three chapters assess the goals, efforts, and impact of missionary and government plans for the Native people of the Yukon Territory and the Natives' response to these initiatives.

Although clergy and government officials can correctly be described, in Ralph Linton's phrase, as agents of directed cultural change,[4] we should not assume that their actions matched their rhetoric. Missionaries and government officials did, at the level of intent and declared policy, seek to assimilate Native people to the standards and customs of Euro-Canadian society. But local conditions, including high costs, a pessimistic forecast of the region's potential for development, difficulty securing suitable personnel, Native mobility, and the activities of non-Natives who seldom shared the idealists' objectives, prevented the quick achievement of national and institutional objectives.

An assessment of religion, education, and federal programming for Native people in the Yukon Territory – the three main elements of institutional activity in the region – demonstrates an ongoing willingness to accommodate, if not accept, a continuation of Native cultural forms. This flexibility did not, however, represent a conscious decision to abandon goals established by the churches or the policy directives outlined in the Indian Act. On the national level, church and state expected that their efforts would accelerate the integration of Natives into the wider Canadian society. Religion, education, and a variety of government programs were designed to mediate between the races, carrying Natives closer to non-Native norms and preparing them for fuller participation. But activities in the Yukon followed a different path. Government agents and missionaries performed their duties with ambivalence, unsure as to whether their Native charges were capable of civilization or whether the limited development prospects for the region justified the restructuring of aboriginal life. They also usually approached the Natives together. Despite national protestations of the separation of church and state, the two arms of colonialism worked closely together in the Yukon. The government financially and morally supported the work of the Christian church, and the missionaries went out of their way to assist with the implementation of government programs. As a Teslin missionary said of his relationship with the local police officer: "Both are aiming to prevent crime and evil. One has law as his weapon while the other has the Gospel."[5]

Natives in the Yukon did not simply accept the dictates of church and state. Instead, consistent with their response to economic and social changes, they adopted those religious components amenable to their culture and responded to government initiatives according to their perception of their best interests. Yet, that said, the impact of church and state on the Yukon's aboriginal population should not be underestimated. Although missionaries and government agents had less of an impact on Natives in the Yukon than in southern Canada, and although they were not single-minded in their pursuit of the goal of cultural assimilation, their programs, ideology, and attitudes were important elements in relegating Yukon Native people to the fringes of territorial society.

CHAPTER SIX

Religion and the Yukon Indians

Although there is considerable historical writing on the role of missionaries and government officials in the north, their activities have seldom been assessed with a critical eye. Studies of the churches, written typically by members of the clergy and published by the missionary or church press, tend toward hagiographic treatment of "wilderness saints" who left the comforts of southern Canada, England, or France to spread the Gospel to the "uncivilized savages" of the far northwest. These accounts seldom advance beyond narratives of the missionaries' time in the north;[1] little effort is made to explain the Natives' response to the work of the church or to assess the impact of Christian teachings on the aboriginal people.

There is a notable exception to this tradition. Kerry Abel's thoughtful and thorough study of relations between missionaries and the Dene of the Mackenzie River basin carefully traces the evolution of spiritual beliefs in the nineteenth century. By adopting an ethnohistorical approach, Abel enters the world view of both the missionaries and the Native people, and argues convincingly that the Dene were not swept passively and unthinkingly into Christianity. She concludes: "The Dene were not easily, automatically and happily 'converted' to Christianity or to other values which the European missionaries attempted to teach. Some rejected the message entirely and openly, some listened cautiously and politely so as not to offend, still others adopted elements of Christian teaching which seemed appropriate to individual cases. There was no single response in this individualistic society. As a pragmatic people, they tested the new ideas and accepted only those which proved their utility."[2]

Abel shows that the Native response to Christianity is one of the central themes in Native-white relations. Through their religious preaching, missionaries of the Catholic and Protestant faiths sought to bring Natives closer to the spiritual enlightenment of the dominant culture. The churches set out to reform, restructure, and ultimately undermine all vestiges of "pagan" traditions; in the case of the Anglican CMS, they also came hoping to create an indigenous church that would quickly supplant the missionary one. The clerics were filled with religious zeal, convinced of the superiority of their spirituality and their civilization. Their motives were sincere and, to them, unquestionable; and their willingness to abandon the cloistered comforts of Europe or the settled colonies for the uncertainties of the frontier originated in a deep desire to bring the truth, both spiritual and cultural, to the "unwashed." If, as recent scholarship has indicated, their religious message included a condemnation of the aboriginal cultures, most missionaries none the less remained convinced of their righteousness.

On an institutional level, church missions sought to eliminate Native spirituality and to lift Native society towards a more civilized norm.[3] These goals remained constant, but it is less clear that organizational imperatives necessarily shaped missionary-Native relations in the field. Policy guidelines sketched in the meeting rooms of the CMS in England, for example, represented ideals, not necessarily workable directives, for missionary operations. An analysis of church activities in the Yukon reveals that the clergy adopted a surprisingly latitudinarian approach to Native spirituality and, like their government counterparts, resisted suggestions that they work swiftly to undermine Native culture. They never wavered in their commitment to the goal of bringing Natives the benefits of Christianity and western civilization, but a realistic consideration of northern conditions and a pessimistic assessment of the church's ability to effect change tempered their lofty ambitions.

This analysis of church-Native relations will, of necessity, focus on the efforts of the Anglican CMS. Beginning in the 1860s, the Anglican Church maintained a continuous presence in the Yukon River basin. In addition to being the only major branch of the Christian church ministering regularly to the Indians, the Anglicans also operated a territory-wide day-school system and administered the region's first two boarding schools. The Roman Catholic Church was more sporadically involved in the region. Members of the Oblate order attempted to breach Anglican domination in the 1860s and 1870s, but were repulsed by the combined efforts of the Anglicans and the HBC. While Catholic clergy continued irregular operations thereafter, particularly in the eastern and southern districts, they did not offer a sustained missionary effort until the 1930s.[4] In the 1940s Anglicans, Catholics, Baptists, and Presbyterians vied for the Indians' attention.[5]

Any consideration of the impact of Christianity must begin with a discussion of Native spirituality. Although the topic, given the dearth of historical sources, has been a field mainly for anthropological inquiry, a description of the Natives' spiritual beliefs is an essential foundation for assessing the balance of persistence or change in the post-contact period.[6] Significantly, unlike many early evangelists in New France and colonial America, the northern missionaries acknowledged the presence and feared the vitality of Indian spirituality. Accordingly, much of their work was a deliberate attempt to supplant Native beliefs.

The central characteristic of Yukon Indian spirituality, common to all sub-Arctic Athapaskans, was the absence of a codified or structured religion. Beliefs were strongly influenced by regional conditions and individual experience, and lacked ceremonial consistency. Among all the groups, however, animism and shamanism dominated spiritual understanding. Natives believed that animals possessed spirits, that inanimate objects had souls, and that humans had to respect the environment in which they lived. There is ethnographic and documentary evidence to suggest that the Natives' interpretation of the religious world culminated in a belief in a supreme supernatural power or deity. Public manifestations of these concepts came principally through the shamans. Possessed with special abilities to control and interpret the spirits, shamans used their power to respond to illness, famine, and bad weather, or to cast spells on enemies.[7] Inland Tlingit religion was more formalized, reflecting their coastal connections, but it differed more in style than substance from the general pattern.[8] Missionaries entering the Yukon encountered a people who had no formalized religion and few regular ceremonies. The Indians' spiritual vision should be characterized more as a world view than as a religion, since it lacked most of the ceremonial regularity associated with the Christian faiths.[9]

The clergy of the CMS represented a particular section of the larger Church of England. They were, in the main, evangelicals, believing in individual salvation and the fundamental importance of each human being's relationship with God. They did not place particular emphasis on the rituals and ceremonies of the church, finding succour in the words of the Bible and personal reaffirmations of faith. William Carpenter Bompas, who would dominate the CMS work in the Yukon during the late nineteeth century, was such an evangelical. He was also, as Kerry Abel has written, "a curious man, who has been revered as the closest thing to a saint that the evangelicals can accept, and reviled as a madman by non-churchmen." He believed in a very simple style of worship and devoted tremendous personal effort to learning Native languages and translating the Bible. Bompas would have a mixed record as a leader of the Anglican Church in the Yukon. While he was a man of notable zeal and unquestioned Christian devotion, he was also inflexible and placed little emphasis on promoting his northern missions among non-Native supporters.[10]

The CMS evangelicals, including Bompas, were not terribly impressed with their Native charges in the Yukon valley. Although believing in the ultimate salvation of even the most unChristian peoples, they had few illusions about the difficulty of their task. Bompas summarized their attitude when he wrote, "These mountain Loucheux [Kutchin] seem 'the lowest of all people,' but I cannot help hoping that they are a 'chosen race.'"[11] The Reverend Flewelling was even more blunt in his characterization of the Natives: "They are in a physical and mental torpor and have neither worldly nor spiritual ambition, but their only object seems to be to exist and that with as little work as possible. They have few or no traditions and have as a race no individuality, and make nothing that be called characteristic. A curio hunter or a collector of legends would have no ground here. They are not vicious but are much like poor human children but do not require obedience, and the children run wild."[12] T.H. Canham offered similarly unflattering descriptions of the Fort Selkirk Indians: "They are we find wretchedly poor, very dark & superstitious & more or less indifferent about matters of religion." They were, he claimed, "the most uncivilized looking Indians I have seen yet."[13]

Under the guidance of Henry Venn, secretary to the CMS, the Anglicans developed a sophisticated approach to evangelism which was intended to soften the cultural clash, overcome the assumed backwardness of Native culture, and bring Christianity swiftly to the centre of aboriginal life. Although the missionaries sought to recast Native traditions, Venn and the CMS cautioned clergy to respect aboriginal societies. Venn argued for the rapid appointment of Native catechists (lay leaders), even if they lacked religious training. Similarly, the translation of the Bible into Native vernacular remained the first order of business. The CMS hoped that maintaining respect for aboriginal culture would prevent a complete social breakdown while evangelism proceeded. Catechists and biblical translations helped make Christianity more culturally relevant and comprehensible, as opposed to the disruptive alternative of imposing a new religious order on an unprepared people.

The CMS planned to build on the expected acceptance of their religious message, using Christianity to bring the Natives closer to the modern, industrializing world. Victorian England, the centrepiece of western civilization, served as both inspiration and model.

Native communicants received more than a new interpretation of the spiritual world; these "child-like" people were also to be exposed to the morals, work habits, and perspectives of western society. Drafted primarily by Henry Venn, the CMS formula provided the basis for missionary education and acted as a practical guide for missions throughout the non-European world. CMS clergymen entering the Yukon River valley after 1861 were dedicated to a program designed to elevate the heathens of the north out of their depraved state.[14]

Proselytizing efforts in the upper Yukon began in 1861, when the Reverend William West Kirkby travelled to Fort Youcon. Kirkby addressed a large group of Natives, assembled at the post to trade, on 6 July. After a lengthy sermon, Kirkby stood by anxiously while several chiefs made speeches which the missionary could not understand. Informed by the post interpreter that they had been favourable, he noted in his journal, "Joy filled my very soul and like Joseph ... I sought my chambers to weep tears of gratitude." Two days later the "great High Priest of Shamanism" renounced his aboriginal beliefs in favour of Christianity. Kirkby found much to celebrate during his stay as Natives came forward to confess their sins, including murder and infanticide, and declare their intention to abandon polygamy. The missionary left before the end of July, convinced that he had laid the foundations for an important new Church of England mission field.[15]

Kirkby returned the following year, anxious to spread CMS influence in the area before the Catholic missionaries arrived. The Natives responded favourably to the second visit:

They were all there waiting for the Boat and 9 days of hard and happy labor I had with them. Full service was held in the open air morning and evening at which all attended, and the intervening times fully occupied by small parties coming to my room to learn a few Hymns and Prayers I had composed for them, to hear my Bible Pictures explained and to be instructed in the way of truth more fully ... The principal Medicine-man, who was formerly the terror of the place, and four other young men belonging to different Tribes, not only knew the Hymns and Prayers, the 10 Commandments, the order of creation, the account of the Deluge, and the principal events in the life of our Blessed Saviour, but could also teach them to others.[16]

Kirkby recommended the establishment of a permanent mission.[17] Robert McDonald, a mixed-blood resident of Red River, answered the call for volunteers. McDonald began his clerical career among the Kutchin in 1862, working along the Porcupine and Yukon rivers and in the lower Mackenzie River region. When McDonald fell ill in 1864,

W.C. Bompas, a London curate, an avid supporter of the CMS, and an often rejected volunteer for missionary work, offered his services. Bompas joined McDonald in the north, dividing his time between the Yukon and the Mackenzie district and becoming bishop of Athabasca in 1870. McDonald directed most of his efforts towards the Yukon, although several new missionaries were recruited to help out. T.H. Canham arrived in 1881, and worked at several stations, including Rampart House and Fortymile. V.C. Sim served along the Porcupine River from 1881 until his death four years later. Robert McDonald's brother Kenneth also worked in the Rampart House area before he resigned to join the HBC. John Ellington joined the missionary corps in 1886 and was assigned to work in the border mining region.[18]

Bompas was unhappy with his Mackenzie River charge and appealed to his superiors for permission to return to the Yukon missions. The church of England and the CMS granted his request in 1891, naming him bishop of Selkirk (later Yukon) and directing him to devote his energies to that district. Working from a rather small base, Bompas attempted to expand his ministry. He remained at Fortymile, assisted by his wife and fellow missionary Benjamin Totty. Bompas dispatched Canham and his wife to Fort Selkirk and newly arrived evangelists Mr and Mrs G.G. Wallis to Rampart House.

By the start of the Klondike gold rush, the CMS could claim an extensive presence among the Indians of the Yukon. Despite, or even because of, the influx of miners, Bompas defended the need to maintain a distinct Native ministry. The church did establish missions to care for the prospectors, but resolved to preserve its mission to the Indians. By 1900 the Anglicans had an extensive Yukon network. Bompas controlled the region from his new diocesan headquarters at Caribou Crossing (Carcross), where he moved to escape the chaos and non-Native dominance of Dawson City. Canham remained at Fort Selkirk, Totty moved to Moosehide, and new recruit John Hawksley ministered to the Fortymile Natives. The church also operated a string of eight temporary missions along the Yukon River between Tagish and Dawson. Sustaining this expansion was not easy, and church officials repeatedly questioned the excessive cost of northern missions: "We spend about £1 for every 17,000 heathen in China and about £1 for every six heathen in the ecclesiastical province of Rupert's Land."[19] In the midst of this expansion, the CMS withdrew from further responsibility for northern missions, although by 1903 that role consisted mainly of routine financial contributions.[20] The Church of England in Canada, operating through the Missionary Society of the Church in Canada (MSCC), assumed control of a network of Native congregations and a growing number of non-Native churches, a reflection of its belief that Indians and whites required separate missions. In the half-century beginning with Kirkby's first efforts, then, the Anglican Church's presence had expanded significantly. Most Yukon Natives came, if only occasionally, under the extended arm of Anglican ministries.

Maintaining, let alone expanding, church operations proved burdensome. Accepting a Native charge in the Yukon did little to speed a clergyman's climb through the ecclesiastical hierarchy. In addition, distance from church power, combined with a firmly entrenched image of the north as a frozen and barren wasteland, hampered recruitment efforts. For men to come north, often bringing their wives, called for considerable devotion and some professional sacrifice. V.C. Sim's death in 1885, attributed to the rigours of his work, offered testimony to conditions in the field.[21] Under such circumstances, the missionaries either showed the total dedication characteristic of Robert McDonald or W.C. Bompas or sought alternative postings soon after coming north. Idealism spawned in the parlour rooms of England often faded in the face of northern social and physical conditions. This was especially true for many clergy of middle-class Canadian or English background. G.G. Wallis's reports from Rampart House commented more on "dust and desolation" than the prospects for Christian work.[22] Following Wallis's resignation after only three years, Bompas requested that the CMS "send only those of an inferior grade [who] in going to the far west generally rise a peg which is mostly pleasant to themselves and their neighbours." Rejecting middle-class idealists, Bompas sought lower-class men of commitment and "hardy constitution" willing to bring their wives and dedicate themselves to the solemn task at hand.[23]

Recruitment efforts, which during Bompas's tenure were targeted primarily at British clerics, occasionally failed. Kenneth McDonald stayed only a short time before leaving for more remunerative employment with the HBC. Benjamin Totty stayed with the church for many years, but was of marginal use since he either came north with a serious ear infection or was infected shortly after his arrival. Anxious to care for the aging missionary, Bompas arranged for Totty to marry a local Indian woman.[24]

Cross-cultural communication proved to be a constant barrier, especially with missionaries newly arrived from England or Canada. R.J. Bowen found himself in charge at Fortymile in 1895 even though he spoke not a word of the local Native language.[25] Similarly, when the Canhams moved to Fort Selkirk from the Porcupine River, they discovered that their hard-earned linguistic skills were useless.[26] The early missionaries, however, attempted to translate the Bible and, in order to make use of the translations, taught some of the Indians to read. Robert McDonald, to take one example, translated the scriptures into the Kutchin language as quickly as he was able, thereby assisting his efforts to have the Natives carry the gospel further afield.[27] These early translations, and especially the compilation of written vocabularies, proved beneficial in easing the work of subsequent missionaries.

Before 1896 evangelistic efforts remained confined to the Porcupine, Fortymile, and Fort Selkirk districts. The church maintained only casual contacts with the rest of the territory, not moving into the southern Yukon until after the gold rush.[28] Although it opened several mission stations, Native mobility and seasonal harvesting cycles limited the utility of central meeting places. Responding to this problem, the clergy began itinerating. Robert McDonald, working out of Fort Youcon and later Fort McPherson, travelled extensively in an attempt to meet his goal of visiting each band at least once a year. His travels, like those of his brother Kenneth and W.C. Bompas, took him as far north as the Arctic Coast, south to Fort Selkirk, and several hundred miles west of Fort Youcon. These regular visitations declined as the mission network and transportation systems expanded. Because itinerating greatly improved the effectiveness of the ministry, however, it was never totally dropped.[29] The Natives' unwillingness to settle at mission sites forced the clergymen to follow their mobile congregations in order, as McDonald phrased it, to "prevent them losing what they have been taught."[30]

The missionaries uniformly lauded the success of itinerating, although they probably confused hospitality with enthusiasm for Christian leadership. The sessions often assumed the external characteristics of a camp revival. "Each day I spent in the Indian camps," Bompas reported in 1872, "was like a Sunday as the Indians were clustered around me from early morning till late at night learning prayers, hymns and Scripture lessons."[31] Missionaries stayed only a few days in each camp, their travels seldom bringing them to a band more than once or twice a year. Yet itinerating, whatever its weaknesses, kept Christianity in front of the Indians, encouraging them to consider at least the elementary principles of the proffered faith.

To enhance the inadequate mission and itinerating efforts, the church relied on the recruitment of Native clergy, another of Henry Venn's central recommendations. Missionaries hoped that the Native clergy, besides enhancing the appeal of Christianity to the aboriginal population, would undermine the authority of local shamans. On Kirkby's first visit to the Yukon valley, he took great pride in announcing that "Doctor," a local shaman, "publicly denounced his past faith." Kirkby put little stock in Doctor's theatrical conversion, but he recognized the potential of offering alternative Native spiritual leadership.[32]

The church devoted considerable effort to recruiting Native catechists in subsequent years. Missionaries identified at least one individual in each band for special religious instruction. Once trained, the man (women were not recruited) held prayer sessions after the band left the mission station.[33] However, these leaders, one appropriately renamed Henry Venn Ketse, seldom fulfilled missionary hopes. In 1875 McDonald noted that only four of the eight catechists proved to be reliable religious leaders.[34] Although they were paid for their efforts – £5 per year and double that if required to leave their band[35] – Native catechists generally lacked commitment and basic understanding of their intended role.[36] Yet remuneration and the attending social status ensured that there was no shortage of potential candidates.

Since catechists worked beyond the supervision of their ecclesiastical superiors, their contributions and impact are difficult to gauge. Soon after the missionaries' arrival, Native spiritual leaders attempted to claim control over the new God: two of the Porcupine River Natives sought "to impose on the credulity of the others by representing themselves as commissioned by the Almighty to teach them."[37] Shamans may have assumed the role of lay leaders, thus maintaining their supremacy as interpreters of the spiritual world.[38] Apparently influenced by the missionary's power – itself an extension of the technological powers of European civilization – various Native men claimed that they had been "commissioned by the Almighty to teach them [the Indians]."[39] The shamen undoubtedly resented the intrusion by missionaries and catechists; that some would try to use the new religion for their own purposes, as "Doctor" seemed willing to do, is likely. There is, as well, some doubt as to what theological wisdom the catechists, shaman or not, were capable of imparting. Marginally literate at best and possessing only a rudimentary comprehension of a complex doctrine, lay readers lacked the knowledge to pass on a comprehensive understanding of Christianity. As catechists, shamen mingled their animist spirituality with the rough outlines of Christianity, using the latter to preserve or enhance their authority.

The church's use of poorly trained catechists to spread its message raises questions about the Natives' adoption of Christianity. Anthropologist Anne Welsh argued that the Old Crow Kutchin accepted the faith with alacrity, "seeing in the various rituals and paraphernalia the probable source of the white man's power."[40] Given haphazard contact, language barriers which slowed if not prevented meaningful communication of basic theological concepts, inconsistent evangelical work by missionaries of varying talents, and the Natives' commitment to their own interpretation of the spiritual world, widespread acceptance of Christianity seems unlikely. When Robert McDonald was at Fort Youcon in 1864, he held several prayer sessions each day to accommodate the constant movement of Natives in and out of the post. He limited his teachings to "the decalogues, the Apostles Creed, and the general confession," as well as a few hymns. He claimed few results: "They certainly know little as yet of the divine power of the Gospel. I am not sure of any one being truly converted to God among the whole of them."[41] On a different journey he limited his instruction to a short hymn, the memorization of a prayer, an abbreviated account of creation and the fall of man, and the story of Jesus.[42]

It is very clear that there was no rapid or unthinking acceptance of the new faith, as has often been asserted. Yet there is evidence for integration. Native and non-Native spirituality were not as different as is commonly believed. There was, as Abel demonstrates in her study of the Dene, considerable overlap between the world views of the Athapaskans and the "low church," evangelical Anglicans; moreover, Native people looked to the church for spiritual elements which were appealing, acceptable, or functional.[43] The Natives did appear to adopt many of the external forms of the faith. Marriages, burials (usually a mingling of both traditions), baptisms, church services, prayers, and hymns offered a ceremonial dimension very different from Athapaskan traditions. Such rituals could be adopted without contradicting aboriginal beliefs.

Whatever the limits of their achievements, most missionaries confidently asserted the success of their efforts. Robert McDonald was initially restrained, noting in 1864 that he refused to baptize Natives since they lacked sufficient knowledge of the ceremony.[44] Catholic pressure on Anglican missions forced many clergymen to lower the standard of knowledge and understanding required for baptism. For the clergy, the rush for souls became of pre-eminent importance. Bompas claimed in 1874 that the Indians now had advanced Christian knowledge and that he had baptized thirty-five adults and eighty children.[45] As time passed, more Natives sang hymns, said prayers, and followed church ceremonies. Such outward manifestations, however, do not prove inner conversion and there is little evidence to suggest that the Natives, *en masse*, experienced spiritual change. The church made much of the exceptions, such as John Ttsiettla of Fort McPherson, who was ordained deacon in 1893.[46] Yet it is likely that before 1900 most Yukon Indians saw Christianity as a focus for celebration and ceremony, not as a repository of the one "true" meaning of the spiritual world.

After the gold rush the Anglican Church attempted to place its scattered mission program on an expanded and firmer footing, adding several permanent missions and sending itinerants into isolated corners of the territory. Bompas's removal of the diocesan headquarters to Carcross and the opening of a church at Whitehorse under R.J. Bowen gave the Anglicans a new presence in the southern Yukon. Following the death of Bompas in 1906, Isaac O. Stringer, a young minister known for his work among the Inuit at Herschel Island, became bishop. Stringer reorganized the diocese, moving its headquarters to Dawson City, expanded the use of Native clergy and catechists, and used theological students to conduct summer missions in poorly served areas. He remained in charge until 1932, when A.H. Sovereign temporarily replaced him. Reorganization followed, with the Yukon placed under the Bishop Geddes of Mackenzie River. In 1941 the Yukon became part of the ecclesiastical province of British Columbia.[47]

Throughout the first half of the century, the Anglican church continued its efforts to expand religious services for the Indians. Indeed, although the church provided the required services for the non-Native population, it maintained a strong and distinct commitment to its Native communicants. The missionaries also intervened in secular matters involving the Indians, appealing to government agents or the police as deemed necessary.[48] Few government officials welcomed the missionaries' activities outside the religious sphere. Yukon Commissioner Frank Congdon wrote, "My complaint with regard to the missionaries is that instead of teaching the Indians self-reliance and independence, they aid most strongly in making them medicants [sic]. I am daily in receipt of letters from Indians, written by a missionary, asking for all sorts of favours."[49] To be sure, representations to the government were frequently tinged by self-interest, as the church sought greater financial support for its own work.[50]

The Yukon diocese attempted to maintain its mission network, although limited by budget and manpower shortages.[51] Yukon bishops encountered continued difficulties recruiting suitable missionaries for northern service. Stringer, unlike Bompas, emphasized Canadian recruiting, and did far more than his predecessor to promote the work of his diocese. He enjoyed limited success; many of those who came to the Yukon stayed only a few years before leaving for more comfortable charges in the south.[52] In recognition of the indifferent results from itinerating, church leaders sought men who, preferably with their wives, would accept year-round placement in

Native camps. In 1911 regular missions operated at eight places: Moosehide (Totty), Fortymile (A.C. Field), Selkirk (Canham and Hawksley), Whitehorse (Blackwell), Teslin and Champagne[53] (C.C. Brett), Carcross (Canham), and Rampart House (Njootli). Lay readers carried the Gospel even further afield. Eleven years later,[54] the network differed little, with six regular missions and five native catechists serving northern and eastern districts.[55] Arrangements varied yearly, depending on the availability of missionaries and the funding provided by the MSCC.

To supplement permanent staff, Isaac Stringer started recruiting students in the 1920s, principally from the Anglican Theological College in Vancouver.[56] The students, who were supported in large part by day-school teacher stipends paid by the DIA, spent several months in outlying villages such as Ross River, Teslin, Carmacks, and Champagne. Their youthful enthusiasm often failed to overcome naive idealism and lack of experience in dealing with Native people.[57] Moreover, they naturally had considerable difficulty with the many languages and dialects in the territory. Max Humphrey, working at Carmacks and Little Salmon in the summer of 1932, observed, "I find that only one or two of those who know English better than their fellows really understand what is said, even if one speaks in the simplest words possible."[58] Shortly after a young student arrived at Teslin in 1923, he sought instruction in basic Tlingit greetings. He was told that "mah-si-ah-ti" meant "good morning," a salutation he tried out the next day on the Teslin chief. The man appeared terribly offended, sending the student off to find out what he had done wrong. He came across a Native woman chastising her son with the same phrase, which apparently meant "What the dickens is the matter with you anyway."[59] The students' reports, typically laden with platitudes, revealed how little they knew of their Native communicants.[60] More important, the students generally acknowledged the limitations of their ministries, and found the experience of more benefit to themselves than the Natives. From the larger perspective of the church, the ventures asserted Anglican territorial claims, an increasingly important objective given the Catholic Church's growing challenge in the Teslin, Lower Post, and Mayo districts.[61]

In the post-gold rush era, Native catechists played a more significant role in church plans to spread the Gospel. Expanding on the practices of the previous century, the Anglican Church recruited and supported Indian field-workers. The use of catechists seemed especially expedient in light of the Natives' mobility and the church's inability to fund more permanent missions. While some hoped that this system would assist evangelical efforts, practical considerations weighed more heavily in the decision to rely on Native lay readers. The church expected catechists to supplement their low stipends through hunting and trapping, something they did not require of their non-Native clergy. The fear that Native leaders might come to depend on salaries led Bishop Bompas to write to John Martin of Mayo that "you will not be expected to give all your time to work at the Church but will be free part of the time to hunt and trap."[62] Catechists typically received only token pay, more to indicate their status to the community than as a means of support.[63] The same did not hold for ordained clergy, although even here there were important differences in salaries. The Reverend Julius Kendi, a Native, received $550 in 1922 for his work near Mayo; a non-Native missionary, the Reverend Moody, at Old Crow was paid $700 a year for much the same work. Anglican clergy used the Native lay and ordained leaders primarily to fill in the blanks on the Yukon mission map, holding little faith in their ability to spread the gospel effectively.[64]

Catechists varied even more widely in effectiveness than did missionaries and students. Some, such as Amos Njootli, remained active for many years but did not have a dramatic impact on their congregations. Njootli's personal problems, the nature of which is only hinted at in the records, undermined his mission.[65] Others similarly discovered that domestic turmoil affected their work as spiritual leaders. The Reverend A.C. McCullum noted from Old Crow in 1930 that quarrels between catechist "Big Joe" Kikavichick and his wife created dissension within the band.[66] Several Native catechists, on the other hand, enjoyed wide respect among the non-Native clergy for their devotion if not for their theological expertise. The efforts of Jospeh Kunizza, John Tizya, Richard Martin, and especially the Reverend Julius Kendi and his wife were greatly appreciated by Anglican clergy.[67]

Anglican clergymen repeatedly commented on the dedication and zeal of the Native catechists. James Pelisse, paid $50 a year for his services in the Ross River area, routinely gathered dozens of local Natives at his weekly meetings. The attraction may have been more than spiritual. According to one witness, "he is a good hunter and generally manages to get some fresh meat-moose or caribou. On Sundays he always counts on making a little feast and the Indians come from miles around in time to eat, and then immediately afterwards James holds his service and of course no one would think of leaving."[68] But even Pelisse's enthusiasm had limits. When Cecil Swanson visited Ross River in 1914, he discovered that Pelisse had not been paid for four years. Not surprisingly, Swanson noted that "his loyalty to the mission cause has been a little strained."[69]

More than any other, John Martin exemplified the problems and promise of utilizing Native catechists. Raised in Fort McPherson and given early Christian training, Martin acceded to Bishop Stringer's request that he take up residence among the Natives of Ross River. Discouraged by his slow progress within the church through the 1930s and the limited attention given his charge by church superiors, Martin petitioned for ordination as a minister in 1932.[70] Bishop Geddes visited his station two years later but, to Martin's dismay, refused him ordination. Martin appealed to Isaac Stringer, then archbishop of Rupert's Land, for help: "I not trouble where I go and stay but I want ordain Priest that all I want I told him (Geddes) and he told me I got to go school for that." His plea, "I want to be Preist Please archbiship tell what am wrong I may try learn more," cut to the heart of the catechists' problems within the church.[71] Stringer cautioned Bishop Sovereign to go slowly: "I would not advise ordaining John to Priest's Orders at present. The only other Indians that have been priested in Yukon and Mackenzie River were John Ttsiettla, Edward Situchinli and Julius Kendi. These three were in Deacon's Orders for many years – perhaps fifteen or twenty. John is a very likely man, perhaps with more ability (natural) than any of the others. Perhaps before he is ordained Priest it might be well to have him spend a Winter with some clergyman and have him taught."[72] Two years later Stringer indicated to Sovereign's successor, Bishop Geddes, that Martin, "one of the most intelligent and most responsible amongst all our Indians," might be ready for ordination.[73]

Inadequately trained, usually working without supervision in isolated corners of the territory, often removed from families and friends, the catechists had few opportunities to study religion or to advance within the church. Martin clearly sought a better salary and social status. But inadequate education prevented him and others from achieving this goal. Martin moved to Mayo after his time in Ross River. Blocked from advancement within the clergy, he seemed preoccupied with the possible material benefits of his position. Martin demanded new furniture for his house, befitting his position as a community leader, and ran up a considerable debt at the local Taylor and Drury store. His superiors repeatedly pointed out that material comforts and "white man's grub" did not go with the job, and they directed him to spend more time trapping.[74] Requesting that Mr Hughes, who ministered to the non-Native residents of Mayo, watch over the catechist, Bishop Sovereign wrote, "You must remember that John Martin is only a native and while in many respects he may be a highly intelligent native yet in many situations he will have the outlook and behaviour of a child."[75] Martin's theological competence was not highly regarded. His task was to ensure that prayers, services, and hymns – the forms but not necessarily the substance of Christianity – remained familiar to the Natives.[76]

Despite his shortcomings as an Anglican cleric, Martin was clearly committed to the spiritual welfare of the Native people. When he died on 8 March 1937, the numerous eulogies praised the deacon for his zeal and good spirit. The *Mayo Miner* said of Martin, "He was a very active man, a very humble man, a brave disciple and a great leader among his people." He was buried in a unique double ceremony, beginning in St Mark's Church at the Indian village and then moving to the non-Native church, St Mary's, in Mayo.[77]

In sum, the Anglican clergy were a mixed lot, including missionaries of such diverse talents as Bishop Bompas and Benjamin Totty, summer students of unquestioned enthusiasm and matching naivety, and Native catechists with the ability of Julius Kendi and the problems of John Martin. Alongside this obvious diversity was a lack of continuity in religious leadership. Transiency, a malady endemic throughout Yukon society,[78] affected the Protestant missionary corps. A constantly shifting church hierarchy ensured rapid movement through the ranks and constant mobility in the field. Benjamin Totty, whose infirmity kept him tied to Moosehide, was an exception among non-Native missionaries. More typical was the case of Cecil Swanson, who served Little Salmon only two years when he was removed to a non-Native pastorate in Whitehorse. Reflecting later on his experience, Swanson wrote, "I felt that I should have been left there [Little Salmon] for at least seven years. It takes time to develop a trusting relationship with the Indians, and a lifetime to learn and use the language. The strength of the Roman Catholic missions is the continuity of pastorate by the fathers of the OMI, the missionary arm of the church. Short-term missionaries are useless."[79] The brief and often ineffectual forays of the summer students into the back country represented only an extension of a problem besetting the entire church effort. Catechists stayed longer in one place, particularly if appointed to serve among their own people, but their insufficient preparation and generally unsophisticated comprehension of Christianity negated the religious impact of their longevity.

Despite impressive baptismal lists and laudatory accounts of their own accomplishments, the missionaries acknowledged their work to be incomplete.[80] Until the 1950s clergymen throughout the Yukon readily admitted the persistence of Native spiritual beliefs and "superstitions."[81] The missionaries could, and did, point to the Natives' adherence to Christian rituals and a general acceptance of western moral standards. Benjamin Totty found much comfort in a

Native woman's comment after attending one of his services: "We never knew how bad we were before; until we heard and read such words as have [read] to us at the classes, we thought our characters fairly good; but now we know the truth, we learn how short we come of what is required of us."[82] Most Natives were married by a clergyman, but only if one was readily available. Even then, missionaries noted with discouragement that such old practices as polygamy, trading of wives, and discarding of partners continued. As Carmacks summer missionary Max Humphrey observed in 1932, "The Indians are quick to notice and respond to what is usually known as 'practical Christianity' but what is hard to overcome is the apparent apathy of the average Indian in church."[83]

The persistence of Native traditions should not be surprising. Despite substantial zeal, the Anglican missionary effort was uneven. Many Natives, particularly in the southern districts, saw missionaries infrequently, and these sporadic contacts bore little fruit. Only in the Porcupine River area, and to a lesser extent at Moosehide and Mayo, could the church claim considerable success. Most of the Native catechists, including Ttsiettla, Richard and John Martin, Amos Njootli, Joe Kikavichick, Julius Kendi, and John Tizya came from the Fort McPherson-Porcupine River district, an area long served by the redoubtable Robert McDonald.[84] Even here, however, shamanism and a variety of non-Christian practices reappeared regularly.[85] In the central Yukon, similarly, it was said that "The efficacy of the medicine man is still believed in, although ... this cult is carried on somewhat furtively."[86] The clergy acknowledged their inability to provide sufficient pastoral care for the Natives, and, although never abandoning their hopes for full conversion, aimed instead at the intermediate goal of outward conformity to church practices. Marriages, baptisms, burial rites, and acceptable moral and social behaviour represented the clergy's real objectives, but the church fell far short on even these counts as Native people continued to follow many aboriginal traditions. The conversion process proved much slower than the Anglican missionaries expected.[87]

Realism forced upon the missionaries an uncharacteristic tolerance in dealing with deviations from Christian practice. A case in point was the Reverend Ashbee's attitude to the Native practice of burying personal effects with the deceased; Ashbee noted that "it was a harmless belief on their part and showed they had, at any rate, a belief in life beyond the grave."[88] Anglican flexibility was perhaps best demonstrated in 1914 when a Champagne Native, Johnny Ned, attracted a large cult following. Claiming to have had a vision and to be miraculously blessed with the ability to speak English (he attended day school for several years), Ned preached a random mixture of Native and Christian beliefs. He said that he had been asleep for a long while. When he awakened, "he had gone through all sorts of torments, had been cast into the fire, and had gone to Heaven, and was [there] for a time. An angel came to him and told him many things, amongst others that he was to teach the people." The charismatic evangelist garnered much support in the southern Yukon through a series of revival-style meetings. One service in Champagne, for example, attracted over 200 while a concurrent Anglican meeting drew but a dozen. At another, held in Whitehorse, he drew a crowd from the surrounding area but was unable to "give them the messages he had promised." Ned's crusade withered abruptly, allegedly (according to Anglican missionaries) because of his immoral behaviour, which contributed to an early death.[89] The Anglican Church looked with disapproval on the threatening sect, but decided not to intervene. As Bishop Stringer commented, "For the most part his teaching is all right. However, he has some fantastic ideas and has mixed up some native superstitions with Christianity. I think it is better to recognize ever[y]thing that is good in his teaching rather than attempt to antagonize him."[90] The Yukon cult experience mirrored revitalization movements among other North American Native peoples and revealed the Anglican clergy's cautious recognition of the persistence of Native spirituality.[91]

An examination of the state of Anglican mission work in the 1930s indicates the extent of conversion and integration. In most communities, a mere handful of Native people had been confirmed as full members of the Anglican Church; and only a few missions could claim even half of the residents as communicants, despite a fairly generous interpretation of Native commitment to the teachings of the church. In Old Crow, an area subjected to almost uninterrupted missionary work for some seventy years and a mission field constantly held up as a model for the work of the church, only 64 of 128 Native members had been confirmed. In Teslin, where the Anglicans faced considerable competition from the Roman Catholics in the 1930s, only 16 of 120 members claimed full church membership. By the Anglican Church's own accounting, therefore, mission work in the Yukon was far from complete.

The Anglican Church faced more barriers than Native resistance. From the 1930s on, the church faced a sustained challenge to its spiritual domination of the Yukon Territory from the Roman Catholic Church. The battle for the Native allegiance began in the 1860s, but, initially, the Catholic Church made few inroads into the Anglican stronghold.[92] Undeterred, the Catholic Church continued its efforts

Table 19
Native People and the Anglican Church, Yukon Territory, 1930s

	Carcross 1936	Kluane & Champagne 1932	Ross River 1932	Ross River 1935	St Mark's Mayo 1932	St Mary's Mayo 1932
Total Members						
White	76	80	13	13		168
Native	60	220	175	175	43	
Non-Christian	0	0	102	57	0	0
Confirmed						
White	12	10				12
Native	20	0	4	4	24	
Communicants						
White	8					12
Native	15		4	4	24	
Marriages						
White	0					3
Native	0		3			
Baptisms						
White	0					2
Native	1		38	3		
Services						
White	52	2				58
Native	52	10	110	50	12	

Year	Moosehide 1932	Old Crow 1936	Fort Selkirk 1932	Teslin 1932	Teslin 1935	Whitehorse 1932	Whitehorse 1936
Total Members							
White	2	15	16	11	7	300	420
Native	71	128	87	129	120	39	45
Confirmed							
White	2	2	3	1	2	28	15
Native	45	64	14	17	16	8	0
Communicants							
White	2	1	2	1	1	17	25
Native	45	62	8	16	12	2	0
Marriages							
White					1	4	4
Native		2			1	1	2
Baptisms							
White				1		5	3
Native	11	5	2	24	7		4
Services							
White				32		114	99
Native	105	99	44	32	22	8	1

Source YTA, Anglican Church, AC79/51, vol. 21, Statistical Reports File.

to break into the area, focusing at first on the Stewart River region as many of the Natives sporadically contacted Catholic missionaries in the Mackenzie River valley.[93] In the 1930s OMI priests moved to Teslin Lake and Burwash, presenting at the former site a direct challenge to an existing Anglican mission.[94] The Natives viewed the expanding doctrinal debate with amusement.[95] The Stikine Indian agent, Harper Reed, noted after visiting Teslin: "They [the Natives] were found divided, some stated that the Mission that paid the highest 'wages' for any work done, would get their attendance. In fact the matter was looked on as a 'joke' in which the Indians would come off best."[96] The battle for souls was waged in large measure as a contest over education as each church sought the right to teach the Natives and thus gain control over the children. The fact that much of the effort would be financed by the federal government was an obvious side benefit.

The competition for souls was not handled with much Christian generosity. At Teslin, Father Drean allegedly kept children away from the Anglican school by taking the boys fishing or having them tend his nets. In time the confrontation grew more serious. Anglican missionary Robert Ward said in 1941 that the Catholics claimed to have talked to Jesus, informing the Indians they should "belong to a church which has so lately been granted such an interview." He further reported that "the RCs have worked up some sort of male SS corps which goes about to the C of E households and attempts to browbeat them."[97] Responding in kind two years later, Anglican Stanley Webb reported that he drew "up a list of some prominint [sic] R.C. errors and am starting an anti-R.C. campaign."[98] Soon education again became the main battleground.[99]

The Anglicans feared that the "Roman Catholics might 'take a knight's move' and try to establish in the central Yukon," and sought to meet the challenge.[100] As the Catholic Church expanded its efforts in the Mayo-Ross River districts, the resulting competition echoed the situation in Teslin a decade earlier. "The New Priest," wrote Norman Wareham of Mayo in 1950, "went all out for the Indians and is still taking advagtage [sic] of every possible opportunity to bribe them into the communion of the Roman Church. The Indians at the village are one hundred per cent behind the Church of England."[101]

The Catholics and later the Baptists slowly penetrated the Anglican mission field. By 1950 about 20 per cent of the Yukon Indian population claimed a religious affiliation other than Anglican. The Roman Catholic effort was, with the exception of Burwash, targeted on the Teslin, Ross River, and Mayo areas. The Baptists enjoyed limited success outside Whitehorse. Throughout most of the territory, the Angli-

Table 20
Religious Affiliation, Yukon Native Population, 1950

Community	Anglican	Roman Catholic	Baptist	Indian
Old Crow	108	–	–	–
Dawson	116	–	–	–
Mayo	80	11	–	–
Stewart R.	15	4	–	–
Selkirk	177	8	–	–
Snag	16	10	–	–
Carmacks	133	3	–	–
Ross River	42	12	–	–
Pelly Lakes	65	13	–	1
Aishihik	39	1	2	–
Burwash Land.	5	22	–	4
La Berge	49	–	–	–
Frances Lake	12	40	–	–
Champagne	93	6	–	–
Whitehorse	116	5	13	2
Carcross	50	6	3	–
Teslin	75	58	–	–
Watson Lake	–	11	–	–
Totals	1191	210	18	7

Source NA, RG10, vol. 8762, file 906/25–1–001, An Educational Survey with Reference to the Relocation of the Carcross Indian Residential School, by C.A. Clark, 8 September 1950.

can Church was the largest denomination, though it no longer enjoyed its earlier pre-eminence.

Doctrinal disputes among denominations centred primarily on education, and emphasized "body counts" more than instruction. The confrontation between the Anglicans and Catholics in particular represented the culmination of a century-long battle over spheres of influence in the mission field. The struggle for converts, unrelenting efforts to discredit the opposing faith, and controversies over schools seriously undermined the credibility of the educational and religious efforts of both denominations. Anglican missionary Robert Ward and Indian Agent Harper Reed both noted that the Teslin debates led to serious community and family dissension, a logical consequence of the vitriolic recriminations.[102] By the late 1940s the Yukon Natives had become caught in the middle of a confrontation of faiths.

The missionaries' goal of converting Yukon Natives to Christianity foundered partly on the difficulties of northern evangelism. Inadequate staff and funding, nomadic Natives, and isolation hampered Anglican efforts to restructure Indian religious beliefs. The Indians became nominal Christians, accepting the outward manifestations of the new faith, but did not entirely abandon their established spiritual beliefs. The two were not incompatible, for the Natives seemingly integrated their ecological interpretation of the spiritual world with the human-based ideas of Christianity. Given the unstructured form of pre-contact beliefs, the missionaries' message provided a framework and ritualistic form for dealing with religious matters.

There were other reasons why Natives maintained much of their spiritual outlook, even after almost a century of proselytizing. Linguistic and cultural barriers hindered the efforts of a small and irregular missionary corps to transmit its message. More important, Native spirituality was largely impervious to the Christian attack. Indian beliefs lacked rigidity and depended on regional and personal interpretation. As well, the manner in which the Natives viewed their human, animal, and geographic landscape was related closely to their spirituality. Since the Christian missions offered no competing, inclusive world view, focusing instead on the limited goal of restructuring the Indians' relationship with the deity, the clergy missed the core of Native spirituality. The Indian world view survived because the Natives' world remained substantially intact; the two were inseparable, and the Anglican missionaries did little to draw them apart. The Indians became ritualistic Christians, accepting the forms of the faith, especially in the presence of a missionary or catechist. Otherwise, they remained Natives, possessors of a different interpretation of the spiritual world.[103]

Anglican evangelism, therefore, encountered both successes and failures in attempts to bring the Natives into Euro-Canadian society. A vague acceptance of Christian morality brought the Natives nearer to the pattern set down by the missionaries. But the survival of Native spirituality, reinforced by the Anglicans' ready admission that their aboriginal communicants remained unprepared for a closer accommodation with the larger Canadian community, ensured that preliminary Christianization did not lead to integration. As late as 1950 Native missions and non-Native churches remained distinct, a mute testimony to the cultural and social gap between the two separate Anglican communities in the Yukon Territory.

CHAPTER SEVEN

Through the Children: Education and Yukon Natives

From its first days in the Yukon River basin, the Anglican Church recognized the potential of education as a tool of assimilation. Together with attempts at Christianization, schooling promised to bring Native people closer to the standards of British/Canadian society. Indeed the two were intricately intertwined, since the curriculum was laced with Christian values. The churches, with financial support from the federal government, directed their effort at the children, who were deemed most vulnerable to cultural transformation. In this realm, as with missionary work, the Anglican church enjoyed a virtual monopoly, proceeding unchallenged until Roman Catholic and Baptist rivals appeared in the 1930s and 1940s.

By bringing knowledge of the world to an intensely localized, allegedly backward, people and highlighting the deficiencies of Native society, educators hoped that children would quickly turn from their "heathen" past. Again, however, the Yukon example illustrates that plans enunciated by federal administrators and church leaders did not prove workable. Despite established assimilationist goals, Native schools in the Yukon did not serve as the catalyst for cultural integration. They functioned rather as a divisive force within Yukon society and in practice deviated substantially from the directives of the federal government and the church.

Historians have recently abandoned uncritical interpretations of the development of Canadian education, questioning the élitist assumptions which governed the establishment of schools and examining the place of education in the evolving capitalist system.[1] Of interest here is the body of literature which links economic and educational considerations under the rubric of cultural imperialism. Rejecting the Whig notion of the educator as liberator, proponents of the new approach argue that schooling served the interests of the internal or external colonizing power. The primary function of education, in this line of analysis, was to prepare the uneducated for participation in the capitalist economy. Martin Carnoy, a leading scholar in this field, argues that "western formal education came to most countries as part of imperial domination. It was consistent with the goals of imperialism and the economic and political control of the people in one country by the dominant class in another." In more specific terms, "the transformation of unskilled man into valuable input for the capitalist production process became an important function for schooling in capitalist society."[2] Educators expressed the values of their own culture and readily depreciated the interests of the people commonly characterized as backward. Anglican mission schools, laden with the aspirations of middle-class England and Canada, clearly fit the cultural imperialist mold.

More useful than this basic formulation, particularly in understanding the impact of schooling on Native peoples, is the "colonial school" model advanced by P. Altbach and G. Kelly. Assessing American missionary schools, they argue that education attempted to remake Natives in the image of the white man while simultaneously usurping or degrading aboriginal society. The colonial school, functioning in church-based Native programs in Canada and still operating in many Third World countries, aimed to draw the Natives to the interests and values of the dominant nation state. Such schools typically limited their offerings to language instruction and moral education, thus providing the perceived prerequisites for social integration. Flaws inherent in the system, however, limited their success and broadened the negative impact of the programs. Restricted by the schools' narrow goals, educators failed to teach the skills necessary for significant economic integration, doing little more than to destroy the children's faith in their own culture.[3] As a consequence, Natives thus educated found themselves unable to compete in a society for which they had in theory been specifically groomed. They remained, instead, entrenched in a subcultural, dependent role, lacking the skills for entry into dominant society while taught to disdain their native culture.[4]

Canadian historians of Native education have divided its history into six phases: pre-contact aboriginal educational systems, early missionary efforts to carry Christianity and western civilization to the Natives; nineteenth-century attempts to use education as the chief means of encouraging the rapid assimilation of Canadian Natives, the retreat in the early twentieth century from the optimism of initial educational efforts; integration of Native students into provincial and territorial education systems after the Second World War; and, starting in the 1960s, Native insistence on educational self-determination. This periodization correctly emphasizes the evolution of Native education policy over time, as educators came to grips with the evidence of their limited ability to transform Native people through schooling. In the case of the Yukon, all six periods are in evidence, the last two occurring after the Second World War, although they are far more compressed in time than was the case elsewhere in Canada.[5]

The new approaches assist with the understanding of the evolution of Native education in the Canadian north. The colonial model over-simplifies the historical complexities of providing education to aboriginal people, but reminds us of the clear and consistent intent that underlay Native schooling. The chronological division corrects this oversight by emphasizing the changing educational tactics and the gradual realization of the flaws in Native educational programs.

The Yukon provides a complex example of the processes of aboriginal education. It is difficult, for example, to identify the overriding hand of the colonizer in the establishment of curriculum.[6] Although federally funded, Native education remained in church hands until after 1950. Limited resources, however, restricted church efforts to an irregular day-school program and several small boarding schools. As with their religious mission, the clergy found themselves continually short of funds and manpower, preventing them from proceeding with education as they would have wished. The church-based education system did not assimilate the Natives of the Yukon; still, it both reflected and assisted the ongoing marginalization of Yukon Indian people.

Bible and slate were virtually indistinguishable from the start. CMS workers offered literacy training to their first congregations, hoping to ensure the continued transmission of their religious teachings, and missionaries, as noted earlier, translated Bibles and attempted to teach a few people in each band to read.[7] Adult education marked the beginnings of a more sustained effort. Until the 1880s, however, the small number of clergy limited educational offerings to basic literacy programs, and these did little more than train a few Natives to understand phonetic translations of biblical passages. In the short term, the clergy's efforts focused on the religious aspects of their mission; education came later.

Inadequate funding slowed any attempt at educational reform. Although Bishop Bompas argued repeatedly that "schooling is the most hopeful branch of mission work,"[8] and ran a small school with the help of his wife and an assistant, the CMS refused to provide the required monies. Bompas's problems emanated from his insistence that education be targeted at mixed-blood children, an acknowledged departure from CMS practice.[9] Answering the repeated rejections by the London Committee of the CMS and the federal DIA, Bompas declared "such half-breed children are liable if untrained and left wild [to become] the bitterest enemies and most formidable obstacles to our mission, whereas if trained in the mission schools they may become our foremost and most useful friends."[10] Bompas proceeded without financial aid and in 1894 had four mixed-blood and two Native girls living in his mission house. The emphasis on Native girls continued for some time, a reflection of the missionaries' belief that the women set the moral and social tone for the community. The practice generated critical observations from a Native man at Little Salmon: "Missionary learn girl – he no learn boy."[11] As the Diocese of Selkirk (Yukon after 1907) expanded through the decade, missionaries attempted to follow Bompas's lead, offering rudimentary education for Native and mixed-blood children.

Limited church funding offered little security, and church leaders sought more reliable backing. In the 1890s the federal government, although reluctant to accept any responsibility in the area, finally surrendered to Bompas's incessant requests.[12] The bishop of the Yukon handled most administrative duties under the new system, although the DIA retained formal responsibility for approving the opening of schools and the appointment of teachers. The church had considerable discretionary power; the only expression of national interest was occasional visits by school inspectors or Indian agents.

Although Bishop Bompas confidently stated that schooling enabled the Natives "to share in the blessings of civilization," federal officials did not share his enthusiasm. Ottawa had only reluctantly provided funding, and only after considerable debate within the civil service about the logic of extending church-administered schools into the far northwest.[13] The Anglican Church, however, demanded that Native education in the Yukon remain in church hands, a position which culminated in a 1908 petition to the DIA for funding for a Native boarding school.[14] Civil servants once more hesitated to entrench Anglican domination, but the church's political power prevailed.[15] In what became a typical pattern, Frank Oliver, minister of the interior, granted the capital and operating budgets while asserting, "I will not undertake in a general way to educate the Indians of the Yukon. In my judgement they can, if left as Indians, earn a better living." The concessions were offered "as a matter of charity toward the Indians as poor citizens." Oliver wished to prevent a repetition of the maladministration and poor results which plagued Native schooling in southern districts.[16] As one of Oliver's employees suggested, boarding schools should "be considered merely as orphanages or refuges for neglected children."[17] The government clearly wished to avoid the financial and moral commitments inherent in a territory-wide education system, but the pressure exerted by the Anglican Church ensured a least a small network of schools for Native children.

The day-school program, expanded from one to five schools in 1910, and the residential school, which opened in new quarters in 1911, rested on false, or at best contradictory, premises. The Anglicans wanted mission schools, but lacked the money. The federal government had the money, but was not convinced that schools were essential and frequently wavered in its support for Native education in the Yukon. To the DIA, the Natives' continued prosperity and mobility obviated the need to alter social and economic patterns through a sustained educational effort, just as providing industrial skills was unsuited to likely future prospects in the territory. Extensive education raised false expectations, provided unmarketable skills, and cost the government a considerable amount of money. The willingness to leave the Natives uneducated, in the colonial sense of that term, lasted until the late 1940s, when a major shift in federal programming led to more universal schooling. Writing in 1933, Indian Agent and former missionary John Hawksley commented,

The Indians, owing to changed circumstances, cannot afford to stay around those villages or leave their families while the men go away to hunt and trap. They are compelled to separate into small parties and live in the woods for the purpose of hunting and trapping in order to make a living. Opportunities for obtaining work from white people are very much reduced. To insist upon the Indian families staying in the villages (which has been suggested) would mean that some of them would have to receive help in the way of provisions. It appears to be a much wiser policy to keep them independent, earning their own living, and they are less liable to get into bad habits.[18]

The federal government, with only a marginal interest in Native education, happily left school administration to the Anglican clergy. Themselves enthusiastic, the missionaries lacked the funding and staff necessary to offer the scale and quality of education desired. The resulting Native school program varied widely over time and by region and accomplished few of the church's stated goals.

Day schools presented the greatest dilemma, because the schools drained the diocese's limited resources without showing an appreciable return. Continuing Native mobility damaged efforts to sustain educational contact. Instead, the day school operated only when Natives were in camp. Government agents challenged the appropriateness of continued expenditures. "Whether such intermittent teaching is of any real value," John Hawksley wrote in 1926, "is open to question, very little progress is possible under such conditions, it leads one to doubt whether the expenditure is justified."[19] The clergy responded that education, however flawed, was better than total neglect. Bishop Geddes claimed that "as citizens of a Christian country we have a duty or a responsibility to the native people of Canada" that could be discharged only through education.[20] Reacting to a reduction in federal funding in 1933, Bishop Sovereign declared, "In an intensive training, these teachers [summer students] have given to the Indian a knowledge of the written and spoken English, a training in simple Arithmetic, a knowledge of the rules of health and sanitation, a love of their country and their Empire and a true loyalty to their Empire's King. Moreover, they are taught the Ten Commandments and knowledge of God, so that they might grow up as law-abiding citizens. Surely such a training is beyond estimation."[21]

Isaac Stringer approached the matter more practically. Regular school attendance, he argued, contradicted the church's and state's determination to keep the Indians away from trading posts and urban centres. The church hoped only that seasonal schools would impart the seeds of learning which the children themselves would nurture. Limiting his claims, Stringer noted that thanks "to the start they received in schools quite a number of Indians in different parts of the Territory are able to write letters and read a letter, and also work out arithmetical problems such as are necessary for trading."[22] Yet, despite his limited enthusiasm for the schools, Stringer believed that they had to be opened whenever attendance warranted, although as much for social as educational reasons. As he noted to a recent recruit, "It is important that the regular day school should be held whenever possible: not only does it benefit the Indians educationally, but also it is a means of getting an influence over them, and of doing them good."[23] Schools were an extension of the religious mission: combining education and proselytizing allowed the church to distribute the financial burden between schoolhouse and mission. They were also the only agency capable of providing schooling on the government's parsimonious budget.

The early day schools operated in conjunction with permanent missions. The first such facility, opened at Buxton Mission (Fortymile), clearly held some attraction. Bompas claimed an attendance of thirty to forty people whenever the Natives visited the settlement; to his dismay, however, many of those in the classroom were adults.[24] The clergy opened schools at Moosehide when the gold rush drew Natives to that point, and at Carcross after Bompas made the village the site of his diocesan headquarters.[25] Thomas Canham similarly maintained a school, irregularly, while at Fort Selkirk. Extended government financing in 1910 allowed the church to place new schools at Champagne, Teslin, and Whitehorse. Over the next forty years the network expanded and contracted, depending on the availability of funds and suitable teachers. The system reached a total of nine schools in 1916–17 and shrunk to as few as two in 1941–42. Only those attached to mission stations attempted year-round programming, although even there Native mobility often forced seasonal closures. Moosehide and Selkirk generally maintained a class, but the schools at Champagne, Teslin, Little Salmon, Old Crow, Ross River, and other locations seldom operated for more than a few months each summer.

Restricted to an erratic network of schools, the Anglican Church consistently contacted less than half of the eligible student population. Initially the schools had had an important social function, and the classes filled with adults, leaving little room for children. Although anxious to attract younger pupils, the missionaries hesitated to discourage any interest in their teaching. During the 1909 summer session, the average age of Teslin students was twenty years and only six of sixteen were of regular school age (six to sixteen years).[26] The children who registered, furthermore, attended sporadically, hampering educational efforts. Not until the implementation of mothers' allowance and enforced school enrollment in the late 1940s did students attend regularly. One disgruntled summer teacher reported that "others use the school more or less as a place in which to pass away a few hours."[27] Registration data illustrates that teachers encountered difficulties forming classes and ensuring that the children came to school.[28]

Native mobility undermined systematic education, forcing teachers to begin virtually anew each session. The church's insistence that the schools be opened whenever possible only compounded its problems. When schools opened at Ross River and Rampart House in 1916, the church hired recent graduates of the Carcross Indian Residential School as teachers. The DIA challenged the appointments and that of Julius Kendi (hired to teach at Mayo even though he spoke little English) on the grounds of academic competence.[29] In defence of Jacob Njootli at Rampart House, Bishop Stringer wrote, "He is perhaps not as well qualified to teach as most of our teachers, but he was the best man available. Again, at this place the Indians have to go off for weeks and months to hunt and fish, so that school can be held only when they come to the Post for a few weeks."[30] Native teachers were seen in the same light as catechists; marginal instruction was better than no instruction at all. The government reluctantly

Table 21
Enrollment of Yukon Native Children in Day Schools, 1920–54
(Five-Year Averages)

Years	Average # Enrolled	Eligible Students[1]	% Enrolled
1920–24	97.2	253	38.4
1925–29	140.4	229	51.3
1930–34	122.6	284	43.2
1935–39	123.8	347	35.7
1940–44	70.6	375	18.8
1945–49	178.0	310	57.4
1950–54[2]	230.0(277)	366	62.8(75.7)

Source DIA, *Annual Reports, 1920–55.*
[1] Ages 7–16 (1924), 6–15 (1929, 1934), 7–16 (1939–54).
[2] Figures in brackets represent average annual day-school enrollment plus average enrollment of Natives in territorial public schools.

Table 22
Day-School Attendance, Yukon Native Children, 1900–54 (Averages)

Years	Schools	Boys	Girls	Total	Average Attendance	% Attending
1900–04[1]	2.5	24.0	31.0	55.0	31.0	56.4
1905–09	1.8	14.6	18.0	32.6	19.0	58.3
1910–14	5.0	70.2	44.8	115.0	39.8	34.6
1915–19	6.0	79.4	58.0	137.4	43.6	31.7
1920–24	4.0	50.0	47.2	97.2	37.4	38.5
1925–29	6.0	72.8	67.6	140.4	58.8	41.9
1930–34	6.0	56.4	66.2	122.6	53.6	43.7
1935–39	5.6	56.8	67.0	123.8	64.0	51.7
1940–44	3.8	32.0	38.6	70.6	42.2	59.8
1945–49	7.2	80.4	97.6	178.0	125.4	70.5
1950–54[2]	6.2	105.4	124.6	230.0	206.7	89.9

Source DIA, *Annual Reports, 1900–55.*
[1] Two years only, 1901–02, 1902–03.
[2] 47 students per year (average) enrolled in territorial public schools are included in the tabulation for 1950–54.

accepted Stringer's appeal, but provided significantly lower stipends for the three Native teachers.

The continued shortage and transiency of teachers forced the church to draw on alternate sources of manpower. The enlistment of summer theology students, beginning early in the twentieth century, aided the church's effort to expand the school network. Enthusiastic beyond their experience, the students received assignments to the most poorly served areas of the territory. They seldom returned to an area more than two successive summers, adding to the Yukon's educational irregularities.[31] Even permanent missionaries added to the overall transiency, circulating freely within the territory and often departing for more prestigious postings.[32] With the exception of Benjamin Totty (twenty-eight years), C.C. Brett (seventeen years at Teslin and Champagne), and Kathleen Martin (an interrupted eight-year stint at Fort Selkirk), teachers seldom remained long in one area.[33]

Nor were the teachers, many of whom had little specific training or experience in education, well qualified for the task at hand. As was the case with the missionary corps, the Anglican Church took what was available. Following complaints about a teacher at Moosehide in the late 1940s, some consideration was given to replacing him with a man working at Carmacks. The Yukon Indian agent rejected the suggestion: "Mr Brownlee is doing a very fine job at Carmacks, he is an honourable bumbling type, painfully punctilious, but lacking the imagination and leadership necessary for the Moosehide. Mr Brownlee's personality is consistent with the Indians of Carmacks."[34] Given the low salaries for church teachers and the less than attractive working conditions, missionary zeal and a willingness to undergo hardships were more important prerequisites than formal training.

The day schools also suffered from a severe shortage of appropriate supplies. The summer students were often informed of their postings only a few weeks before they departed for the north, leaving little time at assemble a proper schooling kit. The Teslin school in 1931, for example, had the following texts: *Morang's Modern Phonic Primer* (fourteen copies); *Morang's Modern Arithmetic* (three copies); *Ontario First Reader's Book* (twenty-four copies); *Ontario Public School Arithmetic* (one copy); *Ontario Reader* (fifteen copies); *Alexandra Reader* (fourteen copies); *Manitoba Supplementary Reader* (four dilapidated copies); and one copy each of *High School History of England, Ontario Public School Grammar, New Canadian Reader, How Canada is Governed,* and *The Religion of Cheerfulness.* The school also had a small stock of pencils, pens, writing tablets, and other materials.[35] Student teachers routinely requested additional supplies, but neither church nor government provided the necessary funds.

Fear of excessive cost, combined with an expectation of minimal return, militated against improvements to the school network until after the Second World War. Indian agents repeatedly challenged church attempts to open new schools and, in 1933, tried to withdraw funding for three seasonal schools. Legislation of 1920 requiring school attendance prodded the DIA to expand educational facilities. The department conducted a series of educational surveys and where appropriate, as at Old Crow in 1950, opened new or long-closed schools.[36]

While money was available for day schools, in the post-war period the government favoured the less expensive option of integrating the children into an expanding territorial public school system. All earlier attempts at integration had been quickly, even rudely, rebuffed by local officials. In the early 1930s several Natives attended the Whitehorse public school but, for reasons that remain unclear, authorities revoked that privilege in 1935.[37] A similar effort at Mayo collapsed in the face of white pressure. The Teslin Joint School, opened in the late 1940s and available to both Native and non-Native children, suggested the kind of educational integration that would come in the following decade.[38]

Seasonal openings, limited attendance, Native mobility, and teacher transiency effectively undermined the already limited potential of Anglican day schools. Children maintained only irregular contact with the education system, even in such comparatively stable settlements as Moosehide and Selkirk.[39] With no standardized instruction and a teaching corps of widely varying talents, the impact of day-school teaching was minimal. Even Archdeacon Canham, active translator and missionary, allegedly said that he placed "very little faith in the work that he was accomplishing in the education of these Indian children and claims that they have not made any improvement since a few years."[40] The teachers acknowledged the limitations of their work and sought to offer only basic literacy and mathematical skills, preferring to mingle education with healthy offerings of practical Christianity and moral training. While a few teachers, exhibiting more enthusiasm than insight, spoke positively of the transformation they had wrought, most admitted the failings of the system.[41]

Day schools did not accomplish their fundamental purpose. Intended to effect a basic alteration of Native interests, the schools actually had little effect. At best, the teachers provided marginal literacy and computational skills, but only to a few of those in attendance. Throughout the territory the schools functioned alternatively as a vehicle of community recreation, drawing many adults and children, or as a baby-sitting service, the children remaining in attendance only as long as their parents were in camp. Few Natives committed their children to the intermittent program, undermining the church's best efforts. In theory, and even according to Anglican intentions, the colonial schools sought to undermine Native culture while offering the skills deemed necessary for integration into the dominant society. However, without federal backing – moral, legal, or financial – the Anglican church's program fell far short of its goal.

The same critique does not apply to the Carcross Indian Residential School. To most educators, residential schools offered the best means of effecting a scholastic and cultural transformation of Native students. By separating the children from their families and environment for an extended period, isolating them in a "total institution" which offered guidance in all areas of moral and social development, boarding establishments provided an opportunity to turn out graduates who were vastly different (administrators said better) than other Natives. Altbach and Kelly's description of the colonial school spoke directly to the residential institution.[42] Although the Anglican Church's Carcross school lacked much of the cultural imperialism typically associated with such facilities, it had a significant impact on those students who passed through its class-rooms.

Bishop Bompas established a boarding school at Fortymile in 1891; most of his early students were orphans or abandoned children.[43] When Bompas moved his diocesan base to Carcross in 1900, he initially left his small school behind. Convinced of the need for a proper boarding school, he appealed to the DIA: "I am wishing now to apply to the Government to open a new Indian Boarding School for orphans and other Destitute Indian children either at Whitehorse or here at Caribou Crossing and to maintain it themselves. I think this the only way to make the remnant of the Indian race in the next generation useful members of society."[44] When the government rejected his request, Bompas transplanted the Fortymile school to Carcross, offering a foster home to approximately two dozen children each year. At Bompas's death in 1906 John Hawksley assumed responsibility for the school. The new bishop, Isaac Stringer, continued his predecessor's campaign for government assistance.[45]

The Anglican Church's appeal for a boarding school came at a most inauspicious time. From 1871, when the federal government signed its first treaty with the Indians of western Canada, education and negotiated land settlements went hand in hand. The government organized boarding schools on reserves, modelled after institutions established earlier in eastern Canada, and, in 1883, opened an industrial school at Battleford. "It is self-evident," the government confidently declared, "that the prime purpose of Indian education is to assist in solving what may be called the Indian problem, to elevate the Indian from his condition of savagery, to make him a self-supporting member of the state and eventually a citizen in good standing."[46] The goals remained intact for many years, but by the early twentieth century many educators and civil servants had acknowledged the failings of the boarding/industrial school.[47]

Typically wary of increased expenditures, the government especially feared further involvement in a flawed experiment. Frank Pedley, deputy minister of Indian affairs, suggested a more flexible program, arguing that "it would seem to be good policy at this juncture to attempt to devise a better system of Indian education, applying to each locality methods which would best achieve the desired result."[48] Particular concern centred on the schools' inability to provide effectively for the "after life of the Indian." Advanced technical training and literary skills served little purpose for Native children destined for a life on a reserve or a trapline. The Anglican church admitted the deficiencies of the institution. A special committee of the MSCC recommended that teaching be limited to basic literacy and arithmetic skills and to "such additional work as will fit the child to take his place as a workman in the locality in which he is to live."[49] Frank Oliver, minister of the interior, offered more explicit criticism. In defence of the (less expensive) day schools, Oliver argued:

My belief is that the attempt to elevate the Indian by separating the child from his parents and educating him as a white man has turned out to be a deplorable failure ... The mutual love between parent and child is the strongest influence for the betterment of the world, and when that influence is absolutely cut apart or is deliberately intended to be cut apart as in the education of Indian children in industrial schools the means taken defeats itself ... To teach an Indian child that his parents are degraded beyond measure and that whatever they did or thought was wrong could only result in the child becoming, as the ex-pupils of the industrial schools have become, admittedly and unquestionably very much less desirable element of society than their parents who never saw the schools.[50]

While both the federal government and the MSCC viewed boarding schools with disfavour, Bishop Stringer proceeded with his appeal. The 1907 synod of the Diocese of the Yukon endorsed the project,[51] as did T.G. Bragg, superintendent of schools for the Yukon.[52] Resistance nevertheless persisted at the national level. DIA Secretary J.L. McLean shared Oliver and Pedley's reservations. He wrote, "The immediate protection of Indian children has too often been considered as the chief end in view, not the final results that are to be achieved and the usefulness of the education to be imparted to enable the children to support themselves when they are thrown upon their own resources."[53] McLean directed two department officials in British Columbia, A.W. Vowell and A.E. Green, to visit the Yukon and assess the need for such a school. Their 1908 submission, tendered after a tour of the main Yukon communities in conjunction with Anglican missionaries and following correspondence with several other missionaries and police officers, seconded Stringer's request.[54]

Oliver reluctantly complied with the recommendations, but he remained unconvinced of the need for such a facility. Completed in 1911 and located on a small farm near Carcross, the facility initially housed thirty students, an increase over the twenty formerly handled in Bompas's quarters. The new building, complete with dormitory and school facilities, remained in use until destroyed by fire in 1939. The school then operated out of temporary quarters until 1954 when, following a protracted debate about the best location for the facilities, the government erected a 120-bed boarding school on the old site.

In attempting to fill the Carcross school, the Anglican Church sought to achieve two divergent goals.[55] Administrators wished to maintain Bompas's original purpose of providing a home for the destitute and orphaned, but they also wanted to use the school as a training ground for future Native leaders. Removed from the influences of a "backward" home environment and protected from the bad influences of non-Natives, boarders would be educationally and morally prepared to elevate their families and communities towards a Canadian ideal. The graduates, it was hoped, would serve as instruments of "civilization" when they returned to their homes. To meet these objectives, the clergy attempted to identify the poor and the deprived while also seeking to recruit "the best both in health and intellect."[56]

Marketing the school proved more difficult than anticipated. Stringer carefully cultivated his territory-wide contacts, often making special allowances in order to attract students. In 1918 administrators allowed the mixed-blood daughter of trader Poole Field to enroll in Carcross because, as Stringer observed, her father had "an immense influence over the Liard and Pelly Indians, and can do a great deal in getting children for our schools."[57] Stringer and the Anglican clergy expended considerable energy in securing the children of prominent people, but often discovered that parents were unwilling to part with their offspring. The bishop expressed dismay that "some of our best and most influential Indians object to sending their children away to school."[58]

The major stumbling-block appeared to be the likelihood of prolonged separation. Children from the Stewart and Porcupine River areas, for example, were compelled to live away from home for as long as ten years, since the school and government would not authorize summer vacation travel to such distant places. The bond between parent and child proved a serious restraint to sending children to Carcross,[59] but other factors also affected the decision to enrol students. Children, particularly as they entered their teens, had an important economic function in the Natives' nomadic world, helping with camp and harvesting activities. Expectation of economic hardship, therefore, added to parental reluctance to answer the church's appeal. Occasionally, children rebelled against parental attempts to send them to school, resisting the unknown in favour of the security of family.[60] Such actions often succeeded but, on the whole, most children seem to have accepted their lot.

The Anglican Church also relied on government representatives, particularly police officers and Indian agents, to encourage school attendance. In 1929 Indian Agent Harper Reed asked Chief Billy Johnston of Teslin to select children for the Carcross school. Interestingly, he asked about "any large families who would like some of their children to go there for say 18 months," a clear appeal to parents in financial hardship.[61]

The missionary and government effort succeeded in keeping the school enrolments close to capacity. A number of parents agreed with the clergy's argument that their children's future depended on literacy, advanced training, and religious guidance. Moreover, many Native catechists, such as Amos Njootli, were heavily influenced by the church's teachings and sent their children to the school.[62] The attempt to attract "better" Natives, however, was not as successful. Initial reluctance hardened in the 1920s after a series of deaths among the student body and rumours about poor food and cramped quarters undermined the respectability of the Carcross school. The facility did much better as a home for destitute and orphaned children. Between 1930 and 1950 a minimum of 30 per cent of all new students came from situations of identifiable family distress.[63]

Missionaries, government agents, and police officers readily identified children in need of special care and ensured that they were sent to the school.[64]

Epidemics hit the school frequently, including an outbreak of influenza which claimed four lives in 1920. The death of children at the institution was not unusual, although they often succumbed to tuberculosis or other diseases contracted before their arrival. The school's reputation as a dangerous place for children gained greater currency with each death and serious illness, impeding further recruitment efforts.[65] The respectable level of attendance despite these problems was the result of additions to the school's capacity and, after 1945, the enforcement of compulsory education.[66]

Table 23
Status of Parents, New Registrants, Carcross Residential School, 1930–50

Year	Both Alive	Both Alive, Destitute[1]	Mother Dead	Father Dead	Both Dead	Total	% Family Distress
30–44	70	4	8	18	7	107	34.6
45–50	69	2	8	18	2	99	30.3

Source NA, RG10, vol. 6481, file 940–10, pts. 4–6, Registration Documents, Carcross School. The collection of registration forms is incomplete.

[1] These numbers, drawn from historical documents, likely understate the extent of destitution.

Registration records reflect the church's difficulties in attracting suitable students. Ideally, educators wanted the children as young as possible and sought to draw them from around the territory. Such a policy, they hoped, would have the greatest possible impact and would ensure that trained leaders would disperse throughout the Yukon. Yet although children as young as six years (and occasionally younger in the case of orphans) came to the school, the average age at entry ranged from nine to eleven years. Most came to Carcross with little educational experience, apart from temporary sessions at one of the day schools.

Registrations in the pre-1944 period suggest that efforts to recruit students from around the territory also fell short. The southern districts accounted for most of the registrants, with more than 70 per cent coming from Whitehorse, Teslin, Champagne, Carcross, and Atlin, BC. Following the gradual introduction of compulsory education in 1945, the geographic distribution shifted. Between 1945 and 1950 fewer than half (45 per cent) came from the south, while Old Crow, which had sent no children to the school in the preceding fifteen years, sent twenty-two, or almost one-quarter of all new registrants. They did so under protest, however, petitioning the federal government in 1945 to provide suitable educational facilities closer to home.[67] Indeed the total number of students from the area north of Fort Selkirk increased almost three times (seventeen to forty-nine) in this period. Government intervention, rather than relentless church appeals, provided the impetus for greater enrolment among the children in outlying areas.

Children from distant locations had difficulty maintaining contact with their parents. Some church administrators, such as W. Barlow, believed that the parents were anxious to transfer responsibility for the children to the church, and were uninterested in their progress in school.[68] Yet, when parents did make an effort to contact their

Table 24
Carcross School Enrollments, Characteristics of Students, 1930–50

Years	Recorded Registrations	Average Age	No Schooling[1]	Less Than One Year[2]	One Year or More	Previous Residential
30–34	40	9.1	25	7	5	3
35–39	30	9.2	14	11	5	0
40–44	51	10.8	29	10	4	8
45–50	99	9.3	67	0	28	4

Source   NA, RG10, vol. 6481, file 940–10, pts. 4–6, Registration Documents, Carcross School.
[1] Either identified as no previous schooling or simply no entry in the relevant blank on the registration form.
[2] Less than one season in a Native day school

children or asked to have them returned, the church was rigidly opposed.

Neither government nor clergy saw the Carcross facility as either an industrial school or an academic institution. When they recommended construction of the facility, A.W. Vowell and A.E. Green suggested: "At the present time, the simplest form of education, such as reading, writing and arithmetic, with instruction as to housekeeping, sanitary measures, and, it may be, carpentry, is all that, in our opinion, is necessary; to go beyond that would be rather to unfit them for their condition in life instead of aiding them to overcome such difficulties as may be met with in their struggle for existence."[69] Educators did not intend to turn out industrial workers. Instead, in recognition of the fact that most would return to their families and a harvesting lifestyle, different priorities took effect. Rather than creating "white Indians," school promoters sought to make "better" Indians, schooled in the necessities of health, hygiene, nutrition, Christian morals, and the Protestant work ethic, but also armed with the requisite skills of the hunter and trapper.

The school program featured a mixture of education and practical training.[70] Instruction in reading, writing, and arithmetic typically occupied the morning, with the remainder of the day spent on work around the school and at vocational lessons. Boys chopped wood, fished, hunted, and worked in the carpentry shop and at small-scale gardening. Girls assisted in the kitchen and with household chores around the school. Teachers also offered the girls training in moccasin-making and bead work, pursuits which would "be useful and profitable to them in after life." There were some deviations from the pattern, including the installation of a student-run printing press, used for several years to publish the church quarterly, Northern Lights, and an expanded industrial workshop. On balance, however, the

Table 25
Origins of New Registrants, Carcross Residential School, 1930–50

Years	Carcross	Peel	Tahltan	Tagish	Big Salmon	Atlin
1930–44	30	6	8	2	2	2
1945–50	8	0	0	0	0	0

	Pelly	Carmacks	Selkirk	Whitehorse	Mayo
1930–44	2	8	5	18	2
1945–50	0	2	14	15	6

	Kluane	Moosehide	Teslin	Champagne	Old Crow
1930–44	2	4	17	9	0
1945–50	1	7	16	1	22

Source   NA, RG10, vol. 6481, file 940–10, pts. 4–6, Registration Documents, Carcross School.

teachers sought to provide necessary skills, as defined by the Anglican clergy, for successful re-entry into Yukon society.[71]

In a major departure from typical Native child-rearing practices, the school insisted upon a strict, often authoritarian code of discipline.[72] Administrators restricted socialization within the school; under most principals, boys and girls were seldom permitted to meet or even to talk to each other, and the students were rarely allowed to visit the Carcross community nearby. Dr Grasset-Smith, principal from 1918–20, allowed virtually no interaction between the sexes, a level of control other missionaries found objectionable.[73] Breaches of school discipline, especially theft or vandalism, were dealt with firmly. In 1940 the students of the school were accused of numerous thefts. After strappings on the hand failed to have the desired effect, the principal, H.C.M. Grant, announced that the next offender would "be laid across the classroom desk in the presence of the whole school, clad only in their night attire, and strapped on a different part of their anatomy than their hands." He carried through on his threat: "So severe was this strapping that the child had to be held down by the Head Matron and the Farm Instructor." Grant later resorted to a different tactic – shaving the head of any child who broke school rules. As he succinctly noted, "It checked stealing at once."[74] Programming varied as principals and staff passed swiftly through the school, but the rigid work schedules, limited socialization, and firm discipline remained intact.

The combination of an apparently flexible instructional program and rigid behavioural control was full of contradictions. Concern for the students' later life was undermined by the residential school regime; social skills were at best not taught, and, at worst, actively repressed; and the firm discipline and work schedules lacked relevance to the Native mode of life – the very environment to which the children were shortly expected to return. Most important, the concerted effort to improve Native hygiene and to inculcate modern work habits and values called into disrepute the habits and standards of the children's parents. Ironically, although supposedly prepared to re-enter Native society, the students had been taught to despise that society, and to look with disrespect, if not disgust, upon their traditional values.

School administrators and government officials were not receptive to parental requests to have their children returned. In the mid-1930s John Semple of Peel River wanted his son to come back home to help with trapping and hunting. DIA officials, displeased with the Semple family and the fact that John Semple had been convicted of minor crimes several times, refused his request.[75] Philip Phelan, chief of the department's training division, observed that "the Department feels that as far as possible the intention of the Indian Act should be recognized, namely, that pupils should be discharged when they reach the age of 16 years."[76] Some parents took matters into their own hands. The Andersons sent three of their children to Carcross; one died in 1930 or 1931. When the surviving children returned home for summer holidays, the parents "positively refused" to send them back to Carcross.[77]

A few children – the total number is unknown – ran away from the school. But the isolated location of Carcross and the difficulties involved in reaching outlying districts limited their chances of success. In 1947 Billy Peter Johnnie of Dawson and Peter Issac of the Pelly band left the school and reached the south end of Lake Laberge before they were stopped. School officials decided to send Billy Johnnie home, "he being a big boy and becoming a bit troublesome at the school"; Peter Issac, age twelve at the time, was returned to Carcross to complete his schooling.[78]

The children leaving Carcross Indian Residential School faced a traumatic transition.[79] Lillian McClusky, deemed by her teachers to be "backward in her studies," was returned to her parents in the winter of 1933. In agreeing to release her from the school, Indian Agent Harper Reed observed, "It was thought better to do that than her to learn so much that when she returned her nomadic way of life she would not be an "outcast."[80] The clergy initially saw the graduation of students as the end of their work, each child representing a new mission worker assisting in the general improvement of Yukon Native people. But as a rule, hope soon turned to despair, and missionaries came to fear the consequences of a student's return to the realities of village life. An Old Crow commentator noted in 1926:

If Caroline Moses['] girl comes back, she is going into the filthiest hovel in the country ... A dirt floor, two tiny windows which cannot be seen for the flies, stinking meat and fish being all over the cabin, the stench unspeakable, six people already there, and now a seventh, and under the willows on the dirt floor, all the filth of a long winter throwing off a deadly effluvia, in a stifling heat ... Bishop, I plead with you not for humanity's sake, but for the sake of the Dear Lord who redeemed us, not to send a decent girl back to untold misery and evil, where she cannot help but curse the very day she was born.[81]

The writer makes the often repeated point that the Carcross graduates faced a difficult challenge. When Eunice Ben reached Fort Yukon on her way back to Rampart House after several years at the school, she refused to leave and took refuge at Hudson Stuck Memorial Hospital.[82]

Not all who left the school had difficulties. The clergy made much of these successes, closely following the careers of such individuals as James Wood, Jacob Njootli, and Maggie Daniels who served the church as day-school teachers or Native catechists. Several others utilized their school skills to make a more complete entry into non-Native society, settling near Whitehorse or Dawson and even applying for enfranchisement.[83] A 1912 survey of several of the graduates found that many had "succeeded," although they had not returned to their communities. Five of the girls worked as domestics, with two living in Victoria. Not all who had the option of domestic labour did so. Annie Smith, who had been returned to her parents at Lower LaBerge after several years in school, was offered a position in Victoria. Indian Agent John Hawksley rejected the request on her behalf, noting that she would likely be married soon. Further, Hawksley warned, such placements would work for only a select few of the graduates. Commenting on the woman who had recommended Annie, he wrote, "I fear she does not quite understand the nature of these northern Indians."[84] Several other girls had married, one to a "man of means" in Seattle.

The boys had fewer options. One, Henry, worked on the railway at Carcross; another worked on a farm outside of Dawson.[85] Other boys were kept at Carcross for several years, working as unpaid labourers as they waited for a position. Officials were reluctant to let these young men return to their communities unless they had the assurance of employment. There was, therefore, considerable disappointment when in 1933 John Tizya refused an offer of work at the school and returned to Old Crow. There was, John Hawksley worried, "nothing up there for him except the backward life of the Indians ... I am inclined to think his decision is, to some extent, influenced by a desire for freedom and the somewhat lazy life of the Old Crow Indians."[86]

The clergy took particular pride in the efforts of one student who, upon returning to Selkirk in 1939, effected a radical change in her family's habits and manners.[87] But such successes were few, noted by the church all the more for their uniqueness. Most of the children found themselves trapped, torn between school values and the realities of camp life. As a summer missionary at Carmacks noted in 1934, "They are potential outcasts of their own people and are not quite up to the standards of the white intellect. In other words, they are 'betwixt and between' – a condition of pitiful helplessness."[88] Sarah-Jane Essau, a Native woman from Moosehide, agreed: "When they are too long at school they won't have anything to do with us; they want to be with white people; they grow away from us."[89]

Because the success of the residential-school program was measured by the activities of the graduates, the Anglican clergy monitored their careers closely. Instead of trusting in the results of their labour, the clergy scrambled to protect the students from the trials of readjustment. To justify their efforts, missionaries endeavoured to keep the young people from the perceived evils of village life and urban centres. Ironically, however, the church ended up guarding the students from the very environment they were intended to reform. Most, including Duncan Scott, the deputy superintendent general of Indian affairs,[90] saw the intermarriage of graduates as the best means of protecting those versed in the new morality and customs. In 1916 Bishop Stringer devoted considerable effort to finding a suitable mate for Jacob, a recent graduate, encouraging him to talk to girls at the school and, when that failed, to write to other graduates. Arranging marriages was, to Stringer, a top priority: "A few years ago I would have laughed at talk like this," he wrote, "but it is only after seeing case after case, and there has been no exception so far, that I have come to this conclusion."[91] The attempt to set up a new class of Natives only highlighted their distinctiveness and compounded the trauma of re-entry. None the less, missionaries and school administrators encouraged suitable marriages, often against the graduates' wishes.[92] While few supported one theology student's recommendation that a separate village be established for young people,[93] most missionaries privately acknowledged that the residential school children could not be left entirely to their own devices.

The ambiguities of the residential-school concept were apparent from the start. Prodded by the federal government, the Anglican Church had modified its curriculum and training program to make them more relevant to the north. The clergy, however, refused to compromise their desire to provide a new – and Christian – outlook on life, health, and work. To do so would deny their central purpose and their aspirations for the Yukon Indians.[94] The problems encountered upon re-entry, therefore, reflected the very structure and purpose of the institution. Conflict between long-separated children and parents, between ideas acquired in school and those of the village, was as inevitable as it was painful. Designed to provide a generation of leaders for the Yukon Indians, the Carcross school instead produced children unsure of their place, uneasy in both Native and non-Native worlds, and unclear about their future in the Yukon.[95]

Residential schools in general, and the Carcross facility in particular, epitomize the destructive effects of "colonial" schools. Altbach and Kelly argue that such institutions "represented a basic denial of the colonized's past and withheld from them the tools to regain the future."[96] Although administrators attempted to make the program relevant to the students' needs, moral and social considerations demanded a rejection of parental values. In sum, the institution failed to provide an obvious route into either Native or non-Native society. Unlike the day schools, which adapted to seasonal movements and remained irregular and virtually inconsequential, the Carcross school forced major changes on its young residents.

Other boarding schools operated in the territory, although none achieved the profile or importance of the Carcross facility. In 1920 the Anglican Church opened St Paul's Hostel in Dawson City, providing a dormitory for mixed-blood children excluded by law from attending Carcross. The students attended public school in Dawson, a matter of considerable concern in town. The hostel differed significantly in that its administrators emphasized the children's non-Native parentage. The explicit goal of the centre was to allow the student "to fit himself to take his place in the community as a white man."[97] The third boarding school opened in army surplus buildings in Whitehorse in 1946, under the Baptist evangelist H.I. Lee, and was connected with the Aberhart Biblical Institute in Alberta.[98] Funded as part of the federal government's post-war program to provide improved educational services, Lee's school placed considerable emphasis on industrial education and regular academic programs. The Whitehorse school was open to all those unable to enter regular public school, including status Indians, mixed-bloods, enfranchised Natives, and a few "poor whites."[99] Lee attracted more than sixty students his first year, including fifty Natives, nine mixed-bloods, and seven enfranchised Indians. The children, forty of whom boarded at the school, came primarily from the Whitehorse and Champagne areas.[100] St Paul's Hostel and the Whitehorse Indian School were markedly different institutions, one serving a distinct clientele, the other entering the scene after the wartime boom and the reordering of federal educational priorities. The establishment of St Paul's indicated the commitment of both church and government to the growing mixed-blood population, while the funding of the Whitehorse school foreshadowed the establishment of a non-sectarian (that is non-Anglican) industrial and assimilationist educational system in the post-war Yukon.[101]

The Catholic Church's decision to enter the territorial education and mission field outweighed the significance of St Paul's and the White-horse school. The Anglicans claimed exclusive educational jurisdiction in the territory, citing a long history of uninterrupted missionary work to substantiate the claim. Responding to a 1902 rumour that the federal government was considering Catholic Native schools, Bishop Bompas wrote angrily: "If the Government are laying a neat plot to take the Education out of our hands and give it to the Roman-ists it is a piece of unjust tyranny and heartless religious persecution which ought to be exposed. No other religious denomination than ours has even made any attempt to ... educate any Yukon Indian children or Indian adults except ours, nor would the Indians attend any other school than ours as they all belong to our church."[102] The Anglicans claimed few areas of exclusive jurisdiction across Canada; they jealously guarded the ones they had.

The Catholics, no less than the Anglicans, felt that education – and especially residential schools – held the key to the ultimate success of their missionary work. Their desire to expand into the Yukon mission field – dormant until the 1930s – first emerged as a demand for government support for day schools. The federal government did not respond with much enthusiasm. When the Oblate priest Father Morrissett requested school supplies for Burwash in 1944, a DIA official warned, "These could, of course, be provided, but our experience is that once this is done we receive a request shortly afterwards for teacher's salary, and rent of buildings, furnishings, etc."[103] The Oblates, claiming 549 adherents in the Yukon and northern British Columbia,[104] were even more anxious to secure funding for a resi-dential school for Catholic children in the northwest. To support their demands, they began in the mid-1940s to protest vigorously against the enrolment of baptized Catholics at Carcross, a contravention of government policy which called for a member of a specific Christian denomination to be educated in a school of like persuasion.[105] In 1945, for instance, Father Charles Hamel of Atlin reported that five students, including three children of Billy Johnson and Martha Sam and two of Bill Hall and Sophie Hamon, were registered at Carcross.[106] Similarly, when Bishop Coudert learned that a young orphan, May Louis of Lansing Creek, had been sent to the boarding school, he wondered why she had not be left with her relatives or, failing that, sent to the Roman Catholic station at Fort St John, BC, for assignment to a Catholic residential school outside the territory.[107] Coudert did not want the children withdrawn from Carcross but he did use these, and other cases, to support his demand for a Catholic residential school in the northwest.[108]

Unhappily provoked by the Anglican-Catholic contest, the DIA reluctantly agreed in 1949 to open a Catholic boarding school for the region. Initially slated for Teslin, the government moved the facility to Lower Post, located along the newly opened Alaska Highway just south of Watson Lake. But the confrontation continued, and even expanded as other denominations entered the field.[109] The establishment of the Reverend Lee's school in Whitehorse, and the Baptists' evangelistic work in the Ross River area, further confused the situation, with Catholics, Anglicans, and now Baptists competing for Native students. Uncharacteristically, Roman Catholic bishop J.L. Coudert appealed that Lee's "propoganda" be stopped as it was "paralyzing both the Catholic and Anglican educational work in the Yukon."[110] This was, of course, more than an educational dispute, as the rival denominations recognized the importance of federal subsidies for schooling in permitting an expansion of missionary work. Not surprisingly, the confrontation served to discredit both education and religion in the Natives' eyes, limiting or reducing the already debatable impact of institutional activities.

In the end, the record of church-run and federally funded education reflected the Native peoples' dissatisfaction with the method and style of boarding and day schools. The continuation of hunting and trapping as the primary mode of life into the 1940s prevented the day schools from having an appreciable impact. The missionaries continued the schools, aiming to gain a toe-hold among the younger generation. There was greater hope, and consequently greater disappointment, surrounding the Carcross Residential School and the Baptist and Catholic boarding schools opened in the late 1940s. The legacy of the boarding schools, and of education generally, was a bitter one, as Yukon Native people recalled their separation from parents and community as well as the rigid discipline, limited socialization, and impractical education that occupied so much of their childhood years. Educational problems did not end after 1950. An interventionist federal state and a renewed determination to bring northern Native people into the Canadian mainstream resulted in a major expansion of educational programs and further challenges to the relationship between Native parents and children.[111]

CHAPTER EIGHT

The Federal Government and Yukon Natives

The federal government played a major role in the evolution of Native-white relations in the Yukon Territory. Its activities, conducted by such officials as police officers, Indian agents, and Ottawa-based civil servants, varied widely, from imposing a legal structure and police force on the region to financing educational programs, and included efforts to restrict Native access to the towns. Since government officials operated without the doctrinal commitment of the clergy, they often served as a buffer between the non-Native and indigenous populations.

Historical assessments of federal Indian policy typically emphasize the British or Canadian origins of programs and initiatives aimed at Native people. Seldom, however, are these policies traced to the level of implementation.[1] But as American historian Francis Paul Prucha has argued, "a policy can be fully understood only by watching it unfold in practice."[2] Commentators on the administration of Indian policy in Canada have concentrated on sketching the broad contours of federal legislation. The policy-oriented analysis employed in these studies, often laced with critical appraisals of the paternalism and colonialism inherent in the Indian Act, has resulted in a characterization of Native policy as unwavering, highly centralized, and goal-oriented. Indian agents in the field, who handled the actual implementation of the federal programs, are described by implication as adhering without question to Ottawa's policies.[3] Yet in reality, the case of the Yukon suggests that federal officials often sought to modify national directives to suit territorial realities and, equally important, that the Natives were often reluctant to accept government services and programs.

The central elements of federal Indian policy, as set out in the Indian Act, were clearly delineated and widely accepted.[4] The government had four goals – promoting Native self-sufficiency, protecting the Indians from the "evils" of non-Native society, encouraging conversion to Christianity, and assimilating the Natives – and it developed a variety of programs in an attempt to achieve these goals.[5] National directives, however, did not translate directly into local initiatives. In the Yukon, scattered settlement, limited development, and continuation of Native mobility interfered with the implementation of national programs. The Yukon experience, all in all, deviated significantly from the patterns suggested by a narrow analysis of federal legislation. The policy guidelines entrenched in the Indian Act never disappeared, but government agents worked with surprising flexibility, altering their programs and emphasis to suit local conditions.

This is not to suggest, however, that the Yukon situation was particularly unique. Government policy for Natives in northern, non-agricultural areas across the country varied considerably from the national norms enunciated in federal legislation. There was, additionally, considerable variation because of the personality, competence, and influence of individual Indian agents. Government officials, moreover, were extremely conscientious managers of their departmental budgets. Funds, particularly for relief payments, were handed out with great reluctance in many quarters. Northern Indians offered a unique opportunity in this respect, in that they could continue to hunt, fish, and trap for much of their sustenance, thus reducing their claim on the government's funds.[6] The pattern of government programming in the Yukon, therefore, is suggestive of a much broader phenomena of the DIA deviating from broad policy goals because of financial constraints or the logic of local circumstance.

The administrative and constitutional structure of the Yukon Territory created special problems and possibilities for the DIA and other federal agencies with northern responsibilities.[7] The district was officially under the control of the North-West Territories (NWT) government from 1870 to 1898, although almost nothing was done to assert that authority.[8] Only the massive influx of prospectors during the Klondike gold rush forced the federal government to assert its control in the region.[9] The federally appointed administration established in 1898 under Commissioner J.M. Walsh ran into conflict with the NWT government over the question of liquor revenues. To resolve the controversy and to assert federal control over the area, Parliament passed the Yukon Territory Act in June 1898, establishing the Yukon as a separate political and administrative unit. The first council consisted of five federally appointed officials. In response to demands for greater local control, the government gradually extended the principle of representative, but not responsible, administration, culminating in the establishment of an elected, ten-member council in 1908. Throughout this period, however, the commissioner exercised dominant authority, frequently overruling the elected council and acting as the agent of his Ottawa-based superiors. With the end of the gold rush and the onset of economic decline, the federal government drastically reduced its financial commitment to the region, cut the size of the elected council to three members in 1918–19, and consolidated administrative power in the commissioner's hands (although that post, too, was down-graded to the position of comptroller after the First World War.). The Yukon Territory retained this administrative form until after the Second World War, when a gradual expansion of representative and responsible government led to the re-establishment of a fully elected territorial council and, in the 1970s, cabinet government.[10]

This political and administrative structure left the federal government all-powerful. The commissioner, gold commissioner (later comptroller), Indian agent, and ranking police officer commanded considerable authority, much more than federal officials exercised in other parts of the country. Even more important, federal officials and politicians had a unique opportunity to shape and control regional programs, with limited interference from regional administrators. Since so much authority rested in federal hands, there were few impediments to the application of national priorities and programs in the Yukon.

That the federal government was unsure of how to deal with the northern territory was evident from the beginning. Between 1870 and 1896 the Canadian government displayed little interest in the northwest corner of its newly acquired territories. Administrators and politicians focused instead on opening the fertile but unsettled lands on the prairies.[11] The Geological Survey of Canada undertook preliminary examinations of the area in the 1880s, but it took the repeated intervention of Bishop Bompas to force the Canadian government into action. Bompas worried that recently arrived miners would harm the local Indians and he repeatedly petitioned the government to dispatch a contingent of the NWMP to the Yukon. The bishop was preoccupied with the controlling the liquor trade; several of the leading miners had, unsuccessfully, tried to limit the sale of spirits to the Natives and, Bompas claimed, would support police efforts to enforce "sobriety among the Indians, as conducive to their own protection."[12] Federal officials sent two men north in 1894, although the decision to act rested only partially on concern for the Natives.[13]

Ottawa gave NWMP Inspector Charles Constantine, commander of the first Yukon contingent, specific instructions on how to deal with the Indians. He was given a copy of Alexander Morris's *Treaties with the Indians of Canada,* a strong indication that the government expected the Natives to place demands before the government. As an official representative of the DIA, however, Constantine was ordered "not to give encouragement to the idea that they [the Yukon Indians] will be received into treaty, and taken under the care of the government."[14] The federal government saw no need to alienate Indian lands through treaty, as was required under the Royal Proclamation of 1763 and as had occurred in southern Canada after 1870, and remained convinced that the northern district held few prospects for significant settlement. Preliminary relief measures were considered, but the government wanted it clearly understood that the Indians were to be accorded no better treatment than any Canadian or immigrant.[15]

Constantine reached the Yukon River valley in the late summer of 1894. At the first major meeting with the local Natives, Chief Charlie told the police officer, "I am quite happy and contented and would like to see the English come and take care of the country. I like the English better than the Americans." Charlie also made some comments regarding the theft of Native dogs, the availability of alcohol, and other matters. Constantine, who did little to hide his dislike of the Natives, told them to look after their dogs more carefully and to avoid alcohol. The local people, Constantine later reported, "appeared to be of a very low order of intelligence." He described them as "a lazy shiftless lot ... content to hang round the mining camps. They suffer much from chest trouble and die young."[16]

The government maintained its policy of negotiating treaties only where and when lands used by the Indians were required for permanent development. Ironically, some government officials used the absence of a treaty to suggest that Ottawa's obligations in the north were minimal. As Hayter Reed, deputy superintendent general of Indian affairs, argued in 1897: "The Department has no jurisdiction over Indians in unsurrendered territory; nor does it appear how – without having entered into any Treaty – the Indians can be otherwise dealt with than white settlers or immigrants."[17] At the same time, the government declared that as far as it was "aware, there is no Indian title to be extinguished in the Yukon."[18] To these arguments, Bishop Bompas responded, "It has been argued that the Indians are no losers by the arrival of the Whites, because they can make money by working for them. This is to persuade one who has been robbed of his property that he is no worse off because he can still make a living by hard labour."[19]

When development pressures emerged in the Mackenzie River valley in 1899–1900 the government provided benefits such as guaranteed access to game, annuity payments, and reservations to compensate for anticipated dislocations.[20] The same concerns were not operative in the Yukon, even after the gold rush. The rapid influx of miners, the concentration of mining activity in the west-central Yukon, and the government's conviction that the territory could not sustain permanent development limited the need, so the government officials thought, for a treaty.[21] The possibility that another "Eldorado" lay somewhere in the district also convinced authorities not to set aside any specific lands for exclusive Native use.

The government's unwillingness to consider a treaty did not end discussion on the matter. Jim Boss, hereditary chief of the southern Yukon Indians (Lake LaBerge),[22] submitted a request for land-ownership negotiations in 1902. Boss demanded financial "compensation because of the taking possession of their [the Indians'] lands and hunting grounds by the white people."[23] Noting that any Natives facing hardships received government relief, federal officials brushed aside Boss's claims.[24] While individual Native people did not press the issue, the Anglican Church picked up the treaty question,[25] supported, on occasion, by territorial politicians such as Dr A. Thompson.[26] Between 1907 and 1910 the Reverend A.E. O'Meara, financial secretary for the Diocese of the Yukon, prepared a fairly comprehensive treaty claim on behalf of the Natives. Reflecting its missionary origins, the claim focused on a request for Anglican-administered day and residential schools, in combination with game preserves and community-improvement projects. The penultimate proposal also called for the appointment of a full-time Indian agent, better medical care, and official recognition of Native marriages.[27] Before the document reached Frank Oliver, minister of the interior, the request for treaty negotiations had been dropped – the clergy had correctly anticipated the government's resistance on this point.[28]

Responding to the church's appeal, Oliver restated the well-known policy: "The Government seeks to protect the interests of all, whether Indian or white, but is not responsible for specifically protecting those of the Indians." The minister rejected the paternalism inherent in expanded government assistance, claiming that it "had been most harmful to the Indians by accentuating their original communism, that is to say, the natural dependance of the Indians upon others." To Oliver, the coming of the non-Natives and the gold rush brought prosperity. Acceding to the Indians' requests would change Native ways; in his judgment, they would "if left as Indians earn a better living."[29]

Subsequent to this debate, the signing of Treaty No. 11 in 1921 with the Indians of the upper Mackenzie River drainage basin brought a small number of Yukon Indians under treaty. But the inclusion of the Liard Indians, due solely to the configuration of the Mackenzie drainage basin, hardly constituted a deliberate recognition of aboriginal title in the territory.[30] Although the Anglican clergy continued their intervention on behalf of their Native charges, they abandoned the idea of a treaty. Following the 1908–10 attempt, no significant effort was made for more than half a century to secure a comprehensive settlement with the government.[31]

Throughout these preliminary discussions, the Yukon Indians remained in the background. The Anglican clergy intervened on their behalf, not always with their permission.[32] A few Native representations were made, typically involving requests for title to specific tracts of land on the basis of traditional occupation. In 1900 Jim Boss asked for a parcel of land on Lake LaBerge, arguing that it "had been occupied by his people from time immemorial."[33] A small parcel of land was set aside for the use of the local Indians. Boss, an entrepreneur of considerable ability, maintained his interest in the land, although by 1917 most of the other Natives in the area had moved away from the area. When a shipping company cut wood on the land for use in its stern-wheelers, Boss demanded, and received, compensation.[34] Such an assertion of control over traditional lands was not unusual. When Kow'h-kha, chief of the Teslin band, died in 1906, his nephew, Billy Johnson, assumed both his position and his name and took "possession of his hunting ground."[35] In 1931 Joe Squam of Teslin similarly claimed lands in the Wolf Lake district because he had "hunted and trapped over this ground since a child." Federal officials doubted both Squam's claim to being the chief of the Teslin Indians[36] and his attachment to the land in question; his request was denied.[37]

The Natives did not hesitate to defend their interests, but they only occasionally based their appeals to government on inherent rights of occupation. Instead, protests over game laws or inappropriate regulations focused on economic hardship or specific instances of non-Native encroachment.[38] That the Natives did not systematically defend their right to game does not suggest a lack of interest. Rather, it indicates their confidence that their use of resources and occupation of the land would continue unchallenged.

The government's concern, illustrated in Oliver's comments, centred on maintaining the Indians in their traditional role as hunters and trappers. From 1894 to 1950 government officials had little commitment to assimilation, except as a distant goal unlikely of accomplishment. Instead, federal authorities attempted to preserve the "Indian way." To achieve this, the government felt it had to insulate the Indians from the questionable benefits of the mining industry and the depredations of the non-Native population. Rather than high-lighting its assimilationist objectives, then, the government empha-sized the need to protect the Natives from destruction. These goals of assimilation and protection contained a number of internal ten-sions. As one scholar has commented:

From its [the Indian Act of 1876] initial promulgation, there have been those who have questioned the sanity of a piece of legislation which actively dis-couraged, and indeed in some areas positively prohibited, the assimilation of the Indian into the social and economic life of the non-native population, while at the same time being the centrepiece of a broad policy of moving the Indians towards full citizenship and full participation in Canadian life. By existing to regulate and systemize the relationship between the Indian and the majority society, the [Indian] Act codifies and often exaggerates the dis-tinctions which it is its functions eventually to eliminate.[39]

In the Yukon Territory the government initially favoured protection over assimilation. They chose to leave the Indians as hunters and trappers until they, and the Yukon, were ready and prepared for incorporation into Canadian society.[40] Government policy focused on two principal objectives: providing Natives with living space on small residential reserves and preserving Indian access to harvestable resources. In the latter case, not surprisingly, Native needs were rou-tinely subordinated to the requirements of the non-Native popula-tion, particularly the resource-development sector.

The desire to enforce social segregation first surfaced in 1896, with the start of the Klondike gold rush. William Bompas requested a small reserve near Dawson City to keep his Native communicants apart from the miners. Over the objections of NWMP Inspector Con-stantine and Yukon Commissioner William Ogilvie, who did not believe that the Indians needed or deserved a special allocation of land near Dawson City, the DIA allocated a small plot for exclusive Native use, having first required the Natives to "relinquish any claim, so far as the Department is concerned, to the site of the old Indian village at Klondak."[41] The 160-acre parcel was three miles downstream from Dawson, not as far away as Constantine and Ogilvie wished.[42] The government rejected repeated requests for an extension of the reserve on the basis of Ogilvie's representation that "discoveries of gold have been made in that vicinity, and before I recommend any extension of the 160 acres, I will await the development of this ground, as gold mining ground."[43]

The federal government followed this policy of establishing resi-dential reserves whenever lands were subjected to development pressure or when Natives moved too close to a non-Native settlement. As noted earlier, when Mayo expanded due to the development of nearby silver and lead mines, several Indians moved into town. The government quickly laid out a residential reserve, two-and-one-half miles downstream, and on the opposite side of the river, a decision the surveyor said "appears to fulfill all local requirements and to satisfy the Indians except, maybe, a few squaws."[44] The Mayo reserve met both of the government's criteria, removing the Indians from potentially valuable land and protecting them from non-Native influences. Over the following years Indian Agent John Hawksley lauded the positive results of the transfer.[45] But securing such a reserve did not guarantee permanence. If the non-Natives demanded access to land granted to the Indians, the government lost no time in relocating the reserve. In the Whitehorse area, for example, the reserve was shifted several times between 1915 and 1921.[46] While non-Native interests determined many reserve allotments, federal authorities occasionally permitted Native needs to govern land selection. In 1898 at Tagish and again at Little Salmon in 1915, the government preserved Native access to community land from non-Native encroachment.[47] As the federal surveyors responsible for laying out the Little Salmon reserve noted, however, "It is a matter of record that the Indians have not made any request for this reserve."[48]

The Yukon situation paralleled experiences elsewhere in Canada: Native reserves were constantly subjected to non-Native encroachment and reallocations.[49] The distinctiveness of the Yukon lay in the use of residential reserves – small parcels of land destined to serve as little more than seasonal homes. In the southern provinces, where hope persisted that the Natives would become agriculturalists, the Natives received larger land allocations.[50] These reserves were targeted as much at the non-Natives as the Natives, as regulations declared all official reserves as off-limits to everyone except the Indians.[51]

The government applied the residential-reserve concept, usually according to the Mayo plan, throughout the territory. In addition to the Mayo, Little Salmon, and Whitehorse allotments, the DIA established reserves at Carcross, Teslin, Selkirk, Carmacks, and Old Crow. The government's attempt to encourage Native settlement on lands removed from centres of non-Native population served as an integral part of a larger plan. Founded on the belief that the future of the nomadic hunting Indians lay in the preservation of their "natural" state, the plan served to enhance the social distance between Natives and non-Natives and to keep the Indians on the fringes of the Yukon's social and economic life.[52]

Table 26
Residential Reserves,[1] Yukon Territory, 1900–58

Location	Acreage	Year Granted
Moosehide Creek no. 2	158.49	1900
Lake Laberge no. 1	320.27	1900
McQueston no. 3	320.00	1904
Carcross no. 4	160.03	1905
Whitehorse no. 8	282.00	1921
Carmacks no. 11	330.80	1926
Teslin Post no. 13	65.23	1941
Nisutlin no. 14	207.40	1941
Burwash Landing	160.00	1953
Old Crow	112.80	1956
Six Mile Creek (Marsh Lake no. 5)	320.00	1956
Mayo no. 5	456.00	1956
Selkirk no. 7	159.98	1956
Little Salmon River no. 10	587.00	1956
Teslin Lake I.R. no. 15	166.49	–
Upper Liard Bridge	120.10	–
Champagne Landing no. 12	15.91	–

Source   Indian Affairs Branch, active files, 801/30–0–1, "Schedule of Lands Reserved for Indians,
Yukon Territory," Bethune to superintendent of reserves and trusts, 1958.
[1] Reserves active as of 1958.

Restricting Native access to the non-Natives world served little purpose without an alternative; the second component of the federal
government objective – preserving Native access to resources – provided the desired substitute. Almost all missionaries, police officers,
and government agents despaired of the prospects of the Natives
accepting "civilization," at least in the foreseeable future. Most
observers accepted the fact that the Natives had to hunt and fish in
order to survive. To that end, Native access to resources had to be
assured. Accomplishing this goal proved relatively easy, in practice
if not in principle, for few non-Natives competed for game stocks.
None the less, there was grave concern that the situation might
change. Market hunters in the Mayo and Dawson areas, and trophy
hunters in the southern Yukon, competed aggressively with the
Natives; the decline of game in these areas foreshadowed future problems.

While most could agree on the need to preserve Native access to
game, finding practical means proved difficult. As evident with residential reserves, Native rights seldom gained high priority within
the government, frequently being pushed aside in favour of concerns
about future development. In the short term, the attention given the

matter aided the Natives' interests. Limited non-settlement and restricted mining activity left the Natives substantially unchallenged in their hunting and trapping pursuits. Several proposals emerged to entrench this Native relationship to the land, including Acting Commissioner J.T. Lithgow's 1907 suggestion that all the Natives in the territory be removed to the Peel-Porcupine district, an area believed to be devoid of mineral resources.[53] It was agreed, early in the twentieth century, that the Natives should be exempt from most provisions – excepting those relating to conservation of threatened game stocks – of the Yukon Territorial Game Act.[54] Not until the 1930s, when increased hunting pressure and improving fur markets threatened Yukon game resources, was serious consideration given to suggestions for Native-only game preserves.

Preserves had been created, allegedly with success, for the Natives in the Mackenzie River valley. Once more, however, the government hesitated to extend such protection to the mineral-rich Yukon.[55] The first proposal for a large-scale preserve emerged in 1935. Indian Agent Harper Reed requested that the DIA take action to protect Native hunting in the upper Liard district.[56] The police failed to substantiate Reed's claims of over-trapping, but his proposal collapsed on other grounds. Charles Camsell, the deputy minister of the Department of Mines and a noted northern surveyor, made the federal government's priorities for the Yukon very clear: "If we are not going to reserve our northern regions exclusively for the use of the native but are looking to encourage the opening up of these regions to the people of Canada generally, then I think we must limit the extent of the preserves to meet the pressing needs of the natives but no more."[57] Development – not Native access to game – took precedence in the Yukon.

When several non-Native trappers began exploiting the Old Crow flats muskrat harvest in 1929 and when others competed for fish and fur resources in the Little Atlin district in 1932, government agents swiftly protected Native interests.[58] There were clear limits to the level of intervention, however. The government maintained a solid commitment to protecting Native hunting and fishing rights, but recoiled at the suggestion that those rights be entrenched through game preserves or special hunting regulations.

Continued non-Native hunting pressure, particularly during the construction of the Alaska Highway, led to increased concern for the future of Native hunting. As already recounted, in 1947 Indian Agent R.J. Meek requested the implementation of registered traplines, a program used to good effect in northern British Columbia. Under Meek's plan, the Natives had first claim to trapping territories, with "half-breeds" and "old-timers" also making their selection before the remaining lands were allocated.[59] The registration program, implemented by the territorial government in 1950, was clearly a second-best option to proposals for Native-only game preserves, but to 1950 it represented the limit of federal generosity and commitment.[60]

Federal authorities, supported by territorial officials, consistently supported the concept of leaving the Natives as hunters and trappers. The imperatives of northern development, however, impinged on the logical application of this idea. The Yukon was viewed as a national resource base. Consequently, the government would not guarantee Native access to game, for to do so would interfere with mineral exploration. Indian interests were regularly subordinated to the more pressing national concern for economic development. Indeed, Native access to game lost out even to sport hunting, which gradually emerged as a potential growth industry. As R.H. Gibson noted, "there has always been a fundamental difference in wild life management in the Yukon and the Northwest Territories. In the Yukon hunting for sport has been encouraged. In the Northwest Territories the wild life is reserved for those who depend on it for a living, chiefly our increasing population of Indians and Eskimos."[61]

As of 1950 most of the Yukon Indians remained hunters and trappers, resorting to towns only as season and need dictated. While the government's program of economic and social segregation appeared successful, more important forces had actually worked to keep Natives and non-Natives apart. Limited mining, the small non-Native population, a strong fur market, and the Natives' affinity for hunting and trapping over industrial labour ensured that the Indians remained Indians. The government succeeded, it seems, in spite of itself; its programs of residential reserves and economic segregation functioned more as symbols than as effective policies. To a certain extent, then, government programs for the Yukon Natives seldom extended beyond accepting the *status quo*. The DIA attempted to solidify and entrench the Natives' position as hunters and gatherers through government initiative, but only to the extent possible within its limited mandate.

Federal government programming for the Yukon Indians strayed significantly from the national priorities outlined in the Indian Act. The encouragement of self-sufficiency and provision of protection from non-Native society are evident in the policies discussed above. The government, moreover, shied away from a commitment to assimilation, allegedly the cornerstone of national Indian policy. The ready acceptance of a "best left as Indians policy" from 1894 to 1950 stands in marked contrast to the cultural imperialism typically associated with federal Indian policy. This contradiction may have been inherent in the government's program, as the dedication to protection and self-sufficiency almost by definition interfered with attempts at assimilation. The guidelines in the Indian Act, however, also allowed for a certain flexibility, permitting government agents in the field and Ottawa to adapt national policy to local conditions. Given the limited development prospects for the territory and the substantial socio-cultural barriers (both Native and non-Native) to Native participation in the industrial economy, the government's acceptance of the Natives as hunters and trappers was no doubt both logical and cost-effective. The creation of residential reserves and the response to Native demands for protection of hunting, fishing, and trapping rights evolved on an *ad hoc* basis amidst changing territorial conditions.

Government agents charged with administering Native affairs spent most of their time and money on more routine matters, including the provision of relief and health care. These benefits were provided in absence of a treaty, which the government studiously avoided. As Clifford Sifton, minister of the interior, commented in 1903, government policy was "to treat them with humanity and with a reasonable degree of liberality, and on the whole that is the most economical policy."[62] This willingness to assist the Indians in times of hardship was based on a general belief that the arrival of whites had caused considerable hardship for the indigenous population.

Indian Affairs' involvement with the Yukon Natives, therefore, stopped short of a negotiated settlement, but went beyond the much more narrow limits suggested by Peter Usher in his study of the Canadian north: "The government had sought to remove any encumbrances to land title and settlement and the police maintained law and order. Beyond these measures, however, the government failed to detect any responsibility on its part for those people over whose territories it had assumed control."[63] Usher's analysis may apply to other northern districts, but it falls short of capturing the nature of government initiatives for Native people in the Yukon Territory.

Government assistance to Native people began with the arrival of the NWMP in 1894. Although Inspector Constantine was enjoined from encouraging treaty negotiations, he was authorized to provide medical care and relief. With the establishment of the Yukon Territory as an administrative unit in 1898, many of the fiscal responsibilities passed to the office of the commissioner, although police officers continued to provide the actual aid.[64] The Anglican Church and other officials tried to convince the government that a full-time agent was required. A.W. Vowell and A.E. Green endorsed the church's demand: "What is required most particularly is an officer whose special duty it will be to look after the Indians, advising them as to all measures calculated to assure their advancement and welfare; protecting them against the machinations of the evilly disposed and to report faithfully to the Department from time to time upon all matters affecting the wards of the Government."[65] Finally, in 1914, the government appointed a full-time Indian agent. The posting fell to John Hawksley, a long-time northern missionary. Hawksley treated his new position as an extension of his former duties, paying particular attention to the Indians' moral and medical condition.[66] Far from being an interventionist, the agent prided himself on the fact that "the Indians feel they have a place to go when they are in trouble where they can be advised and helped; they appreciate it very much."[67] Following Hawksley's retirement in 1933, the duties of Indian Agent reverted to the police. Each year the force delegated one officer to be responsible for territorial Indian matters, a task that it tried to pass on to other government agencies.[68] Clearly, the limited priority given territorial Native affairs had slipped further.[69] From 1914 to 1946 the office of the Indian agent served primarily as an administrative centre, dispensing relief, organizing medical and educational programs, and reporting regularly to the Ottawa office. When R.J. Meek, a former BC provincial police officer from the Telegraph Creek area, received an appointment as full-time agent in 1946, the position took on greater importance as a result of changing government priorities and Meek's activism. From Constantine to Meek, however, individuals responsible for the administration of Indian affairs found themselves preoccupied with assisting the Indians in adjusting to the dislocations attending non-Native expansion.

The most important of these duties involved the dispensing of relief payments or emergency supplies. A myth developed in the 1900 to 1950 period concerning the Natives' willingness to accept relief. The standard impression was that the Indians readily surrendered to the convenience of government assistance, abandoning more rigorous pursuits in favour of begging for scraps at the Indian agent's table. Those administering the relief program in the Yukon almost universally shared this belief and their attitudes played a major role in shaping the program. But the image misrepresented Native interest in government handouts.

Federal officials were extremely reluctant to make relief payments too readily available. They clung to the assumption – not dissimilar to that held about charity and the non-Native poor – that easy access to government support would invite laziness and dependence.[70] Further, the commissioner of the Yukon argued in 1900, "The Indian knows that if any help is to be extended to him at all he will simply sit down and almost starve before he makes any effort to help himself."[71] Functioning without official commitment, police officers provided only occasional relief supplies to truly destitute individuals. Faced with the potential starvation of a small band of Indians at Moosehide in 1900, however, regional officials were forced into more substantial and precedent-setting action. NWMP Inspector Z.T. Wood of Dawson authorized immediate disbursements of food (ten lbs of flour, five lbs of oats and rice, and two lbs of tea for ten or twelve Natives)[72] to contain the crisis, applying for official permission later.[73] The government insisted that "whenever possible the Indians would be required to perform labour or supply game, skins or other commodities in return for the provisions issued to them." In the short term, however, police officers were authorized to "provide against anything like destitution."[74]

From the turn of the century, the government provided relief to those who could demonstrate need. Not many took up the offer, and so the welfare rolls were limited to a few widowed, aged, or infirm Natives.[75] The list of people receiving relief at Carcross in 1902 included William, an invalid; Maggie, a widow with two girls to support; Ellen, an elderly widow with a single child; and David, an old man without any surviving family members.[76] In 1925 the only people receiving relief allotments at Old Crow were several elderly couples, including "John Kwatlatee and his wife, Charlie Ilsoo and his wife, Baalam's mother (who is nearly totally blind) and Matilda."[77] The relief system occasionally responded to more serious destitution, as occurred in 1905 near McQuesten and in 1912 in the southern Yukon, when game supplies unexpectedly declined.[78] Despite the fact that few laid claim to the government's generosity, the police officers in charge of the program before 1914 believed that the availability of relief rendered the Indians beggars. The commanding officer of the Whitehorse detachment commented in 1908, "It is evident that the government assistance given to sick and destitute Indians at Whitehorse is most injurious to the well-being and morale of the Indians." He then proceeded to ascribe alcohol abuse, prostitution, and general laziness to the "pernicious effect" of relief.[79] As a countermeasure, the police imposed mechanisms to guard against anticipated abuse. Inspector Horrigan noted in 1912 that "young husky Indians asking for provisions were asked to split some stove wood. Needless to say in every case they found that after all they did not require provisions. This plan has worked admirably in weeding out the undeserving cases."[80] Those in need received government assistance but, convinced that the Natives were inveterate malingerers, police officers closely regulated their allotments.

Under Hawksley, the relief program expanded considerably. The new Indian agent relied on his former missionary colleagues to assist him, also allowing police officers and even fur traders to allocate supplies when deemed necessary.[81] The relief allotments were not, in any case, particularly generous.[82] Orders issued in 1915 to Anglican missionaries, who were authorized by the Indian agent to distribute relief, indicate the scope of the assistance. One ration could cost from $10 to $15 and was to include flour, tea, sugar, bacon or lard, beans, rice, pilot bread, and prunes or dried applies. No more than ten pounds of sugar could be given per month and no tobacco was to be given. Up to three boxes of ammunition could be given to "an able bodied Indian." Any requests for clothing had first to be cleared through the Indian agent.[83] Neil MacDonald, a trader at Old Crow, complained about the parsimonious grant of $5 a month per family for rations, claiming that it fell far short of the cost of basic necessities.[84]

Even with the expanded networks, there is no indication that the Natives found relief irresistible. Faced with rigorous government strictures on assistance, only the truly destitute applied for aid; as Assistant Commissioner Wood noted in 1904, "There is very little poverty among them, and absolute want is unknown. When necessary, rations are issued to the old and indigent."[85] The news from Dawson City, where there was far more intense competition for game, was different: "The necessity of providing some fixed government assistance is becoming more apparent with the lapse of time and the more marked inability of the Indians to provide for themselves."[86] Here the Natives were hardly different from those few non-Natives who depended on wild game for sustenance. When resources were exhausted or grubstakes dwindled, non-Native trappers and prospectors similarly fell back on meagre government handouts. For Natives and non-Natives alike, the relief system provided an important safety net during those times when other means of support failed.

In offering such aid, the government did not assume a great responsibility. Yet it did accept an obligation to compensate those who suffered through non-Native expansion. This willingness to assist the Indians was not a declared national objective. Instead, as with much government activity on the Natives' behalf, federal authorities responded to local exigencies. In these administrative areas, as with broader policy concerns, regional realities conditioned the scope and effectiveness of federal Native programs.

While few Natives appear to have suffered persistent economic distress, many felt the ravages of imported diseases; a sizeable majority of those on relief accepted aid due to illness. The government provided what was, under the circumstances, a relatively comprehensive medical care program. NWMP surgeons offered assistance to Natives whenever required. By 1905 the government had replaced the *ad hoc* reliance on police personnel with a more permanent and professional system. The DIA placed four doctors on permanent retainer. The doctors then treated Natives as required, receiving $2 per consultation. When authorized to do so by a government official, Indians could visit the doctor, receive free medicine, treatments, and even hospitalization. The Natives patronized the system. In 1902 the two busiest doctors, NWMP surgeon G. Madore and L.S. Sugden, received $1,516 and $1,113 respectively, accounting for more than 1,300 visits between them.[87] By the time John Hawksley became Indian agent in 1914, the government had decided to put two doctors, W.B. Clark of Whitehorse and J.O. Lachapelle of Dawson, on $1200-a-year retainers.[88] All Natives were covered, although those of means were expected to pay their own bills. When Skookum Jim Mason, co-discoverer of the Klondike strike, fell ill in 1916, the DIA refused to pay the $100 hospital charge.[89]

The provision of medical care was not restricted to the major settlements, for the doctors occasionally visited the outlying settlements. Visitations did not always proceed smoothly, as Dr Lachapelle discovered when he arrived at Little Salmon in 1916. The doctor had not warned the resident missionary, Cecil Swanson, of his visit, nor did he include him on his rounds. Swanson was angered by the slight, by LaChapelle's failure to draw on his knowledge of the Indians, and by the doctor's handling of local cases: "If the government prefer to have tubercular patients examined, and glands lanced, and so forth, in the midst of eatables, I will not say them nay."[90] This particular venture was apparently less than successful, but at least doctors were making an effort to extend their activities beyond the largest centres.

The federal government's provision of medical care was particularly evident during epidemics. Recognizing these diseases as non-Native importations, the government did whatever possible to limit or prevent the devastation commonly associated with the attacks. As with most programs for the Indians, other considerations also came into play. Diseases carried by the nomadic Natives threatened the more sedentary non-Native population; therefore, it served everyone's interest to prevent the spread of illness, because containing the epidemics in the Indian camps functioned as an important form of preventative medicine for the entire territory.[91] Still although its motives may have been mixed, the government responded quickly to each appearance of a potential epidemic. Quarantines served to limit the spread of disease; grants of food rations and medical care assisted those under surveillance. This system, imposed regularly throughout the territory, worked in combination with regular medical attendance to provide for the immediate health-care needs of those Natives close enough to non-Native settlements to receive attention.[92] It also deviated from the central tenets of the government's Native policy. Instead of "improving" Native life, it served primarily to offset dislocations resulting from non-Native expansion.

While the federal government had some latitude in the area of medical care, it had less freedom with regard to enforcing Canadian laws. From 1894, when the first representatives of the NWMP reached the Yukon River valley, through to 1950, federal authorities insisted that the national police force bring the Natives under the protection and control of the Canadian legal system. Policing the Natives was usually a small component of the NWMP's duties in the territory, particularly during the Klondike gold rush, when its efforts focused on controlling the mass influx of miners and camp followers. None the less, the police had more extensive contact with the Yukon Natives than did the representatives of any other federal agency.[93]

The police undertook Indian work in the north with little enthusiasm. Inspector Constantine's early assessment of the Yukon Natives as a "lazy and shiftless lot" was echoed by other officers and this perception changed little over time.[94] Consistently prodded by missionaries and government representatives, however, the police reluctantly accepted a supervisory role over the Native population. Over the next half-century, the force attempted to maintain a vigilant watch over its Native charges, and soon came to appreciate their generally law-abiding character. As one government official noted of the Copper Indians in a particularly telling comment, "They are fairly intelligent, and were quite honest before they were influenced by the white man."[95]

Hindered by their small numbers, the vast distances of the territory, and the scattered Native population, the NWMP could offer only a cursory supervision of Native activities. Posts were established primarily with the needs of the non-Native population in mind (although stations were opened at Teslin and Dalton Post with a view to stopping cross-border traffic in alcohol). The network of posts was supplemented by an extensive patrolling system, with police officers undertaking lengthy journeys through poorly served areas in order to deliver mail, provide relief or medical supplies, assert Canadian sovereignty, or investigate reported crimes. The NWMP thus reached into every corner of the territory, although back-country districts were generally poorly supervised.[96]

Working under such limitations, the police took care not to push the letter of the law too firmly. When dealing with Dawson City prostitutes, for example, the NWMP surrendered to public pressure and allowed the ladies to ply their trade in specified districts.[97] The police were particularly lenient with the Natives, in recognition of their generally law-abiding nature and of the impracticality of providing direct supervision over a widely dispersed population. Every effort was made, although not always successfully, to convince governments to exclude the Natives from the provisions of territorial game laws. When individual Natives breached the official regulations, the police treated the offenders with discretion.[98] Like other government agencies, the NWMP believed that the Natives should remain as hunters and trappers, an attitude revealed both in their flexibility concerning game laws and in their willingness to comply with extralegal attempts to keep the Indians out of the towns.

The Natives generally respected the NWMP and acknowledged that the police frequently acted in their interests. Missionaries and government agents similarly believed the police to be a positive influence. In 1931 John Hawksley requested that the Fort Selkirk detachment be reopened. The departure of the police, the Indian agent argued, had led to a serious increase in drinking and violent behaviour.[99] Inspector Horrigan's intervention in a near-battle between Blind Creek and Pelly River Indian bands in 1909 illustrated a more direct approach. The crisis had developed after Liard Bob of the Pelly Indians killed Jonathan, from Blind Creek, allegedly in self-defence. Jonathan's kin arrived *en masse* at Ross River, demanding retribution in the form of 1,000 blankets and 30 rifles. Horrigan arranged a meeting between the bands. His threat of incarceration for the band leaders, and a promise by the Pelly Creek band to provide 500 blankets and 5 rifles, led to a negotiated peace.[100] In this and other cases, the Natives accepted policemen in their role as law enforcers.

Natives did not, however, offer unquestioning obedience to all the dictates of the Canadian police force. The continual flouting of the liquor laws was only the most obvious sign that the Natives did not always abide by police direction. Government officials knew of the problem, among both Natives and non-Natives, but rejected suggestions that penalties for alcohol-related offences be increased.[101] When the NWMP opened an establishment at Dalton Post, the Indians simply ignored the authorities, crossed into American territory, and consumed alcohol beyond police control.[102] Similarly, the force's occasional inability to punish offenders restricted its effectiveness. Knowing themselves to be far from the Dawson courts, the Old Crow Indians repeatedly and publicly ignored proscriptions on gambling and drinking. The Natives had correctly identified a weakness in the Canadian legal system – in this case, the police's unwillingness to incur heavy costs to punish those charged with minor offences.[103] The federal government moved to resolve the problem by appointing Anglican clergyman A.C. McCullum as justice of the peace, but the missionary left the area before his commission arrived.[104] The threat of punishment, particularly incarceration, was a powerful deterrent to the Natives. Without the effective use of this deterrent, however, the Indians cheerfully ignored the local police.

Government officials hoped that the Indians could be convinced to control their own communities.[105] In March 1921 the Moosehide Indians established a village council to regulate the behaviour of their community. The seven-member council was not structured along traditional lines. It was headed by Esau Harper, while Chief Isaac was vice-chairman. The council gave itself authority to keep the village clean, care for the sick and aged, enforce school attendance, supervise relations between husbands and wives, and punish men and women who broke community standards, particularly as regards drinking.[106]

At its first meeting, the Moosehide council passed a number of resolutions which no doubt pleased John Hawksley. It ordered girls to stop "going with white people" and ordered all non-Natives to stay off the reserve. Children were to attend school regularly and were to be in bed by 9 p.m. In addition, all Natives had to leave Dawson City an hour before that curfew. Single women were not allowed to stay in Dawson after 7 p.m. unless they were with a married woman. Men could not stay in town overnight unless they were accompanied by a "comrade." Men were ordered to collect wood and water for their families. Nor was this all. Chewing tobacco, allegedly a form of spreading disease, was not to be shared; dogs were not permitted in houses; each home was to have a slop-pail in the house and was to dispose of the water in a safe fashion. Other regulations were added as conditions warranted.

Over the coming months, the council met regularly and carried out its mandate. It was a remarkably intrusive agency, ordering men to pay attention to their wives, fining individuals known to have been drinking, and interceding in a case involving a Native girl and her non-Native employer. Still, the all-male council acted in a consistent fashion. Its priorities, as demonstrated by its decisions, were to keep families together, limit Native access to Dawson City, and enforce certain standards of behaviour on the people of Moosehide.

Within a year of its formation, community members were grumbling openly about the council's authoritarian activities. According to the minutes for 23 March 1922, Chief Isaac called for the selection of new councillors to overcome some of the bitterness of the first year. Although Tom Young supported the council, he noted that "the people don't like Council because they want to do what they like. They don't like council telling them to keep their home clean and clean the village." Sam Smith argued, "When I first came here Government helped the people, when hungry when sick and died, they have taken good care of the people & I think that the people should do what the gov't wants them to do."

The criticisms were evidently heard, for the Moosehide council was not nearly as interventionist in subsequent years. In as much as the minutes (which run to 1936) indicate the scope of its activities, the council became less prone to hand out stiff fines or intercede in domestic struggles. It tried to prevent alcohol consumption, encouraged people to maintain clean houses, and devoted particular effort to keeping the village tidy. Council also served as a major focus for community collections, celebrations (usually Christian festivals), and improvement projects. There were occasionally more direct interventions. At a meeting on 8 April 1929, council considered a complaint from C. Mason that his wife, Annie, refused to accompany him to Twelve Mile. In December 1935 the council met with Indian Agent G. Binning to discuss the possible replacement of Chief Charlie Isaac, who was charged with being out of town too often. Although Isaac was not terribly enthusiastic about holding onto the position, he was reconfirmed, only to be replaced by Jonas John one month later.

The federal government could not, and did not, always rely on such formal structures as a means of influencing the Native people of the Yukon. Political-administrative structures were only partially formed. In a 1932 review of the band-and-council structure in the Yukon, Hawksley found that Moosehide now had a chief and three-person council; Old Crow had a chief and two councillors; Mayo had a chief and a single councillor; and at Selkirk, Whitehorse, and Teslin Lake, there was only a chief (the election of a chief for Carmacks was pending). At the other settlements, the "bands have no chiefs, usually one of the older men take the lead but cannot be called chiefs."[107] The government did not favour regular elections for Yukon Indians; as the territorial Indian agent declared in 1929, "When an Indian is elected and approved as Chief he is the recognized chief for the rest of his life."[108]

A territory-wide system of elected band councils was created gradually after the Second World War. When the structure came into general use, the band councils did not have complete independence. In 1950 Indian Agent R.J. Meek learned that Joe Netro, a councillor with the Old Crow, had been publicly criticizing Chief Peter Moses. Meek reminded Netro that Moses was well regarded by the government (he had been named to the Order of the British Empire for his fundraising efforts during the war). Making no attempt to disguise his threat, Meek told Netro, "I have heard of men losing their appointments as Councillor for things like that."[109] Clearly, Native councillors were not expected to exercise much independence; from the beginning, their task was to explain the work of the government to the local Natives.

With a few modest exceptions, therefore, the task of administering and controlling the Native population fell to the police who, initially, had grave reservations about their Native charges. Following the murder of a miner in the southern Yukon in 1899, Superintendent Sam Steele noted, "The Indians of this country are as treacherous as any in the North-West Territories."[110] However, these fears proved groundless, since the incidence of serious crime among the Yukon Indians proved remarkably low.[111] It is, of course, difficult to assess the actual extent of Native crime, especially given the glaring gaps in the police network and court records. Indian offences against non-Natives were generally recorded; indeed, the tendency was to attribute most unsolved minor thefts to the Natives, often without cause.[112] Conversely, crimes against Natives normally attracted attention only if violence was involved. Prospectors' reports, such as the 1921 rumour that the White River Indians were planning a raid on the Tanana,[113] led to the commissioning of special investigative patrols, which overwhelmingly refuted the miners' accounts.

The number of recorded crimes involving Natives remained small throughout the period in question. There were, as would be expected, occasional murders, assaults, and thefts. Acts of violence were usually directed against other Natives. The murder of Pelly Jim by Jackie Mackintosh in Whitehorse in 1926 and Paddy Duncan's slaying of Martin Kane at Champagne the next year were rare events and, like most others, involved drunkenness.[114] Natives were seldom implicated in serious crimes against non-Natives, and the reverse was also true. A notable exception occurred in 1899 when two prospectors were attacked, apparently without provocation. One died, while the other, feigning death, escaped to report the crime. Five Natives were apprehended, with the assistance of Chief Jim Boss, who convinced the suspects to surrender to police.[115] The five were delivered to Dawson City where they were speedily tried and all but one executed.[116] This case notwithstanding, the low incidence of interracial crime is a

Table 27
Native Crimes, Whitehorse Police Court, 1900–49

Year	Whites Supplying Liquor	Natives Supplying Liquor	Drunk	Possession of Liquor	Theft	Assault	Other
1900–04	26	3	29	2	3	5	4
1905–09	23	2	30	1	1	4	–
1910–14	22	5	27	10	1	3	4
1915–19	6	–	6	–	–	–	–
1920–24	4	1	4	3	1	–	7
1925–29	15	6	35	9	–	1	1
1930–34	9	7	24	2	3	1	6
1935–39	8	4	32	2	–	1	3
1940–44	27	5	86	6	3	4	10
1945–49	52	5	265	31	–	1	15

Source NA, RG18, Whitehorse Police Court Register, 1899–1949.

further indication of the limited amount of contact between Natives and non-Natives in the Yukon.

Evidence in police-court records points to a consistently low crime rate (although a caveat must be entered: reported and punished crime represents an unknown portion of actual offences). The 744 prisoners who passed through the Dawson jail during 1900 included only 7 Natives and 3 mixed-bloods. Three years later, only 2 of 365 were Native; in 1904 the comparable figures were 7 of 292. Even following the decline of Dawson City's population after 1904, which left the police free to devote more attention to the Natives, the incidence of Native crime remained low. In 1909 the number of Native convictions rose to 19 of 171; in 1912, 32 of 233, and in 1916 only 13 of 197.[117] The Whitehorse police court register for 1900 to 1949 reveals a similar pattern. In sum, court records, supported by police reports, suggest that the Natives were non-violent (especially towards non-Natives) and law-abiding. Most Native convictions in both Whitehorse and Dawson involved the consumption of alcohol, an offence treated by the police more as a nuisance than as a serious breach of the law.

The courts treated Native offenders leniently, partly because of the positive relationship between Natives and the police. Aware that punishments for the numerous alcohol-related offences were of limited deterrence-valve, and reluctant to blame the Natives for depredations inflicted by non-Natives, court officials viewed penalties for such offences as little more than a drinking tax. The Natives rarely challenged the charges, most pleading guilty, paying their fines, and taking their leave. For Natives, penalties for alcohol-related offences

Table 28
Royal Canadian Mounted Police, Distribution of Officers, 1904–50
(Selected Years and Posts)

Year	Dawson	Whitehorse	Old Crow	Selkirk	Teslin	Carcross	Yukon Total
1904	96	70	0	6	0	2	296
1910	33	12	0	1	0	1	60
1917	27	9	1	0	0	1	45
1925	15	9	2	0	1	1	38
1930	22	8	3	0	1	1	46
1935	20	3	1	1	1	1	33
1940	11	3	2	1	1	0	20
1943	12	7	3	2	2	2	34
1945	3	17	2	1	3	1	33
1947	4	19	2	1	2	0	38
1950	4	18	2	0	1	0	32

Source   RCMP, *Annual Reports* 1904–50.

usually consisted of a $5 to $10 fine, although repeat offenders faced short-term imprisonment – a punishment that the Natives did not view as seriously as did non-Natives. The courts and the police dealt more firmly with non-Natives accused of giving or selling liquor to the Indians. In such instances the standard sentence included a $100 fine (still really just a tax, given the high profits to be made bootlegging), six months in jail, or both. In 1900, to provide but one example, two non-Natives charged with giving liquor to Indians received fines of $100 and $10 costs; another individual, D. Ripstein, charged with selling alcohol to Natives, was fined $200 and $10 costs, and was sentenced to two months of hard labour.[118] Repeat offenders faced even more serious penalties.[119]

Under the Indian Act of 1876, Natives in Canada were barred from consuming alcoholic beverages.[120] The interdiction was designed to protect the Natives from the negative influences of liquor while simultaneously protecting the non-Native population from the unpredictable actions of inebriated Indians.[121] Non-Natives in the Yukon, particularly government agents and Anglican clergymen, shared the widely held view that alcohol debauched the Indians and instigated anti-social and violent behaviour. They therefore insisted that the police control the liquor trade.[122] From 1894 to 1950 the bulk of police activities relating to Natives revolved around the ongoing and largely unsuccessful attempt to prevent Native consumption of alcohol, an effort directed largely at the non-Natives supplying the Indians.

The police did not always prosecute offenders with the zeal that missionaries and temperance advocates would have liked. In 1908

Dawson Charlie, co-discoverer of the Klondike gold-fields and a man noted for sharing his wealth with friends and relatives,[123] was drinking at the Caribou Hotel. He left, very intoxicated, and tried to cross the railway bridge to the Indian village on the other side of the river, only to fall to his death. The local clergy petitioned the police to prosecute the hotel for serving a Native person in breach of the Indian Act. Major Snyder of the Whitehorse detachment visited Carcross but, to the missionaries' fury, decided not to press charges.[124]

Nevertheless, the police did investigate reports of Native alcohol-use expeditiously, particularly those instances involving violence or death.[125] All police patrols paid special attention to the availability of liquor in remote districts.[126] Efforts to regulate the trade concentrated on two areas, Dalton Post and Teslin. The former was close to Haines, Alaska, where lax American enforcement ensured a ready supply of liquor. The Teslin Indians, similarly, had comparatively easy access through Atlin, BC. Reports of blatant use of alcohol in both areas led the police to open small detachments in Dalton Post in 1918 and Teslin in 1925.[127] Such efforts were successful in limiting the public consumption and sale of liquor, but the officers were not so naive as to believe they had eliminated the "evil." Wherever the police moved to restrict the use of alcohol, the Indians apparently responded by moving their drinking to private quarters or to camps away from the settlements.[128] Police enforcement of laws restricting Native access to alcohol did little more than push drinking out of the public view and back into the cabins and tents of the Indians and their non-Native drinking partners.

Through its legal and ancillary activities, the NWMP was actively involved with Natives throughout the Yukon Territory. Its attitudes and actions mirrored those of the larger civil service; it perceived its role as that of a buffer between the encroaching non-Native population and the still "unprepared" Natives. The Indians accepted the police's leadership, both because they respected the force and because they feared imprisonment. There were, none the less, limitations on police power. This was particularly evident in the attempts to regulate alcohol-use, which, despite a half-century of vigilance, continued as an important recreational activity among the Indians. Yet in general, federal police work in the north, like so many government programs before the Second World War, served as a palliative, designed to keep Natives and non-Natives apart and to counter the negative effects of non-Native expansion.

After 1945 federal activities in the Yukon underwent a dramatic shift, ushering in a new era of government-Native relations. Whereas the administration of Native affairs before the war had emerged out of a pessimistic assessment of territorial prospects, the striking increase in interventionism after 1945 reflected new national imperatives. The post-war commitment of the Liberal government to a national social-welfare system foreshadowed major new directions in government initiatives for all Canada.[129] While much of the increased intervention stemmed from national policies, including the introduction of the family allowance in 1944, other programs reflected changed conditions in the Yukon[130] and a very different federal attitude toward the Canadian north.[131] The construction of the Alaska Highway and the Canol Pipeline during the war altered social and economic realities just as a precipitous decline in fur prices undermined the viability of the Natives' hunting and trapping pursuits.

Much of the new policy involved an expansion of existing programs. The period 1945–50 saw the extension of medical care outside the Whitehorse-Dawson corridor, a territory-wide tuberculosis survey, the construction of a special tuberculosis wing at the Whitehorse General Hospital, the hiring of a public health nurse to administer routine medical services and offer health education, an immunization program, and special Native dental clinics. The government also fleshed out relief measures, particularly in the aftermath of the collapse of the fur trade,[132] although some of the imperatives of the old system, particularly those requiring able-bodied Native men to continue hunting and trapping, remained in place.[133] Indian agents tried to divert Natives from the welfare rolls, instead "assisting the Indians to be self-supporting and reliant." "Whenever possible," Meek stated, financial aid was "given to Indians to assist them in possible worthwhile fields of endeavour, in preference to direct relief."[134] The government moved with equal speed to expand educational offerings. Two new boarding schools opened between 1946 and 1950, and funding for day schools increased markedly. Significantly, schooling shifted its focus from basic literacy and arithmetic skills to an emphasis on industrial and technical training. As before, the myriad of medical and welfare programs available to Indians far exceeded those provided to the non-Native population.

Of all of the new federal initiatives in this period, the family allowance had the greatest impact. To qualify for the monthly allotment (variable by age of child), one had only to be a citizen of Canada and have children under the age of sixteen registered and attending school. The latter requirement was not immediately enforced in the Yukon, although as the school system expanded in the 1950s the government applied the regulations with increasing severity. Unlike most Canadians, including Indians in the provinces, Yukon Natives did not receive a regular cash payment. Afraid that the Indians'

Table 29
Federal Expenditures on Yukon Indians, 1900–50 (Yearly Averages in Current $)

Year	Admin.	Relief & Medical	Day Schools	Resid. Schools	Welfare	Medical	Total
1900–04[1]	–	4503	2139	–	–	–	6642
1905–09	–	5725	2996	–	–	–	8721
1910–14	1302[2]	18007[3]	2251	15916[4]	–	–	37476[5]
1915–19	3946	11698	3072	7833	–	–	26550
1920–24	3425	12276	2333	12966	–	–	31000
1925–29	3614	13296	3058	15895	–	–	35863
1930–34	2785[6]	–	2872	20972[7]	8836	9076	44541
1935–39	1011	–	4366	15459	9950	11572	42358
1940–44	665	–	4844	11145	11719	13309	41682
1945–49	7227[8]	–	23988[9]	17884	18287	–[10]	67385

Source   DIA, Annual Reports, 1900–50.
[1] Four years only. Net expenditures in 1900–01.
[2] Indian Agent hired in 1914.
[3] Includes expenses relating to Rampart House smallpox epidemic; 1911–12 – $25,000; 1912–13 – $15,100.
[4] Expenditure of more than $40,000 for construction of Carcross Residential School, 1911.
[5] Does not include incidental expenses.
[6] Indian agent retired in 1933; not replaced until 1946.
[7] Expenditure in excess of $48,000 in 1930–31 on construction.
[8] New Indian agent appointed in 1946.
[9] Expenditures increased by almost three times between 1946–47 and 1947–48.
[10] On 1 November 1945, Indian Health Services were transferred to the newly created Department of National Health and Welfare.

nomadic lifestyle would lead to waste of the federal grant, the federal government insisted upon issuing payments in kind. Although admitting that "because we know so little about actual conditions in the Yukon and Northwest Territories, we are thinking about this more or less in a vacuum," D.C. Rowat, in charge of the family allowances, concluded that "if allowances were paid in cash, they would not go to the benefit of the children."[135] Offering food and clothing instead of a cheque allowed the government to dictate Native purchases. Seeing little value in Native eating habits, authorities insisted that canned milk, tomatoes, and prepared baby foods be included in individual allocations.[136] The program had even larger implications than major alterations in diet and material culture. The requirement from the 1950s on that children attend schools regularly forced a difficult choice between seasonal mobility and a more sedentary existence. Father Dream described the impact on the Teslin Indians: "Other parents are sending their children to the Territorial School and making the vast sacrifice of staying here instead of being on their trapping grounds where they could live much better, until better provisions can be made for their children."[137] The government expanded its day-school and residential-school programs in the same period, drawing more and more children into its educational network and more families into permanent residence near the towns.

The federal government had started in a new direction in social programs after 1945 – for all Canadians, not just for the Native people. In the Yukon, government intervention increased as the federal bureaucracy sought new ways to improve the Natives' condition. Mothers' allowance, payments for the aged, housing projects, educational support, employment programs, and expanded welfare and medical care offered greatly enhanced government assistance to Native people and led to a general abandonment of the nomadic lifestyle. For the Yukon Natives, it was only in this later period that the federal government's Native policy approached the interventionist-assimilation program long assumed to have typified government-Native relations.[138]

In conclusion, the policy guidelines sketched in the Indian Act provided a framework within which government-Native relations functioned in the Yukon. Regional and national administrators exercised considerable latitude in relating national policy to local conditions. Of the four main elements of national policy, encouraging self-sufficiency (although in non-agricultural and non-industrial pursuits) and protecting Natives from the non-Native population dominated Yukon programming until the late 1940s. The creation of residential reserves and the protection of Native access to resources were the central features of the DIA's administration in the territory. Although Natives were constantly subordinated to a continued government concern for development, limited mining activity precluded any significant conflict over land or resources. The government avoided assimilationist programs, altering its schooling and expectations considerably, and asserting as late as 1950 that hunting and trapping offered the best prospects for the Yukon Indians. For their part, the Natives agreed with the government's position. The majority continued to prefer the still-economical pursuit of game over the meagre returns from occasional wage labour and government handouts.

Government Native policy in the Yukon both reflected and enhanced the Natives' continuing marginalization. Residential reserves represented a response to the exclusionist pressures from the non-Native community and the Indians' expectation of a seasonal home near population centres. Similarly, limited federal initiatives to protect Native access to game indicated the continuing importance of hunting, fishing, trapping, and gathering in the Indians' economic life. Like religious and educational encroachments, federal government programs did not serve to draw the Indians closer to the centre of the non-Native dominated regional order. Instead, non-Native exclusionism and the Natives' affinity for the harvesting lifestyle undermined the practicality of any programs that did not take into account continued Native mobility and the limited social and economic accommodation between the races in the Yukon.

Yukon Indians and the Changing North, 1950–1990

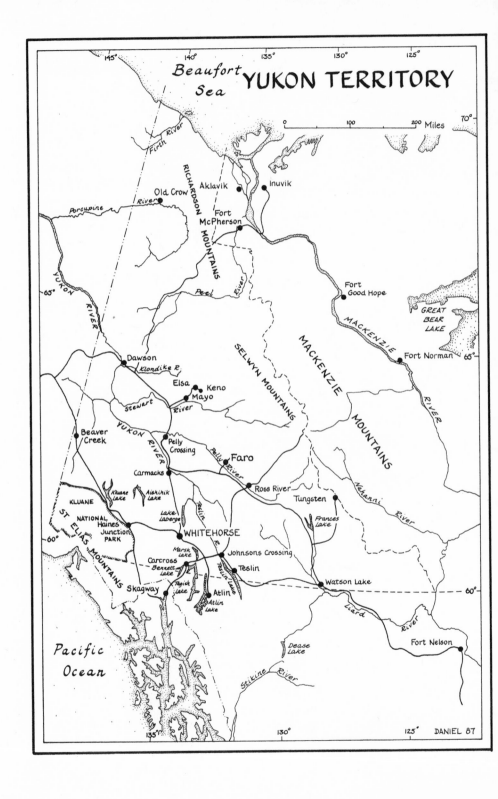

Yukon Indians and the Changing North, 1950–1990

With the completion of the Alaska Highway, the CANOL pipeline project, and the Northwest Staging Route airfields (collectively known as the Northwest Defence Projects) during the Second World War, the old order in the Yukon Territory quickly passed.[1] The construction of the Alaska Highway and Canol pipeline, combined with new airfields, additional roads, telephone lines, and ancillary projects, tore the region from its pre-war isolation and ensured that it would become an integral part of what Canadian promoters enthusiastically labelled the "New North."[2] One official wrote of this invasion: "The boom days of the war when the Alaska Highway and the Alcan pipeline were built accelerated the entire tempo of the North: standards were distorted, values skyrocketed, employment was easy (too easy), and the old values were never resumed."[3] Government and business anticipated that war-time construction would result in a resource boom.

Native people were not afforded pride of place in the new north. In the past, their mobile, harvesting lifestyle had been accepted as inevitable by government officials, missionaries, and others. But now, the non-Natives proclaimed, that would have to change. There would be no role in the modern north for "primitive" peoples; the long-delayed assimilation of Yukon Indians to Canadian norms would have to occur. Natives, the argument went, would need to accommodate themselves to the new order.

Between 1950 and 1973, the date of the tabling of the Yukon Indians' land claim, Natives in the territory experienced a drastic transformation. The harvesting economy declined precipitously, reflecting falling fur prices and changing attitudes towards the marketing of game. Natives were, by circumstance and economic change, pushed off their land and into a sedentary life on small residential reserves.

The small settlements were soon crowded. The aboriginal population increased steadily through the years; the number of status Indians doubled from 1,533 in 1951 to over 3,000 by 1973.[4] Native children were compelled to attend government-funded schools, which adopted the vigorous assimilationist agenda that the missionaries had long favoured. Yukon Indians were also swept up in the expansion of the Canadian welfare state, which provided an array of government programs and hastened the bureaucratization of aboriginal life in the north. In less than two decades, the accommodation that the Natives had reached with non-Native society in the territory, an arrangement which had preserved many of their customs and values, was dramatically altered. Yukon Indians now became an administered people, subject to the control of government officials, segregated from the non-Native population, and suffering the trauma of being separated from their culture.

CHAPTER NINE

The Modern Economy

After the Second World War Yukon Native people discovered that, despite the rhetoric of government agents and politicians, non-Indian society had little room for them. This was particularly true on the economic front, where traditional aboriginal skills seemed archaic and useless. Their marginalization, by itself, was nothing novel, for Native people had only been peripherally attached to the industrial or wage economy in the past. A serious decline in the harvesting economy, however, weakened the major underpinnings of Native life in the Yukon and forced a new response to the rapidly changing conditions.

The decline of the fur trade began shortly after the end of the war. Markets fell precipitously in the late 1940s, and did not soon rebound. The Natives continued to trap, and actually brought in more furs in an attempt to sustain their income, but the returns continued to drop. The implementation of a system of trapline registration in 1950 was intended to ensure Native control of trapping territory; instead, the legalistic structures, combined with the $10 annual fee and declining markets, created circumstances in which a significant number of Natives allowed their trapline registrations to lapse, permitting non-Natives, who usually combined trapping with other work, to step in and claim the territories.

The fur trade continued, of course, particularly in outlying areas, even with the substantially lower prices. All but the most stable traders were forced out of business, however, undercutting what had once been a very competitive market. The absence of competition further reduced aboriginal returns and limited the prospect of a secure return from the trade. The situation at Ross River in 1958 was typical: "These Indians derive their livelihood from trapping. They make their headquarters at Ross River, where they are at the mercy of one trader who charges high prices for food and gives low returns for furs."[1] There were some solutions to this problem. In 1961 constant complaints convinced the Indian agent, Bill Grant, to arrange to ship the Indians' pelts to outside markets, thus ensuring a higher return for the trappers.[2] But such efforts did little to mitigate the structural decline in the fur sector.

Other sectors of the Yukon economy expanded rapidly, but Natives reaped little of the benefit. Prospectors fanned out across the territory, and some of them, including Al Kulan, who made the crucial Anvil lead-zinc discovery, relied heavily on Native assistants.[3] A few Natives found work along the Alaska Highway and with construction crews on the roads being built to Mayo and Dawson in the 1950s. Only a small number were regularly employed in Whitehorse, which remained the territory's largest town after the war and experienced considerable growth as government investment in the region expanded. The mining industry, then the Yukon's largest employer, continued a pattern of excluding Indian workers. It was rare for an Indian to work at the United Keno property at Elsa, on the Yukon Consolidated Gold Corporation dredges at Dawson (which closed down in 1966), or at the New Imperial copper property near Whitehorse. "The Indian," wrote one government official, "is predominately an outside man, who enjoys the bush, fresh air and wide open space. He has done so for generations and to suddenly find himself in a confined space of a few feet, would I am sure result in a fear that he would not too readily admit to anyone else."[4] If Natives found a position with these companies, it was rarely in the mine; rather, they worked on "the ancillary jobs which keep the mines operating."[5] Even then, major employers were "disillusioned and not at all sympathetic about hiring Indians to any great extent."[6]

Native people, of course, needed a cash income, and continued to search for temporary, seasonal work as they had in the past. They could find jobs throughout the territorial economy as labourers on the highways and woodcutters for the riverboats (until the steamboats, too, stopped working in 1955. They could also work as loggers, sell firewood in towns, operate small stores, restaurants, or hotels, and act as guides. A report in 1955 concluded that "employment, insofar as the Indians is concerned, was considered very good throughout the summer and fall. Increased construction and mining activity, provided most opportunities. A large number found employment prospecting or as guides and labourers with survey and hunting parties. Generally speaking, it could be said that anyone who is so inclined, is able to engage in some remunerative employment."[7] But the prospects for Native workers were severely limited. One official observed that "practically all menial tasks – garbage trucks, street cleaners, forest fire fighters – are Indian. They do not mind, in fact they relish the vagaries of their employment, preferring it to the monotony of a steady job."[8]

Indians continued to run up against a deeply entrenched belief, one that was not altogether incorrect, that they would not accept permanent wage labour. By the early 1960s the Department of National Defence was seriously questioning the practice of employing Native seasonal labour on the Alaska Highway: "Many have displayed poor work habits, poor attendance records, and in some cases social habits which have caused them to be considered unacceptable for living in close quarters with the white crews. All these faults can be corrected in time with training but the usual employer has not the time nor the patience to institute any special procedures during the rush season."[9]

Native women, in contrast, had somewhat better prospects. In Whitehorse, it was said, "probably every dishwasher in every cafe in the Yukon is an Indian. Some have graduated by their own ability and personality to waitress or cook."[10] Others made and sold handicrafts. But such trade offered little security: "even at its best, it may be considered pin-money, something for the distaff members to amuse themselves with while the men are away at their tasks ... There is an unfortunate trend to cheap imported beadwork and pseudo Indian carvings by some of the Whitehorse traders."[11]

The federal government continued to hope that the Natives would move into the mainstream economy. In 1949 the Yukon Indian agent attempted to encourage "the Indians to be self-supporting and reliant," offering financial aid to assist them "in possible worthwhile fields of endeavour, in preference to direct relief."[12] Meek's analysis ignored the obvious point that Yukon Natives had been "self-supporting and reliant" for generations; he continued his efforts to integrate the Indians into the non-traditional economy. These initiatives, minor and sporadic, enjoyed little success, as chastened officials noted in the decade that followed.

In 1958 W.S. Arnell, Indian commissioner for BC, provided a detailed assessment of Native employment in the Yukon. He noted that most of the Indians continued to live off the land, although a declining fur trade had severely hurt their incomes: "while many of the more progressive families moved to take advantage of available seasonal labour to augment their income, others insisted on retaining their nomadic life in the bush, remaining near trading posts of a relief basis in the hope of experiencing higher receipts for fur catches in the future and meantime continuing to live mainly off the land."

The remainder (Arnell called them the "working Indians") obtained occasional employment near the towns. Those near Whitehorse found considerable seasonal labour, which employed approximately 100 Native men. The United Keno Hill Mines employed about twelve Indian men on various surface projects; the Klondike dredges, in contrast, rarely hired Indians. In Dawson only two families had full-time work; the other seven or eight families found occasional labouring positions. On the road south to Whitehorse, twelve to fourteen Natives staffed the ferries, although bridge construction soon rendered those positions redundant. Carmacks and Haines Junction each had eight Natives employed on an irregular basis in coal mines and the federal experimental farm. Indians in the Burwash area had few options, although several cut wood for cash. Cassiar Mines hired between twnety-five and thirty Natives to cut wood for their northern BC mine. The Indians, Arnell reported, "are steadily improving in their ability to work alongside others and remain on the job without undue absenteeism."[13] Much as he attempted to put a positive light on the situation, the integration of Native people in the work-force was evidently going to be a slow process.

The mining sector continued to expand through the 1960s, serving as the engine for a resurgent Yukon economy. As before, however, there were few places for Native workers. Because the federal government was heavily involved in subsidizing the new projects, it could insist on a formal "hire Native policy." The Cyprus Anvil Mining Corporation, for example, agreed as part of its complex financial arrangement with the federal government to hire a substantial portion of its work-force from the Native population. The promise looked good on paper, but was not kept. When the mine opened in 1969, there were few Natives on staff, and only a tiny number were hired in subsequent years. The corporation had plentiful explanations for this failure, most related to the Indians' work habits and their difficulties within the Faro community, but the mine operators clearly made few efforts to improve the situation.[14]

Others attempts were made to recruit Natives for mine work, but again with little success. Employers were not particularly keen, believing that the Indians were poorly suited for industrial labour. Government officials seemed to agree: "A very large number of the present generation of Indian people of working force age are not temperamentally equipped for regular industrial employment. They have been raised in a way of life which did not give them the very necessary tolerance for the boredom of regular industrial employment which one must have to succeed as a wage earner in an increasingly technological industry."[15]

For a handful of Native people, the new economy provided an opportunity for individual entrepreneurship, but realistic prospects were few. The small number of Native businesses were effectively ghettoized, serving a largely Native clientele. There were only a few prominent Native business people. In the 1960s Joe Netro established a successful retail operation at Old Crow, although it was far from a typical business: "A crafty dealer, he does not understand the principles of good business and makes blunders and omissions which lose money. He nevertheless does a healthy business and is not only respected, but feared by many trappers. His bookkeeping is weird and wonderful with some ingenious little devices of his own to overcome his business illiteracy."[16]

The exceptions were the big-game guides, the "aristocrats" of the aboriginal population – at least in the eyes of white people. Led by Johnny Johns, and including such men as Paul Fox, Watson Smarch, and George Sidney, the Native guides attracted a steady clientele among outside sports hunters. The territorial government encouraged the industry, and provided considerable assistance to Native guides and outfitters, including writing to major hunting publications in an attempt to secure publicity.[17] The business was uncertain and depended on "word of mouth" advertising; favourable coverage in an American hunting magazine would bring a rush of bookings. Work was, of course, very seasonal.

There were other efforts to capitalize on "traditional" aboriginal skills. Native craftspeople, particularly women, were encouraged to produce mukluks, mittens, coats, and other items for trade. In the early 1960s the Indian superintendent in Whitehorse sought southern outlets for Native handicrafts and even sold these goods through his office.[18] Such efforts were only marginally successful, although a small number of Yukon Indians continued to produce items for the local market. Further development awaited the establishment of a more commercial approach to aboriginal handicrafts.

Unlike the Northwest Territories, where evangelists of the southern cooperative movement established a series of successful ventures, few co-ops were started in the Yukon Territory. A marketing cooperative, Yukon Indian Craft Co-operative Association, was established in 1962 to handle handicrafts, although it enjoyed little of the success associated with the art cooperatives in the eastern Arctic. After management difficulties, the DIA assumed responsibility for it, but the cooperative closed in 1966.[19] As one observer commented, "This operation is not a 'co-op' in the sense of Indian participation. It fact it is not a 'co-op' in any sense – it is an Indian Affairs branch operated service to the native handicraft producers in the Yukon Indian

Agency."[20] The craft industry continued, however, and the idea of a cooperative did not disappear. The Yukon Native Brotherhood, formed in 1968, was very supportive of the handicraft industry, arguing that it would "make the Indian people self-sufficient, independent, and make welfare unecessary [sic]."[21] A new handicraft cooperative, Yukon Native Products, opened in the 1970s. Government support was forthcoming, but the process was slow and difficult.[22] There were some small cooperatives created, including the Ross River Co-operative Sawmill and the Burwash Cooperative, although they usually had constant financial difficulties and seldom remained in operation for long.[23]

The Old Crow Co-operative Association was more successful. In 1970 Joe Netro agreed to sell his retail operations to the band for $46,000. The DIA provided a $50,000 loan, hired a management instructor, and arranged with Saskatchewan Co-op College to host a week-long seminar in the village. A local person completed a management and bookkeeping course in 1972 and was subsequently employed by the cooperative. By 1973, after only three years of operation, the Old Crow Co-operative Association had repaid almost half of the original loan and had paid small dividends each year to the shareholders.[24] It also assumed new duties, including the operation of the Old Crow weather station.[25]

Through the 1960s the Indians, male and female, continued their previous pattern of accommodation with the wage and industrial economy. The main economic problem lay with the fact that the fur trade no longer provided the much-needed income to supplement their summer earnings and their returns from hunting and fishing. Despite the many promises by promoters of the new north, the wage economy provided few openings for Native people. Even if Indians were willing to secure full-time, regular work, and not all of them were, employers and managers were unlikely to hire them in significant numbers.

In the new north, however, the welfare state offered other sources of income. The family allowance, first offered in 1944, and old age pensions provided a basis of support. The government also moved quickly in the early 1950s to provide direct assistance to would-be Native entrepreneurs.[26] When the few subsidized business ventures produced, at best, indifferent results, the government fell back on expanded welfare payments. Between 1940 and 1944 annual government expenditures on relief for Native people and the Yukon Territory averaged less than $12,000. That figure grew to $30,000 by 1949[27] and to $90,000 in 1954–55. By the mid-1960s the DIA was spending $200,000 each year on Native welfare payments. In the past, Native people had been reluctant to accept the government handouts; most recipients had been old or infirm. But now, with their economic opportunities severely limited and their access to the land disrupted, many Yukon Indians felt that they had no choice but to accept assistance.

Both Natives and non-Natives continued to look for alternatives to welfare payments. Training programs were offered, particularly through the Whitehorse Vocational School, for Natives interested in technical careers.[28] Consideration was given to a wide range of projects, from establishing a tannery to buying a working farm on the Pelly River and operating it as an instructional venture.[29] Harry Joe and several others from Champagne approached the federal government in 1961 for assistance in starting a cattle ranch. The government commissioned a variety of reports on the chances for success, and moved quickly to set aside the land, fearing that non-Native ranchers or big-game guides would lay claim to what was believed to be a prime piece of ranch land. Within a year, 21,000 acres had been set aside to provide the land base for the enterprise, but a viable ranch was never established.[30]

The federal government sponsored many make-work projects, offering short-term employment to a small number of Native people, mostly men.[31] In 1963, for example, the Department of Public Works hired a crew of 105 workers, 97 of whom were Indians, to slash and burn the right-of-way on the road from Watson Lake to Ross River. This project, undertaken in the dead of winter, lasted only a few weeks and did not provide regular work for the Natives of Lower Post, Upper Liard, and Ross River.[32] Moreover, such labour-intensive work was not terribly efficient. Public Works officials were on record as noting that "this uneconomical type of hand labour project can only be justified on the basis of the benefits to the native population who have little opportunity for wage labour in winter."[33] Indian Agent A.E. Fry noted that the Indian men were gainfully employed on their traplines and were not actively seeking work. What is more, he argued that "it would be very disruptive to pull people in off traplines for a short term project, the proceeds of which usually went 'down the drain' in one gigantic binge at the end of the job."[34]

In the 1960s increasing Native activism and governmental concern about the deepening poverty of northern Indians prompted the establishment of affirmative action and on-the-job training programs.[35] Within the federal and territorial governments, a certain number of positions were designated for Native people and efforts were made to recruit suitable candidates. Progress in recruiting Natives was very slow. In 1976, in response to public criticisms of the small number of Natives employed by the DIA, the minister, Warren Almand, asked for a list of Indians workers. There were only nine, including a janitor and three security people at Lower Post Residential School, an accounts supervisor, a program clerk, and three workers attached to the Yukon Hall Residence.[36] Affirmative action clearly had some way to go.

Unemployment rates (although specific figures for Native people were not routinely reported) remained extremely high through the 1960s. There were more jobs near Whitehorse than elsewhere in the territory, sparking a substantial migration of families from the community to the capital city. Also, increased traffic along the Alaska Highway provided additional jobs in highway maintenance and tourist-related activities, but few Natives participated in either sector. In the outlying communities, their economies ravaged by a weakened fur trade, there were virtually no jobs for Indians.

Government transfer payments expanded rapidly through this decade. The federal government established an elaborate program of welfare payments and other subsidies, and created an elaborate bureaucracy to administer the funds. Some of the money came with strings attached. Mothers' allowances, for instance, were payable only if the children attended school, and so became a major incentive for relocating to one of the increased number of residential reserves scattered around the territory. Similarly, funds for housing construction had to be spent on the same reserves, thus further encouraging settlement on the lands set aside for Native use.

Government programs were frequently criticized for not respecting the unique circumstances facing the northern Indian. A.E. Fry arranged to move several families in 1963, hoping that the relocation would assist them in finding work. His request for financial help with the moving expenses ran into an administrative road-block. With ill-disguised contempt, Fry wrote: "It is impossible for people living on Indian Affairs relief in an area where there are NO JOBS, and it costs MORE TO LIVE than we give in assistance to save any money toward moving out. On the other hand, unless they move out they will be forever on assistance."[37]

Shortages of cash did not mean that the Indians were without food, for the harvesting economy proved to be extremely resilient. Most Yukon Indians continued to hunt, fish and gather a significant portion of their food. Indian Agent R.J. Meek reported in 1955: "In a bygone day, a family could pretty well live off the country. Only a generation back, a few pounds of tea, flour, sugar and salt seemed sufficient to take a family group back to their trap-line from the trading-post, and the country supported them until the[y] returned the next year. Most of the present-day Indians depend on 'store grub' for their food. But when hard pressed they turn to traditional fare, and manage to get along tolerably well."[38] The people of Old Crow lived off their annual caribou hunts and the proceeds of the community's muskrat harvest in Old Crow Flats. In southern areas the Indians faced increasing competition from non-Native recreational hunters, but their knowledge of the region and their commitment to the hunt ensured a reasonable return. Although children leaving the territory's residential schools often lacked the skills and knowledge necessary to contribute to the food harvest, there were enough skilled hunters and gatherers to ensure a regular supply of food. It would take governments more than two decades to accept country produce as a significant component of the territorial economy, but Indian people knew it to be one of the few reliable sources of food. Bill Grant, Yukon Indian agent, observed in 1961, "The largest group of Indian adults still live 'off the land.' By this I mean the support of the family comes from fishing, trapping and hunting."[39]

Despite the persistence of Native harvesting, non-Natives assumed that the modernization of the territorial economy would continue. The federal government, while expressing some concern for the impact on the Native population, accepted economic expansion and dislocation as being inevitable. Discussing proposed oil exploration in the Old Crow Flats area in 1969, DIA Deputy Minister John Macdonald observed: "By this very token, traditional ways of life will change, in time, as they have in other parts of the country as development progressed, and this will be looked upon by some with apprehension. There is, of course, historical background for this apprehension, but the lessons of history have not been lost upon society at large and will be given full weight in our planning. We cannot prevent change; we can, however, ensure that its net effect is one of genuine and general benefit."[40]

Given this pro-development atmosphere, it is not surprising that the 1950s and 1960s witnessed a widening of the economic gap between Natives and non-Natives in the territory. The resource boom in this period attracted substantial numbers of well-paid, transient workers into the region – yet another migration of people looking to "make a killing, not a living." Through this period the northern civil service expanded exponentially; ironically, many of the new well-paid jobs involved providing services to Yukon Indians, but only a tiny percentage went to them. As the income of aboriginal people stagnated, non-Native wages and living conditions improved appreciably, furnishing graphic evidence of the racial differences in the territory.

The Yukon Native Brotherhood declared in 1972: "Many people of native descent in the Yukon are searching for the means whereby they can become self sufficient members of to-day's society. Many have good ideas about how this can be accomplished through private enterprise. They need the help and guidance necessary to get started."[41]

Such help was a long time coming. Yukon Indian Agent A.E. Fry commented in 1967, "I know the Indian people are themselves frustrated at the great gap between what they have and what they see others around them enjoying. But Government and a well-intended public can do only so much. There comes a time when the improvement of the whole lot of a people can only be substantially improved by the hard work, the very unrelenting hard, hard work of the people themselves as individuals."[42] Fry provided an excellent summary of the individualistic, capitalist ethos that had taken firm root in the new north; Natives would have to conform if they were to share in the prosperity of the resource boom. It was not an accommodation most were able or prepared to make. Government initiatives that attempted to encourage economic integration enjoyed little success, leaving the Natives on the margins of the territorial economy.

CHAPTER TEN

Religion and Education

Before 1950 religion and education had been the pillars of a fitful effort to assimilate the Native people of the Yukon Territory. Although the federal government generally ignored church appeals that Indians be integrated into the Canadian mainstream, it felt obliged to respond to the missionaries' demands that the rudiments of a formal education be provided. The residential school in Carcross and unstable network of day schools created across the territory did little to speed the Natives' entry into non-Native society, but they did prove somewhat disruptive of aboriginal life. The clergy enjoyed greater success with their spiritual message, although the Natives' conception of the universe and their place in it remained strong and distinct. Full Christianization of the aboriginal population remained an elusive goal for the Anglican, Catholic, and other missionaries.

The missionary impulse remained strong after 1945. The Catholic Church expanded its mission base, building on its work in the southern Yukon. Yet not all its ventures were successful. Having checked with the people of Old Crow to see if there was enough interest in a Catholic church, the Oblates decided to send two priests to the isolated town. Their expectations went unrealized, however, as Old Crow remained a strongly Anglican settlement. Few people attended the Catholic church, although the missionaries stayed in town – one of their number, Father Mouchet, a former competitive skier, introduced cross-country skiing to the town's young people.

In the southern Yukon the Anglican Church found its hegemony challenged by the Catholics and the Baptists. Native people attended churches, but many observers continued to wonder if the Indians had, in fact, internalized the new faith. R.J. Meek observed, "How deep Christianity has penetrated is a matter of conjecture. Dr. [Catherine] McLellan is inclined to think it is very superficial, and I believe an objective enquiry would corroborate this. A cynical observer might facetiously remark that the group having the best Sunday school picnic has the biggest congregation."[1]

The Yukon never approached a theocracy, for the churches were not able to exert much authority over the government and could not compel the Indians to follow their dictates. What measure of authority and influence they had, moreover, declined rapidly in the years after 1950. Ironically, the demands of Anglican and Catholic missionaries for greater government attention to aboriginal needs were heeded after the war, resulting in the usurpation by the state of many missionary functions. In particular, the missionaries lost control of the education system, and thus their primary access to Native children. Social workers and Indian agents, the secular missionaries of the post-war era, took over most of their functions. As well, the continued questioning of the missionary enterprise within the Christian churches led to declining support for missionary work.[2] Both the Anglican and Catholic churches maintained their mission stations, although on a reduced level. By the late 1960s the Anglican church at Haines Junction, for example, was operated on an occasional basis by priests travelling from Whitehorse.

In some communities, the Indians' interest in the church remained strong. At Old Crow, the Kutchin remained very supportive of the Anglican Church. In some of the smaller settlements – Mayo, Burwash, and Teslin – the churches maintained a high profile and continued to attract a regular following. But around the larger communities, where social and economic disruptions were profound and distance between whites and Natives the greatest, church attendance dropped off. The younger people, in particular, demonstrated little interest in the church. Many, particularly graduates of the residential schools, were openly hostile to the work of the established denominations.[3]

These changes in the missionary field also affected the churches' work in the residential schools. The Catholic Church had finally built its own school at Lower Post, and ensured that Catholic children from throughout the Yukon and northern British Columbia attended. The Anglicans continued to operate the Carcross Residential School, which was rebuilt and expanded. The schools still functioned much as they had in the past, demanding that the Natives abandon their aboriginal language, accept Christian teachings, and abide by the strict social codes of the school.[4]

Efforts to educate the Native children were aided by the government's willingness to compel attendance. The mothers' allowance was available only to families who had their school-age children attending class regularly.[5] Parents unable or unwilling to send their children to a day school on a regular basis were required to send them to the Anglican residential school at Carcross, the Baptist school in White-horse, or the Catholic facility at Lower Post. Any families failing to comply with these regulations were cut off from mothers' allowance payments.[6] There were cracks in this apparently rigid policy. As Yukon Superintendent W.E. Grant noted: "We have not yet arrived at the stage where we try to force Indian people to stop earning a living in the only manner they know (hunting and trapping) and stay at home to look after their children while they attend day school. We believe and actually have seen some very good examples elsewhere where this is done, resulting in the parents becoming permanent relief cases. We feel the demoralizing effect of continuous relief on a household far outweighs the benefits of day school attendance."[7] In such circumstances, he did not say, the children were by this time required to enrol in one of the territory's residential schools.

So the children went to school, often over the protests of their parents. Numerous stories circulate of Native children being forcibly removed from their families by DIA officials and police officers. The Indian Superintendent reported in 1962, as evidence of Native anger, that he "had just had an Indian woman in my office cursing and swearing because her children were being taken away and sent to Lower Post."[8] Many Yukon Natives still remember, with bitterness and sadness, the arrival of the school bus each fall, which signalled their departure to Whitehorse, Carcross, or Lower Post.

At the Baptist school in Whitehorse, the Reverend Harold Lee, described in the press as a "veritable God-send to the Indian popu-lation,"[9] did not wish to distinguish between status, non-status, mixed-blood, and non-Native students. Over time, however, as the school came to be increasingly dependent on government funding, the Baptists had to adapt the more rigid racial policy of the other residential schools and restrict its operations to status Indians.[10] Stu-dents excluded from the residential schools found spaces in one of the growing number of reserve-based day schools. These once-irreg-ular institutions were placed on a permanent footing in 1948, when the federal government decided to hire regular, full-time teachers for the day schools.[11] Native students were also permitted to enrol in the territorial public schools.

The Native student body expanded tremendously. The number of Native students enrolled in Yukon Indian day schools tripled between 1940 and 1955. In 1950, the first year Native students entered the territorial school system, 21 children occupied desks in the predom-inantly non-Native class-rooms. Five years later, 110 Native children were in the territorial system. The number of children enrolled in Indian day, residential, and territorial public schools jumped from 181 in 1945 to 387 in 1955. Attendance continued to increase thereafter. In 1962, 686 Native children from the Yukon Indian Agency (which included portions of northern BC) attended school. Lower Post had 143 and Carcross 102; another 132 lived in Whitehorse hostels and attended the territorial schools (the Baptist boarding school had closed the previous year). Altogether, 441 Native children attended British Columbia or Yukon public schools.[12] Equally important, attendance at schools, as required by law, became increasingly regular. In 1940, 40 per cent of those on the school lists were absent each day; by 1955, almost 95 per cent of registered students attended classes regularly. "It appears to us," wrote L. Jampolsky, regional superintendent of Indian schools in 1962, "that the day is not far off when most pupils in the Yukon could be integrated into the Territorial school system either through day school attendance or attendance from hostels."[13]

In many communities the integration of Native students into regular classrooms caused considerable difficulties, as education officials openly admitted.[14] The missionaries often argued against integrated schools, preferring to have the students enrol in church-run boarding schools. This, they noted, permitted the parents to return to their traplines,[15] would result in fewer failures in school, and would remove the children from "the environment of the reserve and the low moral standards of the people in the surrounding area."[16] The Catholic missionaries in particular protested against the effort to recruit "their" children for non-denominational schools.[17] The Baptists, for their part, were angry that the decision to close their school in Whitehorse was not matched by a government determination to shut down the Anglican and Catholic residential schools.[18]

When a hostel for Protestant children was opened in Whitehorse, logic suggested that the students attend the nearby Selkirk school. Regional officials agreed that this arrangement would be convenient, but noted that "we would prefer to have our children distributed so that there is no high percentage of Indian children in any of your classrooms."[19] Considerable debate arose over the Selkirk situation, focusing particularly on the preponderance of Native children in the senior elementary grades. A parents' meeting on the issue ended with a unanimous resolution that the number of Indian children in any one grade not be permitted to exceed 50 per cent of the total class.[20]

Teslin and Mayo were significant exceptions to the general pattern. The Mayo school prided itself on being the "first to accept and encourage full integration."[21] In Teslin, Native and non-Native parents had long supported the maintenance of a joint school. In 1963 the Teslin Band went so far as to offer six acres of its reserve land for the construction of single community school. The project was strongly supported by Indians and whites alike.[22]

The curriculum offered to Native students also underwent a dramatic transformation in this period. Before 1945 the government had left responsibility for Native education to the churches and expressed little interest in school programming. All this changed in the postwar era. As the children entered the day, residential, and territorial schools in the 1950s, they encountered an aggressively assimilationist system. The increasingly secular instruction disparaged Native languages, taught "practical" education skills, and attempted to give the students a grounding in the southern Canadian curriculum. The effort offered little real preparation for the world the children discovered when they returned to their communities, and served primarily to distance the students from their culture and way of life.[23]

The children who attended these schools experienced many personal and social problems. Many rebelled, often silently, and left the residential schools angry and embittered.[24] Their performance was poor by southern standards. Few students proceeded beyond grade nine. R.J. Meek wrote in 1955: "It is not improbable that some of these failures are psychological, especially if the boy or girl must go 'Outside.' There may also be complexes which are not understood by lay administrators. Much patience must be shown, as higher education can no more be forced on them than anyone else."[25]

Natives had been critical of the residential schools for decades, but few heeded their complaints. When non-Natives began to complain about the institutionalization of Native children, however, action was forthcoming. In 1967 Richard King, an educational anthropologist, published The School at Mopass, a scathing indictment of the Carcross Residential School where he had worked for two years. The chorus of criticism, combined with continued resistance by parents and children and indifferent educational results, convinced the federal government to phase out the schools. The Baptist Mission School in Whitehorse, housed in army-surplus buildings that the local fire marshall called "a ruddy fire trap,"[26] was the first to shut down.[27] The Carcross school shut down in 1968; Lower Post followed in 1975.[28]

This meant, of course, that the Native children had to be completely integrated into the territorial education system. Non-Natives and Natives alike were wary of such integration: "Only very recently has white prejudice broken down sufficiently to accept Indian children in Provincial and Territorial schools. There is, therefore, an awareness of being closely watched; any accusation that standards of cleanliness, etc. are falling is usually felt by the entire Indian community, whose mobility was advanced by the acceptance of their children into white institutions."[29]

By the early 1960s most communities had elementary schools, open to Natives and non-Natives alike. Older children presented a different problem, for only Whitehorse, Dawson, Watson Lake, and Mayo-Elsa had enough students for high schools. Students from other areas were brought to Whitehorse, primarily for secondary school. Catholic students boarded in a church-run dormitory downtown; the remaining students lived in government-run dormitories near the town's main high school. Children from Old Crow attended school in Inuvik, NWT; only a very few out-of-town students went to school at the territory's other high schools.

The territorial schools proved to be almost as unfriendly as the residential institutions. Imported non-Native teachers had little understanding of the cultural and historical situation of Native people in the Yukon Territory and seldom stayed long enough to learn. They also carried with them the rigid and hostile North American stereotypes about aboriginal people, and often allowed these attitudes to affect their work in the class-room. The school curriculum, moreover, was as culturally insensitive as the missionaries' offerings. Native languages and culture were not taught, nor was there any systematic description of Yukon history.

Native attendance and completion rates were far below those of the non-Native student body. Reflecting the expectations of teachers and administrators, Native students generally performed poorly. Few graduated from high school; most stayed only as long as the law required. Records from the territorial school system in 1973, for example, indicated that there were more than 50 Native children in each of grades from 1 to 7; only 13 children were in grade 11 and only 5 in grade 12.[30] Discipline problems were endemic, as Native children resisted the structure and form of non-Native pedagogy. Poor academic performance and disciplinary difficulties only reinforced the attitudes of the teachers and administrators. A few officials identified the broader social causes: "Their children cannot go to local day schools from shacks so crowded there is no room for homework, or cleanliness, or proper sleep or light to see by. Social change in desirable directions will not come about in this fashion."[31] Teachers were troubled by the dismal showing of their Native children but exhibited little willingness or ability to adapt the school system to suit aboriginal needs and interests.

Some teachers made minor additions to the curriculum, adding a bit of aboriginal culture or history to an overwhelmingly Euro-centric school program. In Old Crow, for example, the school year was altered to accommodate the community's important spring muskrat hunt. A Yukon teacher proposed adding several Native legends to the curriculum in 1973. Her suggestion was greeted with the rather disingenuous response: "It would probably be a good thing to have Indian legends as supplementary reading rather than Fairy Tales stories which do not pertain to them or their environment but I'm not sure that these legends should be the ones used. I think legends with more of a theme or moral would be better for students."[32] Put simply, only Native legends that read like fairy tales would be acceptable.

Native organizations demanded greater changes, including the hiring of more Native teachers, improved curriculum and, in particular, greater Indian control of the education system. Some improvements were forthcoming in the early 1970s,[33] although they fell far short of Native expectations and left most in the communities feeling educationally disenfranchised.[34] The Native residents of Ross River, requesting improvements in the education system, asked that "Indian culture and history and the Ross River Indian language, along with prescribed curriculum be taught to our children in school, so that our children will develop to become flexible, independent, reliable and proud Indian people and not white Indians."[35]

Judged by the educational standards of the dominant culture, Native children were described as failures and were labelled as such. Their inability to adapt to a culturally insensitive school system was generally taken as a sign of limited intelligence. By dropping out of school, they limited their chances of finding regular employment and unwittingly provided further justification for those who argued that the Indians lacked the ability to adjust to the modern world. For the Native children, failure at school further weakened their self-esteem, already suffering by the widespread denigration of their heritage.

Indian Superintendent A.E. Fry offered his summary of the impact of integrated schools on Native children:

The Indian youngster from a bush camp background and then a Residential School setting perhaps for the first few years of school increasingly discovers in the integrated classroom that his or her set of understandings and concepts and values do not seem to be appropriate to the many situations which occur. As a gradual loss of confidence sets in the problem aggravates itself until finally you have a personality facing every situation with trembling anxiety. I have had young Indian men and women who have apparently made a tremendous success in the 'Euro-Canadian' culture tell me that they still go into a store or a restaurant or face a new task at their job with these same anxieties hanging over them.[36]

Religion and education were supposed to prepare Native children for integration into the now-dominant non-Native world. For the churches, the failure of this effort in the pre-Second World War era was attributable to a lack of financial and human resources. They therefore welcomed the educational interventions of the government after 1950, even though the expansion of secular schooling eventually pushed them to the sidelines. Despite government action in the post-war period, however, the "civilizing" impulse still fell far short of its goal. The Indians were not fully integrated into the Christian world, although there were pockets of strong loyalty to the churches. Nor did education prove to be the panacea its promoters had intended. Native children reacted with bitterness and anger to their experiences at the residential schools and to their treatment by the non-Native territorial school system.

By the late 1960s the churches were beginning to admit the limitations of their work among the Yukon Indians,[37] although both the Anglicans and Catholics continued to celebrate the accomplishments of the first missionaries – the "wilderness saints." The churches were genuinely troubled by the social distress in the Native communities. Yet, at the same time, the growth of the non-Native population had led to a greater than ever separation between Native and non-Native church work and to an increased emphasis on non-Native congregations. The churches were caught in a painful dilemma, wanting to assist the Native peoples but only too aware of their responsibility for much of the anger and tension in the aboriginal communities. Since the effort to Christianize and "civilize" the Indians through missions and schools had been a decided failure, the churches began to work in a different direction. The Anglican and Catholic churches became active supporters of the Native land-claims movement and of aboriginal rights generally, deciding to stand with the Indians rather than attempting to speak for them, as they had attempted to do in the past.

Notwithstanding the decline in the churches' role, which was matched by the secularization of northern society generally, the missionary impulse did not die. Instead, it was embraced by the secular missionaries of the post-war era – the social workers and government officials who, with their own agenda and ideology, came north to assist the Indians with their adaptation to the modern world.

CHAPTER ELEVEN

Government and Indians in the Modern North

The Indians' continued resistance to efforts at assimilation, combined with the increasing poverty and social distress evident on reserves across the country, provided stark evidence of the failure of government policy to effect "positive" changes among the Indians. The establishment in 1946 of a special joint committee of the Senate and House of Commons to investigate the Indian Act and make recommendations for improvement was but the most public sign of a clear malaise within the administration of Indian affairs in Canada. The committee's report, implemented legislatively in 1951, changed little. Earlier coercive measures, against such Native rituals as the potlatch and sun dance, were removed, but the assimilationist thrust remained much in evidence.[1]

The government was still determined to speed the integration of Canada's Indian people into the mainstream. As Indian Agent Meek observed of his charges: "Indians are about one fifth of the total population of the Yukon. They are with us for the present and the future, so they might as well be raised to our economic and cultural level. This is the theme that most officials take."[2] Faced with the evidence of continued social and economic problems among Native people, and armed with the resources and ideology of an increasingly interventionist state, the government moved rapidly to expand its programs for all native people. The Indians of the Yukon would experience the full brunt of government activism and efforts to speed the Natives' social, economic, and cultural integration.

The interventions began in the late 1940s, with the establishment of the mothers' allowance and special pensions for Native elders. Other subsidy programs soon followed: small loans for Native entrepreneurs, housing construction on Native reserves, often using Native labour, larger welfare payments, greatly expanded medical care, including preventative measures, and various forms of emergency assistance. The government's agenda represented a marked break with the past. Acceptance of mobility, a cornerstone of the DIA's cost-conscious plan for the Yukon since the late nineteenth century, had been replaced by an encouragement of a more sedentary existence and the integration of Native people into the mainstream of territorial economic and social life. Yukon Indian Agent Alan Fry recalled in a letter to the author: "The fifties and sixties were damned tough times for Indian people. The fur market had gone to hell, the riverboats and the associated life along the rivers to which Indian people had accommodated reasonably well, had given way to the highways and the highway settlements, and a whole lot more white people with no understanding of Indian people had come into the country. Overwhelming change was underway. Hopelessly misguided though government might have been as to how to go about it, the policy of government quite simply was to help Indian people adjust to it all and learn to live as best they could in new ways."

These programs were not always implemented without difficulty, particularly as the territorial administration became more assertive. In 1961 federal officials discovered that the territorial government had denied Yukon Indians supplementary payments for old age, blind, and disabled pensions; "their ridiculous reason for not paying the Allowance to Indians is that '*it has never been done.*'"[3] The territorial government defended its action by arguing that Indians were a federal responsibility and that the Natives did not contribute enough taxes to justify such an expenditure.[4] It resisted the federal government entreaties to amend its procedures and decided in the spring of 1961 to suspend the supplementary allowance payments for all Yukoners; hitherto, whites needing additional funds had to apply to the welfare department, while Indians needing more assistance were to approach the DIA.[5]

A central element in the government's policy was the expansion of the residential-reserve system. The first reserves had been established during the Klondike gold rush. Many had, however, fallen into disuse. Some, such as the one in Mayo, were too far away from the nearby settlement for the convenience of government officials. Beginning in the mid-1950s, the DIA created a series of new reserves, consolidated and centralized existing ones, and otherwise encouraged the Natives to move onto the small parcels of land on a permanent basis. In the same letter to the author quoted above, Alan Fry offered this description of the government's agenda: "As for the 'residential reserves' or villages, these were not some grand design by government to gain control of Indians. Some of the sites date from use in earlier days but many came about as Indian people, by choice, began to camp in proximity to latter day highway settlements. As the camps became somewhat permanent, land was set aside where houses could be built. Encouraging further people to move to these sites, or to relocate to those which seemed to offer better economic opportunity, may have been misguided but it was hardly a grand design by government to force people off the land."

In 1953 the territorial Indian agent was asked to investigate the need for new reserves in areas facing development pressure. R.J. Meek requested a reserve for Ross River because "recent mining discoveries in the area will probably create a change in the economic set-up of the Indians which up to this year has been based entirely on trapping and hunting."[6] Meek also requested a new reserve for Snag, recommended that the Fort Selkirk site be maintained, and observed that the Indians did not need a reserve at Stewart River.[7] Additional reserves were surveyed at Burwash, Old Crow, Upper Liard Bridge, and Marsh Lake; the claim to several dormant reserves was re-established in the 1950s as well.[8]

A 1958 overview of the status of Yukon Native reserves revealed that the reserve program had still not worked and that many of the Yukon bands remained semi-nomadic. The report also spelled out the government's continuing intent to alter the residential patterns of the isolated bands. Regarding the Aishihik band, which lived about fifty miles north of the Alaska Highway, the superintendent of Indian affairs noted, "We will investigate the possibilities of these Indians moving from the remote area to the parcel of land reserved at Haines Junction." The Burwash Indians lived on private land, not the government reserve. It was hoped that they, too, could be moved. The members of the Champagne band faced similar pressure: "Some of the younger Indians are being encouraged to locate on the Haines Junction Reserve to improve employment opportunities and to be closer to services." Indians in the Dawson area, formerly of the Moosehide reserve, were moved into Dawson City and provided with government housing; the homes were placed together, creating what one official called a potential "Indian ghetto."[9] Superintendent M.G. Jutras suggested that the Indians at White River and Ross River be consulted before their reserves were moved. The White River reserve was "to be close to the highway and services." The recommendation for the Ross River band concluded: "These Indians derived their livelihood from trapping. They make their headquarters at Ross River, where they are at the mercy of one trader who charges high prices for food and gives low returns for furs. After consultation with the Indians, stake a few acres at Ross River as a village site and proceed with limited housing. This Ross River area is a welfare problem and the younger Indians are to be encouraged to move to Upper Liard Bridge permanently and to transfer to that band."[10]

Not all the Indians were anxious to relocate to the new residential reserves. In 1966, following the closure of the Aishihik Lake airport and the decision of most of the Native community to move, an elderly couple declared their intention to remain behind. The man, an official observed, had accepted the "inescapable fact that if he moves to 1016, Canyon Creek or Kloo Lake his relatives will go through his winter's grub in short dispatch and his whole mode of living will be upset by the drinking and constant quarreling which goes on now in the places along the highway."[11] The Indian agent then arranged for bush pilots flying through the region to check on the couple from time to time, thus ensuring that they did not fall on hard times. The following year, they moved from Aishihik Lake to Burwash Landing.

The Whitehorse reserve, home to an increasing number of Indians from around the territory, remained north of the industrial district, on the most unattractive piece of land in the town. A number of small, poorly insulated homes were built, most with only rudimentary facilities. The houses were often overcrowded and badly maintained, adding to the inhabitants' social and medical problems. The Indians repeatedly petitioned for the relocation of their reserve, and requested that a new plot of land be set aside across the river.[12] The government refused the Natives' request, arguing that it would be too expensive to build a second bridge across the Yukon River. The Indians continued to demand a better location and more useful housing, but for years the government turned a deaf ear to their appeals.[13]

The reserve system served to keep Natives and whites apart, an arrangement much to the liking of the latter. The Yukon Indian agent in the early 1950s tried to make something of the "safe and sacred retreat of an Indian reserve," particularly as it protected Native women from white men.[14] The arrangement was not, however, without its difficulties and complications. The concentration of the rapidly growing Native population on small residential reserves soon created serious housing shortages.[15] Public officials and concerned citizens increasingly spoke out about the very poor housing stock for Native people and demanded quick government attention to the problem.[16]

The issue burst into the public eye in 1965, when Bill Grant, former Yukon Indian agent, and his assistant, James Armishaw, were charged with diverting DIA funding from authorized projects for use on Native housing. There is, however, another side to the Grant affair, one that was not fully developed in the public accounts of the trial and related events. Government funding for Native housing provided only for basic framing and finishing. Improvements, such as plumbing and wiring, were the responsibility of individual families. Housing for Natives in Dawson City, the origins of the Grant controversy, caused particular problems: "The dilemma in Dawson City stemmed from the fact that while the funds in the Indian Affairs housing budget could be used to frame and finish but not to plumb the houses, the City of Dawson would not issue an occupancy permit until the houses were plumbed, a unique problem in the national picture since nowhere else did any local authority have any jurisdiction over houses built for Indians." Unable to change the policy, Grant proceed with his less direct, and controversial means of funding.[17]

The court case, which proceeded over several weeks, revolved around the charge that Grant and Armishaw had used DIA funds for unintended purposes, the most highly publicized (but by no means the only) of which was improvements to Native homes. Grant was praised by some Yukoners, including several ministers who attested that his honesty and truthfulness were "excellent, beyond reproach."[18] The charges against Armishaw were dismissed; Bill Grant was found guilty and fined $10 on each of six counts.[19] The crown appealed, and Grant's fine was subsequently increased to $500.[20] Local residents, Native and non-Native alike, donated money to help Grant pay his fine. Public debate on the court case focused on the housing, thus oversimplifying a rather more complex situation but ensuring that Grant emerged as something of a local folk hero.

In the wake of regional and national controversy over the exceptionally poor condition of reserve housing, the federal government decided in the mid-1960s to launch an aggressive housing-construction program. Called the Reserve Improvement Program, the $112-million national initiative was "basically aimed at eliminating the known backlog of housing and meeting new family formations in a five year period."[21] The program was much needed in the Yukon, where dozens of homes were required to replace the sub-standard housing on the territory's reserves.[22] The construction program for 1966 called for the erection of forty-one houses in the Yukon Indian agency, including seven each at Whitehorse and Burwash and six at Ross River.[23]

Local agents frequently expressed frustration and anger at the unwillingness of federal politicians and officials to deal with what was clearly a social emergency. A.E. Fry had great difficulty with the slowness of officialdom. Responding to a request for a formal assessment of housing needs, he commented to his superior, "I do not need to make further 'reviews of specific known needs insofar as reasonably possible.' Everytime I go into a village I am confronted with critical needs."[24] When two federal politicians visited the Whitehorse reserve and demanded that the shacks be removed, the Indian superintendent refused to countenance the building of Potemkin villages for politicians: "I will not concentrate funds at Whitehorse to window dress for Minister's inspections. When these shacks go, they must go as part of a program which is fair to all people in the Agency on a basis of straight need, not location in the window of public views."[25] Fry petitioned for more funds in 1967, arguing that the allotted $100,000 would meet less than half of the immediate needs. His requests were rejected.[26] As Fry wrote, dejectedly, "If, in fact, the Government of Canada cannot afford to carry out what we understand to be the intended improvement program for the Yukon Territory, then the Indian people of the Territory and I will have to accept that fact."[27]

Federal officials reacted with some anger to Fry's strongly worded representations. As an Ottawa official noted on the margin of one of Fry's memos: "How far can we go to support Mr Fry?"[28] Describing the Yukon superintendent's memos as "typically Fry," the regional superintendent continued, "He is irrevocably committed to the nonsensical notion that he and he alone knows how to row a boat – or that he is the only one in this league who has had his feet wet."[29]

Budgets for housing increased rapidly in the early 1970s. The community affairs budget almost doubled, from $350,000 to $660,000, between 1973 and 1975, a sign of the government's belated acknowledgement of the need to improve the Indians' living conditions.[30] Housing construction continued through the years, although not at a particularly rapid pace: in 1967–68, thirty-one houses were constructed, twenty-five were built in 1971–72 and twenty-three the following year.[31] A report covering the years 1967–70 showed, further, that Indians were contributing little toward the cost of construction. A total of $610,276 was spent on the 116 new homes built in these years; $7,150 came in the form of personal contributions. The government attempted to get the Indians to pay for improvements, but with little success. Of the $44,532 paid for repairs to 147 homes, $850 came from Native people.[32]

But spending substantial sums did not solve all the Natives' housing problems. The Indians continually argued that building southern-style, "whiteman's" homes was not what was required. The Yukon Native Brotherhood argued, for example, that Indians felt "space between houses is more important than some services which the whiteman thinks are." They also pointed out that Indians typically had more than one home, particularly on the trapline, something the new housing policy did not take into account. The YNB argued, not successfully, "that any housing policy must be started in the Yukon by the Indian people."[33]

The housing projects were constantly entangled in budgetary and administrative considerations. Natives requiring housing had to apply to the Indian agents, who, in conjunction with the bands, decided who would get new homes. An application by some Ross River Indians for off-reserve housing in the new community of Faro was rejected because, in the words of Regional Director I.F. Kirkby, the people "do not have steady work and unfortunately spend a lot of their time in the local bar."[34] Yukon Indians continued to demand greater expenditures on housing, and more control over the construction process, but to little avail.

While the government, by its agents' admission, moved slowly on housing, health programs developed more quickly. In the 1940s and early 1950s, the government had concentrated on efforts to eradicate tuberculosis among the Indians. Many Natives were forcibly removed to the Whitehorse hospital or, for more serious cases, to the Charles Camsell Hospital in Edmonton. Public-health nurses made routine visits to the scattered reserves, offering advice on nutrition, sanitation, and personal hygiene. As the Indians became more sedentary, permanent nursing stations were opened in the villages. By the mid-1950s a substantial network was in place: doctors on a fee-for-service basis in Mayo and Cassiar, and on salary in Whitehorse and Dawson; general hospitals open to Indians in Mayo, Whitehorse, and Dawson; a military hospital in Whitehorse; field matrons at Old Crow and Minto; registered nurses at the Carcross and Lower Post residential schools; and two travelling nurses with the Indian Health Service.[35] This expansion continued in the 1960s as the Indian Health Service developed new facilities, added staff, and promoted preventative health care.[36]

The increased intervention did not ensure the Natives better health, because radical changes in diet, the abandonment of the mobile lifestyle, and other alterations in Indian life added to existing health problems. In addition, the extension of the health-care system came complete with the intrusive ideology of non-Native health-care. The doctors and nurses gave no credence to aboriginal medicines, treatments, or spirituality, and placed high priority on the direct intervention of medical professionals.[37] It was yet another instance of non-Native agents asserting control over aboriginal life. Despite these efforts, however, Native healers, calling on aboriginal spirits and medicines, continued to practise in secret.[38]

The government expanded into all areas of aboriginal life, eventually adding Native culture to the list of programs and initiatives.

In 1970, responding to Native demands for support to local cultural programs, the government provided the YNB with a $5,000 subsidy to hire a short-term coordinator. The following year, grants of almost $28,000 were made to the Dawson and Liard councils, the Kutchin Dancers, and the YNB for various cultural programs.[39] Having worked for years to discredit aboriginal culture, the DIA was now financially encouraging Native music, dance, and art – an irony that was clearly lost on the civil servants working in the area.

Expanded government programs hastened the bureaucratization of aboriginal life, and signalled a further loss of control by Yukon Native people. As late as the mid-1950s the Yukon Indian Agency consisted of a single agent and a small secretarial staff. The number of employees grew rapidly through the rest of the decade and into the 1960s; each new program – housing, health, education, economic development – required a small secretariat. In 1973 the Yukon Indian Affairs agency included officials in the following areas (numbers in brackets indicates the number of person-years assigned): general administration (6), support services (7.5), engineering (2), federal schools (.5), employment and relocation (1), student residence (44), economic-development services (2), community-affairs administration (2), social services (1). Indian people became increasingly dependent upon civil servants, who controlled everything from welfare payments and pensions to school attendance and reserve housing.

Some of the government workers were compassionate, caring people who were much affected by the difficult circumstances the Indians faced. Others, secular missionaries and zealots in their own way, intervened in Native lives with considerable enthusiasm but little cultural awareness. As one observer wrote in 1964, "There seems to be more than just a slight bit of 'Gestapo' methods used here, that is the native WILL do this or that on the say of these people [Indian Agents], the threats always being implied and in many cases real ... I personally have only seen ... the local Indian agent once, but was impressed by the fact that he was in the wrong spot, being more suitable for the haunts of Greenwich Village and mentally, should be at once transferred to the School of Fine Arts at Banff, where he would be much more at home."[40] The Indians were not afraid to express their dissatisfaction. Scurvy Shorty complained in 1966 that the Indian superintendent "seems to be unwilling to associate with us, or discuss matters openly. I have been visiting several villages and they all think it is time that we had a new Superintendent."[41]

The Yukon agents in turn were responsible to superiors in Ottawa, who managed an increasingly expensive and interventionist nation-wide program of aboriginal affairs, and who rarely had direct experience of conditions in the sub-Arctic. There were often tensions, as evidenced by Bill Grant's trial over the diversion of funds and A.E. Fry's regular criticisms of federal policy and bureaucracy. The field agents believed that, because they were in the field and in direct contact with the difficulties people encountered, they were better able to design and implement useful programs than bureaucrats sitting in Ottawa offices. The people in the field, the Yukon agents asserted, had a particular sense of urgency. The oppressive reality of distance – Whitehorse was over 3,000 miles from Ottawa – and the centralization of power in the nation's capital contributed to the Yukon agents' increasing sense of isolation and powerlessness.

The Indians became increasingly bitter about the expanding role of Indian government officials. The activities of child-care workers,[42] particularly the removal of children from the villages, was a source of great dissatisfaction. Native cases made up close to half of all child-welfare interventions (a territorial responsibility) in the Yukon in 1965, even though the Native people made up much less than that portion of the total population.[43] There were numerous requests to officials in Ottawa for greater band control of aboriginal affairs. In general, however, the Natives discovered that they had little ability to influence the government workers. Federal Indian agents and territorial officials encouraged children to attend residential school, controlled the flow of cash into the communities, decided who would get housing or support for a planned business, managed many of the bands' affairs, and in countless other ways affected the lives of communities and individual Indians.

Completing forms and applications, interviews, and appeals to officials became a routine part of Native life, a constant reminder of the Indians' subordinate role in territorial life and their continued status as wards of the state. Much of the frustration was directed at the Department of DIA's officials. As Alan Fry told the author: "The burden lay in the fact that so many services were channelled through one agency. We were a single window for a wide range of services for which non-natives would deal with an equally wide range of different agencies and department. Because for natives almost everything came through one agency, that agency became omnipresent in their lives. I don't think government per se was the problem, it was the concentration of every service through one agency of government that grew horrendous."

Government agents, who bore the brunt of the criticism and animosity, gradually came to the realization that their interventions were not always welcome. The rhetoric remained more substantial than the practice, but government officials talked openly of the need to consult with Native people. Bill Grant observed in 1961

We must recognize that it is not enough to do something for Indians; we must be prepared to work with them. Unless the Indians themselves come to understand the need for better education, better housing, better sanitation and, indeed, a better community and want to obtain these things of their own accord because they feel they should have them, rather than because it is something that the non-Indian believes is good for them, very little progress will be achieved. Therefore every effort is being made so, whenever possible, the Indian people assume responsibility and control of their own affairs.[44]

By the early 1970s there was a growing awareness of the need to pay closer attention to the Native people. J.V. Boys of the Yukon Indian Agency, commenting on a plan to build community freezers in the smaller communities, observed, "The main problem has always been that when we entertain 'change' we suggest such things ... without knowing the full ramifications of their impact. Any programme which we institute should first be preceded by education and instruction in the operation of the programme and then followed up to ensure success. We have been at fault in this in the past.[45]

By the late 1960s the federal government was moving to fulfill the assimilationist agenda that was explicit in the Indian Act. Through a complex web of social, economic, educational, and cultural initiatives, it sought to draw the Yukon Indians into the mainstream of Canadian society. The effort worked – but only in a physical sense. The Indians largely abandoned their mobile ways; many moved into the Whitehorse area or near permanent non-Native communities. But government initiatives, paternalistic and unsympathetic to aboriginal aspirations, did little to reduce barriers between the races. Government agents discovered that Yukon Indians did not particularly want to become white men. The Native determination to preserve their culture undermined the foundation of government programs for Indian people.

CHAPTER TWELVE

Indians and
Non-Native Society

The rapid expansion of mining, road-building, and government services in the Yukon Territory pushed the Indians into the background of territorial society. By 1971 the Yukon's population stood at 18,235, of whom 2,590 were status Indians. As before, the non-Native remained extremely transient in the post-war era, passing quickly in and out of the north on government or military service or working temporarily in the expanding service and mining industries. Yukon Indians found themselves unwelcome in the increasingly middle-class territorial society, where fewer and fewer of the non-Natives had more than passing contact with the Native people.

There was a regional dimension to this racial balance. Whites numerically dominated in Whitehorse, but in many of the smaller communities Indians remained in the majority. This also changed over time, as the economic and social attractions of the new capital (as of 1953) drew many Natives to the city. By 1961 over 410 of the territory's estimated 2,046 status Indians lived in the capital city.[1] By the early 1970s that number had increased by approximately three times, making the Whitehorse reserve the largest Native community in the Yukon.

The social accommodation between the races did not quickly change from its pre-war pattern. Indian Agent R.J. Meek, in an intriguing description of race relations in the Yukon, indicated the continuing complexity of Native-white interaction:

As in most communities, certain stores and restaurants are patronized by nearly all the Indians. I know of no business place in Northern BC or the Yukon where their patronage is refused ... At Whitehorse, Taylor & Drury Ltd. have actively sought Indian trade for over 50 years, they have by far the largest Indian custom. Some restaurants do not seek Indian trade, but in the only case I had referred to me, the management quickly apologized and the staff received instructions of non-discrimination. In the Dawson cinema it has been the custom for many years past for Indian patrons to sit on the left side of the aisle and non-Indians on the right. No stigma is attached, it is simply accepted as the order of things.[2]

In Whitehorse, where discriminatory patterns were most noticeable, Natives and whites remained apart. Most of the Indians lived on the Whitehorse Indian reserve, located a considerable distance from the main settlement. A number of other Indians joined the urban squatter settlements on Whiskey and Moccasin flats. In all locations, Native homes were poorly constructed, crowded, and lacking such basic amenities as running water[3] and oil heating. As late as 1966 water was delivered by truck to a central tank on the reserve; families had to collect their water from the tank.[4] Throughout the reserve, outdoor privies and wood stoves remained the norm.

The Indians remained a subclass within Whitehorse society, continually perceived in stereotypic terms. Derogatory comments were common: "Indians are useless and lazy," "They can't hold down a steady job," "They're always begging," "They expect you to do everything for them," "They're just a bunch of drunken bums."[5] There was some interracial contact, but only rarely on an equal basis. A government official visiting Whitehorse in 1972 observed Indians "who have no regular employment and whose daily occupation is walking to the town centre, sitting on the river bank near the station, hanging around the corner of Drury and Taylor's store, sitting in shop doorways or drinking in the taverns. Although a number of people look down on this group of Indians they are not entirely ostracized by white people and many of them have white friends with whom they pass the time of day."[6]

Non-Natives occupied the better built homes in the main city district and in Camp Takhini, many of them left over from the wartime construction projects. In the late 1950s the government built new residential suburbs atop the cliffs west of the city; most of the military workers and civil servants were housed in these standard-issue duplexes. As the city grew, private suburban developments opened across the Yukon River in Riverdale, and northwest of town at Porter Creek. Until the 1970s these new housing areas remained almost exclusively non-Native.

The opening of a new civic centre in Whitehorse in 1950 brought the racial issue into sharp relief. As the facility was being erected, the local newspaper contained considerable commentary on the appropriateness of allowing Native children to use it. Several observers suggested that permitting Natives into the facility would harm fundraising efforts.[7] The general thrust of the debate, however, was that the Indians should be accepted; one commentator wrote that it would be "only an ill-bred white that can wish to keep the Indian illiterate and low."[8] The discussion went on for several weeks. The North Star Civic Centre Committee noted that all were welcome, provided they behaved themselves;[9] an "onlooker" wondered if the Indians were actually to be welcomed or only tolerated.[10] Natives were ultimately permitted into the facility, but the fact that there had been a debate said a great deal about community attitudes.

The situation was not much different in the mining communities, where Native employees often lived in tents outside the bunkhouse.[11] A.E. Fry wrote, "Indian men find bunkhouses particularly distressing. We have instances where men have given up good employment for which the company in question found them completely satisfactory, simply because they could not tolerate the indignity of bunkhouse living, coupled with the periods of separation from their family and community."[12]

The United Keno Hill mine at Elsa seldom hired Natives, and instead was home to an ever changing population of Canadian, American, and European miners. The distinction between Native and white settlements was graphic in the Ross River area, where in 1969 the Cyprus Anvil Mining Corporation opened a mine and built a new company town.[13] During the construction period, the workers stayed at Ross River, a largely Native community forty miles away, an arrangement which worked poorly and caused considerable racial strife. When the town site was ready, the whites moved to modern new homes, complete with the amenities common to company towns in that era. Ross River, impoverished in comparison, remained home to Natives unable to find work in the mines and those denied the right to live within the Faro town limits.[14] A survey conducted by the Indians in the early 1970s demonstrated that "there are no building or sanitation and Public Health standards in effect. People have to do their own wiring. Electricity is not hooked up, extension cords run from one house to another, walls are painted for the top 5 feet with not enough paint supplied for the rest of the walls. People are still living in tents."[15] The contrast to the modern settlement at Faro was painfully apparent.

In most communities Natives and whites lived separately. In the newer ones, especially along the Alaska Highway, the federal government created new residential reserves, often some distance away from the main settlement. Watson Lake, for instance, was predominantly non-Native; the Indians lived at Upper Liard or Lower Post. In the smaller centres, such as Haines Junction, Burwash, and Beaver Creek, Native villages were constructed near to, but separate from, white housing. In Carcross the Indian reserve was on the opposite side of the river from the main non-Native settlement. This arrangement was partially a reflection of legal realities – non-Natives could not build houses on Indian reserves – but also an indication of the persistent social gulf between the races in the territory.

In these mixed settings, Indians and non-Natives did not socialize freely. The Anglican pattern of using Native leaders continued in several Indian settlements,[16] partly because the church experienced difficulty attracting clergy to its northern postings. In several congregations Native women participated in the "lower echelons" of the women's auxiliary. In the Anglican church in Whitehorse the white population attended the cathedral, while Native communicants rarely did so, although they were served for much of the decade by Deaconess Hilda Hellaby, who had worked in Mayo for much of the 1950s before moving to Whitehorse.[17]

A cautious accommodation was reached in most of the outlying communities. Schools, churches, and businesses were generally integrated, but relations were not always easy or particularly polite. Watson Lake, for example, was notorious for the tensions between the white and Indian sectors. On the other hand, Johnny Johns, the highly esteemed big-game guide and enfranchised Indian, played a prominent role in the Yukon Fish and Game Association and the Guides and Outfitters Association. Yet mixed-race organizations were rare. An attempt to form a Native-white community association in Carcross got off to a promising start in 1948 but soon foundered.[18] In general, the Natives and whites moved in very different social circles, even when the people shared a single, small community.

In spite of this, there were many opportunities for Natives and non-Natives to meet. A handful of Indian veterans of the Second World War joined the Dawson City Legion, and several of the territories' scout troops were integrated. Territorial businesses occasionally sponsored various social events for Native children, particularly those at residential schools.[19] Sports also became an important meeting ground. Indian and white teams played baseball in Teslin and basketball in Mayo and met each other on various playing fields and surfaces in Whitehorse. Native people became very active in cross-country skiing, especially in Old Crow where the program was integrated into the community and produced a number of national-class competitors.[20] Although the Indian agents took these games as a sign of harmony – "there is no racial feeling whatever," one wrote – the fact that teams were routinely segregated by race shows again the social gap between the races.[21]

Only a few almost exclusively Native villages remained – Old Crow in the far north, Pelly Crossing, and Ross River. In these settlements there were noticeable differences between the housing and facilities available to the police officers, missionaries, school teachers, or government agents and those provided for Native residents. The non-Natives did not occupy residential compounds, as was the case on some reserves in the prairie provinces, but they had larger, more comfortable, and better equipped homes than did the Indians. The few non-Natives in these settlements often had considerable authority over the Indians and, in the pattern of the "marginal men" described by sociologist W. Dunning, did not hesitate to use their power to establish social and cultural distance between themselves and the Natives.[22]

The non-Native population had numerous explanations for this pattern of segregation. According to one government official, it originated in the different standard of living of Native and non-Natives: "Being representative of economic and culturally deprived minorities everywhere, they are clannish, shy and suspicious. Cleanliness standards are low. Abuse of alcohol is endemic and many adults have served gaol terms for drunkenness, fighting and petty theft."[23] Commissioner F.H. Collins was even more blunt, saying that the Indians "brood, breed and drink, mostly."[24] Collins also argued that racial discrimination was a two-way street; Natives, he argued, had to refrain from drinking if they hoped for acceptance by the non-Natives.[25]

Complaints about Native drinking became an increasingly common refrain. Public drunkenness, particularly around the "Indian bars" in Whitehorse and the outlying communities, was relatively commonplace and, for many non-Natives, symbolized Native behaviour. For many years most Native drinking was of the "spree" variety, usually occurring when the Indians came to the trading posts.[26] This changed as the laws were amended. In 1955, for example, Indians were permitted to drink beer in taverns, although they could not purchase beer to consume off the premises.[27] Among the non-Natives, stories abounded about the Indians' inability to handle liquor and the lengths to which they would go to purchase it. In Whitehorse, the stories went, one could buy Native welfare-food vouchers for 50 cents on the dollar or purchase most of a moose carcass for a couple of cases of beer. A territorial councillor complained in 1960 that "there should be a welfare officer sitting in the [Carmacks] beer parlour when they hand out family allowance cheques. They ran out of beer for four days after the cheques were released."[28]

While the pattern of aboriginal drinking gives some support to Nancy Lurie's analysis that alcohol abuse was a way of demonstrating one's Nativeness – Indians were expected to be drunk, after all – the problem went much deeper.[29] James Miller's analysis of the relationship between social crisis and drinking in the St Lawrence valley in the eighteenth century appears to be on the mark: "Whether Indians became demoralized because they drank too much, or whether they drank too much because they had been demoralized by other influences can never be known for sure. What is beyond doubt is that alcohol, whether cause or effect, was associated with demoralization."[30]

Under the Indian Act, Natives had routinely been imprisoned for doing what whites did legally.[31] As a direct consequence of this illogical arrangement, the Yukon Indians attached little stigma to such punishments. According to R.J. Meek, "instead of being abashed at seeing their names associated with a criminal charge, most Indians seemed to be flattered when their names were mentioned, and proudly sent copies of the paper to their friends far and wide."[32] The rituals of aboriginal drinking, which often provided Natives with their first contact with the law, served only to discredit the legal and judicial process in their eyes.

In the 1950s the pattern of interracial sexual relations remained as in the past: short-term liaisons between white men and Native women, only occasionally sanctified by church marriages.[33] As the Indian agent wrote, "The towns beckon the girls where, if they are even slightly attractive, they enjoy a gay time."[34] "Generally," R.J. Meek observed, "only the most attractive or seductive of Indian girls marry white men. In a number of exceptions, Indian girls of outstanding morals and character have married white men of good repute. It is almost a truism in the north that Indians marry 'poor whites'. The few cases I have known of Indian men marrying white women have not been successful."[35]

A 1972 government official's report of a visit to Whitehorse suggested that the pattern was still in place: "A number of girls are 'shacked up' with white men in various parts of the city. The biological division between white and Indian is also nebulous. When asked how many Indians there were in Whitehorse one Indian replied 'two or three thousand because of guys like you that fool around with Indian girls.' It is apparent that for many people the question of being Indian or white is largely a matter of personal choice, association, dress and interests."[36]

There was an even darker side to this interaction, particularly in settings where race, sex, and alcohol mixed. Dr O. Schaefar described the situation at Lower Post, a few miles south of Watson Lake:

Lower Post now appears to have the reputation of being extremely lawless. No doubt because of this, workers from Cassiar and Canada Tungsten and others flock there. The Lower Post Hotel is their hangout ... it appears the Lower Post Hotel is being used as a 'brothel.' The Lower Post Indians have only been in contact with civilization for the last 25 or 30 years and they certainly have not built up an immunity to liquor. Because of this the Indian girls and women can, after a few drinks, become the victim of unscrupulous 'White Trash.'[37]

Although racial segregation and discrimination remained an important feature of Yukon life in the 1950s, there were signs of significant changes in attitudes. By the later part of the decade, non-Natives were beginning to express concern about the Indians' condition. While the original impulse was quite paternalistic, expressions of interest formed the basis for a more balanced approach to aboriginal affairs. Once largely the preserve of the churches, the impulse to "help" the Indians gradually expanded into the secular world. In November 1956 the Indian Advancement Association was formed in Whitehorse, under the leadership of Commissioner F.H. Collins and Indian Agent M.G. Jutras. The group retained an assimilationist agenda; it hoped to foster racial understanding, assist the Natives' entry into Canadian society, encourage aboriginal handicraft production, and lobby for improved educational opportunities.[38] The Society sponsored speakers, films, and discussions on aboriginal affairs, and helped to raise the profile of Native issues in the capital city. Over time, Native people assumed leadership of the organization; in 1963 Clara Tizya became its president.[39] Two years later Mrs Tizya was appointed the Yukon representative to the Indian Advisory Council for BC and the Yukon.[40]

The increased attention to Native affairs was partially the result of their gradual integration into the political system. Although Native people in Canada received the right to vote in federal elections in 1960 and the territorial franchise the following year,[41] they did not immediately seek to exercise it. A small number of Indians had presented themselves to vote on several earlier occasions. During the 1957 election, for instance, an indeterminate number of Indians attempted to vote; they were, after all, not legally registered on reserves and felt they could exercise their franchise.[42] Erik Nielsen, Yukon Member of Parliament from 1957, was one of the first territorial politicians to solicit the Native vote successfully.[43] But the Natives would not, as a group, begin to exercise their considerable political might for another decade, and it was not until the 1980s that the Yukon Territorial Council had a sizeable aboriginal caucus.

Astute politicians realized, however, that Native issues were increasingly important, and Nielsen made aboriginal issues a major part of his political career. He often spoke out on Native matters, particularly in the early 1960s. In 1960 he labelled the DIA a "dictatorship" and suggested that the Natives be given far greater control over their own affairs.[44] His repeated and wide-ranging attacks, which often drew on Yukon examples, continued over the following years[45] and were often successful in drawing government attention to territorial conditions.

Conditions changed slowly in the 1960s, as contact increased between the races, particularly in the larger centres. There were more interracial marriages than in previous decades and much greater interaction between Natives and non-Natives, as new social and racial values took root across Canada. The communities, large and small, remained divided along racial lines, but steps toward a greater accommodation were evident. Yukon society would not be remade overnight, especially since the non-Native population remained extremely transient, but the established pattern of racial discrimination and segregation was, by the early 1970s, beginning to break down.

What effect did this pattern of social change, confrontation, and discrimination have on Yukon Native people? There had been problems in Indian society before 1950, but the difficulties increased exponentially in the years that followed. Major changes, which swept the Indians from the land and made them an administered people, occurred rapidly through the 1950s and early 1960s. Even in isolated villages such as Ross River and Old Crow, where many of the Natives continued to hunt and trap for much of their food and cash, the omnipresent hand of government was in evidence. Native peoples, having lived for generations on the land, following the seasons, the animals, and the fish, found themselves relegated to tiny reserves, with few controls over their own affairs and little freedom.

Many Indians continued to return to the land for spiritual renewal and for the food that was so important for their survival. But the mobile habits of the past had, largely through circumstances beyond the Indians' immediate control, been abandoned. Men hunted alone or with other men; women and children remained in the villages so that the youngsters could attend school, as the government demanded. Long-established seasonal rhythms were substantially broken, and young people, often assigned to residential schools, grew up with little experience of life on the land.

These changes also struck at the heart of aboriginal gender roles, particularly that of men. Their primary role had been to hunt and trap, providing much of the food and cash income for their families. Both of these functions were now taken over by the government, which became most women's "old man," at least in financial terms. The government's willingness to support single and unwed mothers seriously interfered with aboriginal marriage patterns. Arranged marriages, common in the north in the 1940s and 1950s, quickly disappeared, for women no longer needed men for support. Women retained responsibility for the care of the children and the nurturing of the community; men had lost their primary function, and found themselves rendered financially impotent under the new rules of the welfare state.[46]

The cumulative impact was truly severe. Consider A.E. Fry's description of Upper Laird in 1966: "Upper Liard is a village of problems. The people are apathetic, unskilled and often unemployed. Children are poorly cared for. Severe drinking is wide spread, reaching down to the *younger* school age group. While the adults drink, night after night, the school children wander the village, sometimes until day break. Violent strife frequently breaks out in manifestation of the ever present hostility between factions and families, husbands and wives. There have been killings. We have reason to expect more."[47]

The cultural loss had been remarkably pervasive. Most Indian children in the Yukon before the 1950s were raised by their parents, lived off the land, and learned, from birth, both their aboriginal language and customs. With the expansion of residential schools, the inclusion of other children in the territorial school system, and increasing government intervention in many aspects of personal and band life, this experience of childhood was lost. Native children learned to speak English in school, and were often punished for speaking their own language. Native culture was deprecated; the school curriculum included virtually no aboriginal content, except as a backdrop to the history of North America. By the early 1970s few Native people under the age of thirty could speak their Native tongue, and by the time Native-language instruction was introduced into the school system in the late 1980s, several of the territory's indigenous languages were in danger of extinction.[48]

The new order also had a damaging effect on aboriginal spirituality. Because of the pervasiveness of Anglican and Catholic missions by the 1940s, Native spiritual expression had been largely hidden from public view. This did not, as a number of anthropologists and ethnographers discovered, mean that aboriginal beliefs had disappeared, although they had clearly changed. As Native people became separated from their land and culture, their spiritual confidence ebbed. Younger people, raised outside their culture and in an oddly despiritualized Christian environment, had little connection to the spiritual beliefs that had long enriched their parents' and grandparents' lives.

Missionaries, teachers, and government agents welcomed all these changes, for they saw the elimination of aboriginal cultures as being essential to the Indians' assimilation into Canadian society. But the cultural, spiritual, and economic losses carried a huge social cost, one that was borne almost entirely by the aboriginal community. The Indians had been forced from the land, cloistered in residential reserves, tied into an assimilationist education system, and bound economically to an interventionist federal government. The result was that Indians suffered an incalculable loss of identity; processes largely held in check in the Yukon until the 1950s had, in only two decades, resulted in the serious but systematic destruction of aboriginal culture and society.

Some elements, of course, remained. The elders, though suffering through the dislocations, maintained a knowledge of their language and culture. They would, when Canadian attitudes changed in the 1970s, enthusiastically share their skills with anthropologists and ethnographers in a systematic attempt to sustain the old cultural forms.[49] Individuals, in declining numbers, remained on the land, continuing the harvesting traditions of their ancestors; isolated settlements, particularly Old Crow, retained their dependence on hunting and trapping and continued decades-old seasonal rhythms.

For most Yukon Indians the years of disintegration brought personal hardship and pain. The statistics of social crisis – unemployment, suicide, infant mortality, arrests and convictions, violent deaths – provided mute testimony of the trauma that ripped through the villages and cultures of the territory. In the 1970s, when the Indians became more politically assertive, non-Natives wondered why the Indians had been comparatively silent in the 1960s – the implication being that outside agitators were solely responsible for the emergence of Native complaints. They misunderstood. Native people did protest through the 1950s and 1960s, but they did so privately and against themselves, rather than publicly and against the white population.

Alcohol-use became a key ingredient in aboriginal protest, serving as either an assertion of Indianness or a self-induced fog that repeatedly blurred the oppressive reality of aboriginal life in the Yukon Territory. Alcohol was a symptom of the cultural identity crisis, and not simply a cause of social decay. Indians in the Yukon drank excessively, it appears, because of the cultural and social dislocations they had experienced; the social problems did not originate with the drinking.

Native drinking also had a significant impact on Indian-white relations. The sight of drunken Indians on the streets of Whitehorse, Dawson, or Watson Lake provided the non-Native population with confirmation that the long-held stereotypes about Indians were based in fact. Because they clearly could not control themselves, the argument went, there was no reason to provide them with special services or programs. There was also no reason to expect the Indians to play an important role in the territory's future.

But alcohol-abuse was only the tip of the proverbial iceberg, readily identified by the non-Native majority because aboriginal drinking was often a public event. The social pathologies of a culture in extreme distress were evident throughout the territory. Native people filled the jail and juvenile detention centre – leading a number of whites to comment, not always inaccurately, that the Indians willingly broke the law to be able to stay in jail. Such criminal behaviour, which almost always involved alcohol, typically occurred within the group, and was seldom directed at the non-Native population. There were other signs of widespread crisis, including high rates of violent death, particularly among young Native men, family disintegration, spousal assault, and a cultural malaise that threatened the entire population.

While the cultural and social crisis was profound and, to many, hopeless, there were Native people fighting for survival and non-Natives anxious to support their efforts. A.E. Fry who, in his capacity as Indian agent between 1961 and 1965, was responsible for implementing many of the government's program, was clearly dissatisfied with the federal agenda and continually lobbied for change. Many church workers, particularly Hilda Hellaby of the Anglican Church and Father Mouchet of the Roman Catholic Church, were horrified by the Indians' social circumstances and worked hard to improve conditions, though their parent institutions, unconvinced of the need for a new approach to aboriginal affairs, were less supportive. But the main impetus, separated from the still colonial ideology of church and state, came from the Native communities. A number of prominent Indian women, including Angela Sidney, Ellen Bruce, Virginia Smarch, Pearl Keenan, and Margaret Thompson, fought within their villages and with the government for basic improvements. There were also several men, including Elijah Smith, Frankie Jim, Johnny Johns, and Art Johns, who played key leadership roles as the Indians drew together to lobby federal and territorial governments for change.

Much emphasis has been placed on the social and cultural ills that descended on Yukon communities in the 1950s and 1960s. There is no question that the combination of economic dislocation, the destruction of nomadic lifestyles, residential schools, alcohol-abuse, and widespread discrimination had a serious effect on the aboriginal people of the territory. In the midst of the pain, however, was a determination – obvious, intentional and unbroken – to remain Indian, and to avoid the assimilationist pull of government and society. As they watched their homeland being divided by non-Native developers and found themselves pushed from the lands that had sustained them for countless generations, Yukon Native people began to turn from their personal suffering and seek greater control over their lives and future.

CHAPTER THIRTEEN

Fighting for Their Place: The Emergence of Native Land Claims

In 1973 the Yukon Native Brotherhood tabled Canada's first comprehensive land claim, collected in a document called *Together Today for Our Children Tomorrow*. The Indians' sweeping demands sent shock waves through the territory.[1] *Together Today* included an angry indictment of the role of non-Natives in Yukon history, from the fur traders and missionaries to contemporary government officials. A number of non-Native Yukoners had clung to the belief that the Indians had accepted the developments of the past, and had developed a respect for the triumvirate of western civilization: religion, education, and government. The land claim set that perception to rest.

Initial reaction by non-Natives was strongly negative. People worried that their land was about to be expropriated by Indians and that Native financial and property demands would emasculate the territorial economy, concerns that political leaders were not able to dispel quickly. Misunderstanding in the Native communities added to the uncertainty. After years of being forced off their homelands, many Indians counted on the claim to give them renewed control over their lives and lands. Many non-Natives, however, refused to credit the Indians for the creation of the land claim. They asserted, generally in private, that the emergence of the land claim was the work of young non-Native radicals, particularly members of the Company of Young Canadians. There was, seemingly, some comfort to be found in the argument that it was non-Native agitators, such as John Hoyt, and not the YNB chief, Elijah Smith, who was responsible for the tabling of the land claim.

This misapprehension lingered through the years, even as the land-claim negotiations became more sophisticated on both sides and the Indians clearly held their own against the government officials. The Yukon land claim, the argument goes, was simply tied to the emergence of Native protest across the country – to such organizations as the American Indian Movement and to the tremendous cross-Canada reaction to the Trudeau government's abortive proposed amendments to the Indian Act in 1969.[2] This view is incorrect. It ignores the indigenous roots of the Yukon land claim and the pattern of Native representations on the question of aboriginal lands that culminated in the 1973 demands.

Until the 1950s Yukon Native people experienced few restrictions on their use of the land. Canadian and territorial laws were enforced with considerable flexibility; exceptions were routinely made if Native subsistence was at stake.[3] Non-Native interest in the land remained limited to small plots of mineralized ground and a few town sites. This did not, however, mean that the Indians did not have a strong sense of territoriality, as Yukon Indian Agent R.J. Meek observed: "As land, in itself is held in low esteem, there are seldom disputes over it. There are disputes, however, over trap-line boundaries ... The minute particle of land used as a fishing station is a jealously guarded possession and there are occasional disputes about these, though they usually devolve into matters of prior rights or inheritance."[4]

The post-war period witnessed the expansion of the capitalist land-and-resource ethic in the Yukon.[5] The Canadian government and the most recent wave of immigrants from the south rejected aboriginal hunting as a viable economic activity and sought to integrate the Indians into the broader Canadian society. For the first time, efforts were made to impose Canadian concepts of land ownership and tenure on the Yukon Indians. The licensing of big-game hunting territories and the implementation of trapline registration in 1950, for example, commercialized aboriginal lands, and created circumstances by which Natives could be separated from lands which they and their ancestors had controlled for generations.

The new system for land tenure was applied rapidly across the territory. Trapline registration, huge oil and gas leases in the northern Yukon, the staking of hundreds of new mineral claims throughout the region, and the purchase of individual plots of lands near the cities and along the lakes, particularly Marsh and Tagish in the southern Yukon, signalled the entrenchment of Canadian methods of land ownership and control. A Native man from Whitehorse was angered by the new system: "This was my father's land and his father's before the white man came. We didn't ask you to come. Once I had a cabin in Whitehorse. The policemen said it was on government land. They tore it down. They laughed. That was my home."[6] This burst of activity in the first two decades after the war threatened the Indians' traditional use of the land, in many areas for the first time. They were now expected to respect non-Native claims to the land, and to refrain from hunting on or otherwise using properties legally assigned to individual use.

The Indians did not, in the 1950s, have the institutional or political structures to respond to this encroachment on their lands in a way that non-Native society would recognize. The initial framework was an elected chief-and-council system for the Yukon bands implemented by the DIA, even though the structure had little aboriginal relevance. As the Hawthorn Report noted, "The band council device was not a spontaneous creation of the Indians, but one that was introduced from the outside ... the system was not congruent with Indian precedent or social organization in most cases."[7] As late as 1955 some bands had never had the formal elections that were required by the DIA. Teslin, Dawson, Mayo, and Old Crow had active councils and regularly petitioned the territorial and federal governments; Whitehorse Indians showed little interest in elections.

The chiefs acknowledged by the DIA were a mixed lot, some claiming hereditary status, others elected by the band. In 1955 R.J. Meek described Patsy Henderson of Carcross as "a patriarch with an outstanding personality"; Mayo Chief David Moses was "a very strong personality, but without the backing of an important family"; Chief Charles Isaac was an "indifferent personality, but is sincere and hardworking with the added qualification of having his father and grandfather chief of the Dawson band." The leaders generally had access to jobs, and often served as employment brokers for mining and construction companies and fire-fighting crews.[8] But many of the chiefs derived their authority almost entirely from their relationship with the DIA and not from traditional sources.

The council system was not, in fact, designed to transfer real authority to Native leaders. Instead, the structure provided an agency through which the government and the DIA could deal with the entire band or settlement. Rather than serving as leaders in the Native sense of the term, band chiefs and councillors functioned as intermediaries, implementing government programs on occasion and representing the group's interests to the DIA. Thus, even in this one apparent gesture towards Indian autonomy, the government had in fact imposed yet another artificial structure and reduced further the power of traditional Native means of social control.[9]

Band chiefs and councils consequently experienced considerable difficulties through the 1960s and 1970s. A number of bands applied to the DIA for new elections and successfully deposed unpopular leaders. There were particular problems with band managers, and both DIA officials and local Natives were often sharply critical of them.[10] There were many other problems. Several bands were, in fact, amalgamations of different cultural groups: Champagne and Aishihik were joined in the early 1970s,[11] Upper Liard-Lower Post was a merger of five bands created in 1961,[12] Kluane represented a grouping of the Indians from Snag, Burwash, and Kloo Lake that started in 1961,[13] and the Whitehorse Indians were joined with those from Lake LaBerge in the mid-1950s.[14] Some newly created bands had developed little of the internal cohesion required for an organized response.[15] There was especially severe tension in the Liard River band, which united the Kaska of northern British Columbia with people who had formerly lived in the Frances Lake area. In 1972 band affairs had come to a "standstill" as a result of dissatisfaction between the groups.[16]

The existence of chiefs and councils did not ensure that Native people were regularly consulted on matters relating to their welfare. In December 1958, for example, a major meeting on the welfare of Yukon Indians was held in Whitehorse. The participants included Erik Nielsen, Commissioner Fred Collins, the Anglican and Catholic bishops, five Yukon territorial councillors, two officials of the Department of Northern Affairs and National Resources, and M.G. Jutras, superintendent of the Yukon Indian Agency. Not a single Native person from the Yukon was invited.[17]

Even though new forms of leadership did not suit aboriginal needs, Yukon Native people did not hesitate to press their cases before government, particularly on questions of land and resources. Years before the tabling of the Yukon land claim in 1973, Yukon Indians were petitioning the territorial and federal government for redress of outstanding grievances. When approached by the Indians on the question of land rights, the government's position was firm: "The Yukon Indians ... have no stipulated land entitlement, land being provided as required to meet their needs."[18] The federal government, which retained control of territorial lands, would provide specific plots of land to meet what it defined as legitimate aboriginal needs; Ottawa would not, however, deal with the broader question of aboriginal rights to the Yukon Territory. Nor did lands set aside have official status. L.L. Brown, superintendent of reserves and trusts, wrote in 1954 that most of the lands "are merely reserved in the records of the Department of Northern Affairs and National Resources for the use of the Indians for so long as required for that purpose."[19] Eight of the eighteen bands in the Yukon were, in government parlance, "squatters on the land."[20]

So long as the Natives' requests did not impede development, the government was generally prepared to accept them.[21] The amount of land set aside was, in any case, minimal. A 1962 estimate of territorial lands allocated for Native use identified less than 4,800 acres: Mayo had a reserve of 728 acres, but it was no longer inhabited; and the second largest reserve, at 640 acres, was a largely unused tract at Moosehide. All but 6 of the 21 properties scattered about the territory were under 250 acres.[22] At the same time, the Native villages were not reserves under the legal meaning of the term, and had to be set aside by Order in Council.[23]

There were members of the civil service who worried that even this *ad hoc* system of land allocation was not in the Indians' best interest. When M.G. Jutras assumed control of the Yukon Indian Agency in 1955, he queried his superiors about the utility of the reserve system, which was linked to the extension of the Indian housing program. He argued that the Indians should be granted land in fee simple, with the department's interest in the property protected by a lien. "It is thought," Jutras speculated, "that in this way, the Yukon Indian might be integrated into the Non-Indian population, in a shorter time than by segregating them by placing them on a reserve."[24] Erik Nielsen took a contrary view, arguing in Whitehorse and the House of Commons as early as 1958 that a treaty was required to settle the Indian land question.[25]

Yukon Native people made a number of requests for specific pieces of ground – for additional housing, cattle grazing, fur-farming, or other uses. A substantial, 21,000-acre block of land was set aside in 1962 for a proposed Indian-run ranch in the Champagne-Mendenhall area.[26] A 6,000-acre piece of grazing land was set aside near Teslin in 1965 at the request of local Indians, another sign that the government was prepared to provide substantial blocks of property – under the right conditions.[27] Most of the appeals were accepted,[28] although these small decisions did not address the larger question of aboriginal rights to the land. Concern was also expressed by government officials about the "ad hoc way land is being set aside for the use of Indians in the Yukon."[29] This was addressed, in part, by reclaiming some lands that "are of absolutely no value or use to the Bands for whom they were originally required."[30] Also, it was widely believed that "The Indians of the Yukon Territory are likely to demand, in time, that they be treated the same as their brothers to the south and the east, and as time goes on the most desirable areas will have been picked up by the non-Indians."[31]

There was clearly a gathering consensus among officials and interested parties that a land settlement was required. A 1958 meeting of federal, territorial, and church officials included the passage of a motion that read: "Be it resolved that inasmuch as no treaty exists between the Indians of the Yukon, and the Government of Canada, it would seem desirable, with the consent of the Indians of the Yukon, to make some arrangements regarding individual and Band land allotments at this time as a measure of security."[32] Indian Superintendent W.E. Grant was even more blunt: "It is my duty to point out that desirable land is being purchased very rapidly. If the future interests of the Indian people are not protected we will be inviting criticism and even worse it will not be possible in a few years to purchase land which will be of any immediate value."[33]

Ottawa was reluctant to accept demands for a Yukon treaty. The explanation for this reluctance, which stood in contrast to the government's willingness to sign treaties across the prairie west and middle north, ironically rested with the sensitive question of aboriginal land rights in British Columbia. The BC government had since 1870 steadfastly refused to consider Native requests for treaty rights. When Treaty No. 8 was negotiated in 1899, it was made clear to the commissioners that no discussions were to be held with Indians to the west of the Rocky mountains not covered by the special conditions of the Treaty No. 8 process, for fear that such discussions would prejudice the BC situation.[34] The Yukon Indians' land rights had, according to government advisers in the 1960s, been sacrificed on the altar of federal-provincial politics.

By the late 1960s that position appeared to be softening. While the official policy remained that the Indians had no aboriginal rights to their ancestral lands, officials within the civil service were considering ways of settling this vexatious question. One government agent, writing in 1967, observed, "Our position should be either to negotiate a treaty with these Indians or have some independent body hear their claims and, if their claim is good, to compensate them on a once-for-all basis. I understand that the proposed Indian Claims Commission is intended to serve this purpose."[35]

The issue assumed greater urgency when the Indians began to protest development activities on their lands. In 1970 Northern Oil Explorers received permission to drill for oil in the Old Crow flats, an area that regularly produced over 10,000 muskrat pelts and was the foundation of the village economy. When the project, promised "as a showpiece for the industry of what can be done in an extremely sensitive environment,"[36] resulted in some localized damage, the Old Crow band sought an injunction against oil exploration in the Porcupine Region.[37] The band resolution stated "in unequivocal terms to the MINISTER of MINES, MINERALS and RESOURCES that we do not consent to the diversion or tempering [sic] with the waters of the

PORCUPINE RIVER VALLEY drainage the LANDS of which we claim as ours by original occupation and possession."[38]

The department's legal adviser, Hugh Fischer, argued, "The fact that no treaties were signed between the Old Crow Indians and the Government of Canada in no way derogates from the Crown's absolute dominion and sovereignty over the land in question ... In my opinion the Old Crow Indians have no right of property or any right or interest either legal or equitable, save their right of occupancy subject to the absolute dominion of the Crown."[39] The Indians were able to extract some concessions from the government and industry concerning future development activities;[40] they had far greater difficulty getting the government to accept the legitimacy of their land claim.

The debate over lands, combined with the many other issues and problems facing Yukon Indians, convinced several leading Natives of the need to organize on a territory-wide basis. Led by Elijah Smith, and with the assistance of such men as Frankie Jim and Art John, Native leaders from throughout the territory began to discuss common issues in the mid-1960s. When the federal government became more sympathetically disposed to Indian organizations, funding was offered for a Yukon assembly. A major meeting of Yukon and northern British Columbia Indian chiefs and representatives was held in Whitehorse in January 1966. At the beginning of the meeting, the assembled Native leaders asked the government officials to leave the room, "the idea being that there might be a freer discussion if they were on their own."[41] The leaders agreed that they should begin work immediately towards the creation of a territory-wide Native organization.[42]

The organizational efforts continued, resulting in a heightened sense of common cause and shared injustice. The leaders, having returned to their communities to generate support for the idea of an umbrella group, met again (this time in the company of several of the nation's leading Indian activists, including John Tootoois, George Manuel, and Duke Redbird) in Whitehorse in June 1966. They formally established the Klondike Indian Association, with Gordon Frank of Telegraph Creek, BC as the first president. The association had a series of specific objectives: the settlement of the Yukon land claim, the election of an Indian to the Yukon Territorial Council, the encouragement of economic development, aboriginal culture, and education, and the improvement of social conditions.[43]

The new Native organization soon found itself busy with a variety of initiatives and activities, including a visit in 1968 by Jean Chrétien, minister of northern development and Indian affairs. Highly publicized meetings – the first serious consultations between ranking federal officials and Yukon Indian representatives – provided clear evidence that Native issues had taken on great political importance.[44]

Yukon Natives used these consultations to voice their complaints about the management of Indian affairs and to demand attention to their outstanding grievances. To Elijah Smith, who was emerging as an important spokesperson for the movement, the primary issue was land claims: "We need a treaty to tell us what our rights are – where our land is – we want to plan for the future of our People. We have no future until we clean up this unfinished business. We have several ideas of what we think the terms of the treaty should be. We intend to put a high price on our right to the land of the Yukon. Every year that goes by, and a new mine opens up, our asking price will go up."[45]

The land-claims issue was primarily responsible for the decision, taken in October 1968, to separate Yukon Indians from those in northern British Columbia (who were also administered out of the Whitehorse office of the DIA). A new organization, the Yukon Indian Brotherhood (later Yukon Native Brotherhood), was formed to represent the interests of all Yukon status Indians.[46] A formal structure was established afterwards, providing the organization with a general council made up of the twelve band chiefs, one additional member from each band, and eight members-at-large. Elijah Smith was elected the first chief of the Brotherhood; Dave Joe was the executive director. John Hoyt, a non-Native, was the consultant and a key organizer for the organization. Funding for the YNB came primarily from the federal government, in the form of a $121,000-core grant and various additional research and administrative contracts, bringing the association's total budget for 1973 to over $360,000.[47]

The YNB had an immediate impact on the Yukon, stirring up debate about such issues as Native education, reserve housing, economic development and, in particular, the Indians' demand for a formal treaty.[48] It inundated the DIA with position papers, requests for assistance, and project proposals. A particularly blunt submission, *Where Grows Hopelessness: A Crisis in Housing*, provided vivid statistical and visual evidence of the problems facing Yukon Native people.[49] W.A. Gryva, chief of the Indian-Eskimo bureau, commented in 1971 that "the Yukon Native Brotherhood is becoming a viable force in the Yukon. Although there is a shortage of qualified people at present, enthusiasm for self-determination, and a willingness to speak out is growing."[50] The YNB was initially rather modest in its demands, arguing in an early position paper, "They are *not* claiming native title to the Yukon but are asking for a cash settlement to help them plan a better future."[51]

In 1973 the combination of aboriginal organization and increased pressure on territorial lands resulted in the tabling of the YNB's land claim, which was set out in a document entitled *Together Today for Our Children Tomorrow*. Non-Native Yukoners reacted to the document with dismay and openly questioned the legitimacy of Native demands. Many Yukon Indians were likewise distressed by the vigorous and unflattering response by non-Natives, and wondered if an accommodation was possible under such circumstances. The following years were marked by intense public debate over land claims and considerable frustration on all sides. But through this period, a substantial shift in the nature of Native-white relations in the Yukon occurred.[52]

Much media and academic attention has been focused on the contemporary social pathology of Native communities in the north. The pictures of Native life that emerge are chilling: the rapid and seemingly inexorable loss of indigenous language skills and traditional knowledge, exceptional rates of teenage suicide, endemic problems with alcohol, family violence, chronic unemployment (particularly outside Whitehorse), and continued difficulties within the educational and criminal-justice systems. Although all these problems are real, there is much more to the story.

Out of the same processes of discrimination, disenfranchisement, and dispossession that resulted in the land-claims movement came a territory-wide Native determination to affect meaningful change in the lot of indigenous peoples. Native women, working through community-based organizations, demanded far greater attention to local health and family concerns. Struggles emerged over the use and management of wildlife resources, with the Natives resisting the imposition of "scientific" management of animals and the fishery. Similar debates developed over other issues: the use of Native languages in the classroom, calls for a separate Native school system, community requests for a restructuring of DIA's methods of band management, improved opportunities for post-secondary education for Yukon Natives, and expanded training and job prospects for Native people.

These demands emerged at a time when the federal and territorial governments were prepared to devote financial and personnel resources to aboriginal issues. The DIA, while remaining the focus of considerable hostility in villages across the territory, provided hundreds of thousands of dollars for housing projects, educational and training initiatives, community development, and language and cultural-retention programs. But the criticisms continued. Federal economic programs, for example, paid particular attention to entrepreneurship and were not well designed to address the economic disadvantages of most indigenous communities. At the same time, a vocal minority of non-Natives openly criticized the government for offering what they considered to be excessive levels of financial support for Native programs, and decried what they viewed as the dependence of Yukon Native society on welfare.

Despite complaints and criticism, and notwithstanding the serious economic, social, and cultural problems that continued to plague Yukon Native peoples, a series of significant changes did occur. Residential segregation, particularly in Whitehorse, began to break down in the 1970s and 1980s as Native professionals settled among the general population and as a series of social-housing projects brought Native and whites together in the same complexes. The Whitehorse reserve, built on the least desirable site in the city, was moved to a new and attractive location overlooking the Yukon River valley.

The blatant and overt racism directed at indigenous peoples in earlier times receded somewhat, although many Native people recount numerous personal experiences that make it clear they remain on the outside in their homeland. With the obvious exception of the Native residential reserves, Indian status, and the land-claims processes that clearly differentiate Natives from non-Natives, official acts of discrimination have ceased. Informal racism, pervasive across North America and not unique to the Yukon Territory, however, remains an integral part of the experience of Native people, and continues to hamper attempts at accommodation.

Improvements were evident on the economic front. Native people entered the civil service, partly as a result of affirmative-action programs and also because a significant number had secured the training and skills necessary to move effectively in the world of public administration. There were sizeable gaps, most noticeably in the mining sector, but Native people gradually moved towards the mainstream of the territorial wage economy. This did not generally hold in the outlying villages, which offered few commercial or employment opportunities for its residents. The drift of Native people, particularly the young, toward Whitehorse and cities "outside" continued. Significant attempts have been made to arrest this process. Native entrepreneurs, led by Paul Birckel and Champagne Aishihik Enterprises Ltd. (the commercial arm of the Champagne-Aishihik band), expanded operations into the tourist sector, manufacturing (particularly through Yukon Native Products), and other business and administrative services.

This does not mean that Yukon Native people have uniformly accepted the structure and assumptions of the Canadian economic system, or that that system is sufficiently flexible to meet the economic needs of all Native people, particularly in the smaller, isolated settlements. Hunting, fishing, and gathering remain an integral part of Native life, providing a sizeable portion of the food consumed by Yukon indigenous people each year; expanding resource development and hunting by non-Natives is seen as a serious threat to this vital component of aboriginal life. For many Yukon Indians, and to the consternation of many non-Natives, government support payments (pensions, welfare cheques, and other financial transfers) remain an integral part of the Native economy.

The greatest effort by the non-Native community to reach out to, and to understand, indigenous societies in the Yukon has come on the cultural front. Supported by federal and territorial programs for Native cultural retention and enhancement, Yukon Native people expanded language training, re-established regular cultural gatherings of related peoples (often extending across boundaries to include relatives from Alaska, British Columbia, or the Northwest Territories), and gave higher profile to aboriginal games, story-telling, and traditional knowledge. Federal funding resulted in the establishment of a Native radio and television company (Northern Native Broadcasting Yukon), an aboriginal magazine, and a variety of other cultural initiatives. Aboriginal cultural events, including the extremely successful story-telling festival established in Whitehorse in the late 1980s, attracted wide support in the Native community and increasing interest among non-Native Yukoners and visitors. Financial hardship, however, provides the best test of the non-Native politicians' commitment to these initiatives; the federal government's decision to cut funding for Native broadcasting and communication in 1989 is a sad, but hardly shocking indication that this commitment is, on the federal level at least, very thin.[53]

The increasing profile of Native issues in territorial affairs through the 1970s and 1980s also resulted in a far greater integration of indigenous people into the political process. Native politicians did not emerge as a significant force in the territory until the mid-1970s. The electoral division of the territory that occurred during the struggle for and attainment of responsible government, which favours the smaller, largely Native settlements over Whitehorse, encouraged this process. All three major parties, Liberal, Conservative, and New Democratic, have made concerted efforts to court the Native vote. First elected with a minority government in 1985, the New Democratic Party under Government Leader Tony Penikett made a most determined effort to integrate Native concerns with the territory-wide political agenda, offering strong encouragement to the land-claims process, bringing Native leaders into positions of prominence, and making a sincere effort to accommodate aboriginal aspirations. The contrast to the 1950s, when Native people lacked the vote and had virtually no place on the pro-development agenda of territorial and federal politicians, is indeed striking, and an excellent indication of the depth of the changes that have engulfed the Yukon Territory.

In the public eye, these more general processes and issues were overshadowed continually by land-claims negotiations. Discussions after 1973 followed a tortuous, difficult, and costly path. Agreements appeared imminent at several stages, only to be dashed by dissension within Native ranks, a change of heart by the federal government, or the intervention of territorial politicians. The federal Liberal government, for example, negotiated an agreement-in-principle with the Council of Yukon Indians in 1984. An election intervened before the final details could be worked out, and the victorious Progressive Conservative administration balked at further discussions on the terms of the arrangement.

Negotiations began once again, building on a lengthy history of debate but shadowed by the apparent uncertainty of the entire process. The federal government's seemingly unalterable demand that the Indians surrender all outstanding aboriginal entitlements in exchange for a final settlement was, in communities such as Mayo and Ross River, rejected as unacceptable. Similarly, the non-Native negotiators were troubled by the Natives' apparent inability to develop and maintain a consensus on the items under discussion. Tempers flared on more than one occasion, leading to a variety of accusations and counter-charges. The territorial government initially provided little help, demanding that its own considerations receive equal billing with Native land claims. The election of a New Democratic government in 1985, and that administration's solid support for the resolution of indigenous land claims, helped expedite discussions.

In April 1990, representatives of the Council of Yukon Indians, the federal government, and the Government of the Yukon signed an agreement in principle. This agreement did not complete the land-claims process. Band-by-band negotiations and discussions on other points continued. The agreement did, however, address the major question facing Yukoners since the early 1970s. Under the accord, Yukon Indians regain control over 16,000 square miles of their traditional lands and a payment of over $230 million. Perhaps most significantly, the land-claims agreement requires the establishment of a series of special boards and committees, with assured Native participation, to oversee such matters as wildlife management, non-renewable resource development, and heritage preservation.

Slightly more than one hundred and fifty years after the first non-Natives ventured into the upper Yukon River basin, the indigenous peoples of the region have, through the land-claims process, secured a significant measure of control over their future. The problems Natives and non-Natives face are still many, rooted in years of struggle, change, and cultural misunderstanding; to expect a quick resolution of such complex difficulties is overly optimistic. Nevertheless, the settlement of the Yukon land claim is a bold new experiment, one of greater significance to the indigenous people than to the non-Native signatories. It is a fitting end to the long, and often painful, story of Native-non-Native encounter in the territory from the 1840s to the late twentieth century.

Conclusion

While the specifics of the Yukon case are, of course, unique to the territory, the general pattern of Native-white relations described herein can be seen across the Canadian north.[1] Canadian academics have begun to examine this process in considerable detail. Charles Bishop's ethnohistorical study of the northern Ojibway,[2] Hugh Brody's examination of the Beaver Indians of northeastern British Columbia,[3] and James Waldram's book on the sweeping dislocations accompanying the construction of hydro-electric dams in northern Manitoba[4] all point to the persistence of Native harvesting practices and values and the clash with non-Native developmental priorities.

Bishop demonstrates that, although the northern Ojibway faced different pressures than the Yukon Indians because of the extended period of contact and the over-harvesting of game, they similarly maintained their reliance on hunting and fishing into the mid-twentieth century. As in the Yukon, however, the combination of expanded government programs, new mineral developments, more roads, and declining returns from the fur trade after the Second World War forced many lifestyle changes on the Ojibway. In a different geographical context, Brody's impassioned description of Native society in northern British Columbia rests on the conviction that aboriginal harvesting remains to this day viable and important. The same is true of the entire Canadian north. After 1945 northern harvesting remained profitable, if variable, and the Natives retained their cultural and economic attachment to the land. The Natives were not living artifacts – non-economic people caught in the bounds of "traditional" society. Instead, they were flexible, adaptable people whose material, moral, and spiritual culture reflected extensive and on-going adaptation to contact with non-Natives.[5]

Although the Yukon situation shares much in common with other northern districts, it stands in noticeable contrast to conditions in the south, where agricultural settlement, resource development, urbanization, and over-hunting undermined the hunting and trapping option.[6] Stripped of their ability to continue hunting, plains Natives in Canada faced dispossession or ghettoization on government-sponsored reserves. Unlike their counterparts in the north, where the continuation of seasonal mobility undercut the influence of agents of acculturation, southern Natives found themselves cloistered with missionaries and often dependent on government agents.[7] Moreover, under the restrictions of bureaucratic control, southern Natives were far more vulnerable to the forces of Christianity and Canadian education, although never as much as missionaries or government agents wished or believed.[8] Of course, both missionaries and officials of the federal government were active in the north, but their impact was diminished by isolation. The northern Ojibway signed a treaty with the Canadian government, and as result experienced relatively regular contact with government agents. Even in this instance, however, continued Native mobility and the isolation of the Osnaburgh reserve limited the impact of these official activities.[9] The Yukon Natives did not sign a treaty[10] and, despite the continuing efforts of Indian agents and missionaries, remained largely outside the influence of government and religious leadership until the 1950s.

The experience of Yukon Indians can also be understood as a microcosm of a global process. Beginning in the nineteenth century and escalating in the years after the Second World War, the rapacious appetite of the industrial economies resulted in the rapid development of long ignored frontier districts. Just as the Yukon Indians were ultimately swamped by the sweeping dislocations of the Klondike gold rush and the construction projects of the Second World War, and the post-1950 period, so did the aborigines of Australia's Northern Territory[11] and the indigenous peoples of Brazil, Central America, Alaska, and other areas experience, often for the first time, the full force of resource development. In this era, the world's last harvesting peoples faced the brunt of the resource-demands of the First World and were pushed off lands that they had long occupied. The experience of Yukon Indians, therefore, is clearly but a small example of a process that has occurred around the world, and across the centuries. This sorry tale, which does not reflect well on the cultural, economic, and political aspirations of the colonial and imperial powers, left an indelible mark on aboriginal peoples everywhere.[12]

The Native people of the Yukon Territory are now living with the painful effects of these historical developments. The same cannot be said of non-Native Yukoners. Because of their economic, political, and demographic domination of the territory, non-Native Yukoners have distanced themselves from the history of their territory. Indeed the Yukon has only a limited historical consciousness, which is ironic given the importance to the tourist industry of Klondike-era reconstructions. There is another reason for this lack of attention to the past among non-Natives. Native people are in the Yukon to stay, for it is their homeland. In contrast, transiency and impermanence are dominant social characteristics of the non-Native population. Temporary northerners, whose frame of reference remains southern Canada, have had little reason to come to grips with the patterns of Yukon history.

Many of the Native issues debated in the 1960s and early 1970s were constantly stalled by difficult land-claim negotiations.[13] The aboriginal people of the Yukon Territory understandably pinned their hopes on the successful conclusion of these discussions. With the money, land, and administrative authority promised through the land-claims process, Yukon Natives aimed to regain control of their future. The discussions were slowed through the 1970s by a recalcitrant pro-development Conservative territorial government which worried about the potential impact of a settlement on resource exploitation. Even the election of a more sympathetic New Democratic Party government in 1985 did not immediately remove the many roadblocks that stood in the way of an acceptable settlement. Happily an agreement has now been reached, ensuring that the Yukon, and Native-white relations in the territory, will be set on a strikingly different course.

But the past twenty years have seen other changes that suggest that Yukon Native people are not content to rely entirely on the land-claims negotiations to solve their economic and social problems. Financially supported by a spate of federal and territorial initiatives, and benefitting from an improved climate of race relations in the territory, Yukon Indians have found a variety of ways to address the social, cultural, and economic difficulties that bedevil their communities. Much of the impetus has become from the villages, where women, organized in the Yukon Indian Women's Association, have been particularly active in responding to pressing social concerns. The same determination can be seen in the work of the Council of Yukon Indians (formed in the early 1970s as a result of a merger of the Yukon Native Brotherhood and Yukon Association of Non-Status Indians), which has played a prominent role in territorial affairs.

The reawakening of the aboriginal spirit is also evident in the expansion of Native art, the development of aboriginal radio, television, and print journalism, Indian demands for greater control of the education system and for improvements to cultural programs in the prisons, and a myriad of other initiatives. Some bands, starting with the Teslin, have sought to re-establish aboriginal leadership-systems, rejecting the imposed elected chief-and-council structure in favour of clan-based councils. In addition, improved educational performance on the part of Natives has resulted in greater Native participation in the territorial economy; and a variety of government programs have provided financial support for many Native businesses, ranging from small individual enterprises to a territory-wide Native crafts cooperative, Yukon Native Products, and several successful band enterprises, including the Han Fishery, Champagne-Aishihik's several ventures, and the development-oriented Kwanlin Dun Enterprises.

Yet, however promising, these initiatives have made only a small dent in the broader social problems facing Yukon Native people. Unemployment remains extremely high, particularly in the smaller communities. There is also a growing disparity in incomes between educated and uneducated Native people; the prospect of substantial class division within the Native communities looms large. Signs of distress are abundant: Indian people still make up a huge percentage of the prison population; and the high suicide rate, particularly among teenagers, is a constant reminder of the level of anxiety among Natives, as are the continued problems with alcohol that plague the entire culture.

Non-Native society has also changed substantially over the last two decades. A new environmental ethos that has drawn many people to the north has expanded to include an acceptance, and even a celebration, of aboriginal culture and traditions. A growing number of permanent non-Native residents have made a concerted effort to understand and include aboriginal aspirations within their own vision of the modern north. At the same time, however, the pro-development lobby continues to view the north from an "us or them" perspective; there is less willingness in this quarter to accept the Indians' demands for control over their future.[14]

The overt discrimination experienced by many Natives in the 1960s has been replaced by greater tolerance. Natives and non-Natives mix more regularly; the racial segregation that long characterized Yukon communities has given way to more substantial integration. Indian children still experience a distressingly high drop-out rate in high school, but the situation has improved significantly. The territorial and federal governments have been more open to the aboriginal perspective; the regular election of Native representatives has no doubt contributed to the improved level of understanding.

The future of Native-white relations in the Yukon Territory is uncertain. Promising signs are offset by evidence of continued social distance and disharmony. There are, in particular, few indications that the non-Native population feels it has much to learn from the Indians in the Yukon. The intensity of the cultural crisis among Natives – emphasized by the imminent disappearance of several aboriginal languages – is not matched by the degree of cultural sensitivity and willingness to change among non-Natives. The dominant society, still firmly in control of the political and administrative apparatus, the education system, and the economy, has yet to reach a consensus on the value of sharing power with the Yukon Indian population.

One hundred and fifty years ago, Native people in the upper Yukon River basin had not yet come in direct contact with Europeans. In short order, fur traders, missionaries, miners, government agents, more non-Native settlers, and many others made their way into the region, upsetting a lifestyle and culture that had developed over thousands of years. Until the 1950s Yukon Native people retained a great deal of freedom, and had the option of remaining outside the economic and social world of the now-dominant white population. The non-Natives, unable to find or provide a place for the indigenous people in their midst, were content to leave the Indians as Indians. This situation changed dramatically in the years after 1950, as development, government intervention, and continued discrimination served to restrict Natives to the territory's social and economic margins. Relations have now shifted in the opposite direction, drawing Natives and non-Natives together and suggesting that the region has a unique opportunity for racial and cultural harmony.

A visitor to the Yukon Territory would, on first glance, no doubt be impressed with the efforts made to reach out to Native people. The Native-run radio station, CHON, is popular throughout the territory; local newspapers regularly contain numerous stories of aboriginal activities. The Whitehorse campus of Yukon College, opened in 1988 in a ceremony complete with aboriginal cultural performances and prayers, has a Native name, Ayamdigut Hall. Yet the level of integration, which stands in stark contrast to most other areas in Canada, is somewhat misleading because it masks the personal suffering and cultural loss that pervades the aboriginal communities and that offers a constant challenge to all northerners, Native and non-Native alike. This said, however, the contemporary situation represents a significant improvement over past decades and holds considerable promise for the years to come.

History, cautiously applied, does not offer lessons for the future; it does, however, tells us how we reached the point where we are now.

This account of the history of Native-white relations in the Yukon Territory has traced the pattern of interaction from first contact to the recent past, and suggests that the current condition of Natives and whites in the territory can be understood only as the outgrowth of the region's history. The explanations for the contemporary challenges facing Yukon Native people can be found in the past – in the experience of children in residential schools, the years of systematic discrimination, the establishment of separate residential reserves, the attitudes of the white majority, and the policies of the federal and territorial governments. Contemporary Canadians, Native and white, have inherited their ancestors' pasts and, however much they might wish to disassociate themselves from their country's historical experience, they retain responsibility for it. The challenge for the modern north is to address the past, accept the reality that was, and seek improvements for the future.

Notes

AC   Anglican Church Records, Yukon Territorial Archives

CMS   Church Missionary Society Records (microfilm copy, National Archives of Canada)

DIA   Department of Indian Affairs Records, National Archives of Canada

GSA   General Synod Archives, Anglican Church of Canada

HBCA   Hudson's Bay Company Archives (Provincial Archives of Manitoba)

Indian Affairs   Records held in Ottawa and Whitehorse offices of Indian and Northern Affairs

MSCC   Missionary Society of the Church of England in Canada

NA   National Archives of Canada

NWMP   North West Mounted Police

PAM   Provincial Archives of Manitoba

RCMP   Royal Canadian Mounted Police Records, National Archives of Canada

RNWMP   Royal Northwest Mounted Police

YRG   Yukon Government Record Group, Yukon Territorial Archives

YTA   Yukon Territorial Archives

PREFACE

1 In recent years, one of the Yukon's primary resources has been its strategic location astride highway and pipeline routes between Alaska and Alberta. As the Lysyk Commission argued in its final report, "geographical location may equally be regarded as a natural endowment." Lysyk, Bohmer, and Phelps, *Alaska Highway Pipeline Inquiry*, 150.

2 Coates, "Limits to Growth," in Coates and Morrison, *For the Purposes of the Dominion*.

3 To be a "sourdough" one had to see the rivers freeze and be in the north to see the ice leave in the spring. Newcomers carried the less flattering title of "Cheechako."

4 Coates and Morrison, "Transiency in the Far Northwest," in Coates and Morrison, eds., *Interpreting the Canadian North*.

5 Zaslow, *The Opening of the Canadian North* and *The Northward Expansion of Canada*.

6 Literature on the Canadian north is reviewed in Coates and Morrison, "Northern Visions."

7 A major exception is Abel, "The Drum and the Cross," although even here the time frame is primarily nineteenth century. See also Yerbury, *The Subarctic Indians*, and Francis and Morantz, *Partners in Furs*. The latter two books, although fine pieces of scholarship, reflect the historical and ethnohistorical emphasis on the nineteenth century. The major study of the Yukon Indians, McClellan *et al.*, *Part of the Land, Part of the Water*, is, in fact, an anthropological analysis targeted at a high-school audience. It is not a history and offers only cursory comments on historical events and processes. For an attempt at a regional history, see Coates and Morrison, *Land of the Midnight Sun*.

8 Zaslow, *The Opening of the Canadian North* and *The Northward Expansion of Canada*. See also major monographs by two of Zaslow's students: Morrison, *Showing the Flag*, and Diubaldo, *Stefansson and the Canadian Arctic*.

9 Ray, "Periodic Shortages." Also useful, albeit with a heavily contemporary and a correspondingly less convincing historical focus, is Brody, *Maps and Dreams*.

10 Recent literature is surveyed in Walker, "The Indian in Canadian Historical Writing," in Getty and Lussier, eds., *As Long as the Sun Shines and Water Flows*; and Fisher, "Historical Writing on Native People in Canada." For a recent review of writing on the fur trade, the strongest thematic field of Native history in Canada, see Peterson and Anfinson, "The Indian and the Fur Trade." One of the best books on Indian-white relations, Fisher's *Contact and Conflict*, is very good for the southern regions of the province but does not do proper justice to developments in the northern and eastern parts of British Columbia, where a much different interaction occurred. See also Milloy, *The Plains Cree*; Elias, *The Dakota of the Canadian Northwest*; and Waldrum, *As Long As the Rivers Run*.

11 Trigger, "The Historians' Indian."

12 Krech, "The Eastern Kutchin and the Fur Trade"; Osgood, *The Han Indians* and *Contributions to the Ethnography of the Kutchin*; Welsh, "Nomads in Town"; McClellan, *My Old People Say*; Honigman, *The Kaska Indians*; Legros, "Structure Socio-culturelle"; Cruikshank, "Becoming a Woman in Athapaskan Society."

13 Axtell, "Ethnohistory: An Historian's Viewpoint," in Axtell, *The European and the Indian*; Martin, "Ethnohistory."

14 Helm, *Handbook of the North American Indian*, particularly vol. 6, *The Subarctic*.

15 Yerbury, *The Subarctic Indians*. One of his major arguments is that "the precontact matriorganization of the Canadian Athapaskans likely changed to a bilateral-matrilocal organization as a result of postcontact fur trade factors." (166).

16 Bishop, *The Northern Ojibway*; Bishop and Ray, "Ethnohistoric Research in the Central Subarctic."

17 This is particularly the case with oral testimony. Collecting such data requires considerable linguistic and anthropological skill. Another complicating factor is the fallibility of human memory, which interferes with full recollection of historical events. A series of interviews I conducted with the aid of an interpreter in the Yukon in 1988 confirmed my concerns both about this process and my ability to handle the task. The elders I interviewed had, in numerous cases, no memories of historically documented events and circumstances. On other themes, such as their relationship to specific pieces of land and harvesting practices, they demonstrated exceptional recall.

18 Fisher, *Contact and Conflict*, xiii.

19 Washburn, "Ethnohistory: History 'In the Round.'"

20 Martin, "Ethnohistory," 56.

21 Two recent books, Trigger's *Natives and Newcomers* and Axtell's *The Invasion Within*, provide excellent examples of the value of ethnohistorical techniques and the historical insights available through careful use of archaeological and anthropological research.

22 The phrase "contact cultures" is used to draw attention to the fact that the techniques of ethnohistory apply as much to reconstructions of European motives and actions as they do to the study of Native people. Thomas Stone's recent articles on northern mining communities reveal the important opportunities thus provided. Stone, "Flux and Authority in a Subarctic Society" and "Whalers and Missionaries at Herschel Island."

23 There is great room for ethnohistorical research on the Yukon Territory and the Canadian north generally. I hope that my study will be of use to those scholars who undertake this valuable work and that it will be accepted for what it is, a piece of historical scholarship on an often neglected area.

24 This issue is addressed in Jaenen, "The Meeting of the French and Amerindians in the Seventeenth Century."

25 Sahlins, *Stone Age Economics*. See especially the chapter "Notes on the Original Affluent Society."

26 And not without good reason. The European option of an agricultural lifestyle seemed, to most North American Natives, impractical and unnecessary, offering poorer living conditions than those under which they traditionally lived. Berkhofer, *The White Man's Indian.*

27 The best statement on this point, although flawed in its argument, is Martin, *Keepers of the Game.* For a critique of Martin's argument, see Krech, ed., *Indians, Animals and the Fur Trade.* For a discussion of this environmental accommodation as it relates to the Yukon, see McClelland *et al., Part of the Land, Part of the Water.*

28 For extremes in the anthropological debate over whether the environmental accommodation determined social organization or whether the social structure reflected more human processes, see Harris, *Cultural Materialism,* and Riches, *Northern Nomadic Hunter-Gatherers.*

29 Brody, *Maps and Dreams.*

30 Asch, "The Ecological-Evolutionary Model," in Turner and Smith, eds., *Challenging Anthropology;* "The Economics of Dene Self-Determination," ibid.; "Capital and Economic Development."

31 Owram, *The Promise of Eden.* Shelagh Grant's chapter, "A Historical Perspective, 1867–1930," in *Sovereignty or Security* provides a good introduction to the non-Native view of the north.

32 For a description of the sojourner society in Alaska, see Hinckley, *The Americanization of Alaska.*

INTRODUCTION

1 Recently some Natives have argued that aboriginal people are indigenous to North America.

2 YA, Anglican Church, New Series, file #3, Particulars Regarding the Copper Indians, July 1908.

3 McClellan *et al., Part of the Land, Part of the Water,* summarizes this material very well. On the similarities between recent scientific discoveries and aboriginal tradition, see Cruikshank, "Legend and Landscape."

4 Rea, *The Political Economy of the Canadian North;* VanStone, *Athapaskan Adaptations,* 17–18; Camu, Weeks, and Sametz, *Economic Geography of Canada;* Putnam and Putnam, *Canada: A Regional Analysis.*

5 Murray, *Journal of the Yukon,* ed. L.J. Burpee; Jones, "The Kutchin Tribes"; Hardisty, "The Loucheux Indians"; Kirkby, "The Indians of the Youcon," in Hind, *Explorations in the Interior of the Labrador Peninsula;* Wesbrook, "A Venture into Ethnohistory"; GSA, M56–2, Series C–23, Canham Papers, T.H. Canham, "undated account of the Indians of the Far Northwest".

6 The best place to start is McClellan *et al., Part of the Land, Part of the Water.* See also Helm, ed., *Handbook of North American Indians, vol. 6:*

The Subarctic; VanStone, *Athapaskan Adaptations*; and the Yukon sources cited in the preface.

7 VanStone, *Athapaskan Adaptations*.

8 Osgood, *Contributions to the Ethnography of the Kutchin*.

9 Osgood, *The Han Indians*.

10 McClelland, *My Old People Say*.

11 The best ethnohistorical study of aboriginal religion in the north is Abel, "The Drum and the Cross."

12 For an excellent example of the need to assess pre-contact population, and how such estimates condition subsequent analysis of Native-white relations, see Jennings, *The Invasion of America*.

13 Ugarenko, "The Distribution of the Kutchin," and Ostenstat, "The Impact of the Fur Trade," establish the importance and fluidity of those contacts.

14 Krech, "On the Aboriginal Population of the Kutchin."

15 The closest is Dall, "On the Distribution and Nomenclature of the Native Tribes of Alaska and the Adjacent Territory." Dall admitted that his study was speculative and incomplete. Of some use, but with similar limitations, is Dawson, "Notes on the Indian Tribes of the Yukon District."

16 Mooney, *The Aboriginal Population of America North of Mexico*. He claimed that there were 2,200 Kutchin and 800 "Nehane."

17 Kroeber, *Cultural and Natural Areas of Native North America*, does not make this conversion. He suggests a density of .87 per 100 sq. km.

18 Osgood, *Contributions to the Ethnography of the Kutchin*. The estimate was based on an 1858 HBC survey.

19 Borah and Cook, *The Aboriginal Population of Central Mexico*.

20 Dobyns, "Estimating Aboriginal American Population."

21 Krech, "On the Aboriginal Population of the Kutchin." While I accept the thrust of Krech's argument, evidence he does not cite supports a possible upward revision of his estimate. A.H. Murray estimated a trading population (Fort Youcon Kutchin and some Han) of some 250–300 Native males in 1847. HBCA, B200/b/22, fol. 15, Murray to McPherson, 20 November 1847. Krech uses a published estimate, also from Murray, of 210 males. Similarly, Bishop Bompas estimated the number of Natives at Fort Youcon, Lapierre's House, and Peel River in 1865 to be "at least 1000." *Church Missionary Intelligencer*, vol. 11 (New Series), 1866. See also YTA, Anglican Church 80/93, "Statement of the Indian Population of Mackenzie River District 1871," which listed a total of 812 persons at the three posts. Further questioning of Krech's approach can be found in Ugarenko, "The Distribution of the Kutchin," 14–15.

22 DIA, *Annual Report, 1896*, suggested a population of 2,600.

23 Deneven, *The Native Population of the Americas in 1492*; Jacobs, "The Tip of the Iceberg"; Crosby, "Virgin Soil Epidemics"; Dobyns, *Native American Historical Demography*.

24 Krech, "On the Aboriginal Population of the Kutchin"; Miller, "The Decline of Nova Scotia Micmac Population."

25 Fisher, *Contact and Conflict*, 20–3, 45.

26 Crosby, "Virgin Soil Epidemics." Interestingly, Crosby uses the Yukon experience in the 1940s to illustrate his case. See also Crosby, *The Columbian Exchange*, and McNeill, *Plagues and People*. For a major statement on this theme, see Crosby, *Ecological Imperialism*.

27 Crosby, *Ecological Imperialism*.

28 Ray, "Diffusion of Diseases," in Shortt, ed., *Medicine in Canadian Society*.

29 On the Alaskan smallpox epidemic, see VanStone, *Ingelik Contact Ecology*, 58–61; Wright, *Prelude to Bonanza*, 18; Zagaskin, *Lieutenant Zagaskin's Travels*; and Stoddard, "Some Ethnological Aspects of the Russian Fur Trade," in *People and Pelts*. On the Pacific coast, see Gibson, "Smallpox on the Northwest Coast." This article offers a perspective different from, and more convincing than, Robin Fisher's.

30 GSA, M56–2, Series C–23, Canham Papers, T.H. Canham, "undated comments on the Indians of the Far North."

31 The transmission of disease in advance of direct contact is at the centre of debate on the size of aboriginal populations. Earlier forecasts originated in the first reports of population size by non-Native observers, despite the fact that such descriptions may have come a century or more after the arrival of Europeans in contiguous regions. Most historians and demographers now agree that significant depopulation often occurred before non-Natives arrived. Dobyns, "Brief Perspectives on a Scholarly Transformation." Crosby, "Virgin Soil Epidemics."

32 HBCA, B240/2/1, fol. 45, Youcon Journal, 27 November 1847.

33 HBCA, B200/b/29, fol. 184, Hardisty to Anderson, 31 May 1852; fol. 183, Hardisty to Anderson, 6 July 1852; fol. 153, Hardisty to Anderson, 5 November 1852; fol. 113, Anderson to Council, 30 November 1852; NA, MG19 A25, Robert Campbell, "Journal of the Yukon," 138.

34 In 1868, for instance, it was casually noted that sickness affected the Indians at Fort Youcon and twenty-two Indians died. HBCA, B200/b/35, fol. 140, McDougall to gentleman in charge, 27 October 1868.

35 HBCA, B200/b/36, fol. 43, McDougall to Hardisty, 25 September 1865.

36 HBCA, B200/b/25, fol. 74, Hardisty to McDougall, 28 August 1866; HBCA, B200/b/35, fol. 158, Hardisty to McDougall, 2 April 1866; ibid., fol. 140, Hardisty to council, 28 November 1865.

37 HBCA, B200/b/36, fol. 58, McDougall to Hardisty, 5 July 1866. On Lapierre's House, see HBCA, B200/b/36, fol. 42, Flett to Hardisty, January 1866. To provide some context, the 1861 population along the Porcupine River was less than 200 persons. HBCA, B200/b/36, fol. 43, McDougall to

Hardisty, 25 September 1865. Inspector Charles Constantine recounted the tale thirty years later, but he claimed that the epidemic had spread from the Chilcat Indians to the south. He had been told that an entire band of Kutchin Indians had perished. NA, RG10, vol. 3906, file 105, 378, Report of Inspector Charles Constantine, 10 October 1894.

38 HBCA, B240/a/1, fol. 14., Youcon Journal, 25 July 1847.

39 Hardisty, "The Loucheux Indians," Jones, "The Kutchin Tribes," and Murray, *Journal of the Yukon*, all describe Natives blaming sorcerers for illnesses. See also the important discussion in Krech, "Throwing Bad Medicine"; On Campbell, see HBCA, B200/b/32, fol. 24, Hardisty to Anderson, 15 October 1853; HBCA, B240/2/1, fol. 14, Youcon Journal, 25 July 1847.

40 Canham, "undated comments"; see also HBCA, B200/b/42, fol. 18, Hardisty to Grahame, 4 August 1876; HBCA, B200/b/43, fol. 35, Camsell to Grahame, 29 July 1879.

41 HBCA, B200/b/35, fol. 186, Hardisty to council, 30 July 1866. For a later example of the same attitude, see NA, RG18, vol. 295, file 273, Cuthbert to asst. comm. Dawson, 30 June 1905.

42 Fisher, *Contact and Conflict*, 21–3. Fisher draws heavily on his understanding of contact situations throughout the Pacific, and in this instance relies on McArthur, *Island Populations of the Pacific*.

43 Gibson, "Smallpox on the Northwest Coast."

44 HBCA, B240/2/1, fol. 45, Youcon Journal, 27 November 1847.

45 HBCA, B200/b/29, fol. 153, Hardisty to Anderson, 5 November 1852. This comment could possibly relate to elders, although the context suggests otherwise.

46 HBCA, B200/b/36, fol. 43, McDougall to Hardisty, 25 September 1865.

47 HBCA, B200/b/32, fol. 24, Hardisty to Anderson, 15 October 1853.

48 Numerous illnesses were reported. NA, MG17, B2, Bompas to CMS, 6 December 1872; HBCA, B200/b/43, Camsell to Grahame, 23 March 1881; NA, MG17, B2, Canham to CMS, November 1889; Bompas to CMS, 19 December 1898; Bompas to CMS, 23 August 1899; Reeve to Baring Gould, 23 July 1900; NA, RG18, vol. 154, file 445, Bowridge to comptroller, NWMP, 1 December 1900; D. Legros, "Structure Socio-Culturelle," provides more detailed discussion of the cycle of disease. See also Wesbrook, "A Venture into Ethnohistory," 41, and especially Krech, "Throwing Bad Medicine."

49 NA, MG17, B2, Bompas to CMS, 19 December 1898.

50 Crosby, "Virgin Soil Epidemics," 294.

PART ONE

1 This debate is now dominated by A.J. Ray. See his *Indians in the Fur Trade*, *Give Us Good Measure* (with Donald Freeman), and *The Canadian*

Fur Trade in the Industrial Age. The argument goes back to earlier interpretations by E.E. Rich, Abraham Rotstein and H.A. Innis.

2 Knight, *Indians at Work*.
3 Elias, *The Dakota of the Canadian Northwest*.
4 Milloy, *The Plains Cree*.
5 Ray, "Periodic Shortages," examines the fur trade in much of the north but not in the Yukon Territory.

CHAPTER ONE

1 The details of fur-trade expansion are covered in Coates, "Furs Along the Yukon." See also the article by the same title in *BC Studies*.
2 HBCA, A. 12/1, fol. 72, Simpson to governor and committee, 10 August 1932. McLeod's journal can be found in HBCA, B200/2/14.
3 HBCA, D5/6 fol. 341, Bell to Simpson, 20 December 1843; and NA, MG30 D39, Burpee Papers, "Letters of John Bell," fol. 27.
4 Franklin, *Thirty Years in the Arctic Regions*, 448. Thomas Simpson and Peter Warren Dease observed similar trading ties when they visited the area in 1837. Simpson, *The Life and Travels of Thomas Simpson*, 119–20.
5 Pre-contact trade networks are described in Susan Ugarenko, "The Distribution of the Kutchin"; Ostenstat, "The Impact of the Fur Trade on the Tlingit"; Tanner, "The Structure of Fur Trade Relations"; Osgood, *Contributions to the Ethnography of the Kutchin*; and McClelland, *My Old People Say*.
6 Krech, "The Eastern Kutchin and the Fur Trade."
7 Karamanski, *Fur Trade and Exploration*. Governor Simpson believed that the Colville was a major river, comparable to the Mackenzie River, draining what he believed to be a major fur preserve.
8 Hammond, "Any Ordinary Degree of System."
9 NA, MG30 D39, Burpee Papers, "Letters of John Bell," 28; HBCA, B200/b/ 11, fol. 15, McPherson to Simpson, 30 November 1838?; Ugarenko, "The Distribution of the Kutchin," 137.
10 HBCA, D5/7, fol. 250, Bell to Simpson, 11 September 1842; HBCA, D/8, fol. 421, Bell to Simpson, 10 August 1843.
11 HBCA, D5/5, fol. 377, Lewes to Simpson, 20 November 1840; HBCA, B200/ b/13, fol. 14, Bell to Lewes, 26 August 1840.
12 HBCA, D5/7, fol. 250, Bell to Simpson, 11 September 1842.
13 HBCA, D4/31, fol. 93, Simpson to Bell, 3 June 1844; HBCA, D5/14, fol. 212–15, Bell to Simpson, 1 August 1845.
14 HBCA, B200/b/22, fol. 15, Murray to McPherson, 30 November 1847; Murray, *Journal of the Yukon*, 35–45.
15 HBCA, B200/b//23, fol. 35, Murray to McPherson, 12 November 1848.

16 Ugarenko, "The Distribution of the Kutchin," 138–42; HBCA, D5/34, fol. 71, Anderson to Simpson, 10 July 1852.

17 Wilson, *Campbell of the Yukon*; Wright, *Prelude to Bonanza*, 27–77; Karamanski, *Fur Trade and Exploration*.

18 HBCA, B200/b/19, fol. 11, Campbell to Lewes, 25 July 1843.

19 HBCA, D5/25, fol. 590, Campbell to Simpson, 28 August 1849.

20 HBCA, D/34, fol. 71, Anderson to Simpson, 10 July 1852. See also the Pelly Banks and Fort Selkirk journals in NA, MG19 H25 and MG19 D13. Part of the company's problem lay in the fact that it was competing against itself. As part of the 1839 accord with the Russian American Fur Company, the HBC leased the Alaskan panhandle. Company traders, operating in the main off trading ships, visited the coastal Indian communities each year. The Tlingit traders competing with Robert Campbell in the Fort Selkirk region were selling their furs to the HBC.

21 HBCA, B200/b/29, fol. 170, Campbell to Anderson, 4 November 1852; NA, MG19 D13, Journal of Occurrences at the Forks of the Pelly and Lewes, 3–9 July.

22 HBCA, B200/b/29, fol. 236, Campbell to gentl. in charge, R. district, 18 October 1851.

23 HBCA, B200/b/24, fol. 60, Campbell to McPherson, 24 July 1850; HBCA, D5/22, fol. 162, Campbell to Simpson, 22 April 1848.

24 Ostenstat, "The Impact of the Fur Trade." For a discussion of Tlingit trade along the Stikine River, see Johnson, "Baron Wrangel and the Russian American Company."

25 The company maintained the outpost at Lapierre's House, but trade was not permitted. Employees directed the Indians to take their furs to Fort Youcon or Peel's River. HBCA, B220/b/29, fol. 34, Anderson to Peers, 25 January 1852.

26 Tanner, "The Structure of Fur Trade Relations," 37–44.

27 HBCA, B200/b/23, fol. 35, Murray to McPherson, 12 November 1848; HBCA, B200/b/19, fol. 183, Hardisty to Anderson, 6 July 1852.

28 HBCA, B200/b/23, fol. 35, Murray to McPherson, 12 November 1848.

29 The "Made Beaver" was the standard unit of exchange in the fur trade. The cost of all goods, furs, and services was expressed in terms of their value compared to one prime beaver pelt. A poor quality beaver pelt, for example, would be worth less than one Made Beaver; a prime mink skin might command several Made Beaver in goods. HBCA, B200/b/35, fol. 94, Circular from W. Hardisty, 10 March 1865. HBCA, B240/d/13, Fort Youcon Accounts, 1869.

30 Murray, *Journal of the Yukon*, 45–69.

31 HBCA, B200/b/23, fol. 9, Murray to McPherson, 24 June 1849.

32 HBCA, B240/a/1. fol. 19, Fort Youcon Journal, 6 August 1847.

33 HBCA, B240/a/1, fol. 45, Fort Youcon Journal, 27 November 1847; fol. 76, 24 May 1848.

34 This observation is based on discussions with K. Arndt, who is currently finishing a Ph.D. dissertation on the Russian American Fur Company.

35 HBCA, E37/9, fol. 40, Anderson to Colville, 16 March 1852. Letters from Fort Youcon regularly included appeals for specific additions to the annual outfit. The post's extreme isolation – there was a seven-year cycle between the time trade goods left London and Yukon furs reached market – meant that it took several years to secure a noticeable modification in the yearly allotment.

36 HBCA, B220/b/37, fol. 277, Hardisty to council, 30 November 1870.

37 HBCA, B200/b/34, fol. 136, Jones to Hardisty, 23 June 1863.

38 NA, MG17, B2, McDonald to "Dear Brother in the Lord", 25 June 1864.

39 Stefansson, *Northwest to Fortune*, 219–20; HBCA, B200/b/34, fol. 57, Jones to Hardisty, 10 November 1863; HBCA, B200/b/37, fol. 28, Hardisty to McDougall, 29 January 1869.

40 HBCA, B200/b/32, fol. 24, Hardisty to Anderson, 15 October 1853; HBCA, B200/b/33, fol. 15, Ross to council, 29 November 1858.

41 HBCA, B200/b/32, fol. 42, Anderson to Hardisty, 1 January 1854.

42 NA, MG19 D13, Pelley and Lewes Forks Journal, vol. 1, 30 September 1849. For Fort Youcon, see HBCA, E37/10, fol. 95, Anderson to Simpson, 25 March 1855.

43 HBCA, B200/b/35, fol. 99, Hardisty to Jones, 1 April 1864. J. Dunlop, an apprentice clerk, also left after incurring the displeasure of the Indians. HBCA, B200/b/33, fol. 15, Ross to council, 29 November 1858.

44 Lain, "The Fort Yukon Affair"; Raymond, "Reconnaissance of the Yukon River."

45 The HBC traders went to considerable lengths to keep competitive traders out of the Mackenzie district. In 1873 James McDougall bought out the furs of Leroy McQuesten on the condition that he abandon the Mackenzie trade for the Yukon basin. HBCA, B200/b/40, fol. 86, Hardisty to Smith, 15 August 1873.

46 Balicki, *Vunta Kutchin Social Change*, 34–6; HBCA, B200/b/37, fol. 272, Hardisty to Smith, 30 November 1870; HBCA, B200/b/40, fol. 5, Hardisty to McDougall, 10 March 1871.

47 Johnson, *Alaska Commercial Company*; McQuesten, "Recollections of Leroy McQuesten". The best description is that by Melody Webb in *The Last Frontier*, 51–76.

48 HBCA, B200/b/38, fol. 15, McDougall to Hardisty, 3 January 1870.

49 HBCA, B200/b/37, fol. 255, Hardisty to council, 2 August 1870.

50 HBCA, B200/b/40, fol. 74, Hardisty to Sinclair, 1871; HBCA, B200/b/37, fol. 272, Hardisty to Smith, 30 November 1870.

51 Coates, "Furs Along the Yukon," 152–75.

52 Ibid. HBC blankets were particularly valued as trade goods. The company was most concerned when, in 1881, the Americans began trading English merchandise at lower prices. HBCA, B200/b/43, fol. 30, Camsell to Grahame, 23 March 1881; Ogilvie, *Klondike Official Guide*, 48.

53 HBCA, B200/b/37, fol. 272, Hardisty to Smith, 30 November 1870; HBCA, B200/b/39, fol. 35, McDougall to Hardisty, 20 December 1873; HBCA, B200/b/40, fol. 120, Hardisty to Wilson, 30 March 1875.

54 NA, MG17, B2 McDonald to CMS, 30 June 1870.

55 NA, MG29 A11, MacFarlane Papers, vol. 1, fol. 607–8, McDonald to MacFarlane, 10 January 1877.

56 NA, MG29 A11, MacFarlane Papers, vol. 1, fol. 817–18, McDonald to MacFarlane, 1 January 1881; and fol. 819–20, Sim to MacFarlane, 4 January 1881.

57 HBCA, B200/b/43, fol. 698, Camsell to Wrigley, 25 March 1891; HBCA, B200/b/43, fol. 719, Camsell to Chipman, 11 September 1891; Peter Usher, "Canadian Western Arctic"; Warner, "Herschel Island"; Stevenson, "Whalers' Wait" and "Herschel Haven."

CHAPTER TWO

1 Country provisions were meat, fish, and other foodstuffs used for trade.

2 Whymper, *Travels in Alaska and the Yukon*, 227; Willson, *The Life of Lord Strathcona*, 427.

3 This summary is based on Webb, *The Last Frontier*, 77–98.

4 Stone, "Flux and Authority in a Subarctic Society."

5 Webb, *The Last Frontier*, 82. See also Ogilvie, *Information Respecting the Yukon District*, 9–15; Hunt, *North of 53*.

6 Fred Hutchinson, a Fortymile miner, and William Ogilvie, a member of the Geological Survey of Canada, have both been given credit for introducing this technique. See Webb, *The Last Frontier*, 82.

7 Evidence on Native labour is widely scattered. This account is drawn from NA, MG17 B2, Bompas to CMS, 20 January 1893, May 1893, and 15 May 1894; NA, MG20 B22, Ogilvie Papers, file 4, Bompas to lt. governor, 3 December 1891; Report of Inspector C. Constantine, 20 January 1896, *Annual Report of the North West Mounted Police, 1896*; YTA, Anglican Church, New Series, file 4, Constantine to minister of the interior, 19 November 1896; Ogilvie, *Information Respecting the Yukon District* and *The Klondike Official Guide*; Dawson, *Report of an Exploration*; NA, MG 29 C92, Bowen Papers, Bowen, "Incidents in the Life of R.J. Bowen," unpublished manuscript.

8 Report of Inspector C. Constantine, 20 January 1896, *Annual Report of North West Mounted Police, 1896*.

9 Interestingly, during the supposedly rampant inflation of the Klondike gold rush, day-labour rates ranged from $10 to $15 per day, a reflection of the vast increase in the size of the labour pool. NA, MG17, B2, Bompas to CMS, 2 March 1898.

10 NA, MG17, B2, Bompas to CMS, 20 January 1893; NA, Ogilvie Papers, Bompas to lt. governor, 3 December 1891.

11 NA, RG10, DIA, vol. 3962, file 147,654–1, pt. 2, Bompas to Indian commissioner, 5 September 1896.

12 NA, RG10, DIA, vol. 3962, file 147, 654–1, pt. 2, Bompas to Indian commissioner, 5 September 1896.

13 NA, MG17, B2, Bompas to CMS, 15 May 1894.

14 Ibid., Bompas to CMS, 3 January 1895.

15 Friesen, *The Chilkoot Pass*.

16 Webb, *The Last Frontier*, 205–24.

17 YTA, AC, New Series, file 4, Constantine to deputy minister of the interior, 19 November 1896.

18 Ibid., Indian Affairs, file 801–30–0–01, Bompas to minister of the interior, 28 October 1896 (extract from William Ogilvie's letter is dated 8 November 1896).

19 The best description of this process is in "Incidents in the Life of R.J. Bowen," 116–33.

20 YTA, AC, New Series, file 4, Constantine to deputy minister of the interior, 19 November 1896. The inspector claimed that the Indians imitated the whites, refusing to hunt and fish unless absolutely necessary. While a few temporarily adopted a more "white" mode of life, his larger generalization is misleading. Importantly, Constantine staunchly defended the miners and had little time for those, such as Bompas, who sought to preserve Indian rights. Constantine's comments on the Indians, appended to a refutation of Bompas's claims that the government should protect Native fishing and land rights, are of questionable validity.

21 Many moneyless miners received a grubstake from local traders, who were promised a share of any gold strike. The availability of goods on credit further reduced the pool of available workers.

22 For an excellent description of the functioning of a casual, seasonal labour market in an industrial setting, see Jones, *Outcast London*.

23 Indians near the mining camps restricted the access of other Natives to the markets and wage-labour opportunities, a course of events reminiscent of earlier Indian attempts to preserve fur-trade monopolies. See "Incidents in the Life of R.J. Bowen" for an excellent description of this process.

24 The Natives' successful adaptation to the nineteenth-century mining frontier in the Yukon is not unique, although it contrasts with most

portraits of the expansion of mining activity. See the portrayals of the British Columbia experience in Fisher, *Contact and Conflict*, and Knight, *Indians at Work*. Also, see Kay, "Indian Responses to a Mining Frontier," in Savage and Thompson, eds., *The Frontier: Comparative Studies*, 193–203. The governing factor appears to be the size and speed of the gold rush. When large numbers of prospectors arrive in a brief period, the Indians are quickly pushed aside, and either dispossessed or ignored, depending on whether or not they live on or near the gold-bearing ground. When development proceeds more gradually, with fewer miners and less dramatic discoveries, the dislocation of Indian society is not as severe.

25 For a good description of the discovery of gold, see Wright, *Prelude to Bonanza*. See also Zaslow, *The Opening of the Canadian North* for an overview of the gold-rush period.

26 Canada, *Census 1901*.

27 Green, *The Gold Hustlers*; Hall, *Clifford Sifton: The Young Napoleon* and *Clifford Sifton: The Lonely Eminence*; Gould and Stuart, "Permafrost Gold."

28 The earlier figure is based on a DIA estimate of 2,600 Natives and approximately 600–700 whites in 1896. The latter ratio is based on Canada, *Census, 1901*.

29 MacGregor, *The Klondike Gold Rush Through Edmonton*.

30 Slobodin, "The Dawson Boys," 24–35 The Porcupine River region was virtually deserted in this period as the Natives departed for Fort McPherson, Herschel Island, or Dawson City. NA, MG17, B2, Bompas to CMS, 18 November 1896; "Report of Inspector Starnes," *North-West Mounted Police Annual Report, 1902*, pt. III, 57; "Report of Inspector Wood," ibid., 18; "Report of Inspector Routledge," *Northwest Mounted Police Annual Report, 1903*, 89.

31 The notable exception is the records of the North-West Mounted Police (NA, RG18). See also Berton, *Klondike*; Clark, *The Developing Canadian Community*; and Innis, *Settlement and the Mining Frontier*. All of these studies reflect the standard Euro-centric focus.

32 Zaslow, *The Opening of the Canadian North*, 144–6; North-West Mounted Police, *Annual Reports*, 1896–1904. Indian Affairs, file 801–30–0–1, Bompas to commissioner of Indian affairs, 12 July 1899; NA, RCMP, vol. 189, file 339, S. Sergt. Pringle to O.C. "B" Division, 7 August 1900, discusses the McQuesten area. NA, RCMP, vol. 154, file 445, Jarvis report re: trip to Dalton trading post, 16 August 1898, describes short-term work in that area. Wages for guides and packers reached $4 per day. See also "Report of Superintendent Wood, NWMP, *Annual Report, 1899*, pt. III, 41.

33 YTA, Anglican Church Records, New Series, file 4, Constantine to deputy minister of the interior, 19 November 1896; Archer, *A Heroine of the North*, 160.

34 See Friesen, *The Chilkoot Pass*.

35 Coates, *The Northern Yukon*, 65–74; MacGregor, *The Klondike Gold Rush Through Edmonton*; Graham, *The Golden Grindstone*; McAdam, *From Duck Lake to Dawson City*; Inman, *Buffalo Jones' Forty Years of Adventure*, 454.

36 Technological advances in transportation are well described in Bennett, *Yukon Transportation*.

37 Zaslow, *The Opening of the Canadian North*, provides a good description of administrative maneuvers. See also Morrison, *Showing the Flag*, 28–49. NA, RG10, vol. 3962, file 147, 6544, pt. 2, Bompas to commissioner for Indian affairs, 5 August 1896.

38 NA, RG10, DIA, vol. 3962, file 147, 6544, pt. 2, Bompas to Indian commissioner, 5 September 1876; YTA, AC, New Series, file 4, Constantine to deputy minister of the interior, 15 November 1896. The government imposed game laws to protect the resources, but exempted Indians. The decision reflected the desire to prevent Natives from becoming public charges. DIA, vol. 6761, file 420–12, J. Smart to Major Z.T. Wood, 17 October 1902. On the decimation of game around the gold-fields, see "Report of Inspector Wood," NWMP *Annual Report, 1902*, pt. III, 10; "Report of Supt. Wood," NWMP *Annual Report, 1903*, 18.

39 Archer, *A Heroine of the North*, 162, suggests Indian women prospered during the gold rush. The NWMP valued many Native products, especially snowshoes, for their suitability to northern conditions. "Report of Supt. Wood," NWMP *Annual Report, 1899*, pt. III, 62.

40 Mason, *The Frozen Northland*; Cody, *Apostle of the North*, 279, states that the prices for dogs reached $250 or, on a rental basis, $1 per dog each day.

41 DIA, vol. 4037, file 317,050, McLean to Jackson, 28 January 1902; DIA, vol. 4001, file 207, 418, Longdon to Pedley, 28 May 1903, White to Smart, 1 January 1901, Accountant to Secretary, Department of Indian Affairs, 1 May 1902.

42 "Report of Supt. Wood," NWMP *Annual Report, 1899*, III, 55; RCMP, vol. 247, file 92, Bompas to Wood, 6 July 1900; Indian Affairs, file 801–30–0–1, Bompas to Commissioner of Indian Affairs, 12 July 1899, "Report of Inspector Jarvis," NWMP *Annual Report, 1902*, pt. III, 70–1; "Report of Inspector Snyder," NWMP *Annual Report, 1903*, 43.

43 "Report of Inspector Routledge, 1 December 1902," NWMP *Annual Report, 1903*, 89; "Report of Supt. Cuthbert," NWMP *Annual Report, 1904*, 43.

44 Slobodin, "The Dawson Boys." Since the author traced Indian involvement in the mining camps beyond the gold-rush period, several of the occupations noted were from the post-Klondike era.

45 Kehoe, *North American Indians*, 500.

46 Asch, "Capital and Economic Development"; and "Some Effects of the Late Nineteenth Century Modernization of the Fur Trade," 7–15.

47 Indians Affairs, 801–30–0–1, Bompas to Commissioner of Indian Affairs, 12 July 1899.

48 NA, RCMP, vol. 251, file 262, Supt. 'H' Division to Asst. Commissioner, 10 July 1903.

49 Zaslow, *The Opening of the Canadian North*, 145.

50 NA, RCMP, vol. 155, file 484, Jarvis to comptroller, NWMP, 11 August 1896; NA, RCMP, vol. 154, file 445, Jarvis report re: trip to Dalton trading post, 16 August 1898; "Report of Inspector Jarvis," NWMP *Annual Report 1899*, pt. III, 63.

51 NWMP officers offered glimpses of the Indians' activities. NA, RCMP, vol. 295, file 273, Cuthbert to asst. commissioner, 30 September 1905; NA, RCMP, vol. 251, file 262, Supt. 'H' Division to asst. commissioner, 7 February 1903; NA, RCMP, vol. 245, file 62, Wood to comptroller, 29 December 1902, Cuthbert to asst. commissioner, 17 December 1902; RCMP, vol. 231, file 188, Inspector Horrigan to asst. comm., 3 November 1902; NA, RCMP, vol. 189, file 339, Pringle to O.C. 'B' Division, 7 August 1900; "Report of Inspector Sternes," NWMP *Annual Report, 1902*, pt. III, 56–7.

52 Exclusionist policies kept Natives out of the mines. Policies designed to prevent competition from cheap labour similarly barred the Chinese. Bishop Bompas and the police encouraged this exclusion. DIA, vol. 3962, file 147,654–1, p. 2; Bompas to Indian commissioner, 5 September 1896; NA, MG17, B2, Bompas to CMS, 2 March 1898.

53 Fisher, in *Contact and Conflict* (19–20, 101, 113, and 128), notes that prostitution in British Columbia ceased with the arrival of a white-settler population.

54 Guest, "Dawson City," especially the chapter "Languorous Lillies of Soulless Love." The police accepted prostitution as a necessary frontier evil, and tried to regulate it, rather than prevent it. See Morrison, *Showing the Flag*. The NWMP adopted similar policies on the southern plains. See McLeod, *Law Enforcement and the Canadian West*.

55 There is little detailed information on the fur trade in this period. See McCandless, *Yukon Wildlife*. Congdon, "Fur Bearing Animals in Canada, and How to Prevent Their Extinction," *First Annual Report of the Commission on Conservation, 1910*. On Dalton Post, NA, RCMP, vol. 251, file 262, Supt. 'H' Division to Asst. Commissioner, 7 February 1903; "Report of Supt. Wood," NWMP *Annual Report, 1904*, 12; "Report by McDonell, Dalton Trail," NWMP *Annual Report, 1904*, 72; "Report of Inspector Jarvis," NWMP *Annual Report 1900*, pt. II, 59; "Report of Inspector Jarvis, NWMP *Annual Report, 1899*, pt. III, 62–3.

CHAPTER THREE

1 Green, *The Gold Hustlers*; Rea, *The Political Economy of the Canadian North*, 96–150.

2 Bennett, *Yukon Transportation*, 94–114.

3 NA, RG10, DIA, vol. 7575, file 19166–6, pt 1, G. Binning to secretary, DIA, 7 November 1936.

4 NA, RG85, vol. 609, file 2657, "Stampede to New Gold Field" (*Vancouver Province* news clipping), E. Blatta to O.C. Whitehorse, 22 October 1924.

5 YTA, Anglican Church, Report of Messrs Vowell and Green, 14 August 1908.

6 "Report of Supt. Snyder, 30 November 1904," RNWMP, *Annual Report, 1904.* Several Indians mined for themselves. See also Northern Administration Branch, vol. 609, file 2657; YTA, AC, New Series, file 2, Vowell and Green to secretary of Indian department, 14 August 1908.

7 YTA, Anglican Church, New Series, file 3, A.E. Green to secretary of the Indian department, 16 April 1909.

8 YTA, AC, New Series, file 3, A.E. Green to secretary, Indian department, 16 April 1909,

9 This description is drawn from the following: NA, RCMP, vol. 514, file 530, Bell to O.C. "B" Division, 2 September 1916; RNWMP *Annual Report 1908*, 209; YTA, AC, Young file, Young to Stringer, 15 October 1920, NA, DIA, vol. 6478, file 930–1, pt. 1; particulars regarding Yukon Indians, Teslin Lake band, June 1907 and Stringer to Hawksley, 31 January 1925; Indian Affairws, file 801–30–0–1,; Taggart to Allen, 3 April 1940; Indian Affairs, file 801–30–0–1; YTA, AC, Selkirk children reports; YTA, AC, Ashbee file, Kirsey to Stringer, 5 October 1927; YTA, AC, Misc. file, Stringer to Welsh, 15 May 1916; YTA, AC, Ashbee file, Ashbee to Stringer, 26 June 1926; YTA, AC, Wood file, James Wood to Stringer, 15 June 1916; YTA, AC, Field file, Stringer to Field, 16 January 1915; YTA, AC, New Series, file 1, particulars regarding Yukon Indians, *c.* 1907; YTA, AC, New Series, file 2, Vowell and Green to secretary of Indian department, 14 August 1908; YTA, YRG1, , series 5, vol. 2, file 198, Mitter to controller, mines, lands and Yukon branch, 6 February 1917. In the same file, see McLean to Rowett, 10 March 1917, Mitter to controller, mines, lands and Yukon branch, 14 May 1917. See also Helm, *Handbook of North American Indians*, vol.6, *Subarctic*, and McClellan, *My Old People Say*.

10 NA, RG18, vol. 514, file 530, A.L. Bell to O.C. "B" Division, 2 September 1916.

11 An attempt was made to replace wood with coal, mined near Carmacks. The effort was dropped because of the poor quality of the Yukon product.

12 Importantly, the YNB identified the cancellation of the Yukon River steamships in the 1950s as a cause of major distress among their people. See YNB, *Together Today*, 12.

13 YTA, YRG1, vol. 9, file 1490, pt. J, Hawksley to Scott, 21 August 1931.

14 McCandless, *Yukon Wildlife*, 47–48. The rationale for this estimate, which McCandless suggests is likely quite low, is unconvincing.

15 See YTA, Cadzow Papers, Account Book, which lists a number of meat purchases from Indians. On the sale of game in Whitehorse, see YTA, YRG1, series 3, vol. 4, file 12–6A, Higgins to Percy, 25 August 1926.

16 YTA, YRG1, series 3, vol. 2, file 12–14B, Game Hunters Licenses Issues, 1921.

17 YTA, YRG1, series 3, vol. 12, file 13–2A, Statement of Game Purchased by Waechter Bros. Co., 1925, Statement of Game Purchased by Waechter Bros. Co., 1927.

18 YTA, YRG1, series 3, vol. 10, file 12–20C, Jeckell to Gibson, 13 January 1944.

19 See, for example, YTA, YRG1, series 3, vol. 10, file 12–20A, Gibson to Jeckell, 9 September 1942.

20 Remley, *Crooked Road*. The essays in Coates, ed., *The Alaska Highway*, address the issues raised in this paragraph.

21 The question of what impact the highway had on the Yukon Indians is the subject of considerable debate. See the articles by Coates and Cruikshank in Coates, ed., *The Alaska Highway*.

22 NA, RG85, vol. 944, file 12743, pt. 1, C. Clarke to Mr Cumming, 3 November 1942.

23 In 1935 the federal government had asked for information on the status of handicraft production in the Yukon. G. Binning, the acting Indian agent, observed that "except for the older people I fear there is not much interest taken in handicrafts, outside of making the necessary moccasins, mitts, etc." NA, RG10, vol. 7554, file 41, #212–1, G. Binning: Questionnaire on Indian Arts, October 1935.

24 NA, DIA, vol. 7553, file 41–166–1, Gibben to Indian Affairs Branch, 10 April 1943. The file contains further details on the project. See in particular, Lowe to Hoey, 15 June 1943.

25 YTA, YRG1, series 1, vol. 61, file 35402, G.A. Jeckell to Gen. W.W. Hoge, 24 July 1942; ibid., vol. 66, file 3525, Yukon Consolidated Gold Corporation, Report for 1942, 2, cited in Stuart, "The Impact of the Alaska Highway," in Coates, ed., *The Alaska Highway*.

26 YTA, YRG1, series 1, vol. 9, file 1490, pt. J, C.K. LeCapelain to R.A. Gibson, 17 July 1943.

27 Osgood, *The Han Indians* and *Contributions to the Ethnography of the Kutchin*; Honigman, *The Kaska Indians*; YTA, YRG1, vol. 9, file 1490, pt. J., J. Hawksley to McLean, 9 January 1929, J. Hawksley to Scott, 18 May

1926; NA, DIA, vol. 4081, file 478, 700, J. Hawksley report on Mayo Band of Indians, 26 August 1917.

28 YTA, YRG1, series 3, vol. 1, file 2019, Wood to Stewart, 2 July 1902; ibid., vol. 17, file 28798, Sandys-Wunsch to secretary, DIA, 28 April 1939, Gibson to Jeckell, 6 October 1943.

29 YTA, YRG1, series 3, vol. 1, file 2019, Silas to Dear Sir, n.d.; McCarvill to O.C. "B" Division, 17 July 1909.

30 YTA, YRG1, vol. 9, file 1490, pt. 7., Hawksley to Mackenzie, 15 November 1933.

31 NA, RG18, vol. 539, file 2, Sergt. Mapley to O.C. Whitehorse Sub-District, 7 February 1917; YTA, Anglican Church, Champagne file, "L.G. Chappell report on missionary work undertaken in Champagne District, Summer 1934." The extremely exploitative American fishery along the Alaska panhandle and at the mouth of the Yukon River had serious implications for upper Yukon and Alsek River fish stocks. YTA, Anglican Church, Hudson Stuck to Isaac Stringer, 29 March 1920.

32 NA, RG18, vol. 549, file 109, Inspector Bell to O.C. "B" Division, 24 October 1918.

33 The best description of the evolution of big-game hunting is McCandless, *Yukon Wildlife*.

34 Yukon Territory, *Ordinances 1923*, chapter 5.

35 YTA, YRG1, series 3, vol. 10, file 12–19B, Jeckell to Slaughter, 9 October 1941.

36 YTA, YRG1, series 3, vol. 10, file 12–19B, Hall to Jeckell, 12 November 1941; Jeckell to Hall, 9 October 1941; Grennan report re: William Hall (Indian), 10 November 1942. George Johnston of Teslin encountered similar difficulties. See YTA, YRG1, series 3, vol. 7, file 12–13B, Jeckell to O.C. "B" Division, 20 June 1934; Irvine to O.C. "B" Division, 18 May 1934. Constable Irving's report was strikingly positive, but Commissioner Jeckell none the less rejected the application.

37 YTA, YRG1, series 3, vol. 4, file 12–7, Higgins to commissioner, 12 August 1927.

38 YTA, YRG1, series 1, vol. 71, file 32, Eugene Jacquot to George Black, 30 March 1947.

39 YTA, YRG1, series 3, vol. 10, file 12–19B, Jeckell to S.D. Slaughter, 9 October 1941.

40 A number of hunters wrote accounts of their Yukon adventures: Auer, *Campfires in the Yukon*; Martindale, *Hunting in the Upper Yukon*; Selous, *Recent Hunting Trips*; Armstrong, *After Big-Game*; Bond, *From Out of the Yukon*.

41 YTA, Anglican Church, Acc. 79/52, W. Fry to Stringer, 26 March 1918.

42 For comparative purposes, Yukon gold production never fell below $529,000 in any one year and reached as high as $3.2 million in 1942.

43 Dan Cadzow of Rampart House left portions of an account for 1907–12, which reveal something of the prices. The source (YTA, Cadzow Papers, Account Book) is very incomplete and unreliable. On Cadzow, see Riggs, "Running the Alaska Boundary."

44 YTA, Anglican Church, C.F. Johnson file 2, Johnson to Stringer, 7 April 1920.

45 NA, RG85, vol. 797, file 6535, Maclean to Cory, 12 October 1928.

46 YTA, Anglican Church, Rampart House, Fort Yukon, and Old Crow file, McCullum to Stringer, 23 July 1930.

47 NA, MG30 E2, N.A.D. Armstrong, Diary 1925 #2, Fur Prices – Priced by A. Klimisch, Selkirk, YT.

48 NA, RG18, vol. 539, file 2, Serg. Mapley to O.C., Whitehorse, 7 February 1917.

49 RG18, vol. 539, file 2, A. Laurent to O.C., Whitehorse, 2 April 1917.

50 *Northern Lights* 28, no. 2 (May 1930): 4–5.

51 This topic is covered in McCandless, *Yukon Wildlife: A Social History*, and Adrian Tanner, "The Structure of Fur Trade Relations." Both works suffer from the general absence of systematic records on the twentieth-century fur trade.

52 NA, RG85, vol. 797, file 6535, Maclean to Cory, 12 October 1926.

53 NA, RG85, vol. 609, file 2657, Extracts from report of Constable Young, 18 March 1925.

54 YTA, Anglican Church, Morris file, Morris to Stringer, 24 June 1926.

55 YTA, Anglican Church, Cadzow file, Cadzow to Stringer, 20 March 1917.

56 YTA, Anglican Church, Brett file, Brett to Stringer, 16 October 1914.

57 Tanner, "The Structure of Fur Trade Relations," 44–72.

58 YTA, YRG1, series 4, vol. 10, file 241A, territorial secretary to Constable Tidd, 30 August 1918; YTA, YRG1, series 3, vol. 3, file 12–58, gold commissioner to J.H. Mervyn, 5 July 1924, gold commissioner to M.R. Jackson, 30 June 1924; YTA, YRG1, series 3, vol. 4, file 12–7B, proclamation dated 1 September 1928; YTA, YRG1, series 3, vol. 3, file 12–5B, Cadzow to gold commissioner, 20 July 1924.

59 See, for example, YTA, YRG1, series 3, vol. 10, file 12–19B, R.A. Gibson to G.A. Jeckell, 9 June 1941, which deals with restrictions on the Old Crow muskrat harvest.

60 YTA, YRG1, series 4, vol. 10, file 241A, territorial secretary to Const. C.B. Tidd, 30 August 1918. Furs trapped outside the territory but traded in the Yukon also received exemptions. Ibid., Isaac Taylor to Geo. Mackenzie, 10 July 1918, Affidavit by Wm. Drury, 24 November 1919.

61 Since some fur bearers were harvested for food, these restrictions had considerable impact. Game caught for sustenance generally escaped the

regulations. YTA, Teslin Band Collection, Hawksley to Dear Sir., 8 November 1923.

62 YTA, YRG1, series 3, vol. 4, file 12–6A, Insp. Caulkin to P. Reid, 2 August 1926; ibid., file 12–6B, Thornthwaite to gold commissioner, 31 January 1927.

63 NA, RG10, DIA, vol. 6761, file 420–12, O.S. Finnie to G.J. MacLean, 28 December 1928; YTA, YRG1, series 3, vol. 5, file 12–8B, Urquhart to O.S. Finnie, 10 August 1929, Constable A.S. Wilson to O.C., RCMP Edmonton, 10 August 1929; ibid., file 12–8A, Thornthwaite to O.C., Dawson, 26 February 1929, Hawksley to McLean, 3 January 1929; NA, RG10, vol. 6761, file 420–12, Inspector Wood to Commissioner, RCMP, 5 August 1929. Further attempts to restrict Native harvesting across territorial or provincial boundaries met similar resistance. Ibid., Ralph Parsons, HBC fur trade commissioner to Dr H.W. McGill, 17 December 1937.

64 YTA, YRG1, series 3, vol. 5, file 12–8A, Maclean to Finnie, 6 February 1929.

65 YTA, YRG1, series 3, vol. 7, file 12–14B, G.A. Jeckell to J. Lorne Turner, 16 April 1935.

66 NA, RG10, DIA, vol. 6761, file 420–12, Thornthwaite to O.C., Dawson, 9 April 1929; YTA, YRG1, series 3, vol. 5, file 12–8A, gold commissioner to O.S. Finnie, 3 January 1929. Eagle, Alaska Natives, closely related to those at Moosehide, were accorded more liberties. YTA, YRG1, series 3, vol. 6, file 10A, Hawksley to gold commissioner, 14 May 1931.

67 For the best statement on this ongoing relationship, see YTA, YRG1, vol. 9, file 1490, pt. J, John Hawksley to Harper Reed, 25 February 1933.

68 NA, RG10, DIA, vol. 6761, file 420–12, Squam to Indian department, 22 August 1932.

69 YTA, YRG1, series 3, vol. 6, file 12–11B, Jeckell to Hume, 21 November 1932.

70 YTA, Teslin Band Collection, Stikine Agency Inspection Report no. 3, 31 July 1935, Simpson to Chief Billy Johnston, 1 October 1942.

71 YTA, YRG1, series 3, vol. 11, file 12–22, Gibson to Gibben, 9 May 1947; NA, RG10, vol. 6761, file 420–12–2–2, Meek Report, 28 February 1947; ibid., file 420–12–2–RT-1, Meek to D.J. Allen, 27 November 1947, Conn to Meek, 4 December 1947.

72 YTA, YRG1, series 3, vol. 11, file 12–22, Extract from Indian Agent R.J. Meek's Quarterly Report, 10 October 1947.

73 NA, RG10, DIA, vol. 6761, file 420–12–2–RT-1, Meek to Hugh Conn, 17 January 1950; YTA, YRG1, series 3, vol. 11, file 12–23B, Meek to Gibson, 27 September 1950.

74 YTA, YRG1, series 3, vol. 11, file 12–23B, director to R.A. Gibson, 14 February 1950.

75 YTA, YRG1, series 3, vol. 11, file 12–23B, Chief Peter Moses, Councillor Moses Tizya, and Councillor Joseph Netro to R.J. Meek, 24 July 1950, Chief Wm. A. Johnston et al. (petition), 7 July 1950.

76 See the comments by Native elders in *The Gravel Magnet*.

77 NA, RG10, DIA, vol. 4081, file 478, 698, John Hawksley, Report of Fortymile Band of Indians, 29 March 1917; YTA, Anglican Church, McCullum file, Wood to Stringer, 14 April 1926; YTA, YRG1, series 3, vol. 4, file 12–6B, Thornthwaite to gold commissioner, 26 April 1927; YTA, YRG1, series 3, vol. 5, file 12–8C, Thornthwaite to gold commissioner, 31 December 1929.

78 This argument is presented in McCandless, *Yukon Wildlife*.

79 YTA, YRG1, series 3, vol. 5, file 12–8C, Thornthwaite to gold commissioner, 31 December 1929; YTA, YRG1, series 3, file 12–5B, gold commissioner to Nelson, 30 June 1924; YTA, RG10, vol. 6761, DIA, file 420–12–2–2, Meek Report, 28 February 1947; YTA, YRG1, series 3, vol. 11, Extract from Indian Agent Meek's Quarterly Report, 10 October 1947; NA, RG10, DIA, vol. 6761, file 420–12, Harper Reed to Sir, 1 September 1934; "Report of Supt. Knight," NWMP, *Annual Report, 1917*, 306.

80 YTA, YRG1, series 3, vol. 9, file 12–18B, Boyerchuck to Dear Sir, 20 June 1939; YTA, YRG1, series 3, vol. 2, file 12–3B, Lloyd to Mackenzie re: complaint by Game Warden T.A. Dickson, 20 May 1920; YTA, YRG1, series 3, vol. 10, file 12–16B, Dahl to Supt. T.B. Caulkin, 5 September 1936, Const. T. Henderson to O.S. RNWMP, "A" Division, 26 October 1910; NA, RG18, vol. 393, Supt. Snyder to Asst. Commissioner, RNWMP, 11 July 1910, Jim Thompson et al. to Major Snyder, 4 July 1910; YTA, YRG1, series 3, vol. 11, file 12–22, Bond to Biggen, 23 June 1943.

81 For an excellent series of descriptions of this mingling of activities, see YTA, Anglican Church, Selkirk Children Reports, which detail movements and economic activities at Fort Selkirk.

82 See RNWMP, *Annual Report, 19*, Sergeant Clay to O.C. "B" Division, 5 March 1915, 200; YTA, YRG1, series 7, vol. 33, file 33937, pt. 9, Report-Patrol from Dawson to Snag, Wellesley Lake, etc. 19 February 1931.

83 YTA, Anglican Church, Amos Njootli file, Njootli to Stringer, 1 April 1917; YTA, Anglican Church, Goldrich file, Cadzow to Stringer, 14 December 1919; YTA, Anglican Church, Rampart House, Fort Yukon, and Old Crow file, H. Anthony to Stringer, 16 November 1925; NA, RG85, vol. 609, file 2657, Thornthwaite to O.C., RCMP Dawson, 17 November 1928; NA, RG10, vol. 6478, file 932–1, pt. 1, Extract from report of G. Binning, 17 July 1935.

84 YTA, Anglican Church, Moosehide file, Sarah Essau to Bishop Stringer, 31 August 1919; YTA, Anglican Church, Leigh file, Leigh to bishop, 24 October 1927.

85 YTA, Anglican Church, Cadzow file, Cadzow to Stringer, 23 December 1917.

86 YTA, RG10, DIA, vol. 3462, file 147, 654–1, pt. 2, Bompas to DIA, 25 May 1906.

87 NA, RG18, DIA, vol. 409, file 109, Const. C.H. Hill to O.C. Sub-Division "B," 25 January 1911; NA, RG18, vol. 599, file 1343, supt. commanding "B" Division to commissioner, RCMP, 15 March 1920. Attached to the letter are depositions by T.S. Dickson, a former RCMP officer, and Ole Dickson (no relation) attesting to the "slaughter." See also YTA, YRG1, series 3, vol. 2, file 12–3B, gold commissioner to Lloyd, 14 June 1920.

88 YTA, YRG1, series 3, vol. 2, file 12–4A, Report of Major N.A.D. Armstrong concerning Game Conditions in the Yukon Territory, 29 November 1920. Armstrong, ironically, is typically dismissed as being anti-Indian and racist. See the comments on Armstrong in McCandless, *Yukon Wildlife*.

89 YTA, YRG1, series 3, vol. 2, file 12–4A, Supt. R.E. Tucker to commissioner, RCMP, 20 April 1921.

90 YTA, YRG1, series 3, vol. 2, file 12–14B, Supt. Tucker to gold commissioner, 20 March 1922; YTA, YRG1, series 4, vol. 27, file 408–4, E. Jacquot to G.A. Jeckell, n.d.; YTA, YRG1, series 3, vol. 10, file 12–20A, J.E. Gibben to R.A. Gibson, 17 December 1942.

91 NA, RG85, vol. 609, file 2657, Const. McCormick to O.C., RCMP, Dawson, 1 August 1924.

92 See McCandless, *Yukon Wildlife*. YTA, YRG1, series 3, vol. 11, file 12–21A, Bostock to Gibson, 28 November 1946.

93 YTA, YRG1, series 3, vol. 11, file 12–22, Summary of the Game and Fishing Regulations, Yukon Territory, 1947; YTA, YRG1, series 3, file 12–23B, Gibson to Simmons, 22 April 1950.

94 YTA, YRG1, series 3, file 12–23B, Morisset to Simmons, 13 April 1950, Morisset to Indian Affairs Branch, 11 April 1950, Gibson to Simmons, 22 April 1950.

95 NA, RG10, DIA, vol. 6761, file 420–12–2–RT-1, Conn to Meek, 22 May 1950; YTA, YRG1, series 3, vol. 11, file 12–23B, Gibben to Gibson, 19 June 1950; NA, RG10, vol. 6761, file 420–12–2–RT-1, Meek to Conn, 20 June 1950.

96 YTA, Anglican Church, Champagne file, Report to the Diocese of the Yukon upon the present state of the Champagne (Y.T.) Mission Field, Summer 1949 by Anthony Guscoyne.

97 For a somewhat different view, see Cruikshank, "The Gravel Magnet," in Coates, ed., *The Alaska Highway*.

98 Records are found in the Yukon Territorial Government, Vital Statistics Branch, active files. The materials could be examined only on the condition that they be sampled randomly and that no names be recorded.

Checkout Receipt
        Kenai Community Library
                283-4378
    You may renew materials online
    at http://www.kenailibrary.org
            03/19/08 02:25PM
    ****

Baby craft /
CALL NO: 745.5 BABY
33430001001726   DUE: 04/14/08

Best left as Indians : native-white relCA
LL NO: ALASKA 971.9 COA
33430000715128   DUE: 04/16/08

The six wives of Henry VIII /
CALL NO: 942.052 WEIR
33430000798306   DUE: 04/16/08

Legends, lies & cherished myths of worlCA
LL NO: 902.07 SHE
33430000597922   DUE: 04/16/08

TOTAL: 4

PART TWO

1 Zaslow, *The Opening of the Canadian North*, chapter 6; Berton, *Klondike*. A recent study, rich in detail but largely inaccessible, is Guest, "A History of the City of Dawson." Morris Zaslow's second book, *The Northward Expansion of Canada*, provides only brief descriptions of the nature of northern society. One exception to this trend is the useful chapter on northern society in the 1930s found in Shelagh Grant, ed., *Sovereignty or Security?* For a general statement on the evolution of Yukon society, see Coates and Morrison, *Land of the Midnight Sun*.
2 The census does not accurately reflect the non-Native population. The non-Native population was exceptionally transient, moving within and out of the territory at will. The census figures represent, at best, a snapshot of territorial demographics.

CHAPTER FOUR

1 Sylvia Van Kirk, *Many Tender Ties*. See also Brown, *Strangers in Blood*.
2 Murray, Journal of the Yukon; HBCA, B240/2/1, fol. 27, Youcon Journal, 31 August 1847.
3 Van Kirk, *Many Tender Ties*. This is also the only Yukon example included in Van Kirk's study.
4 Dall, *Alaska and Its Resources*, 106.
5 HBCA, B200/b/43, fol. 209, Camsell to Grahame, 24 March 1884. Firth's wife may have been a Métis. Crowe, *A History of the Original Peoples of Northern Canada*.
6 Dall, *Alaska*, 104.
7 Kennicott, "The Journal of Robert Kennicott."
8 YTA, Anglican Church, AC 79/51, vol. 21, Statistical Reports file, Baptisms, Rampart House.
9 NA, MG17, B2, Bompas to Baring Gould, 13 January 1896.
10 Van Kirk, *Many Tender Ties*, 75–94, expands on the notion of Indian wives as "women in between" in the context of economic relations.
11 Experience elsewhere in North America illustrates that, when non-Native women were not available, males enthusiastically turned to women of other races. Regarding whites and blacks, see Jordan's *White Over Black*, 140. Nash, *Red, White and Black*, deals with the issue more broadly. Morner, *Race Mixture in the History of Latin America*.
12 Jones, "The Kutchin Tribes"; Hardisty, "The Loucheux Indians"; HBCA, B200/b/33, fol. 15, Ross to council, 29 November 1858; HBCA, B200/b/34, fol. 130, Jones to Hardisty, 23 June 1863; HBCA, B200/b/35, fol. 106, Hardisty to McDougall, 4 April 1865; NA, MG19, D13, Pelly and Lewes Journal, vol. 1, 9 June 1848; PAM, MG7 (Archives of the

Ecclesiastical Province of Rupertsland), A1, Box 4001, "Rev. W.W. Kirkby's Journey to Fort Youcon"; NA, MG17, B2, Bompas to CMS, 6 December 1872.

13 See Berkhofer, *White Man's Indian,* for the broader context suggested here.

14 Cody, *An Apostle of the North,* 253–72.

15 NA, MG29 C92, Bowen Papers, "Incidents in the Life of R.J. Bowen."

16 NA, MG29 C92, Bowen Papers, "Incidents in the Life of R.J. Bowen"; Archer, *A Heroine of the North;* Cody, *An Apostle of the North.*

17 Coates and Morrison, "More than a Matter of Blood," in Barron and Waldrum, eds, *1885 and After.*

18 Cody, *An Apostle of the North;* Archer, *A Heroine of the North;* NA, MG17, B2, Bompas to CMS, 24 May 1895, Bompas to Dear Sirs, 2 March 1895, Bompas to CMS, 15 May 1894; Bompas to CMS, 26 July 1895, Bompas to CMS, 3 January 1894, Diocese of Selkirk by Bompas, c. 1893, Bompas to CMS, 20 January 1893; NA, RG10, DIA, vol. 3906, file 105, 378, Bompas to minister of the interior, 5 June 1894, deputy supt. general to Hon. T. Mayne Daly, 18 September 1893.

19 Usher, "Canadian Western Arctic"; Warner, "Herschel Island"; Coates and Morrison, *Land of the Midnight Sun,* chapter five.

20 NA, MG30 E55, Constantine Papers, Constantine to O.C., Regina, 20 November 1896; See also, NA, RG18, vol. 336, file 254–07, Whittaker to Col. White, c. 1905; NA, MG17, B2, Bompas to CMS, 24 May 1895.

21 NA, MG29 C92, Bowen Papers, "Incidents in the Life of R.J. Bowen," 133.

22 Berkhofer, *The White Man's Indian.* One of the best examples of this attitude is contained in "Report of John Hawksley," DIA, *Annual Report, 1915–1916,* 117. Hawksley came to the Yukon as a missionary in the period in question.

23 NA, MG30 E55, Constantine Papers, vol. 4, fol. 120–1, Constantine to MacIntosh, 25 June 1896.

24 The police refused to accept Native testimony. The difficulty this caused in securing convictions did not dampen the policemen's ardour. NA, RG18, vol. 485, file 221, Moodie to Commissioner, 4 August 1918. See also NA, RG18, vol. 549, file 109, Report of Serg Mapley, 28 September 1918.

25 On the relation of this to contemporary America, see May, "Arrests, Alcohol and Alcohol Legalization."

26 Horton, "The Function of Alcohol in Primitive Societies."

27 Washburne, *Primitive Drinking;* Lemert, "The Use of Alcohol in Three Salish Indian Tribes"; Honigmann and Honigmann, "Drinking in an Indian-White Community."

28 Field, "A New Cross-Cultural Study of Drunkenness," in Pittman and Snyder, eds., *Society, Culture and Drinking Patterns.*

29 Dozier, "Problem Drinking Among American Indians"; Homer and Steinbring, eds., *Alcohol and Native Peoples of the North*.

30 Daly, "The Role of Alcohol Among North American Indian Tribes."

31 Lurie, "The World's Oldest On-Going Protest Demonstration." Lurie's argument is supported by a major work on Indians in New France, C. Jaenan's *Friends and Foe*.

32 Edgerton and MacAndrews, *Drunken Comportment*.

33 Levy and Kunitz, *Indian Drinking*.

34 NA, RG18, vol. 514, file 521, A.C. Bell to O.C. "B" Division, 12 August 1916.

35 Again, see Nash, *Red, White and Black*; Morner, *Race Mixture*.

36 George Carmacks, co-discoverer of the Klondike fields, was a "squaw man" and encountered significant discrimination as a result. A.A. Wright, *Prelude to Bonanza*, discusses the problems he encountered because of this status.

37 NA, MG29 C92, Bowen Papers, "Incidents in the Life of R.J. Bowen," 99.

38 Fisher, *Contact and Conflict*, 95–118.

39 Note the almost complete absence of discussions of Native people in Berton, *Klondike*, and Guest, "Dawson City."

40 NA, MG17, B2, Bompas to CMS, 4 May 1898.

41 NWMP, *Annual Report, 1902*, pt III, "Report of Supt. Wood," 10–11.

42 NA, MG17, B2S, Bompas to CMS, 23 August 1898.

43 NA, RG18, vol. 189, file 339, Davis to O.C., Dawson, 2 October 1900.

44 Slobodin, "The Dawson City Boys." Slobodin's essay is drawn from interviews with elders at Fort McPherson. There is little archival evidence to suggest that Natives participated in, rather than observed, the social round at Dawson. See also Knight, *Indians at Work*, 174–6.

45 Guest, "Dawson City," has the best discussion on this topic. See also Harris, "Prostitution in the Klondike." On the NWMP generally, see Morrison, *Showing the Flag*, and Stone, "The Mounties as Vigilantes."

46 Newell, "Importance of Information and Misinformation in the Making of the Klondike Gold Rush."

47 See Guest, "Dawson City: San Francisco of the North," and Friesen, "The Chilkoot Pass," for discussions of available materials.

48 Adney, "The Indian Hunter of the Far Northwest," and "Moose Hunting with the Tro-Chu-Tin."

49 Service, *Rhymes of a Rolling Stone*.

CHAPTER FIVE

1 *Across the Rockies*, vol. V, no. 7 (July 1914), Letter from, Rev. C.C. Brett.

2 NA, RG18, vol. 387, file 181, Macdonald to asst. comm., 1 September 1910; ibid., vol. 549, file 109, Report of Sergt. Mapley, 28 September 1918.

3 Riggs, "Running the Alaska Boundary."

4 YTA, Anglican Church, Fort Yukon file, Grafton Burke to J. Hawksley, 21 May 1926.

5 NA, MG30 E2, vol. 3, N.A.D. Armstrong Papers, Diary 1921, 8 July, 2 September.

6 "Report of Asst. Comm. Wood," RNWMP, *Annual Report, 1909*, 209.

7 NA, RG18, vol. 369, file 133, supt. commanding "H" Division to asst. comm., RNWMP, 29 February 1909.

8 Berton, *I Married the Klondike*, 169.

9 One of the most popular folk songs in the territory, typically sung with little awareness of the implicit racism, was long "Squaws Along the Yukon." For words and music, see YTA, Musical Scores #1, Cam Smith, "Squaws Along the Yukon," copyright 1936.

10 See, for example, the account of the work of Fred Watt, who lived between Pleasant Camp, BC and Dalton Post, Yukon. NA, RG18, vol. 539, file 2, Report to O.C. "B" Division, RNWMP, 29 September 1917.

11 NA, RG18, vol. 369, file 133, supt. commanding "H" Division to asst. comm. RWNMP, 29 February 1909, Frank Pedley to Fred White, 3 March 1909.

12 NA, RG10, DIA, vol. 6477, file 929–1, pt. 1, Meek to Indian Affairs Branch, 25 October 1947.

13 NA, RG10, DIA, vol. 6479, file 940–1, pt. 1, Stringer to DIA, 5 March 1912; YTA, Anglican Church, Johnson file 1, Stringer to C.F. Johnson; YTA, Anglican Church, Contributions: St Paul's Hostel file, St Paul's Hostel, 14 February 1947.

14 NA, RG10, DIA, vol. 6481, file 941–1, pt. 1, Duncan Scott to Sir James Lougheed, 2 May 1921.

15 YTA, Anglican Church, St Agnes Hostel file, Extract from Mayo-Keno Bulletin, 8 September 1925.

16 NA, RG18, vol. 369, file 133, Snyder to asst. comm., 29 January 1909.

17 NA, RG10, DIA, vol. 6479, file 940–1, pt. 1, Stringer to Secretary, DIA, 5 March 1917.

18 YTA, Vital Statistics Branch. Marriage registrations to 1950 did not indicate ethnicity.

19 This issue was not adequately resolved before 1950. As long as there was no formal marriage, the government considered the women to be Native. Children remained legally Native unless their fathers assumed full and public responsibility for their care. See NA, RG18, vol. 369, file 133, Pedley to White, 3 March 1909; YTA, YRG1, vol. 9, file 1490, pt. J., Meek to Gibben, 28 May 1947, Gibben to Hoey, 4 June 1947, Gibben to Hoey, 20 June 1947, McCrammon for supt. reserves and trusts to Gibben, 19 August 1947. See also Coates and Morrison, "More than a Matter of Blood."

20 YTA, YRG1, series 3, vol. 11, file 12–21A, H. Bostock to R.A. Gibson, 28 November 1946.
21 GSA, M74–3, 1–A-2, Henderson to Stringer, 6 March 1911.
22 YTA, Anglican Church, Whittaker file, Stringer to archdeacon, 20 February 1915.
23 This pattern of marriage represents a marked change from pre-contact conditions. See McClellan, *My Old People Say*; Helm, ed., *Handbook of North American Indians, vol. 6: The Subarctic.*
24 NA, RG85, vol. 797, file 6535, G.J. McLean to W.W. Cory, 26 September 1928; YTA, Anglican Church, Old Crow file, P.E. Moore to H.A. Alderwood, 17 December 1946.
25 On Indians near towns, see NA, RG18, vol. 352, file 128, supt. "H" Division to asst. comm., 3 March 1908, 1 May 1908; NA, RG18, vol. 316, file 241, Cuthbert to O.C., RNWMP, 30 April 1906; NA, RG18, vol. 192, file 995, Primrose to O.C., 1 November 1902; NA, RG18, vol. 335, file 191, supt. "H" Division to asst. comm., 6 May 1907; NA, RG18, vol. 315, file 228, supt. "H" Division to asst. comm., 7 August 1906.
26 NA, RG10, DIA, vol. 3962, file 147, 654–1, T. Bragg to secretary, DIA, 23 June 1910. See also "Report of Supt. Moodie," RNWMP, *Annual Report 1914*, 274.
27 YTA, YRG1, series 1, vol. 29, file 13014, W.C. Bompas to commissioner of Y.T., 29 November 1904.
28 YTA, YRG1, series 1, vol. 9, file 1490, pt. J, J. Hawksley to Black, 23 October 1916.
29 NA, RG10, DIA, vol. 4081, file 478, 700, Hawksley to J.D. McLean, 7 April 1915.
30 See also YTA, YRG1, series 1, vol. 29, file 13014, F.J.A. Demeres to asst. comm, RNWMP, 6 January 1905; YTA, YRG1, series 1, vol. 46, file 29967, McDonald to Black, 23 July 1915.
31 GSA, M74–3, 1–A-2, Box 1, Stringer Papers, A. Henderson to I. Stringer, 6 March 1911.
32 YTA, YRG1, series 1, vol. 9, file 1490, pt. J, Hawksley to Puckett, 29 December 1927.
33 "Report of Supt. Moodie," NWMP, *Annual Report, 1914*, 274.
34 NA, RG10, DIA, vol. 4081, file 478, 700, John Hawksley Report on Mayo Band of Indians, 27 July 1916.
35 YTA, Moosehide Band Council Minute Book, 1920s.
36 YTA, YRG1, series 1, vol. 9, file 1490, pt. J, J. Hawksley to E.A. Packett, 29 December 1927.
37 YTA, YRG1, series 1, vol. 9, file 1490, pt. J, Hawksley to McLean, 17 April 1929; NA, RG10, DIA, vol. 7155, file 801/3–10, pt. 1, Hawksley to McLean, Notice by John Hawksley, 1929.

38 YTA, YRG1, series 1, vol. 9, file 1490, pt. J, Hawksley to A.F. Mackenzie, 16 November 1933.

39 NA, RG10, DIA, vol. 6477, file 927–11, pt. 1, Meek Report, 28 February 1947. The curfew was marked by the ringing of a loud bell (as it was in Mayo), which directed the Indians to return to the reserve. The bell remained in use into the 1960s.

40 Berton, *I Married the Klondike*.

41 YTA, Anglican Church, Totty file, B. Totty to committee of the CMS, 29 January 1917.

42 Berton, *I Married the Klondike*, 59–60.

43 NA, RG10, DIA, vol. 6478, file 930–1, pt. 1, Extract from report submitted by Supt. R. Meek, 1 April–30 June 1949.

44 NA, RG10, DIA, vol. 6478, file 929–11, pt. 1, Meek to Indian Affairs Branch, 24 November 1949.

45 NA, RG18, vol. 296, file 274, supt. "A" Division to asst. comm., 6 March 1905.

46 YTA, YRG1, series 4, vol. 24, file 403–2, G[di] MacLean to O.S. Finnie, 18 August 1928.

47 YTA, YRG1, series 4, vol. 24, file 403–2, E.L. Stone Memorandum re: Mayo General Hospital, 6 September 1932.

48 YTA, Anglican Church, Commissioner of Yukon file, W.B. Clarke to Commissioner Black, 1 March 1913.

49 YTA, YRG1, series 7, vol. 7, file 1490–19, pt. 1, G.A. Jeckell to E.L. Stone, 25 October 1939.

50 YTA, YRG1, series 7, vol. 7, file 1490–19, pt. 1, G.A. Jeckell to E.L. Stone, 25 October 1939.

51 YTA, YRG1, series 1, vol. 65, file 813, Report of a Tuberculosis Survey in the Yukon Territory, c 1947.

52 NA, MG19 A25, Pelly and Lewes Journal, vol. 1, 9 June 1848; HBCA, B200/b/33, fol. 15, Ross to council, 29 November 1858; HBCA, B200/b/34, fol. 130, Jones to Hardisty, 23 June 1863; HBCA, B200/b/35, fol. 106, Hardisty to McDougall, 4 April 1865; Hardisty, "The Loucheux Indians," Jones, "The Kutchin Indians."

53 Berkhofer, *The White Man's Indian*. On the function of changing non-Native images of the Indian, see Jennings, *The Invasion of America*.

54 YTA, YRG1, series 2, vol. 44, file 36496, L. Locke to J.G. Gibben, 28 Sept. 1949; NA, RG18, vol. 295, file 273, H. Cuthbert to asst. comm., 20 June 1905; NA, MG30 E2, N.A.D. Armstrong Papers, vol. 3, Diary 1920, fol. 47, 20 June 1920.

55 "Report of Supt. Snyder," RNWMP, *Annual Report 1909*, 223.

56 YTA, YRG1, series 1, vol. 9, file 1490, pt. J, J. Gibben to Indian Affairs Branch, 1 March 1946.

57 NA, RG10, DIA, vol. 6477, file 927–1, pt. 1, R.J. Meek report, 28 February 1947.

58 See the articles by Coates and Cruikshank in Coates, ed., *The Alaska Highway*. See also Remley, *The Crooked Road*.

59 Cruikshank, "The Gravel Magnet," in Coates, ed., *The Alaska Highway*.

60 Honigmann and Honigmann, "Drinking in an Indian-White Community." See also Honigmann, "On the Alaska Highway." Most of the Honigmanns' work related to the Kaska Indians in the Liard River district.

61 NA, RG10, DIA, vol. 8762, file 906/25–1–005, pt. 1, Meek to Indian Affairs Branch, 8 February 1950.

62 NA, RG10, DIA, vol. 6479, file 940–1, pt. 2, Extract from report of R.A.J. Meek, 9 April 1948.

63 This question is discussed in Coates and Morrison, *The Sinking of the Princess Sophia*.

64 YTA, YRG1, series 1, vol. 34, file 22052, Dr D. Lenman to Dr W.T. Barnett, 2 December 1907.

65 YTA, Anglican Church, Cadzow file, 20 March 1917.

66 YTA, YRG1, series 1, vol. 9, file 1490, pt. J, C.K. Le Capelain to R.A. Gibson, 17 July 1943.

67 Marchand, "Tribal Epidemics in the Yukon."

68 *Northern Lights*, vol. XXX (August 1941).

69 Honigmann, letter to the editor, *Journal of the American Medical Association*, CXXIII (1944), 386. Honigmann noted that the diseases Marchand saw at Teslin did not appear among the Liard River bands.

70 Romaniuk and Piche, "Natality Estimates for the Canadian Indians."

71 Note that these figures are for status Indians and do not include similar increases in non-status Native populations.

72 This description is drawn from Rich, *The Pathogenisis of Tuberculosis*; Robbins and Cotram, *Pathologic Basis of Disease*.

73 Robbins and Cotran, *Pathologic Basis of Disease*, 403.

74 McNeill, *Plagues and People*; Young, "Changing Patterns of Health and Sickness." On the question of pre-Columbian tuberculosis, see Buikstra, ed., *Pre-Historic Tuberculosis in the Americas*.

75 For a discussion of the impact of tuberculosis on Canadian Native people, see DIA, *Annual Report 1931*, 940; DIA, *Annual Report 1926*, 8–11; Graham-Cumming, "Health of the Original Canadians."

76 See, for example, NA, RG10, DIA, vol. 4501, file 207, 418, Inspector Taylor to officer commanding, "B" Division, 22 May 1903; "Report of Asst. Commissioner Wood, 1 December 1904," RNWMP, *Annual Report, 1905*, 19; YTA, Anglican Church, Old Crow file, McCabe to Coldrick, 4 December 1937.

77 "Report of Asst. Surgeon L.A. Pare," NWMP, *Annual Report, 1903*, appendix D.

78 NA, RG10, DIA, vol. 4081, file 478, 698, Report of Forty-Mile Band of Indians, 7 June 1915.

79 GSA, M74–5, 1–A–1, Stringer to commissioner, YT, 11 April 1912; on the larger campaign, see Wharett, *The Miracle of the Empty Beds*.

80 See GSA, M74–5, 1–A–1, Stringer to commissioner, 11 April 1912; NA, RG18, vol. 5049, file 109, Knight to commissioner, 16 October 1918.

81 The federal government authorized compulsory hospitalization of those affected. Since the Yukon lacked adequate facilities, the regulations were seldom enforced. YTA, YRG1, vol. 9, file 1490, pt. J, J. Gibben to Indian Affairs Branch, 1 March 1946; ibid., P.E. Morre to R.A. Gibson, 5 April 1946.

82 YTA, YRG1, series 1, vol. 65, file 813, Summary of x-ray survey, Yukon Territory Indians, June 1948.

83 YTA, YRG1, series 1, vol. 65, file 813, Summary x-ray survey, Indian Residents, Whitehorse, July 1949. In the same file, see Summary x-ray survey, Yukon-Whitehorse, 4 February–11 February 1949; Summary x-ray survey–Old Crow Band, Yukon Agency, 15 December 1948; Summary x-ray survey–Yukon Territory Indians, June 1948. See also Gibben to Keenleyside, 4 September 1947, Gibben to Meltiex, 10 March 1949; Report on a Tuberculosis Survey in the Yukon Territory by J. Locke (1949). For a personal account of the surveys, see Wilson, *No man Stands Alone*.

84 DIA, *Annual Reports, 1948–1950*.

85 Robbins and Cotran, *Pathologic Basis of Disease*, 397.

86 For an excellent socio-economic study of the regional impact of disease, see Rutman and Rutman, "Of Aques and Fevers."

PART THREE

1 The best example of this is the work of Zaslow, *The Opening of the Canadian North*, and *The Northward Expansion of Canada*. See also Morrison, *Showing the Flag*, and Grant, *Sovereignty or Security?*

2 See, for example, Titley, *A Narrow Vision*.

3 This perspective is set out at greater length in Coates and Morrison, "Northern Visions."

4 Linton, *Acculturation in Seven American Indian Tribes*. For an application of this theory in a Canadian context, see Fisher, *Contact and Conflict*.

5 YTA, Anglican Church, Teslin file, Report on Teslin Mission, May-September 1932.

CHAPTER SIX

1 See Cody, *An Apostle of the North*, and Archer, *A Heroine of the North*. Peake, *The Bishop Who Ate His Boots*, is less hagiographic, but still narrative in approach. See also Whittaker, *Arctic Eskimo*, Boon, *The Anglican Church*, and Swanson, *The Days of My Sojourning*. For a more analytical approach, see Coates, "Send Only Those Who Rise a Peg."

2 Abel, "The Drum and the Cross," 323–324.

3 Berkhofer, *Salvation and the Savage*, and "Protestants, Pagans and Sequences." In a northern setting, see Van Stone, *Ingalik Contact Ecology*. On British Columbia, see Usher, *William Duncan of Metlakatla*. On the CMS generally, see Usher, "Apostles and Aborigines". On the Catholic Church, see Mulhull, *Will to Power*. More useful, because of the editor's willingness to abandon high-profile clerics in favour of a more "average" missionary, is Whitehead, *They Call Me Father*.

4 For a cursory history of the Catholic Church in the Yukon, see Monnet, "The Oblates and the Yukon".

5 Different denominations were, of course, active during the Klondike gold rush, but they ministered primarily to the non-Native population. Catholic records in the Yukon, which would have facilitated an analysis of the church's activities, are currently closed to researchers.

6 The outline sketched here does not, as anthropologists properly do, pay heed to minor variations in structure and practice between Native groups.

7 One of the best descriptions of aboriginal beliefs is in NA, MG17, B2, W.W. Kirkby's Journal, 25 May 1861–2 May 1862, entries dated 3–28 July. Osgood, *The Han Indians*, 161; Jones, "The Kutchin Tribes," 325; Hardisty, "The Loucheux Indians," 318; See also GSA, M56–2, Series C–23, Canham Papers, "undated account of the Indians of the Far North." Canham said that the Kutchin referred to God as "Vittukwii-chanchyo," a name they previously applied to the "Good Spirit." See also NA, MG17, B2, McDonald to Long, 31 January 1865; Peake, "Robert McDonald"; W.W. Kirkby, the first missionary in the Yukon, said that the Indians had only medicine men and no idea of a superior "God." Kirkby, "A Journey to the Youcon." NA, MG17, B2, McDonald to Long, 31 January 1865.

8 McClellan, *My Old People Say*.

9 For a more complete analysis, the best place to begin is June Helm, ed., *Handbook of North American Indians, vol. 6: Subarctic*. See also more detailed studies by McClellan, *My Old People Say*, especially chapters 2, 12, 17; Osgood, *Contributions to the Ethnology of the Kutchin*, and *The Han Indians*; Honingmann, *Culture and Ethos of Kaska Society*.

10 Bompas has received an uncritical press among church historians. For a balanced assessment of his northern career, see Abel, "The Drum and the Cross."

11 NA, MG17, B2, Bompas to CMS, 6 December 1872.

12 YTA, Acc. 82/176, Flewelling Diary, 29 May 1897 (Thlondick).

13 NA, MG17, B2, Canham to Mr Fenn, 17 February 1893.

14 The above description is based on Usher, "Apostles and Aborigines." See also Usher, *William Duncan of Metlakatla*. Usher's description broadly conforms to the conclusions in Berkhofer, "Protestants, Pagans and Sequences."

15 NA, MG17, B2, W.W. Kirkby's Journal, 25 May 1861–2 May 1862, entries dated 3–28 July.

16 Ibid., W.W. Kirkby to CMS, 29 November 1862.

17 Boon, "William West Kirkby"; NA, MG17, B2, Kirkby to CMS, 29 November 1862; Ibid., Kirkby's Journal, 25 May 1861–May 1862; Kirkby, "A Journey to the Youcon."

18 This chronological survey is based on several works. The place to start is Boon, *The Anglican Church*, 204–23; Archer, *A Heroine of the North*; Cody, *An Apostle of the North*; Peake, *The Anglican Church in British Columbia*, and "Robert McDonald"; *Northern Lights*, vol. 30 (August 1941); Wesbrook, "A Venture into Ethnohistory"; *Church Missionary Intelligencer*, various issues starting in 1865.

19 Coates, "Send Only Those Who Rise a Peg."

20 NA, MG17, B2, List of Missions in Selkirk Diocese, 1900. On the ending of the relationship with the CMS, see ibid., Bompas to CMS, 18 January 1897, 3 May 1898.

21 Wesbrook, "A Venture into Ethnohistory."

22 NA, MG17, B2, Wallis to CMS, 30 December 1892.

23 Ibid., Bompas to CMS, 3 January 1895. This question is explored in depth in Coates, "Send Only Those Who Rise a Peg."

24 Berton, *I Married the Klondike*, 61; CMS, Bompas to CMS, 13 January 1896, tells the story differently, suggesting that the bishop had tried to stop a budding interracial romance but had failed.

25 *Northern Lights*, vol. 30 (August 1941).

26 NA, MG17, B2, Canham to Fenn, 17 February 1893.

27 Peake, "Robert McDonald"; NA, MG17, B2, McDonald to Lond, 31 January 1865; ibid., McDonald to Brother in the Lord, 25 June 1864, McDonald to CMS, 20 June 1870 re: translation efforts by Bompas and HBC trader James Flett.

28 Ibid., Bompas to CMS, 3 September 1896 re: his insistence on being allowed to open a mission in the south.

29 Coates, *The Northern Yukon, 38–43*. The list of journeys is very long; all of the trips were described in vague terms. *Church Missionary Record*, vol. 14, New Series, no. 6 (June 1869), 172–79; *Church Missionary Intelli-*

gencer, no. 7, New Series (1871), 333–41; *Church Missionary Intelligencer*, vol. 11, New Series (1875), 63; NA, MG17, B2, Bompas to CMS, 6 December 1872, Kenneth McDonald to Bompas, 30 December 1874, R. McDonald to CMS, 7 January 1870, R. McDonald to CMS, 30 June 1870.

30 Ibid., R. McDonald to Dear Friend, 26 March 1877.

31 Ibid., Bompas to CMS, 6 December 1872.

32 NA, MG17, B2, Kirkby's Journal, 25 May 1861–7 May 1862, entry for 8 July 1861.

33 Ibid., McDonald to CMS, 25 January 1876.

34 Ibid., McDonald CMS, 25 January 1875.

35 Bompas's report, *Church Missionaries Intelligencer and Record*, vol. 11, no. 122 (February 1886), 104–5.

36 NA, MG17, B2, V.C. Sim to CMS, 9 January 1882.

37 Ibid., McDonald to Dear Brother, 25 June 1865.

38 Welsh, "Community Pattern and Settlement Pattern," 24.

39 NA, MG17, B2, McDonald to Dear Brother, 25 June 1864. This practice of Natives asserting control over the "new Gods" is not uncommon. See Upton, *Micmacs and Colonists*, 154; Chamberlain, "New Religions among the North American Indians," Wallace, "Revitalization Movements."

40 Welsh, "Community Pattern and Settlement Pattern," 24. A similar argument, tied to the impact of disease, is advanced in Martin, "The European Impact."

41 NA, MG17, B2, McDonald to Dear Brother, 25 June 1864.

42 Ibid., McDonald to CMS, 30 June 1870.

43 Abel, "The Drum and the Cross."

44 NA, MG17, B2, McDonald to Dear Brother, 25 June 1864.

45 Ibid., Bompas to CMS, 17 July 1873.

46 *Church Missionary Society Proceedings, 1893–1894*, 246–49.

47 Boon, *The Anglican Church*, 221–31; Peake, *The Anglican Church in British Columbia*, 179–91; Cody, *An Apostle of the North*; Peake, *The Bishop Who Ate His Boots*.

48 See Coates, "Asking for All Sorts of Favours." See also McCullum and McCullum, *This Land is Not for Sale*.

49 NA, RG10, DIA, vol. 4001, file 207, 418, Congdon to Pedley, 28 May 1903.

50 In an era when few non-Natives had much concern for aboriginal people, this vigilance was of considerable importance. In areas where the aboriginal people lacked the support of missionaries, they suffered considerably. See the argument advanced in Upton, "The Extermination of the Beotucks," in Fisher and Coates, eds., *Out of the Background*.

51 Obtaining financial support was not easy and had plagued Bompas for years. NA, MG17, B2, CMS to Bompas, 4 May 1899; YTA, Anglican Church, New Series, file 2, O'Meara's memorandum, 15 January 1908.

52 Coates, "Send Only Those Who Rise a Peg."

53 The two stations, close to 200 miles apart, were often administered by the same missionary who changed his base depending on the movements of the Natives. NA, RG10, vol. 6477, file 925–1, pt. 1, Bragg to secretary, DIA, 30 October 1913.

54 YTA, Anglican Church, New Series, file 1, "Indian Work in the Diocese of Yukon," by I. Stringer, 14 September 1911.

55 YTA, Anglican Church, MSCC, file #2, Stringer to Dr Gould, 16 February 1922.

56 The program began in earnest in the 1930s, but a few students came north the previous decade. YTA, Anglican Church, Unsworth file, J. Unsworth, "Report of Students' Visit to Ross River, July 1923."

57 NA, RG10, DIA, vol. 6477, file 925–11, pt. 1, Hawksley to Mackenzie, 15 June 1933.

58 YTA, Anglican Church, Diocese-Synod file, Max Humphrey, "Carmacks and Little Salmon, 1932."

59 YTA, Anglican Church, Helen Wilkinson file, "Impressions of my work amongst Indians at Teslin Lake during Summer of 1923."

60 YTA, Anglican Church, Teslin file, "What Place has the Church in the Lives of the Teslin Indians, 1932"; YTA, Anglican Church, Carmacks–Little Salmon file, G.W. Long, "A Report of the Missionary Work Carried on From May 23 to August 31, 1934 in and about Carmacks, Yukon"; YTA, Anglican Church, Teslin file, "Report on Teslin Missions–June–September 1931"; YTA, Anglican Church, Champagne file, L.G. Chappell, "Missionary Work Undertaken in Champagne District, Summer 1934"; YTA, Anglican Church, Teslin file, "Report on Teslin Mission, May–June 1932"; YTA, Anglican Church, Champagne file, W.S. Jenkins, "Report on Champagne-Klukchu School and Mission, 1936"; YTA, Anglican Church, Champagne file, Anthony W. Gascogne, "Report to the Diocese of the Yukon upon the present state of the Champagne (Y.T.) mission field, Summer 1949.

61 On the latter, see YTA, Anglican Church, New Series, file #1, B. Totty to O'Meara, 20 August 1908.

62 YTA, Anglican Church, Martin file, Bishop to John Martin, 29 July 1935; GSA, M74–3, 1–A–4, Semple to Stringer, 10 July 1932; YTA, Anglican Church, Amos Njootli file, Stringer to Njootli, 26 January 1917.

63 "Jim," who may have been James Pelisse, received only $50 a year – and had trouble collecting that amount. His problem was complicated by the fact that his initial agreement was with the Mackenzie River Diocese. YTA, Anglican Church file, Cecil Swanson to bishop, 30 July 1914.

64 In 1922 only Julius Kendi received a full salary of $550. Native catechists received less: John Tinzya, Old Crow, $100; Joseph Kunnizzi, Peel River, $100; Richard Martin, Porcupine, $75; Jonathan Wood, Moose-

hide, and James Pelisse, Ross River, $50. YTA, Anglican Church, MSCC file #2, Stringer to Gould, 16 February 1922.

65 YTA, Anglican Church, Amos Njootli file, Stringer to Njootli, 26 January 1917; YTA, Anglican Church, Totty file, Totty to bishop, 17 September 1918; YTA, Anglican Church, Amos Njootli file, Njootli to bishop, 1 April 1917. Regarding his death in 1923, see YTA, Anglican Church, Eunice Njootli file, Eunice Njootli to I.O. Stringer, 20 February 1923.

66 YTA, Anglican Church, Rampart House, Fort Yukon, and Old Crow file, A.C. McCullum to Stringer, 23 July 1930.

67 YTA, Anglican Church, MSCC file #2, Stringer to Gould, 16 February 1922; YTA, Anglican Church, Buck file, F.H. Buck to superintendent, Church Camp Mission, 9 September 1920.

68 YTA, Anglican Church, MSCC file #2, Stringer to Gould, 16 February 1922.

69 YTA, Anglican Church, Swanson file, Swanson to bishop, 30 July 1914.

70 YTA, Anglican Church, John Martin file, Martin to Gaddes (Geddes), 10 January 1934.

71 GSA, M74–1, 1–A–4, Martin to Stringer, 16 July 1934.

72 GSA, M74–1, 1–A–1, Box 1, Stringer to Sovereign, 24 February 1932.

73 GSA, M74–3, 1–A–1, Box 1, Stringer to Geddes, 2 August 1934.

74 YTA, Anglican Church, Sovereign file, Coldrich to Bishop Sovereign, 16 February 1932; YTA, Anglican Church, Martin file, bishop to Rev. John Martin, 29 July 1935.

75 YTA, Anglican Church, Hughes file, bishop of Yukon to Mr Hughes, 22 August 1935.

76 A change for the worse in the Mayo band after Martin's death suggests that he had had a positive impact on the community. NA, RG10, vol. 6478, file 935–1, pt. 1, Binning Report, 7 July 1937.

77 *Northern Lights*, vol. XXVI, no. 2 (May 1937), 7.

78 Coates and Morrison, "Transiency in the Far Northwest after the Gold Rush."

79 Swanson, *The Days of My Sojourning*, 36.

80 NA, RG10, DIA, vol. 6478, file 930–1, Additional Memo re: Teslin Lake Indians, c. February 1909. As part of a general survey in 1908–9 conducted by the Anglican Church and the Canadian government to ascertain the need for increased educational and mission work, police officers and missionaries were requested to provide summaries of conditions among local Native bands. Almost all of the reports explicitly mention the continuing importance of Native religion. See the reports in YTA, Anglican Church, New Series.

81 YTA, Anglican Church, New Series, file 2, Particulars Regarding Little Salmon Indians, June 1908.

82 YTA, Anglican Church, Totty file, Benjamin Totty to committee of the CMS, 29 January 1917.

83 YTA, Diocese-Synod file, Humphrey to Your Lordship and Members of the Synod, 1932. Examples of the persistence of traditional beliefs are far too numerous to list. Most summer student reports and many internal documents of the Anglican Church echoed Humphrey's claim. See also letter from Rev. C.C. Brett, *Across the Rockies*, vol. 5, no. 7 (July 1914). Amy Wilson, a nurse in the southern Yukon in the 1940s and 1950s, noted repeated expressions of established aboriginal spiritual beliefs, especially as regards healing. Wilson, *No Man Stands Alone*. That ethnographers such as McClelland were able to reconstruct such a vivid portrait of pre-contact beliefs is further evidence of spiritual persistence. McClelland, *My Old People Say*.

84 And even here coverage was not continuous. There was a ten-year hiatus following the departure of the HBC from Rampart House in 1893. Coates, *The Northern Yukon*, 41–2.

85 See various comments from Lucy, a nurse sent to Old Crow in the late 1940s. *GSA, Lucy Papers*.

86 YTA, Anglican Church, Diocese-Synod file, Max Humphrey, "Carmacks and Little Salmon, 1932."

87 On religious persistence generally, see Spicer, *Cycles of Conquest*; Bowden, *American Indians and Christian Missions*.

88 YTA, Anglican Church, Ashbee file, Ashbee to lord bishop, 8 July 1926.

89 GSA, M74–3, 1–D–18, Re: Indian reported to have seen visions and spoken in unknown languages, c. 1917.

90 YTA, Anglican Church, Young file, Stringer to W.D. Young, 25 April 1917; GSA, M74–3, 1–D–18, Re: Indian reported to have seen visions and spoken in unknown languages, c. 1917; Swanson, *The Days of My Sojourning*, 40–9; YTA, Anglican Church, Bennett file, Stringer to Bennett, 13 July 1918.

91 A similar "sect," led by "Father Divine," developed around Teslin in 1936. *Northern Lights*, vol. XXV, no. 4 (November 1936), 5–6. Upton, *Micmacs and Colonists*, 154; Chamberlain, "New Religions Among the North American Indians"; Wallace, "Revitalization Movements."

92 Regarding this struggle, see Coates, *The Northern Yukon*, 38–9; Coates, "Mixed Blessings"; CMS Kirkby to CMS, 29 November 1862; PAM, Archives of the Ecclesiastical Province of Rupertsland, #4001, Box J, C.T. Best, "Biography of Robert McDonald," (unpublished manuscript), 105, *Proceedings of the Church Missionary Society* (1864), 214; *Church Missionary Gleaner*, vol. 18 (1868), 45–7; NA, MG17, B2, McDonald to CMS, 6 February 1879, Bompas to Wigram, 14 July 1890; Breynat, *The Flying Bishop*, 122–3.

93 YTA, Anglican Church, New Series, file 1, Totty to O'Meara, 20 August 1908; YTA, Anglican Church, Leigh file, G.F. Leigh to bishop, 24 October 1927.

94 *Northern Lights*, vol. XXVIII, no. 3 (August 1939). The competition was used, as it had been in the past, as the foundation for an appeal for funds for the work of the diocese.

95 NA, RG10, vol. 6482, file 942–1, pt. 1, Harper Reed Report for February 1939.

96 Ibid., Reed to secretary, Indian Affairs Branch, 16 August 1939.

97 YTA, Anglican Church, Teslin file, Ward to Mr Lord, 7 March 1941.

98 YTA, Anglican Church, Teslin file, Ward to Right Reverend W.A. Geddes, 9 July 1941.

99 The battle continued through 1950. NA, RG10, vol. 6478, file 933–1, pt. 1, Albert Dream to Mon. Rev., 21 December 1949, Dream to Mon. Rev., 4 January 1950, Dream to Meek, 24 February 1950.

100 YTA, Anglican Church, Carcross Property file, Henry Cook to Canon L.A. Dixon, 11 July 1950.

101 YTA, Anglican Church, Wareham file, Norman Wareham to W.R. Adams, 10 February 1950, Wareham to Adams, 17 December 1950.

102 YTA, Anglican Church, Teslin file, R. Ward to Harper Reed, 7 March 1941, Reed to secretary, Indian Affairs Branch, 16 August 1939.

103 For an excellent analysis of this concept of spiritual persistence as based on a relationship with the physical world, see Clendinnen, "Landscape and World View." See also Spicer, *Cycles of Conquest*, 502–39.

CHAPTER SEVEN

1 Jean Barman, et al., eds., *Indian Education in Canada, vol. 1: The Legacy*. On non-Native education, see Prentice, *The School Promoters*; Katz and Mattingly, *Education and Social Change*.

2 Carnoy, *Education as Cultural Imperialism*, 3–4.

3 Kelley and Altbach, "Introduction," in Altbach and Kelley, ed., *Education and Colonialism*, 15.

4 Iverson, "Civilization and Assimilation," in Altbach and Kelley, ed., *Civilization and Assimilation*; Szasz, *Education and the American Indians*. For a forcibly argued Canadian example, see Fisher, "A Colonial Education System."

5 Barman et al., ed., *Indian Education in Canada, vol. 1: The Legacy*, "The Legacy of the Past: An Overview."

6 Altbach and Kelley correctly identify the importance of a "national" component in the formation of a colonial education system (*Education and Colonialism*, 43). The Yukon educational network lacked this overrid-

ing control, but did not deviate in theoretical terms from accepted patterns and programs.

7 On the importance of literacy to the CMS, see Jean Usher, "Apostles and Aborigines," Peake, "Robert McDonald."

8 NA, MA17, B2, Bompas to CMS, 3 January 1894.

9 Cody, *An Apostle of the North*, 253–72; Boon, *The Anglican Church*, 222–3.

10 NA, RG10, DIA, vol. 3906, file 3078, Bompas to minister of the interior, 18 June 1896.

11 YTA, Anglican Church, New Series, file 2, Additional Particulars Regarding Little Salmon Indians, June 1908.

12 NA, RG10, DIA, vol. 3906, file 3078, Duncan Scott, Memorandum to Deputy Superintendent General, 2 January 1908.

13 The complex issue of industrial and boarding schools is described in Hall, "Clifford Sifton and Canadian Indian Administration," and Titley, "Indian Industrial Schools," in Sheehan *et al.*, ed., *Schools of the West*. GSA, M75–103, series 2–14, MSCC, Memorandum on Indian Mission Schools by R. Mackay, *c.* 1906.

14 YTA, Anglican Church, New Series, file 1, Notes made from interview with Rev. Mr O'Meara, re: Indians in the Yukon, 1908; ibid., file 2, O'Meara to Stringer, 6 January 1909; ibid., file 3, Memo for Archbishop regarding Yukon Indians Work, *c.* 1909; ibid, file 3, Indian Matters: Recommendations of Messrs Hawksley and O'Meara, *c.* 1908; ibid., file 3, Requests regarding Yukon Indians, *c.* 1908; ibid., A.E. O'Meara to Stringer, 15 January 1908; ibid., file 1, Memorandum for Minister regarding Yukon Indians.

15 GSA, M74–3, 1–A–2, F. Pedley to F. Oliver, 23 January 1908.

16 YTA, Anglican Church, New Series, file 2, Notes of Interview, 26 February 1909.

17 NA, RG10, DIA, vol. 3906, file 105, 378, Scott, Memorandum to Deputy Superintendent General, 21 January 1908.

18 YTA, series 1, vol. 9, file 1491, John Hawksley to A.F. Mackenzie, 29 August 1933.

19 YTA, series 1, vol. 74, Hawksley to J.D. McLean, 20 November 1926; see also ibid., Russell Fernier, superintendent of Indian education to J. Hawksley, 27 October 1925.

20 NA, RG10, DIA, vol. 6477, file 925–1, pt. 1, W.A. Geddes to Secretary, DIA, 23 January 1934.

21 YTA, Anglican Church, Indian Affairs file, Tr. Rev. A.H. Sovereign to secretary, DIA, 21 August 1933.

22 NA, RG10, DIA, vol. 6478, file 931–1, pt. 1, Stringer to Hawksley, 9 February 1925, Stringer to Hawksley, 31 January 1925; YTA, Anglican Church, Hipp file, Stringer to T. Hipp, 14 February 1930.

23 YTA, Anglican Church, Middleton file, Stringer to Middleton, 25 April 1917.

24 NA, RG10, DIA, vol. 3962, file 147, 654–1, pt. 2, Bompas to deputy minister of the interior, 15 June 1905; NA, MG17, B2, Bompas to CMS, 20 January 1893.

25 Ibid.

26 NA, RG10, DIA, vol. 6478, file 930–1, pt. 1, Report of the Teslin Lake Mission School, 5 July to 19 August 1909.

27 YTA, Anglican Church, Champagne file, W.S. Jenkins, Report of Champagne-Klukshu School and Mission, 1936.

28 DIA files and the records of the Yukon Diocese of the Anglican Church of Canada contain many day-school returns documenting attendance irregularities. See Bythell's enthusiastic report on the Teslin school in NA, RG10, DIA, vol. 6478, file 930–1, pt. 1, Report of Teslin Lake Mission School, 5 July–19 August 1909. Despite Bythell's optimism for the school program, only seven of thirty-seven students attended more than half of the classes. Sixteen students showed up for fewer than ten of the thirty-three sessions.

29 NA, RG10, DIA, vol. 3962, file 147, 654–1, pt. 2, J.D. McLean to John Hawksley, 30 August 1916; ibid., Hawksley to McLean, 1 August 1916.

30 NA, RG10, DIA, vol. 3962, file 147, 654–1, pt. 2, Stringer to Hawksley, 24 October 1916.

31 YTA, Anglican Church, New Series, file 4, Hawksley to bishop of the Yukon, 15 December 1916.

32 NA, RG10, DIA, vol. 6477, file 925.1, pt. 1, A.F. MacKenzie to Arthur Sovereign, 19 June 1933.

33 Ken Coates, "Send Only Those Who Rise a Peg."

34 NA, RG10, DIA, vol. 6477, file 927–1, pt. 1, Meek to Indian Affairs Branch, 29 June 1949, Meek to Indian Affairs Branch, 23 March 1947. The second letter refers to conditions at Reverend Lee's school at Whitehorse.

35 YTA, Anglican Church, Teslin File, Report on Teslin Mission, June–September 1931.

36 YTA, Anglican Church, Old Crow, E.A. Kirk to O.C., Whitehorse Sub-Division, 13 November 1947; NA, RG10, vol. 8762, file 906–25–007, pt. 1, Extract from Supt Meek's Quarterly Report, 25 October 1950; ibid., L.J. Lucy to Indian Affairs Branch, 30 April 1951.

37 NA, RG10, DIA, vol. 6477, file 925–1, pt. 1, W.A. Geddes to secretary, DIA, 6 February 1935.

38 NA, RG10, DIA, vol. 6478, file 930–1, pt. 1, R.J. Meek to Indian Affairs Branch, 16 October 1948, Meek to Indian Affairs Branch, 25 January 1950, Extract from Quarterly Report of R.J. Meek, 1 April–30 June 1949.

39 Moosehide encountered particular difficulties attracting suitable teachers: the long-time missionary had serious hearing problems. YTA,
Anglican Church, Totty file, Stringer to Totty, 26 March 1918; NA, RG10,
DIA, vol. 3962, file 147, 654–1, pt. 2, Ross to secretary, DIA, 18 December 1903. In the 1940s M.J. Bridge operated the school. Parents complained about his teaching and the fact that the children were required
to do work in his home. NA, RG10, DIA, vol. 6477, file 927–1, pt. 1,
Agent's Report, Moosehide Indian School, May 1948, Meek to Indian
Affairs Branch, 29 June 1949, C.A. Clark Report re: Moosehide School,
11 July 1947; YTA, Anglican Church, Moosehide file #2, B. Neary to
W.R. Adams, 6 July 1949.

40 NA, RG10, DIA, vol. 3962, file 147, 654–1, pt. 2, John Ross to F.T. Congdon, 18 April 1904.

41 For positive comments, see NA, RG10, DIA, vol. 6477, file 925–1, pt. 1,
A.H. Sovereign to secretary, DIA, 21 August 1933; YTA, Anglican
Church, Parsons file, Arthur Parsons to Coldrick, 10 November 1933.
For more critical and accurate assessments, see NA, RG10, DIA,
vol. 3962, file 147, 654–1, pt. 2, Ross to Congdon, 18 April 1904, Ross
to secretary, DIA, 16 December 1902; GSA, M74–3, 1–A–1, Stringer to
secretary, DIA, 7 October 1911; NA, RG10, DIA, vol. 6478, file 930–1,
pt. 1, Stringer to secretary, DIA, 22 March 1911; NA, RG10, DIA, vol.
6042, file 166–10–1, pt. 1, Stringer to Hawksley, 19 November 1914;
NA, RG10, DIA, vol. 4081, file 478, 698, Report of the Forty-Mile Band
of Indians, 29 March 1917; NA, RG10, DIA, vol 4081, file 478, 700,
Report of the Mayo Band of Indians, 28 August 1917; NA, RG10, DIA,
vol. 6478, file 931–1, pt. 2, Report of Ross River Band of Indians, c.
1917; NA, RG10, DIA, vol. 6477, file 928, pt. 1, Report on the Work of
the Pupils of the Moosehide Day School, 25 March 1918; NA, RG10,
DIA, vol. 6477, file 927–1, pt. 1, Hawksley to Mackenzie, 3 April 1933;
YTA, Anglican Church, Teslin File, "What Place has the Church in the
Lives of the Teslin Indians, 1932"; YTA, Anglican Church, Carmacks–
Little Salmon, G.W. Long, "A Report of the Missionary Work"; YTA,
Anglican Church, Teslin file, "Report of Teslin Mission, June–Septem-
ber 1931"; YTA, Anglican Church, Champagne file, L.G. Chappell,
"Missionary Work Undertaken in Champagne District, Summer 1934";
YTA, Anglican Church, Teslin file, "Report on Teslin Mission, May–
June 1932"; YTA, Anglican Church, Champagne file, W.S. Jenkins,
"Report of Champagne-Klukshu School and Mission, 1936"; YTA,
Anglican Church, Champagne file, A.W. Gascognye, "Report upon
the present state of the Champagne (Y.T.) mission field, summer
1949."

42 Altbach and Kelly, ed., *Education and Colonialism*, "Introduction."

43 Boon, *The Anglican Church*, 222–3; Cody, *An Apostle of the North*, 253–73; NA, Bowen Papers, "Incidents in the Life of R.J. Bowen," 100.

44 NA, RG10, DIA, vol. 3962, file 147, 654–1, pt. 2, Bompas to Hon. J.H. Ross, 7 March 1903.

45 Cody, 310–336; YTA, Acc. 82/77, Preliminary Manuscripts, "History of Chouttla School"; M. Gibbs, "History of Chouttla School"; David Greig, "The Anglican Mission Schools and the Beginning of the Carcross Residential School from 1890 to 1907"; YTA Acc. 82/526, J.A. Wilson, "Schooling on a Distant Frontier," (unpublished manuscript).

46 GSA, M75–103, series 2–14, MSCC, F. Pedley to Rev. L.N. Tucker, 21 March 1906. J. Gresko, "White 'Rites' and Indian 'Rites'," Gresko argues that the Qu'Appelle Industrial School reinforced Native identity and stimulated Native cultural awareness. The point is made again in Tennant, "Native Political Organization in British Columbia." Many of the leaders of the Native-rights movement came of the residential school environment.

47 This was part of a general malaise in the Christian missions to the Native people of Canada. See Grant, *The Moon of Wintertime*.

48 GSA, M75–102, series 2–14, Pedley to Tucker, 21 March 1906.

49 GSA, *Memorandum on Indian Missions and Indian Schools*, submitted on behalf of the Special Indian Committee of MSCC, 14 March 1906. Evidence of the concurrence of the Anglican, Presbyterians, and Methodists (the Roman Catholics refused to participate in the interdenominational conference) with Pedley's comments is found in GSA, M75–103, MSCC, "Memorandum of a Conference, 24–7 March 1908, S.H. Blake, Chairman.

50 GSA, M75–103, series 2–14, MSCC, Frank Oliver to Anglican Church of Canada, 28 January 1908.

51 Vancouver School of Theology, Anglican Church Archives, Journal of the Synod of the Diocese of the Yukon, Whitehorse, 1907.

52 YTA, YRG1, series 4, vol. 13, file 308, T.G. Bragg to Hon. Alexander Henderson, commissioner, 14 December 1907.

53 NA, RG10, vol. 3962, file 147, 654–1, J.D. McLean to A.W. Vowell, 4 April 1908. The comments come directly from a subordinate's letter. See ibid., Accountant, Memorandum to Deputy Superintendent General, 20 February 1908.

54 YTA, Anglican Church, New Series, file 2, Vowell and Green to secretaries, DIA, 14 April 1908.

55 Gibbs, "History of Chouttla School"; Church of England in Canada, *Chouttla Indian School*; King, *The School at Mopass*, 36–38. The last book, a study of the school in the 1960s, contains sketchy and unreliable historical sections. On the debate to relocate the school, see NA, RG10,

DIA, vol. 6479, file 940–1, pt. 2, McGill to deputy minister, 25 November 1942, Geddes to McGill, 11 November 1942; YTA, Anglican Church, Carcross Property file, various letters; NA, RG10, DIA, vol. 8762, file 906/25–1–001, C. Clark, "An Educational Survey with Reference to the Relocation of Carcross Residential School," 8 September 1950.

56 Gibbs, "History of Chouttla School," 12.

57 YTA, Anglican Church, Acc. 79/52, Stringer to Johnson, 24 August 1918. He also arranged at the same time for the entry of Jeff van Gorder, a mixed blood, from Ross River.

58 YTA, Anglican Church, Westgate file, Stringer to Dr Westgate, 19 April 1923.

59 YTA, Anglican Church, New Series, file 2, Additional particulars regarding Little Salmon Indians, June 1908; NA, RG10, vol. 6479, file 940–1, pt. 1, Hawksley to McLean, 16 April 1923.

60 YTA, Anglican Church, AC 79/52, Stringer to Johnson, 24 August 1923.

61 YTA, Acc. 77/2, Teslin Band Collection, H. Reed to Chief Billy Johnston, 15 December 1929.

62 On the children of Amos Njootli, see YTA, Anglican Church, Amos Njootli file, Stringer to Njootli, 26 January 1947.

63 NA, RG10, DIA, vol. 6479, file 940–1, pt. 1, Hawksley to McLean, 16 April 1923; YTA, YRG1, series 1, vol. 9, file 1491, pt. 4, Hawksley to McLean, 15 October 1929; NA, RG10, DIA, vol. 6481, file 940–10, pt. 5, Meek to Welfare and Training, DIA, 17 January 1947. On one occasion agents received instructions to recruit children from close to Carcross to reduce transportation costs. NA, RG10, DIA, vol. 6481, file 940–10, pt. 4, Philip Phelan to commissioner, RCMP, 9 September 1940.

64 See, for example, the correspondence regarding the Chitzi children of Old Crow, who were sent to the school following their parent's separation. NA, RG10, DIA, vol. 6481, file 940–10, pt. 5, J.E. Gibben to secretary, Indian Affairs Branch, 23 May 1945, 16 July 1946. There was concern expressed that some parents would "dump" their children on the school's care. YTA, Anglican Church, Barlow file, Barlow to bishop of Yukon, 18 March 1925.

65 Gibbs, "History of Chouttla School," 11; NA, RG10, vol. 6479, file 940–1, pt. 1, Stockton to deputy superintendent general, 19 November 1912; King, The School at Mopass.

66 NA, RG10, DIA, vol. 6481, file 940–10, pt. 6, B. Neary to R. Meek, 19 August 1949.

67 NA, RG10, DIA, vol. 6478, file 932–1, pt. 1, Peter Moses et al. (petition) to Indian agent, Dawson City, 28 August 1945.

68 YTA, Anglican Church, Barlow file, Barlow to bishop of Yukon, 18 March 1925.

69 YTA, Anglican Church, New Series, file 2, Vowell and Green to secretary, DIA, 14 August 1908.

70 For reports on the program in practice, see YTA, Anglican Church, Carcross School file #2, Report of E.D. Evans, 29 April 1912, Report of W.T. Townsend, 31 March 1914; YTA, Anglican Church, C.F. Johnson file #2, Report of Chas. Johnson, 31 March 1918, and frequent reports in *Northern Lights*.

71 The summary is based on the citations given in note 70 plus "Report of the Superintendent of Indian Education," DIA, *Annual Report 1909–1910*, 351; NA, RG10, DIA, vol. 3962, file 147, 654–1, pt. 2, Ross to Congdon, 16 April 1904, Ross to DIA, 2 April 1906, T.C. Bragg to McLean, 1 May 1907, Bragg to secretary, DIA, 21 April 1910; NA, RG10, DIA, vol. 6479, file 940–1, pt. 1, Stockton to deputy superintendent general, 29 November 1912, Stringer to secretary, DIA, 31 March 1913 (a reply to Stockton's harsh criticism), Hawksley to J.D. McLean, 7 January 1915; ibid., pt. 2, Hawksley to A.F. Mackenzie, 25 March 1931, H.C.M. Grant to superintendent of Indian affairs, 5 February 1940; YTA, Anglican Church, Carcross School file #1, E.D. Evans to J.D. McLean, 29 April 1912; "Report of Venerable Archdeacon T.H. Canham, 31 March 1913," DIA, *Annual Report 1912/1913*, 618; GSA, M75–103, series 2–14, MSCC, Collins to Blake, 27 April 1904, 13 March 1909, 11 February 1909; *Northern Lights* (various issues); Gibbs "History of Chouttla School."

72 YTA, Anglican Church, Johnson file #2, Report of Chas. F. Johnson, 31 March 1918.

73 YTA, Anglican Church, Carcross file, C.E. Whittaker to Dr Smith, 2 July 1919.

74 NA, RG10, DIA, vol. 6479, file 940–1, pt. 2, Grant to superintendent of Indian affairs, 5 February 1940. The punishment was meted out for such "serious" offences as stealing bread from the kitchen.

75 NA, RG10, DIA, vol. 6481, file 940–10, G. Binning to secretary, DIA, 11 April 1936, P. Phelan to Inspector G. Binning, 1 September 1937, G. Binning to P. Phelan, 9 November 1937.

76 NA, RG10, DIA, vol. 6481, file 940–10, pt. 4, P. Phelan to H.C.M. Grant, 17 April 1940.

77 NA, RG10, DIA, vol. 6479, file 940–1, pt. 1, Ditchburn to secretary, DIA, 26 August 1931.

78 NA, RG10, DIA, vol. 6481, file 940–10, pt. 6, R.J. Meek to Indian Affairs Branch, 29 August 1947.

79 On specific cases, see YTA, Anglican Church, Moosehide file, Sarah Jane Essau to Bishop, 31 August 1919; NA, RG10, vol. 6481, file 940–10, pt. 4, Frant to Dewdney, 17 November 1941, Phelan to Grant, 8 August 1938, Grant to Phelan, 24 August 1938, Binning to secretary, DIA, 11

April 1938, Grant to O.C., RCMP, 2 March 1934, Meek to Indian Affairs Branch, 18 August 1947; ibid., pt. 4, T.B. Caulkin to principal, 16 March 1935, Binning to secretary, DIA, 15 December 1937; NA, RG10, DIA, vol. 6481, file 940–10, pt. 6, Meek to Indian Affairs Branch, 19 August 1947, Meek to Indian Affairs Branch, 4 April 1949; ibid., pt. 4, Grant to Binning, 12 May 1938.

80 NA, RG10, DIA, vol. 6481, file 940–10, pt. 4, Reed to J.D. Sutherland, 7 October 1933.

81 YTA, Anglican Church, McCullum file, E.D. Wood to Stringer, 14 April 1926.

82 YTA, Anglican Church, Fort Yukon file, Grafton Burke to Hawksley, 21 May 1926.

83 Gibbs, "History of Chouttla School," 13–14; YTA, YRG1, series 1, vol. 9, file 1490, pt. 5, Hawksley to Mackenzie, 7 March 1930. The government viewed a Carcross graduate favourably when reviewing applications for enfranchisement.

84 YTA, YRG1, series 1, vol. 9, file 1490, pt. J, Hawksley to W. Ditchburn, 6 October 1930.

85 YTA, Anglican Church, Carcross School file 1, E.D. Evans to J.D. McLean, 29 April 1912.

86 YTA, YRG1, series 1, vol. 11, file 2335, pt. 6, John Hawksley to Rev. Principal, Chouttla Indian School, 27 May 1933.

87 YTA, Anglican Church, Selkirk Children Reports, Robinson to Dickson, 7 March 1939.

88 YTA, Anglican Church, Carmacks–Little Salmon file, Report of Missionary Work Carried on from 23 May–31 August 1934 in and about Carmacks. See also YTA, Anglican Church, Carcross file, C.E. Whittaker to Dr Smith, 2 July 1919; YTA, Anglican Church, C.F. Johnson file, Stringer to Johnson, 31 October 1917; NA, RG10, vol. 3962, file 147, 654–1, pt. 2, T.G. Bragg to secretary, DIA, 23 June 1910; NA, RG10, DIA, vol. 6479, file 940–1, pt. 2, J.E. Gibben to Clarence, 12 January 1942; YTA, YRG1, series 1, vol. 11, file 2335, pt. 6, Hawksley to principal, Chouttla School, 27 May 1933; YTA, Anglican Church, Old Crow file, McCabe to Coldrich, 11 December 1937; YTA, Anglican Church, McCullum file, E.D. Wood to Stringer, 14 April 1926.

89 YTA, Anglican Church, Moosehide file, Sarah Jane Essau to Bishop, 31 August 1919.

90 YTA, Anglican Church, C.F. Johnson file #2, Duncan C. Scott to Sir, 12 March 1914.

91 YTA, Anglican Church, Townsend file, Stringer to Townsend, 28 January 1916.

92 YTA, Anglican Church, Whittaker Papers, Stringer to Archdeacon Whittaker, 20 February 1915; YTA, Anglican Church, Townsend file, Stringer

to Townsend, 28 January 1916; YTA, Anglican Church, Bennett file, Stringer to Miss Bennett, 13 July 1918.

93 YTA, Anglican Church, Carmacks–Little Salmon file, Report of Missionary Work, 23 May–31 August 1934.

94 The government did not abandon the residential program. As a result of the Joint Parliamentary Committee on Indian Affairs, established in 1946, it was decided to expand and alter the boarding-school program. The Carcross School was enlarged in 1953–54 to accommodate 125 students. Anglican control was weakened and finally eliminated, and more assimilationist curriculum was implemented. GSA, M75–103, series 3–3, Indian Work Investigation Committee, 1947–74, "Indian Work Investigation Commission Report of the General Synod, Winnipeg, 1946"; Gibbs, 'History of Chouttla School"; King, *The School at Mopass.*

95 Marginality is not an uncommon consequence of colonial education systems. See Memmi, *Dominated Man.*

96 Altbach and Kelley, ed., *Education and Colonialism*, 15. On American Indian Education, see Fuchs and Havinghurst, *To Live On This Earth;* Szasz, *Education and the American Indian.* For an earlier period, see Berkhofer, *Salvation and the Savage.* See also Prucha, *Americanizing the American Indians,* and *The Churches and the Indian Schools.* On Alaska, see Smith, "Education for the Natives of Alaska."

97 NA, RG10, DIA, vol. 6481, file 941–1, pt. 1, Geddes to Dr H.W. McGill, 27 January 1943; NA, RG10, DIA, vol. 6479, file 940–1, pt. 1, Stringer to secretary, DIA, 5 March 1912; YTA, Anglican Church, Contributions–St Paul's Hostel, "St. Paul's Hostel-Dawson, Y.T.," 14 February 1947; YTA, Anglican Church, Johnson file #1, Stringer to C.F. Johnson, 28 December 1926; NA, RG10, DIA, vol. 6479, file 940–1, pt. 2, director to J.E. Gibben, 19 February 1943; YTA, Anglican Church, St Paul's Hostel, Matron to Mrs A. Stockton, 14 October 1946.

98 NA, RG10, DIA, vol. 6477, file 929–1, pt. 1, C.A. Clark re: Whitehorse Indian School, 17 May 1947.

99 This interracial character changed in the 1950s, and the Whitehorse Indian Baptist School became a more formal Native-oriented institution. See *The Mission School Syndrome.*

100 NA, RG10, DIA, vol. 6477, file 929–1, pt. 1, R.J. Meek to R.A. Hoey, 5 September 1946, Meek to Indian Affairs Branch, 14 October 1946, Hackett to Moore, 24 January 1947, Meek to Welfare and Training, Indian Affairs Branch, 15 January 1947, C.A.F. Clark re: Whitehorse Indian School, May 1947, H.I. Lee to Meek, 18 August 1947, Meek to Indian Affairs Branch, 30 October 1947. Lee's school received full residential-school status in 1949. Ibid., arrangement between Indian Affairs Branch and Rev. H.I. Lee, 12 January 1949, Meek to Indian Affairs Branch, 25 October 1947, Meek to Indian Affairs Branch, 23 March 1948.

101 On the new assimilationist programming, see: NA, RG10, vol. 6478, file
929–11, pt. 1, C.A.F. Clark to superintendent of education, 11 November 1949, Meek to Indian Affairs Branch, 24 November 1949; NA, RG10,
DIA, vol. 6478, file 933–1, pt. 1, Clark to superintendent of education,
11 November 1949; NA, RG10, vol. 8782, file 906/25–1–005, pt. 1, Phelan
to Meek, 1 December 1950.

102 NA, RG10, DIA, vol. 3962, file 147, 654–1, pt. 2, Bompas to secretary,
DIA, 18 June 1902.

103 NA, RG10, DIA, vol. 6478, file 934–1, pt. 1, R.A. Hoey to J.E. Gibben, 4
August 1944; ibid., J.L. Coudert to Philip Phelan, 17 March 1945.

104 Ibid., J.O. Plourde to H.W. McGill, 10 February 1940.

105 NA, RG10, DIA, vol. 6482, file 924–1, pt. 1, Father Charles Hamel to J.L.
Coudert, 29 January 1945; NA, RG10, DIA, vol. 6481, file 940–10, pt. 5,
Coudert to Phelan, 31 December 1945, Coudert to Phelan, 31 December
1945 (a different letter), Coudert to Phelan, 26 January 1946, H.M.S.
Grant to Indian agent, 25 January 1946.

106 NA, RG10, DIA, vol. 6482, file 942–1, pt. 1, Hamel to Rev. J.L. Coudert,
29 January 1945.

107 NA, RG10, DIA, vol. 6481, file 940–10, pt. 5, Coudert to Philip Phelan, 31
December 1945.

108 NA, RG10, DIA, vol. 6481, file 940–10, pt. 5, Coudert to Philip Phelan, 26
January 1946.

109 NA, RG10, DIA, vol. 6482, file 942–5, pt. 1, G.F. Kingston to C. Gibson,
24 June 1949, W.H. Adams to Gibson, 4 July 1949; NA, RG10, DIA, vol.
8762, file 906/25–1–001, Coudert to Bernard Neary, 27 September 1950;
NA, RG10, DIA, vol. 6482, file 942–10, pt. 1, F.A. Clark's Annual Report,
31 December 1950; NA, RG10, DIA, vol. 6482, file 942–1, pt. 1, Privy
Council Minute 5218, 12 August 1947, Lauchlan, Chief Treasury Post
Office to B.C. Donnelly, Central Accounts Payable, 22 March 1950.

110 NA, RG10, DIA, vol. 8782, file 906/25–1–006, pt. 1, J.L. Coudert to Philip
Phelan, 15 February 1951, Coudert to Neary, 27 January 1951.

111 See *The Mission School Syndrome*, which documents Native reactions to
residential schools.

CHAPTER EIGHT

1 See, for example, Titley, *A Narrow Vision*.

2 Prucha, *Indian Policy in the United States*, 14.

3 For a review of the literature, see Surtees, *Canadian Indian Policy*. On the
post-Confederation period, see Ponting and Gibbins, *Out of Irrelevance*.
The assessment of the activities of Indian agents is beginning to
change. See, in particular, Barron, "Indian Agents and the North-West
Rebellion," in Barron and Waldram, eds., *1885 and After*.

4 Upton, "The Origins of Canadian Indian Policy"; Leighton, "The Development of Federal Indian Policy in Canada"; Weaver, *Making Canadian Indian Policy*; Miller, *Skyscrapers Hide the Heavens*.

5 Ponting and Gibbins, *Out of Irrelevance*, 3–30.

6 As A.J. Ray has shown, however, the government was often called on to assist with relief payments in trading districts. See "Periodic Shortages," in Krech, ed., *The Subarctic Fur Trade*.

7 On a technical level, see Elliott, *Some Constitutional Aspects*.

8 Thomas, *The Struggle for Responsible Government*.

9 This issue is examined in Morrison, *Showing the Flag*.

10 Zaslow, *The Opening of the Canadian North*, 108–9, 143–4. See also Coates and Morrison, *The Land of the Midnight Sun*, and Coates and Powell, *The Modern North*.

11 On government activities in the north, see Zaslow, *The Opening of the Canadian North*, 77–100; Zaslow, *Reading the Rocks*.

12 NA, MG17, B2, Bompas to chief commissioner of Indian affairs, May 1893.

13 Bompas's petitions include: NA, RG10, DIA, vol. 3906, file 105, 378, deputy superintendent general to Hon. T. Mayne Daly, 18 September 1893, Bompas to Dear Sir, 26 August 1893, Bompas to minister of the interior, 5 June 1894, Native Races and Liquor Traffic United Committee to Hon. Sir Charles Rupper, 1894; NA, MG17, B2, Bompas to CMS, 15 May 1894. On the dispatching of the NWMP, see NA, MG30, E55, Constantine Papers. For a descriptive summary, see Wright, *Prelude to Bonanza*, 256–71. Concern for the Indians was secondary to the government's desire to assert Canadian sovereignty in the face of American incursions and to collect customs duties on resources being exported from the district. Morrison, *Showing the Flag*.

14 NA, RG10, DIA, vol 1115, Deputy Superintendent's Letterbook, 27 April 1894–16 November 1894, H. Reed to Charles Constantine, 29 May 1894.

15 NA, RG10, DIA, vol. 1121. Letterbook 10, Memorandum, 2 December 1897; YTA, Anglican Church, New Series, file 4, Hayter Reed to bishop of Selkirk, 19 March 1897; *House of Commons Debates*, vol. 46 (1898), 814.

16 NA, RG10, DIA, vol. 3906, file 103, 378, Report of Inspector Constantine, 10 October 1894.

17 YTA, Anglican Church, New Series, file 4, Hayter Reed to bishop of Selkirk, 19 March 1897.

18 *House of Commons Debates*, vol. 46 (1898), 824.

19 Indian Affairs, file 801-30-0-1, Bompas to commissioner of Indian affairs, 12 July 1899.

20 Fumoleau, *As Long As This Land Shall Last*, 30–9. On northern Manitoba, see Coates and Morrison, *Treaty 5*; on northern Saskatchewan, see Coates and Morrison, *Treaty 10*.

21 This attitude to the north is best described in Hall, *Clifford Sifton: The Young Napoleon*.

22 In 1948 Indian Agent R.J. Meek wrote of Boss, "Chief Jim Boss is not recognized by most of the Indians [from Whitehorse]." Indian Affairs, file 801/30–18–8, Meek to Indian Affairs Branch, 17 February 1948.

23 NA, RG10, DIA, vol. 4037, file 317,050, Jackson to superintendent general of Indian affairs, 30 June 1902.

24 NA, RG10, DIA, vol. 4037, file 317, 050, J.D. McLean to Jackson, 28 January 1902, Congdon to Sifton, 10 September 1904, assistant secretary, Memorandum to Mr Pedley, 19 October 1904.

25 NA, RG10, DIA, vol. 3962, file 147, 654–1 pt. 2, Bompas to J. Ross, 7 March 1903. NA, RG10, DIA, vol. 4037, file 317, 050, T. Congdon to C. Sifton, 10 September 1904.

26 YTA, Anglican Church, New Series, file #3, Memo Regarding Trip to Dawson, 21 July to 8 August 1908.

27 Coates, "Asking for All Sorts of Favours." YTA, Anglican Church, New Series, file 2, Memo for the Minister re: Yukon Indians, *c.* 1907; YTA, Anglican Church, Carcross Property file, Pedley to Oliver, 23 January 1908; YTA, Anglican Church, New Series, file 1, Notes made from interview with Reverend A.E. O'Meara re: Indians in the Yukon, 1908; Proposed requests regarding Indians, 1908, Indian Matters–Recommendations of Messrs Hawksley and O'Meara, 1908; Memo for Archbishop regarding Yukon Indian work, 1908.

28 YTA, Anglican Church, file 3, Requests regarding Yukon Indians, 1908.

29 YTA, Anglican Church, file 2, Notes on interview with Mr Pedley and Mr Oliver, 26 February 1909.

30 Fumoleau, *As Long As This Land Shall Last*, 150–215. For a brief statement of the Yukon treaty issue, see DIAND, Indian Affairs Branch, Indian Affairs, file 801/30–0–1, "Land Entitlement of Indians of the Yukon and North West Territories" by Col. H.M. Jones, director.

31 On Anglican activities, see YTA, Anglican Church, New Series, file 2, Roberts to Stringer, 7 January 1910. That interest has remained to the present; McCullum and McCullum, *This Land Is Not for Sale*. Native interest in land entitlement in the Yukon, as it did in much of Canada, took on new life in the 1960s, culminating in the 1973 release of a comprehensive land claim. YNB, *Together Today for Our Children Tomorrow*.

32 NA, RG10, DIA, vol. 4001, file 207, 481, Congdon to Pedley, 28 May 1903.

33 NA, RG91, DIA, vol. 7, file 1331, Miller to Ogilvie, 10 April 1900, commissioner to deputy minister of the interior, 1 May 1900.

34 YTA, YRG1, series 5, vol. 1, file 1298, Miller to controller, mines, lands and Yukon branch, 14 May 1917, McLean to Rowatt, 10 March 1917, Miller to controller, 6 February 1917.

35 YTA, Acc. 77/2, Teslin Band Collection, J.A. Fraser, stipendiary magistrate, To Whom It May Concern, 14 July 1906.

36 Chief Daniel Johnson and Chief Joe Squam both claimed official status, a source of some disagreement in the community. But Squam was listed as the Teslin chief in an official report in 1932. Several years earlier a debate had arisen about whether or not Squam had been enfranchised in Atlin, BC YTA, YRG1, series 1, vol. 9, file 1490, pt. J, Hawksley to McLean, 2 August 1926. YTA, YRG1, series 1, vol. 9, file 1490, pt. J, Hawksley to Mackenzie, 4 November 1932. YTA, YRG1, series 1, vol. 9, file 1490, pt. J, J. Hawksley to J.D. McLean, 6 December 1929.

37 The confusion over the position of chief was complicated by the fact that there were two Teslin Lake bands, one based on the southern, British Columbian portion of the lake, the other to the north. YTA, YRG1, series 3, vol. 6, file 12–10A, Squam to DIA, 26 March 1931. NA, RG10, DIA, vol. 5761, file 420–1, Squam to Indian department, 22 August 1922. YTA, YRG1, series 1, vol. 9, file 1490, pt. J, Hawksley to Mackenzie, 1 October 1931; YTA, YRG1, series 3, vol. 6, file 12–13b, Jeckell to Hume, 21 November 1932.

38 When trapline registration was introduced in 1950, for example, the main Native protest was over the annual $10 fee. YTA, YRG1, series 3, vol. 11, file 12–23B, Meek to Gibson, 27 September 1950, Moses, Tizya, and Netro to Meek, 24 July 1950, petition from Chief William Johnson et al., 7 July 1950.

39 Chamberlin, *The Harrowing of Eden*.

40 On this issue, see Tobias, "Protection, Civilization, Assimilation."

41 YTA, Anglican Church, New Series, file 4, J.A. Smart to bishop of Selkirk, 12 August 1897.

42 Indian Affairs, file, 801/30–0–1, Constantine to deputy minister of the interior, 19 November 1896, Extract from William Ogilvie's letter, 8 November 1896; NA, MG30, E55, Constantine Papers, Constantine Letterbook, Constantine to Dear Sir, 13 November 1896; YTA, Anglican Church, New Series, file 4, Smart to Bompas, 12 August 1897; Indian Affairs, files 801/30–0–1, McLean Memorandum, 26 April 1897; YTA, YRG1, series 1, vol. 7, file 1187, McGee to minister of the interior, 27 March 1900.

43 YTA, YRG1, series 1, vol. 7, file 1187, Ogilvie to secretary, Department of the Interior, 11 December 1900, commissioner to Bompas, 27 September 1900.

44 YTA, YRG1, series 1, vol. 46, file 29967, Brownlee to Black, 23 July 1915.

45 NA, RG10, DIA, vol. 4081, file 478, 700, Hawksley to McLean, 7 April 1915, Moddie to Sir, 1 April 1915; YTA, YRG1, series 1, vol. 46, file 29, 967, Brownlee to McLean, 19 October 1915.

46 Indian Affairs, file 801/30–0–1, Hawksley to McLean, 25 November 1915; Indian Affairs, files 801/30–18–8, Hawksley to McLean, 19 October 1917, Bethune to superintendent of trusts and reserves, 14 May 1858, Meek to Indian Affairs Branch, 17 February 1948. The relocations originated in non-Native demands for the land. As of 1950 those Natives living near Whitehorse no longer inhabited the reserve.

47 Indian Affairs, file, 801/30–3–5, Strickland to officer in command, Upper Yukon, 16 August 1898, Pereira to White, 14 September 1898.

48 YTA, YRG1, series 1, vol. 46, file 29, 995, C. Swanson to commissioner, 1 September 1915; Indian Affairs, file 801/30–4–10, Brownlee to secretary, DIA, 19 August 1915, Report of Survey of Little Salmon Indian Reserve, c. 1915. A number of Yukon Native reserves were laid out in the summer of 1915. See YTA, YRG1, series 1, vol. 46, file 29995, from J.H. Brownlee's diary, 16 June–26 July.

49 The best example is the erosion of prairie reserves during the First World War, when, in the interests of the national war effort, substantial segments of reserves were leased to farmers.

50 YTA, YRG1, series 1, vol. 29, file 13, 013, Bompas to commission, 29 November 1904, Indian Affairs, file 801/30–0–1, J.J. Wright to superintendent general of Indian affairs, 4 February 1902.

51 YTA, YRG1, series 1, vol. 29, file 13014, J.A. Demeres to asst. comm, RNWMP, 6 January 1905.

52 NA, RG10, DIA, vol. 3962, file 147, 654–1, pt. 1, Congdon to F. Pedley, 28 April 1903; NA, RG10, DIA, vol. 4062, file 398, 746–1, secretary, Dawson Board of Trade, to Rt. Hon Frank Oliver, 19 August 1911. The latter document refers to a suggestion by the Dawson Board of Trade, seconded by Bishop Bompas, that the government import reindeer and hire the Indians to tend the herds. Like other proposals, this one focused on keeping Natives and whites apart.

53 NA, RG10, DIA, vol. 6479, file 940–1, pt. 1, Bursar to deputy superintendent general, 17 June 1907.

54 NA, RG10, DIA, vol. 6761, file 420–12, James Smart to Major Wood, 17 October 1902.

55 YTA, YRG1, series 3, vol. 2, file 12–14B, commissioner of Y.T. to J.B. Harken, 16 March 1922, ibid., file 12–13C, Report by A.W. Elling, 16 January 1923. When game preserves were established in the NWT, part of the Peel River valley was incorporated into a game reservation. This action in 1923 was designed to serve the needs of the Natives of the Mackenzie River basin, not those of the Yukon. Fumoleau, As Long As This Land Shall Last, 245–50; YTA, YRG1, series 3, vol. 2, file 12–4C, O.S. Finnie to Inspector Wood, 6 June 1925.

56 YTA, YRG1, series 3, vol. 8, file 12–15A, Extract from a report by Harper Reed, 8 May 1935.

57 YTA, YRG1, series 3, vol. 8, file 12–15, Camsell to Gibson, 14 September 1935, Reed to Perry, 12 July 1935; NA, RG10, DIA, vol. 6761, file 420–12, Binning to Jeckell, 18 October 1935, Jeckell to director, lands, N.W.T., and Yukon branch, 18 October 1935, Summary: Proposed Yukon Preserve For Sole Use of Indians, 1938.

58 Indian Affairs, file 801/30–10–10, Hawksley to McLean, 23 August 1929; YTA, YRG1, series 1, vol. 9, file 1490, pt. J, J. Henderson *et al.* to Mackenzie, 26 May 1932; YTA, YRG1, series 3, vol. 6, file 12–11B, Hawksley to Jeckell, 11 July 1932; YTA, YRG1, series 3, vol. 6, file 12–11B, Jeckell to chairman, Dominion Lands Board, 15 July 1932.

59 NA, RG10, DIA, vol. 6761, file 420–12–2RT–1, Meek to Indian Affairs Branch, 27 November 1947, Conn to Meek, 4 December 1947; NA, RG10, DIA, vol. 6742, file 420–6–1–1, Gibson to Gibben, 17 December 1947, NA, RG10, vol. 6761, file 420–12–2–2–RT–1, Meek to Indian Affairs Branch, Hugh Conn, 17 January 1950.

60 NA, RG10, DIA, vol. 6761, file 420–12–2–RT–1, Meek to Indian Affairs Branch, 27 November 1947, Conn to Meek, 4 December 1947, NA, RG10, DIA, vol. 6742, file 420–6–1–1, Gibson to Gibben, 17 December 1947; NA, RG10, DIA, vol. 6761, file 420–12–2–RT–1, Meek to Indian Affairs Branch, Hugh Conn, 17 January 1950.

61 YTA, YRG1, series 3, vol. 10, file 12–20B, Gibson to Hoffmaster, 23 January 1943.

62 *House of Commons Debates, 1903*, vol. 3, 7270–3.

63 Usher, "The North," in McCann, ed., *Heartland and Hinterland*, 427.

64 GSA, M74–2, file 1–A–2, Pedley to Oliver, 23 January 1908. As late as 1903 Clifford Sifton, minister of the interior, believed there to be only 700 Natives in the Yukon. *House of Commons Debates 1901*, vol. 11, 5449–5450; Ibid., (1903 session), vol. 3, 7270–3.

65 YTA, Anglican Church, New Series #2, Report of Messrs Vowell and Green, 14 August 1908.

66 YTA, YRG1, series 2, file 29, 299, J.D. McLean to John Hawksley, 4 March 1914; NA, RG10, DIA, vol. 1129, superintendent general to governor general in council, 12 January 1914; NA, RG10, DIA, vol. 7155, file 801/3–10, pt. 1, Hawksley to McLean, 17 April 1929, Hawksley to McLean, 13 June 1919. See also Hawksley's reports in DIA, *Annual Reports*, especially 1915–16, 115–17, and 1917, 30.

67 DIA, *Annual Report, 1915–1916*, Report of John Hawksley, 117.

68 YTA, YRG1, series 1, vol. 9, file 1490, pt. J, MacInnes to Gibson, 23 July 1938.

69 YTA, YRG1, series 2, file 29, 299, Jeckell to chairman, Dominion Lands Branch, 17 November 1933; YTA, YRG1, series 1, vol. 9, file 1490, pt. 7, T.E.L. MacInnes to R.A. Gibson, 23 July 1939. That the RCMP would accept such a task was in keeping with their tradition of handling a

variety of government duties in frontier settings. See Betke, "Pioneers and Police on the Canadian Prairies." See also W.R. Morrison, *Showing the Flag.*

70 *House of Commons Debates*, vol. 46 (1989), 824.

71 YTA, YRG1, series 1, vol. 7, file 1331, commissioner to deputy minister of the interior, 17 July 1900.

72 NA, RG18, vol. 247m file 92, Bompas to Capt. Wood, 6 July 1900.

73 NA, RG18, vol. 247, file 92, Bompas to Wood, 6 July 1900, Wood to comptroller, 5 July 1900.

74 NA, RG10, DIA, vol. 4001, file 207, 418, Smart to McLean, 30 April 1902, White to Smart, 1 January 1901, accountant to secretary, 1 May 1902.

75 NA, RG18, vol. 147, file 92, Hawksley to Wood, 24 June 1902; NA, RG10, DIA, vol. 4001, file 207, 418, Snyder to asst. commissioner, 19 November 1902; "Report of Superintendent Wood, 1 December 1901," NWMP, *Annual Report, 1902*, pt. III, 10; NA, RG10, DIA, vol. 3962, file 147, 654, pt. 2, Wood to superintendent general of Indian affairs, 22 March 1903; "Report of Asst. Commissioner Wood, 1 December 1904," NWMP, *Annual Report 1950*, 19; "Report of Asst. Commissioner Wood, 1 December 1903," NWMP, *Annual Report, 1904*, 12; NA, RG18, vol. 295, file 173, Cuthbert to asst. commissioner, 31 January 1905; NA, RG18, vol. 352, file 128, superintendent "H" Division to asst. commissioner, 3 March 1908, ibid., 1 May 1908; "Report of Asst. Commissioner Wood, 1 October 1909," RNWMP, *Annual Report, 1910*, 217.

76 NA, RG18, vol. 247, file 92, Hawksley to Major Wood, 24 June 1902.

77 YTA, Anglican Church, Rampart House, Fort Yukon, and Old Crow file, H. Anthony to Stringer, 16 November 1925.

78 NA, RG18, vol. 195, file 273, Cuthbert to asst. commissioner, 30 September 1905, RNWMP, *Annual Report, 1912*, 222.

79 NA, RG18, vol. 352, file 128, superintendent "H" Division to asst. commissioner, 1 June 1908. See also "Report of Inspector Routledge, 1 December 1902," NWMP, *Annual Report, 1902*, 89. Not all police officers shared this view, several argued for greater government assistance. NA, RG18, vol. 272, file 267, superintendent "B" Division to asst. commissioner, 31 January 1904.

80 "Report of Inspector Horrigan, 30 September 1911," RNWMP, *Annual Report, 1911*, 212.

81 "Report of Superintendent Moodie, 30 September 1913," RNWMP, *Annual Report 1914*, 274; YTA, YRG1, series 2, file 29, 299, McLean to Hawksley, 4 March 1914; YTA, Anglican Church, Carcross file, Stringer to Townsend, 9 February 1915; GSA, M74–3, file 1–A–5A, Stringer to Martin, 13 November 1916; "Report of Corporal Mocking, 6 March 1914," RNWMP, *Annual Report, 1915*, 740; YTA, Anglican Church, Chambers file, Stringer

to Chambers, 17 May 1916; YTA, Anglican Church, Young file, Stringer
to W.D. (Young), 25 April 1917. Allowing fur traders to dispense relief
supplies led to occasional cries of conflict of interest. In those areas
without police or mission stations, however, the government permitted
the resident trader to determine need.

82 See Canada, *Sessional Papers, Auditor General Annual Reports*. Auditor
General's reports, which provide a dollar by dollar listing of expenditures in the early years of the twentieth century, demonstrate that government agents authorized everything from house construction for the
elderly to the provision of rifle shells.

83 YTA, Anglican Church, Carcross file, Isaac Stringer to Mr Townsend, 9
February 1915.

84 YTA, YRG1, series 3, vol. 5, file 12–8A, A.B. Thorntwaite to O.C., RCMP,
Dawson, 17 November 1928.

85 "Report of Assistant Commissioner Wood, 1 December 1904," RNWMP,
Annual Report, 1905, 19.

86 "Report of Supt Cuthbert, 30 November 1904," RNWMP, *Annual Report,
1905*, 39.

87 Auditor General of Canada, *Annual Report, 1902–1903*, J–78; Auditor
General of Canada, *Annual Report, 1904–1905*, J–62. See other annual
reports for continuing data.

88 YTA, YRG1, series 2, file 29299, J.D. McLean to Hawksley, 4 March 1914.

89 YTA, Phelps Papers, Phelps to Peele, 6 March 1916.

90 YTA, Anglican Church, Swanson File, Swanson to bishop, 16 June
1916.

91 The Yukon presented unique opportunities in the area of disease control. When the Spanish Flu epidemic spread across North America in
1918, the Yukon government established a quarantine in Skagway, stopping all people who planned to enter the territory.

92 NA, RG18, vol. 247, file 91, Bompas to Wood, 6 July 1900; NA, RG18, vol.
514, file 530, Bell to O.C. "B" Division, 2 September 1916. One of the
most serious outbreaks involved a smallpox epidemic at Rampart House
in 1911–12. See Coates, *The Northern Yukon*, 80–1. Green, *The Boundary
Hunters*; YNA, RG18, vol. 532, file 206–17, Fyfe to C.O. "B" Division, 7
September 1911.

93 Morrison, *Showing the Flag*. For a provocative study of the role of the
police in the gold-rush era, see Stone, "The Mounties as Vigilantes."

94 Morrison, "The Natives of the Northern Frontier," in Dempsey, ed., *Men
in Scarlet*.

95 YTA, Anglican Church, New Series, file 3, Particulars Regarding Copper
Indians, July 1908.

96 Morrison, *Showing the Flag*.

97 Guest, "A History of Dawson City."

98 NA, RG10, DIA, vol. 6761, file 410–12, J.A. Smart to Major Z.T. Wood, 17 October 1902; NA, RG85, vol. 905, file 10, 442, Report re: Tanana Joe, 25 November 1942; YTA, YRG1, series 1, vol. 62, file 35, 411, file re: J. Sheldon–Trapping Beaver Without Permit, 21 June 1950. There are many such examples of leniency.

99 YTA, YRG1, series 1, vol. 9, file 1490, pt. J, John Hawksley to A.F. Mackenzie, 27 August 1931.

100 The story was blown up in the southern press. Horrigan was alleged to have taken twenty officers with him to prevent an uprising. RNWMP, *Annual Report 1909*, 210, 243–4. For a more readable, if less reliable, account, see National Museum of Man, Canadian Ethnology Service Archives, Poole Field Letters, Field to Dear Jask, *c.* 1909.

101 NA, RG18, vol. 331, file 116, deputy superintendent general of Indian affairs to Fred White, 23 February 1907.

102 "Report of Assistant Surgeon Fraser," RWMP, *Annual Report, 1901*, pt. III, 54; "Report of Inspector McDonnell," NWMP, *Annual Report, 1902*, pt. III, 101–3.

103 NA, RG85, vol. 774, file 5589, Thorntwaite to superintendent of Indian affairs, *c.* 1927, Allard to commissioner, 5 February 1927; ibid., vol. 609, file 2657, Extracts from report of Corp. Thorntwaite, 8 November 1927.

104 YTA, YRG1, series 2, vol. 34, file 33, 989, Minute of Privy Council, 13 February 1928.

105 Indian Agent Hawksley clearly saw the Moosehide council as an experiment, and resisted efforts by Ottawa civil servants to give the council permanent status. NA, RG10, DIA, vol. 7155, file 801/3–10, pt. 1, A.F. Mackenzie to Hawksley, 18 July 1921, Hawksley to J.D. McLean, 8 August 1921.

106 *Northern Lights*, vol. IX, no. 3 (August 1921), 6.

107 YTA, YRG1, series 1, vol. 9, file 1490, pt. J, Hawksley to A.F. Mackenzie, 4 November 1932.

108 YTA, YRG1, series 1, vol. 9, file 1490, pt. J, Hawksley to Jacquot, 12 February 1929.

109 NA, RG10, DIA, vol. 6761, file 420–12–2–RT–1, Meek to Netro, 25 May 1950.

110 "Report of Superintendent S.B. Steele," NWMP, *Annual Report, 1899*, pt. III, 20.

111 The police were soon commenting that the Natives were law-abiding and peaceable. NA, RG10, DIA, vol. 4081, file 478, 700, Report of Mayo Indians, 28 August 1917; "Report of Superintendent Wood," NWMP, *Annual Report, 1904*, 21; "Report of Inspector Snyder," RWMP, *Annual Report, 1907–1908*; "Report of Inspector Macdonald," RWMP, *Annual Report, 1911*, 225.

112 A good example is the general indictment of the Hootchi near Dalton Post in "Report of Inspector Jarvis," NWMP, *Annual Report, 1900*, pt. II, 58.

113 NA, RG10, DIA, vol. 7475, file 19, 166–3, pt. 1, Superintendent Tucker to commissioner, 11 April 1921, Hawksley to O.C. "B" Division, 27 April 1921. See also "Report of Inspector Constantine," NWMP, *Annual Report, 1896*, 13.

114 NA, RG10, DIA, vol. 7475, file 19166–6, pt. 1, Binning to secretary of Indian affairs, 7 November 1936. Andrew Paull of the North American Indian Brotherhood appealed for Duncan's release from prison in 1947, arguing that he was an old man and could tell Natives in the Yukon "what British Justice is" as a result of his experience. Yukon officials were reluctant to have him brought back to the territory, because they feared that his victim's brothers would seek revenge. NA, RG10, DIA, vol. 7475, file 19166–6, pt. 1, Meek to Indian Affairs Branch, 18 April 1947, Andrew Paull to J.G. Gelm, MP, 11 March 1947.

115 YTA, YRG1, series 5, vol. 2, file 198, R. Miller to controller, Mines, Lands and Yukon branch, 6 February 1917.

116 "Report of Inspector Wood," NWMP, *Annual Report, 1899*, pt. III, 42–3.

117 Figures are from NWMP and RNWMP, *Annual Reports* (various years).

118 "Report of Supt Primrose," NWMP, *Annual Report, 1900*, pt. II, Return of Criminal and Other Cases.

119 NA, RG10, DIA, vol. 3906, file 105, 378, Extract from monthly report of Superintendent G.E. Snyder, December 1906.

120 Leslie and Maguire, *The Historical Development of the Indian Act*.

121 McLeod, *The NWMP and Law Enforcement*, 32.

122 NA, RG10, DIA, vol. 3906, file 105, 378 has a number of letters, particularly from Bishop Bompas, on this topic. See also NA, MG30, E55, Constantine Papers, Constantine to O.C., Regina, 20 November 1896.

123 "Report of Supt Primrose," NWMP, *Annual Report, 1901*, pt. III, 28.

124 GSA, M56–4, series E–7, Cody Papers, Hawksley to Cody, 31 December 1908.

125 NA, RG18, vol. 539, file 2, Bell to O.C. "B" Division, 20 January 1917, Mapley to O.C., Whitehorse Sub-Division, 28 February 1917; NA, RG10, DIA, vol. 549, Scott to McLean, 30 January 1916, Bell to commissioner, 18 February 1918.

126 Most patrol reports, except for those dealing with the Porcupine River area, routinely included comments on local liquor traffic. For one such example, see YTA, YRG1, series 7, vol. 33, file 33, 937, pt. 9, Report of superintendent H.H. Cronkhite re: Patrol from Dawson to Coffee Creek, 7 March 1929.

127 Efforts to establish posts at these locations in 1905 were thwarted by manpower shortages. NA, RG18, vol. 300, file 443, Wood to comptroller,

13 August 1905, controller to Wood, 26 August 1905. For Teslin, see NA, RG18, vol. 301, file 583, Wood to controller, 11 November 1905; NA, RG18, vol. 315, file 228, superintendent "H" Division to asst. commissioner, 8 October 1906. YTA, YRG1, series 3, vol. 10, file 12–19A, Jeckell to Mayfield, 31 August 1940. For Dalton Post, see NA, RG18, vol. 516, file 607, Knight to Ironside, 19 October 1916; NA, RG18, vol. 539, file 2, Knight to commissioner, 14 April 1917, Report re: Liquor to Indians in Dalton Trail district, 29 September 1917, Extract from report of Inspector Bell, 4 February 1918, Extract from report of Superintendent Knight, January 1918.

128 NA, RG18, vol. 352, file 128, superintendent "H" Division to asst. commissioner, RNWMP, 1 April 1900. On the high priority ascribed to this problem by the police, see NA, MG30 E98, Z.T. Wood Papers, Report re: Law and Order in the Yukon, 14 May 1909.

129 Guest, *The Emergence of Social Security in Canada*. For a detailed examination of the war period and Native affairs in the Yukon, see Coates, "The Alaska Highway and the Indians of the Southern Yukon," in Coates, ed., *The Alaska Highway*.

130 Coates and Morrison, *Land of the Midnight Sun*.

131 Grant, ed., *Sovereignty or Security*.

132 YTA, YRG1, series 1, vol. 65, file 813, Gibben to Keenleyside, 4 September 1947; NA, RG10, DIA, vol. 8762, file 906/25–1–005, pt. 1, Quarterly Report of R.J. Meek, 1 October–31 December 1949; *Public Accounts of the Government of the Yukon Territory, 1949–1950*, 41. Wilson, *No Man Stands Alone*.

133 YTA, YRG1, series 9, vol. 4, file 5, Revised Scale of Rations for Indigent Indians, 4 March 1952. Under the new scale, two adults received the following each month: 36 lbs of flour, 9 lbs rolled oats, 1 ¾ lbs baking powder, 1 ½ lbs of tea, 4 lbs of sugar, 5 lbs lard, 5 lbs beans, 5 lbs of rice (or potatoes to equivalent value), 1 ½ lbs of cheese, $3.75 worth of fish or meat, 10–15 cents worth of salt per family, 10–20 cents worth of matches per family, and one pint of evaporated or powdered milk per day for each child under the age of 12. Dried fruit could be substituted for beans.

134 Canada, Department of Mines and Resources, Indian Affairs Branch, *Annual Report, 1949*, 200. NA, RG10, vol. 6761, file 420–12–1–RT–1, Meek to Kjar, 15 March 1950. See the Indian Affairs Branch, *Annual Reports, 1949–1951* for details on Native employment projects.

135 YTA, YRG1, series 4, vol. 33, file 689, D.C. Rowat to G.A. Jeckell, 4 June 1945.

136 Indian Affairs Branch, *Annual Report, 1946*, 211; Guest, *The Emergence of Social Security in Canada*, 128–33.

137 NA, RG10, DIA, vol. 6478, file 933–3, pt. 1, Father Dream to R.J. Meek, 24 February 1950.
138 This description of the post-Second World War activism of the federal government in Native matters is widely accepted by commentators. See Usher, "The North," in Leacock and Lurie, eds., *North American Indians;* Kehoe, *North American Indians,* 487–504; Riches, *Northern Nomadic Hunter-Gatherers.*

PART FOUR

1 See Coates and Morrison, *The Army of Occupation.*
2 On this post-war enthusiasm, see Grant, *Sovereignty or Security?*
3 Meek, *Report on the Yukon Indian Agency,* 57.
4 Indian Affairs, file 801/19–4, vol. 4, Briefing Material on the Yukon Region, 10 April 1973.

CHAPTER NINE

1 Indian Affairs, 801/30–0–1, Jutras re: Reserves–Yukon Territory, 9 June 1958.
2 *Whitehorse Star,* 6 July 1961, 18.
3 Griffin, *Cashing In.*
4 NA, RG10, DIA, vol. 8423, 801/2–1, Jutras to Indian Affairs Branch, 22 February 1966.
5 Meek, "Report on the Yukon Indian Agency," 27.
6 Indian Affairs, file 801/21–1, vol. 2, Cole to superintendent, Yukon Indian Agency, 21 August 1962.
7 NA, RG10, DIA, vol. 8423, 801/2–1, Quarterly Report, September 1955.
8 Meek, "Report on the Yukon Indian Agency," 27.
9 Indian Affairs, file 801/21–1, vol. 2, Cole to Indian commissioner, 2 May 1963.
10 Meek, "Report on the Yukon Indian Agency," 27.
11 Meek, "Report on the Yukon Indian Agency," 25.
12 DIA, *Annual Report,* 1949, 200.
13 Indian Affairs, file 801/29–2, vol. 2, W.S. Arneil to Jones, 10 March 1958.
14 YTA, series 10, vol. 87, file 6, A. Stevenson to employment liaison officer, 28 September 1971. Nor was the federal government anxious to force compliance. See NA, RG10, DIA, vol. 8423, 801/21–1, Jones to Silverta, 27 August 1958.
15 Indian Affairs, file 801, 21–1, vol. 2, Fry to Indian commissioner, 21 July 1967.

16 Meek, "Report on the Yukon Indian Agency," 19.
17 Indian Affairs, file 801/20–15, vol. 1, David Gimmer to Jack O'Connor, 1 October 1971.
18 Indian Affairs, file 801/14–5, Grant to Garner, 10 March 1961.
19 Indian Affairs, file 801/14–1, vol. 1, V. Vokes to Industries Section, 3 June 1966. See also Indian Affairs, file 801/19–8, vol. 1, passim.
20 Indian Affairs, file 801/19–8, vol. 1, memo by C.H. Larsen, 16 March 1967.
21 Indian Affairs, file 801/20–15, vol. 1, Ron Chambers to Peter Lesaux, 1 November 1972.
22 Indian Affairs, file 801/14–1, vol. 1, draft proposal, Grant to Co-operative Union of Canada; see also Indian Arts and Crafts Advisory Committee, Terms of Reference.
23 Indian Affairs, file 801/19–8–1, vol. 1, H.B. Robinson to W. Smith, 21 January 1974.
24 Indian Affairs, file 801/19–1, vol. 1, Old Crow Co-operative Association Limited.
25 Indian Affairs, file 801/19–8–1, vol. 1, Press Release: Weather Station to be Operated by Indians, December 1970.
26 Indian Affairs, file 801/19–7, vol. 1, contains correspondence relating to a variety of such applications and loans.
27 In 1948 the Yukon Territorial government's budget was $943,400. *Whitehorse Star*, 26 March 1948, 3.
28 *Whitehorse Star*, 18 April 1963, 22. In 1963 twenty-four Native people enrolled in the school, the women in courses for nursing assistants, hair-dressers, and cooking, the men in carpentry, mechanics, and welding programs. *Whitehorse Star*, 19 September 1963, 9.
29 Indian Affairs, file 801/15–1, vol. 1, Meek to Abbott, 31 January 1951.
30 Indian Affairs, file 801/30–0–1, vol. 2, Grant to chief, reserves and trusts, 2 November 1961.
31 NA, RG10, DIA, vol. 8432, 801/21–6–1, passim.
32 Indian Affairs, file 801/21–6–1, vol. 4, Gordon to Clarke, 14 June 1963.
33 Indian Affairs, file 801/21–6–1, vol. 4, Memo re: Winter Clearing Ross River–Watson Lake Road, 16 October 1963.
34 Indian Affairs, file 801/21–6–1, vol. 4, Memo re: Watson Lake–Ross River Road Project, 9 December 1963.
35 Indian Affairs, file 801/21–1, vol. 2, passim.
36 Indian Affairs, file 801/21–1, vol. 2, Mackie to minister, 19 November 1976.
37 Indian Affairs, file 801/19–4, vol. 1, Fry to Indian commissioner for BC, 8 April 1963. The family, in this instance, lived in northern BC.
38 Meek, "Report on the Yukon Indian Agency," 6.
39 *Whitehorse Star*, 6 July 1961, 18.

40 YTA, series 10, vol. 146, file 6, John A. MacDonald to J. Smith, 22 April 1969.

41 For a detailed statement on the Indians' hopes for the future, see Indian Affairs 801/19–1, vol. 1, YNB, *Economic Development for Indians in Yukon Territory.*

42 Indian Affairs, file 801/21–2, vol. 2, Fry to Indian commissioner, 21 July 1967.

CHAPTER TEN

1 Meek, "Report on the Yukon Indian Agency," 16. Catherine McClellan was doing anthropological field-work in the southern Yukon.

2 For a discussion of this issue on a national scale, see Grant, *Moon of Wintertime.*

3 Two decades later, in the 1980s, the main Christian denominations would confront their history of evangelizing among the Indians and begin to apologize for their deliberate efforts to destroy aboriginal cultures. There were hints of this self-awareness in the 1960s, particularly among younger clergy, who opted for social and political activism over the cultural intervention of the past. See, for example, the work of Hugh and Karmel McCullum, *This Land Is Not For Sale,* a biting indictment of the impact of development on northern Natives. For the most part, however, supporters of the missionary enterprise were concerned about the obvious limitations of their work among the Yukon Indians, but generally unrepentant.

4 For a very critical, and influential, study of residential schools in the Yukon, see King, *The School at Mopass.*

5 Indian Affairs, file 801/29–8, vol. 3, F.H. Collins to Erik Nielsen, 5 April 1961.

6 *Indian Affairs Branch, Annual Report, 1946,* 212; NA, RG10, DIA, vol. 8762, file 906/25–1–005, pt. 1, Meek to Indian Affairs Branch, 8 February 1950.

7 Indian Affairs, file 801/25–1, Education, March 62–Nov. 63, Grant to Tizya and Whyard, 23 July 1962. See also Indian Affairs, file 801/25–1, Education, April 63–Jan. 65, Fry to Father Guiliband, 14 August 1963.

8 Indian Affairs, file 801/25–1, Education, March 62–Nov. 63, Grant to Coudert, 3 September 1962.

9 *Whitehorse Star,* 18 June 1948, 1.

10 See the extended description in *Whitehorse Star,* 7 January 1949, 5.

11 *Whitehorse Star,* 20 February 1948, 4.

12 Indian Affairs, file 906/25–1, vol. 4, Jampolsky to Indian commissioner, 21 September 1962.

13 Indian Affairs, file 906/25–1, vol. 4, Jampolsky to Indian commissioner, 21 September 1962.

14 Indian Affairs, file 906/25–1, vol. 4, Jampolsky to Davey, 13 October 1963.

15 Indian Affairs, file 906/25–1, vol. 4, Sivertz to Gordon, 30 September 1963.

16 Indian Affairs, file 906/25–1, vol. 4, Coudert to Verywat, 2 August 1963, McAllister to Sheppard, 9 August 1963.

17 Indian Affairs, file 801/25–1, Education, March 62–Nov. 63, Coudert to Grant, 31 August 1962.

18 Indian Affairs, file 801/25–1, Education, Jan. 59–Feb. 62, Hill to Nielson, 9 March 1961.

19 Indian Affairs, file 801/25–1, Education, Jan. 1959–Feb. 1962, Parminter to Collins, 16 January 1961.

20 *Whitehorse Star*, 17 November 1960, 1.

21 Indian Affairs, file 801/7–2, vol. 1, Gordon to Grant, 11 March 1961.

22 Indian Affairs, file 801/30–0–1, vol. 6, Fry to Boys, 18 June 1963.

23 King, *The School at Mopass*.

24 See ibid., and also *The Mission School Syndrome*, a documentary produced by Northern Native Broadcasting Yukon, 1988.

25 Meek, "Report on the Yukon Indian Agency," 30.

26 Indian Affairs, file 801/25–1, Education, Jan. 59–Feb. 62, Grant to chief, Education Division–Ottawa, 18 May 1961. See also, ibid., Blaker to DIA, 9 June 1961.

27 Indian Affairs, file 801/25–1, Education, Jan. 59–Feb. 62, Hill to Nielson, 9 March 1961.

28 The Anglican Church ran the Carcross Residential School as an alternative school for a few years, but that experiment failed and the institution was closed. It was finally torn down in the 1980s. See Indian Affairs, file 801/25–1, vol. 6, "The Carcross Community Education Centre," 1975.

29 Meek, "Report on the Yukon Indian Agency," 34.

30 Indian Affairs, file 801/19–4, vol. 4, Briefing Material on the Yukon Region, 10 April 1973.

31 Indian Affairs, file 801/29–2, vol. 2, Fry to Indian commissioner, 3 May 1966.

32 Indian Affairs, file 801/43–1, vol. 2, Cote to Jamieson, 29 June 1973.

33 For a summary of programs extant in 1973, see Indian Affairs, file 801/25–1, vol. 4, J. Smith to P.B. Lexaux, 22 October 1973.

34 Indian Affairs, file 801/25–1, vol. 7, Chrétien to Smith, 10 May 1974, Gooderham to Robinson, 23 May 1974.

35 Indian Affairs, file 801/25–1, Education, Jan. 71–Feb. 72, E. Smith to Mr Ferguson, n.d. See also ibid., Resolution 1, First Yukon Native Education Conference, 10–14 Jan. 1972.

36 Indian Affairs, file 801/25–1, Education, April 63–Jan. 65, Fry to Sister Agnes Dolores, 23 July 1963.

37 See, for example, Hendry, *Beyond Traplines*, and Hugh and Karmel McCullum, *This Land Is Not for Sale*.

CHAPTER ELEVEN

1 Miller, *Skyscrapers Hide the Heavens*, 221–2.
2 Meek, "Report on the Yukon Indian Agency," 54.
3 Indian Affairs, file 801/29–5, vol. 2, W.E. Grant to Indian commissioner, 11 January 1961. Emphasis in original.
4 Indian Affairs, file 801/29–5, vol. 2, B. Sivertz to H.M. Jones, 19 April 1961.
5 Indian Affairs, file 801/29–5, vol. 2, Walter Dinsdale to Ellen Fairclough, 21 April 1961.
6 Indian Affairs, file 801–30–0–1, Meek to Arneil, 21 October 1953.
7 Ibid.
8 Indian Affairs and Northern Development, active files, file 801–30–0–1, Bethune to supt of reserves and trusts, Schedule of Lands Reserved for Indians, Yukon Territory, 14 May 1958.
9 Indian Affairs, file 801/29–2, vol. 2, Fry to Indian commissioner, 19 November 1965.
10 Indian Affairs, file 801–30–0–1, Jutras, superintendent of Indian affairs, reserves – Yukon, 9 June 1958.
11 Indian Affairs, file 801/19–4, vol. 1, Fry to Nielsen, 14 December 1966.
12 There is a large amount of correspondence on this issue. See Indian Affairs, file 801/19–4, vol. 1, passim.
13 In the 1980s, after the collapse of the Alaska Highway Pipeline project left the municipal and territorial governments with a substantial subdivision that they could not sell, the Indians requested that this land be made available to them as a reserve. After much prevaricating, the Kwanlin Dun band's appeal was finally accepted, and new homes were constructed.
14 Meek, "Report on the Yukon Indian Agency," 18.
15 This was common across the North. See Nixon, "Eskimo Housing Programs."
16 *Whitehorse Star*, 4 December 1958, 10. See also *Whitehorse Star*, 2 March 1961, 6.
17 Alan Fry to author, personal correspondence, 3 January 1991.
18 *Whitehorse Star*, 24 June 1965, 19.
19 *Whitehorse Star*, 26 July 1965, 1.
20 *Whitehorse*, 16 September 1965, 1.
21 Indian Affairs, file 801/29–2, vols. 4 and 5, G.J. Bowen to Indian commissioner for BC, 18 January 1967.
22 Programs also involved connecting existing houses to the electrical network. Indian Affairs, file 801/29–2, vols. 4 and 5, Munro to Robillard, 9 January 1969.

23 Indian Affairs, file 801/29–2, vols. 4 and 5, Battle to Minister, 31 August 1966.

24 Indian Affairs, file 801/29–2, vol. 2, Fry to Indian commissioner, 22 April 1966.

25 Indian Affairs, file 801/29–2, vol. 9, Fry to Indian commissioner, 3 May 1966.

26 Indian Affairs, file 801/29–2, vol. 9, Fry to Indian commissioner, 19 April 1967, Clark to Fry, 1 May 1967.

27 Indian Affairs, file 801/29–2, vol. 9, Fry to Indian commissioner, 5 May 1967.

28 Indian Affairs, file 801/29–2, vol. 2, Fry to Indian commissioner, 3 May 1966.

29 Indian Affairs, file 801/29–2, vol. 2, D. Clark to commissioner, 25 May 1966.

30 Indian Affairs, file 801/29–2, vols. 4 and 5, Connelly Departmental Secretariat, 21 November 1972. See the attached reply to Elijah Smith.

31 Indian Affairs, file 801/29–2, vols. 4 and 5, Indian Housing–Yukon Region (Community Affairs Program).

32 Indian Affairs, file 801/29–1, vol. 11, Housing–Yukon Indian Agency.

33 Indian Affairs, file 801/19–4, vol. 4, "Housing Policy for Yukon Native Brotherhood," by Chief Elijah Smith, YNB.

34 Indian Affairs, file 801/29–2, vols. 4 and 5, Kirkby to director, Community Affairs, 29 June 1972.

35 Meek, "Report on the Yukon Indian Agency," 38.

36 For a report on the status of Indian health-care services in 1963, see YTA, series RG 1, vol. 86, file 8, Department of National Health and Welfare, Medical Services, "Annual Report," 1963.

37 O'Neill, "The Politics of Health in the Fourth World," in Coates and Morrison, *Interpreting Canada's North*.

38 Meek, "Report on the Yukon Indian Agency," 38. See also the report in *Whitehorse Star*, 11 January 1946, 5.

39 Indian Affairs, file 801/43–1, Cultural Grants–Yukon.

40 Indian Affairs, file 801/3–8, vol. 1, letter to Rene Tremblay, 5 August 1964.

41 Indian Affairs, file 801/3–8, vol. 1, Shorty to deputy minister, 12 April 1966.

42 Indian Affairs, file 801/18–1, vol. 1, Indian supt., Yukon Agency, to Indian Affairs Branch, 21 March 1960.

43 Indian Affairs, file 801/42–2, vol. 1, Yukon Territorial Government, Child Welfare Services, 1965.

44 *Whitehorse Star*, 13 July 1961, 8. See also 6 November 1991, 1–2.

45 Indian Affairs, file 801/7–7, vol. 1, Boys to director of operations, 1 November 1968.

CHAPTER TWELVE

1 YTA, series 1, vol. 19, file 1, Indian Population in the Yukon Territory, 1 June 1961.
2 Meek, "Report on the Yukon Indian Agency," 23.
3 See Indian Affairs, file 801/29–2, vols. 4 and 5, Fry to Indian commissioner for BC, 15 November 1966, Re: the difficulty of getting the reserve connected to the Whitehorse water system.
4 Indian Affairs, file 801/29–2, vols. 4 and 5, R.F. Battle to minister, 31 August 1966. This issue was not soon resolved. Indian Affairs, file 801/19–4, vol. 1, Jean Chrétien to T.C. Douglas, 30 July 1970.
5 *Whitehorse Star*, 14 December 1961, 19. This item is a commentary on Native affairs by Rev. A. Hallidie Smith of Carmacks.
6 Indian Affairs, Peter Edridge, re: Whitehorse Indian Village, 1972.
7 *Whitehorse Star*, 7 July 1950, 6.
8 *Whitehorse Star*, 14 July 1950, 10, see also 2.
9 *Whitehorse Star*, 21 July 1950, 12.
10 *Whitehorse Star*, 28 July 1950, 10.
11 Meek, "Report on the Yukon Indian Agency," 30.
12 Indian Affairs, file 801/29–2, vols. 4 and 5, A.E. Fry to G.R. Cameron, 21 April 1966.
13 The initial town site was destroyed in a fire and had to be entirely rebuilt.
14 Indian Affairs, file 801/29–2, vols. 4 and 5, Band Council Resolution, Ross River, 17 May 1972.
15 Indian Affairs, file 801/19–4, vol. 4, "Housing Policy for Yukon Native Brotherhood: Proposed."
16 Old Crow, where Ellen Bruce continued her work on behalf of the church, remained a solid example of this process.
17 *Whitehorse Star*, 22 September 1960, 9.
18 Meek, "Report on the Yukon Indian Agency," 53.
19 *Whitehorse Star*, 9 July 1948, 3.
20 See Indian Affairs, file 801/24–4, vol. 1, passim.
21 Meek, "Report on the Yukon Indian Agency," 60.
22 Dunning, "Ethnic Relations and the Marginal Man."
23 Indian Affairs, file 801/1–1, vol. 2, Battle to Gibson, 15 November 1966.
24 *Whitehorse Star*, 17 November 1960, 4.
25 *Whitehorse Star*, 13 February 1958, 11.
26 Indian Affairs, file 801/18–6–0, Laval Fortier to Robertson, 10 August 1955.
27 Indian Affairs, file 801/18–6–0, J.T. Parsons to officer commanding, 10 December 1957. *Whitehorse Star*, 20 October 1955, 9. Some Indians were not pleased with these changes. Chief Albert Isaac of Haines Junction petitioned the federal government in 1968 to restrict the sale of liquor

to Indians. Indian Affairs, file 801/16–6, vol. 6, McClellan to Arthur Laing, 9 March 1968, and passim.

28 *Whitehorse Star*, 24 November 1960, 26.

29 Lurie, "The World's Oldest On-Going Protest Demonstration."

30 Miller, *Skyscrapers Hide the Heavens*, 49.

31 Indian Affairs, file 801/18–6, vol. 6, J. Smith to A. Laing, 8 December 1966, Arthur Laing to James Smith, 24 February 1967.

32 Meek, "Report on the Yukon Indian Agency," 48.

33 Ibid., 13–14.

34 Ibid., 38.

35 Ibid., 41.

36 Indian Affairs, file 801/19–4, vol. 5, Peter Edridge re: Whitehorse Indian Village, 1972.

37 Indian Affairs, file 801/18–1, vol. 1, quoted in J.V. Boys to R. Bonner, 9 May 1962. See also *Vancouver Sun*, 8 May 1962. Such problems were not uncommon. In 1961 two runaways from the Roman Catholic hostel in Whitehorse were picked up by several white men. When they were finally found by the RCMP, both of the girls, fourteen and fifteen years old, had venereal disease. *Whitehorse Star*, 9 November 1961, 1–2.

38 *Whitehorse Star*, 24 January 1957, 9.

39 *Whitehorse Star*, 6 January 1963, 3.

40 *Whitehorse Star*, 14 June 1965, 11.

41 Linda Johnson,

42 Indian Affairs, file 801–30–0–1, vol. 1, marginal notes, Fortier to acting minister, 27 November 1957.

43 Nielsen, *The House is Not a Home*.

44 *Whitehorse Star*, 24 March 1960, 20.

45 *Whitehorse Star*, 25 August 1960, 22.

46 For an analysis of this process in the NWT, see Lange "The changing Structure of Dene Elders, and of Marriage, in the context of colonialism," in Dacks and Coates, eds., *Northern Communities*.

47 Indian Affairs, file 801/7–1, vol. 1, Fry to Indian commissioner for BC, 9 November 1966.

48 There is only a single surviving speaker of the Tagish language; the Han language is also in serious difficulty.

49 The major force in this process has been John Ritter, a linguist, and the Yukon Native Languages Project, a remarkable enterprise dedicated to the preservation of aboriginal languages and culture.

CHAPTER THIRTEEN

1 See, for example, Indian Affairs, 801/3–8, Hector Lang to Jean Chrétien, May 1973.

2 Weaver, *Making Indian Policy*. There was, of course, a Yukon dimension to this debate, not mentioned in Weaver's excellent study. See YTA, series 10, vol. 141, file 6, for correspondence on this issue.

3 Coates, "Sinews of Their Lives," in Abel and Friesen, eds., *Aboriginal Resource Use*.

4 Meek, "Report on the Yukon Indian Agency," 26.

5 McCandless, *Yukon Wildlife*.

6 *Whitehorse Star*, 14 December 1961, 19.

7 Hawthorn, ed., *A Survey of the Contemporary Indians of Canada*, pt. 2.

8 Meek, "Report on the Yukon Indian Agency," 53.

9 There are important signs of a Native reassertion of cultural values in this area. The Teslin band recently re-established a clan-based council system and Carcross is implementing a similar traditional structure.

10 Indian Affairs records are replete with debates over chiefs, councillors, and band administrators. On the Liard band, see Indian Affairs, file N10001–1/0, vol. 4, passim.

11 Indian Affairs, file 801/1–1, vol. 2, Chapman to regional director, 14 April 1972.

12 Indian Affairs, file 801/1–1, vol. 2, Ciaccia to Smith, 23 May 1972; ibid., vol. 1, Jones to deputy minister, 21 April 1961.

13 Indian Affairs, file 801/1–2, vol. 1, superintendent to Indian commissioner, 7 February 1967.

14 Indian Affairs, file 801/1–1, vol. 1, Meek to Indian Affairs, 20 April 1954.

15 Meek, "Report on the Yukon Indian Agency," 52.

16 Indian Affairs, file 801/1–1, vol. 2, Smith to Chrétien, 11 April 1972.

17 Indian Affairs, file 801/30–0–1, vol. 1, Meeting to Discuss the Welfare of Yukon Indians, 29 December 1958.

18 Indian Affairs, file 801/30–0–1, vol. 1, Jones to Nielsen, 24 July 1958.

19 Indian Affairs, file 801/30–0–1, vol. 1, Brown to J.H. Gordon, 9 June 1954.

20 Indian Affairs, file 801/30–0–1, vol. 1, Jones to deputy minister, 29 June 1955.

21 The issue of land rights was discussed within the civil service. See Indian Affairs, file 801/30–0–1, vol. 1, Land Entitlement of Indians of the Yukon and Northwest Territories.

22 Indian Affairs, file 801/30–0–1, vol. 2, 1962 acreage estimate.

23 Indian Affairs, file 801/30–0–1, vol. 1, Jones to deputy minister, 29 June 1955.

24 Indian Affairs, file 801/30–0–1, vol. 1, Quarterly Report, 1 July–Sept. 1955, M.G. Jutras. See also, ibid., Fortier to acting minister, 27 November 1957.

25 *Whitehorse Star*, 9 October 1958, 2; ibid., 12 March 1959, 4.

26 Indian Affairs, file 801/30–0–1, vol. 2, director to Jones, 26 March 1962.
27 Indian Affairs, file 801/30–0–1, vol. 3, Carter to Battle, 9 September 1965.
28 As of 1971 there were forty-one parcels of land set aside by notations on territorial land records and another twenty established by Order in Council. Indian Affairs, file 801/30–0–1, vol. 3, Vergette to chief, Admin. Div., 8 January 1971.
29 Indian Affairs, file 801/30–0–1, McGilp to Leaux, 29 August 1972.
30 Indian Affairs, file 801/30–0–1, Jones to deputy minister, 29 June 1955.
31 Indian Affairs, file 801/30–0–1, Jones to Nielsen, 24 July 1958.
32 Indian Affairs, file 801/30–0–1, vol. 1, Meeting to Discuss the Welfare of Yukon Indians, 29 December 1958.
33 Indian Affairs, file 801/30–0–1, vol. 2, Grant to A/Indian commissioner for BC, 31 May 1961.
34 Indian Affairs, file 801/30–0–1, vol. 3, R.G. Young to director of operations, 25 November 1968. Land for settlement of Treaty No. 8 in northern British Columbia came out of lands held by Ottawa as part of the Peace River block.
35 Indian Affairs, file 801/30–0–1, vol. 3, H.T. Vergetter to head, Land, Surveys and Titles Section, 28 June 1967.
36 YTA, series 10, vol. 146, file 6, A.B. Yates to J. Smith, 27 February 1970.
37 YTA, series 10, vol. 146, file 6, Chief Charles Abel to Commissioner Smith, 3 November 1970.
38 Indian Affairs, file 10/148/3, Band Council Resolution, 25 October 1971.
39 YTA, series 10, vol. 146, file 6, H. Fischer to director, Territorial Relations Branch, 16 November 1970.
40 YTA, series 10, vol. 146, file 6, David Miles, Chevron-Standard, to A.J. Reeve, 7 January 1971.
41 *Whitehorse Star*, 27 January 1966.
42 *Whitehorse Star*, 3 February 1966, 11.
43 *Whitehorse Star*, 23 June 1966, 13.
44 The Indians might well have wondered if Chrétien was listening, for the following year his White Paper called for the elimination of special status for Native people and the closure of the DIA. This issue, which provoked massive protests and anguished cries of frustration from Native groups, galvanized Indians across the country into action. See Weaver, *The Making of Canadian Indian Policy*. For the Yukon reaction, see *Whitehorse Star*, 26 June 1969, 1–2.
45 *Whitehorse Star*, 24 October 1968, 10.
46 *Whitehorse Star*, 24 October 1968, 16.
47 Indian Affairs, file 801/19–4, vol. 4, Briefing Material on the Yukon Region, 10 April 1973.

48 For an excellent statement on the YNB's agenda, see Indian Affairs, file 801/25–1, vol. 6, Brief presented to the Special Senate Committee on Poverty, by the YNB, 23 July 1970.

49 Indian Affairs, file 801/29–2, vol. 7, Raymond Obomsawin, "Where Grows Hopelessness: A Crisis in Housing," c. 1974.

50 Indian Affairs, file 801/43–1, vol. 2, Gryba to churchman, 2 March 1971.

51 Indian Affairs, file 801/19–4, vol. 4, Yukon Paper – Summary, c. 1972.

52 The following discussion of post-1973 developments is drawn from Coates and Powell, *The Modern North*.

53 For a statement of conservative philosophy on Native affairs, see Nielsen, *The House Is Not a Home*.

CONCLUSION

1 On the Yukon Natives generally, see Catherine McClellan, *et al.*, *Part of the Land, Part of the Water*.

2 Bishop, *The Northern Ojibway*, especially chapters 3–5.

3 Brody, *Maps and Dreams*.

4 Waldram, *As Long As the Rivers Run*.

5 This theme, for many different cultural groups, is developed in June Helm, ed., *Handbook of North American Indians*, vol. 6: *The Subarctic*.

6 See Milloy, *Plains Cree*, and Elias, *The Dakota of the Canadian Northwest*.

7 Barron, "Indian Agents."

8 On the question of the Native response to education, see Barman *et al.*, eds., *Indian Education in Canada*, vol. 1: *The Legacy*. On missionaries, see Grant, *The Moon of Wintertime*.

9 Bishop, *The Northern Ojibway*, 84–87.

10 The Indians of the upper Liard technically came under Treaty eleven. The Yukon Natives did not, however, sign the treaty and received few benefits from it. Fumoleau, *As Long As This Land Shall Last*; Coates and Morrison, *Treaty 11*.

11 This comparison is particularly telling because of the striking similarities between conditions in the Yukon Territory and Australia. See Powell, *Far Country*.

12 Two of the more interesting examinations of this global phenomenon are Crosby, *Ecological Imperialism*, and Bodley, *Victims of Progress*.

13 Indian Affairs, file 801/43–1, vols. 1 and 2, A. Kroeger to James Smith, 23 October 1975.

14 These issues are addressed in Coates and Powell, *The Modern North*.

Bibliography

ARCHIVAL SOURCES

ARCHIVES OF THE ECCLESIASTICAL PROVINCE OF RUPERTSLAND
(PROVINCIAL ARCHIVES OF MANITOBA, WINNIPEG, MAN.)
Kirkby Journal, C. Whittaker Collection, Robert McDonald Collection

GENERAL SYNOD ARCHIVES, ANGLICAN CHURCH OF CANADA
(TORONTO, ONT.)
M56–2, Series C–23, T.H. Canham Papers
M56-4, Series E–7, Cody Papers
M68–1, Lucy Papers
M75–103, Missionary Society of the Church of England in Canada Records
M74–5, 1–A–1, Stringer Papers
M74–4, C. Whittaker Papers

GOVERNMENT OF YUKON, ACTIVE FILES
(WHITEHORSE, YUKON TERRITORY)
Vital Statistics Branch Records

HUDSON'S BAY COMPANY ARCHIVES
(PROVINCIAL ARCHIVES OF MANITOBA, WINNIPEG, MAN.)
E.37, James Anderson Papers
D.19/1–27, Commissioner's Inward Correspondence
D.13/1–21, Commissioner's Outward Correspondence
B.200/d, Fort Simpson Accounts
B.200/b/5–44, Fort Simpson Correspondence
B.240/d/1–13, Fort Youcon Accounts
B.114/d/1–19, La Pierre House Accounts
A.6/23–92, London Committee's Outward Correspondence

E.38, James McDougall Papers

B.173/d/1–15, Rampart House Accounts

D.5/3–52, Governor Simpson's Inward Correspondence

D.1–17–19, Governor Simpson's Outward Correspondence and Official Reports to the London Committee

D.12/1–21, Donald A. Smith's Inward Correspondence

D.11/1–18, Donald A. Smith's Outward Correspondence

B.356/e, Teslin Post Journals

INDIAN AFFAIRS AND NORTHERN DEVELOPMENT, ACTIVE FILES (HULL, QUE.)

Yukon Indian Agency records (These documents will eventually be transferred to the National Archives.)

INDIAN AFFAIRS AND NORTHERN DEVELOPMENT, ACTIVE FILES (WHITEHORSE, YUKON TERRITORY)

Yukon Indian Agency Records (These documents, kindly made available by departmental officials in Whitehorse, were examined in the Yukon. They have since been transferred to Ottawa and are destined for the National Archives.)

NATIONAL ARCHIVES OF CANADA (OTTAWA, ONT.)

MG30 E2, N.A.D. Armstrong Papers

MG29 C92, R.J. Bowen Papers

MG30 D39, L.J. Burpee Papers

MG17 B2, Church Missionary Society Papers

MG30 E55, C. Constantine Papers

RG10, Indian Affairs Records

RG22, Indian and Northern Affairs Records

MG29 A11, R. MacFarlane Papers

RG126, Mackenzie Valley Pipeline Inquiry Records

RG85, Northern Administration Branch Records

MG19 A25, Pelly Banks and Fort Selkirk Journals

MG19 D13, Pelly Banks and Fort Selkirk Journals

RG18, Royal Canadian Mounted Police Records

RG36/7, Special Commissioner on Defence Projects in the Canadian Northwest Records

RG91, Yukon Territorial Government Records

NATIONAL MUSEUM OF CIVILIZATION (HULL, QUE.), ETHNOLOGY ARCHIVES, DAVID BLACKJACK COLLECTION (USED WITH PERMISSION OF D. LEGROS)

Poole Field Letters

SMITHSONIAN INSTITUTION ARCHIVES (WASHINGTON, DC)
Record Unit 7215, Kennicott Collection, Collected Notes, Lists, and Catalogue
  on Birds, 1839, 1849–51, 1855–1965, Box 13, Kennicott #8. Copies in possession of Greg Thomas, Parks Canada, Winnipeg, Man.

YUKON DIOCESE, ANGLICAN CHURCH OF CANADA (WHITEHORSE,
YUKON TERRITORY)
Materials in the Office of the Bishop

YUKON TERRITORIAL ARCHIVES (WHITEHORSE, YUKON TERRITORY)
Anglican Church Records
Dan Cadzow Papers
AC #82/188, Connolly Family Papers
W. Dempster Papers
AC #82/176, Flewelling Family Collection
AC #82/415, Frank Foster Papers
AC #77/8, Ida May Meek Goulter Papers
Phelps Family Papers
St Mary's Hospital Records
Teslin Band Collection
YRG1, Series 1–8, Yukon Territorial Government Records

PRINTED PRIMARY SOURCES

Adney, Tappan. "The Indian Hunter of the Far Northwest: On the Trail to
  the Klondike." *Outing*, vol. 39, no. 6 (1907), 623–33.
– *The Klondike Stampede of 1897–98*. New York: Harper 1899.
– "Moose Hunting with the Tro-chu-tin." *Harper's New Monthly Magazine*, vol.
  100 (1900), 495–507.
Archer, A.S. *A Heroine of the North: Memoirs of Charlotte Selina Bompas*. London:
  Macmillan 1929.
Armstrong, N.A.D. *After Big Game in the Upper Yukon*. London: John Long
  1937.
Auer, Harry. *Camp Fires in the Yukon*. Cincinnati: Stewart and Kidd 1917 [*c*.
  1916].
Baltzell, Dent. *The Alcan Journal*. New York: Rockford Press 1967.
Berton, Laura. *I Married the Klondike*. Boston: Little, Brown 1954.
Bond, James H. *From Out of the Yukon*. Portland: Binfords and Mort 1948.
Bostock, H.S. "Yukon Territory: Selected Field Reports of the Geological Sur-
  vey of Canada, 1898–1933." *Geological Survey of Canada, Memoir 284*. Ottawa:
  Queen's Printer 1957.
Bovet, L.A. *Moose Hunting in Alaska, Wyoming and Yukon Territory*. Philadel-
  phia *c*. 1933.

Cadzow, D. "Habitat of Loucheux Bands." *Indian Notes*, vol. 2, no. 3 (1925), 172–7.

Campbell, Robert. *Two Journals of Robert Campbell, 1808–1853*. Seattle: John W. Todd, Jr 1951.

Canada, Auditor General. *Annual Reports*, 1897–1930. Ottawa: 1898–1931.

Canada. *Census of Canada* 1901, 1911, 1921, 1931, 1941, 1951. Ottawa: 1902–52.

Canada, Department of the Interior. *The Yukon Territory: Its History and Resources*. Ottawa: Department of the Interior 1907. Revised and republished, 1909, 1916.

Canada. Indian Affairs Branch. *Annual Reports*, 1896–1955. Ottawa: 1897–1956.

Canada. North West Mounted Police. *Annual Reports*, 1890–1903. Ottawa: 1891–1904.

Canada. Parliament. House of Commons. *Debates*, 1896–1950.

Canada. Royal Canadian Mounted Police. *Annual Reports*, 1920–50. Ottawa 1921–51.

Canada. Royal North-West Mounted Police. *Annual Reports*, 1904–19. Ottawa: 1905–20.

Canada. Vital Statistics Branch. *Annual Reports*, 1928–51. Ottawa: 1929–1952.

Church of England in Canada. *Chouttla Indian Residential School*. Missionary Society, Indian Residential School Commission, n.d.

Coe, Douglas. *Road to Alaska: The Story of the Alaska Highway*. New York: J. Messner 1943.

Congdon, F.T. "Fur Bearing Animals in Canada, and How to Prevent Their Extinction." *First Annual Report of the Commission on Conservation*, 1910.

Constantine, C.P. *I Was a Mountie*. New York: Exposition Press 1958.

Dall, W.H. *Alaska and Its Resources*. Boston: Lee and Shepard 1870.

– "On the Distribution and Nomenclature of the Native Tribes of Alaska and the Adjacent Territory," in *Contributions to North American Ethnology*, vol. 1, 7–40. Washington: Government Printing Office 1877.

– "Reminiscence of Yukon Exploration, 1865–1868." *Popular Science Monthly*, vol. 69, no. 9 (1906).

Davidson, George. "Explanation of an Indian Map of the Rivers, Lakes, Trails and Mountains of the Chilkat to the Yukon Drawn by the Chilkat Chief, Kohklux, in 1869." *Mazama* (April 1901), 75–82.

Dawson, George. "Notes on the Indian Tribes of the Yukon District." *Annual Report of the Geological Survey, 1887*. Montreal: Government Printing Office 1888.

– *Report on an Exploration in the Yukon District, N.W.T. and Adjacent Northern Portion of British Columbia, 1887*. Ottawa: Queen's Printer 1898.

Ebbutt, F. "The Gravel River Indians." *Canadian Geographical Journal*, vol. 2, no. 4 (1931).

Field, Poole. "The Poole Field Letters," ed. June Helm MacNeish. *Anthropologica*, vol. 4 (1957), 47–60.

Finnie, Richard. *Canol*. San Francisco: Taylor and Taylor 1945.

Franklin, John. *Thirty Years in the Arctic Regions: or the Adventures of Sir John Franklin*. New York: H. Dayton 1859.

Glave, E.J. "The Alaska Expedition." *Frank Leslie's Illustrated Weekly Newspaper*, 28 June, 12 July, 19 July, 9 August, 16 August, 6 September, 15 November, 22 November, 29 November, 6 December, 13 December, 20 December, 27 December 1890; 3 January, 10 January 1891.

Graham, Angus. *The Golden Grindstone: The Adventures of George M. Mitchell*. London: Chatto & Windus 1935.

Harbottle, Jeanne and Fern Credeur. *Woman in the Bush*. Pelican 1966.

Hardisty, William. "The Loucheux Indians." *Smithsonian Institution Annual Report, 1866*, Washington, DC, 311–20.

Honigmann, J.J. "On the Alaska Highway." *Dalhousie Review*, vol. 23 (April 1943–Jan. 1944), 400–8.

– "Tribal Epidemics in the Yukon: Comment." *Journal of the American Medical Association*, vol. 124 (1944), 386.

Hunter, Farley. *Frances Lake, Yukon*. Fleshing: Marion Press 1924.

Inman, Henry. *Buffalo Jones' Forty Years of Adventure*. London: Crane and Company 1899.

Isbister, A. "Some Account of the Peel River, N. America." *Journal of the Royal Geographical Society*, vol. 15 (1845), 332–45.

James, James Alton. *The First Scientific Exploration of Russian America and the Purchase of Alaska*. Evanston and Chicago: Northwestern University 1942.

Jones, Strachan. "The Kutchin Tribes." *Smithsonian Institution Annual Report, 1866*, Washington, DC, 303–10.

Keele, Joseph. "Reconnaissance across the Mackenzie Mountains on the Pelly, Ross and Gravel Rivers, 1907–08," in H.S. Bostock, ed., *Yukon Territory: Selected Field Reports of the Geological Survey of Canada, 1898 to 1933*. Ottawa: Queen's Printer, 1957, 283–314.

Kirkby, W.W. "The Indians of the Youcon," in H.Y. Hind, *Explorations in the Interior of the Labrador Peninsula: The Country of the Montagnais and Nasquapee Indians*. London: Longmans, Roberts and Green 1863, 254–75.

– "A Journey to the Youcon, Russian America." *Smithsonian Institution, Annual Report, 1864*, Washington, DC, 416–20.

Lynch, J. *Three Years in the Klondike*. Chicago: Lakeside Press 1967.

McAdam, Ebenezer. *From Duck Lake to Dawson City: The Diary of Eben McAdam's Journey to the Klondike, 1898–1899*. Saskatoon: Western Producer Prairie Books 1977.

McConnell, R.G. "Report on an Exploration in the Yukon and Mackenzie Basins, N.W.T.," Geological Survey of Canada, *Annual Report, Vol. 4, 1888–1889*. Montreal: William Foster Brown & Co. 1890.

MacDonald, Malcolm. *Down North*. Toronto: Oxford University Press 1943.

McQuesten, Leroy. "Recollections of Leroy McQuesten," YTA Pamphlet 1952–3.

Marchand, J.F. "Tribal Epidemics in the Yukon." *Journal of the American Medical Association*, vol. 123 (1943), 1019–20.

Martindale, Thomas. *Hunting in the Upper Yukon*. Philadelphia: G.W. Jacobs and Co. 1913.

Mason, W. *The Frozen Northland*. Cincinnati: Jennings and Graham 1910.

Menzies, Don. *The Alaska Highway*. Stuart Douglas 1943.

Michael, Henry, ed. *Lieutenant Zagoskin's Travels in Russian America, 1842–1844: The First Ethnographic and Geographic Investigations on the Yukon and Kuskkwim Valleys of Alaska*. Toronto: University of Toronto Press 1967.

Murray, A.H. *Journal of the Yukon, 1847–1848*, ed. L.J. Burpee. Ottawa: Government Printing Bureau 1910.

Ogilvie, William. *Early Days on the Yukon and the Story of Its Gold Finds*. Ottawa: Thorburn and Abbott 1913.

– *Exploratory Survey of Part of the Lewes, Tat-on-duc, Porcupine, Bell, Trout, Peel and Mackenzie Rivers*. Ottawa: Queen's Printer 1890.

– *Information Respecting the Yukon District from the Reports of William Ogilvie, Dominion Land Surveyor and from Other Sources*. Ottawa: Department of the Interior 1897.

– *Klondike Official Guide*. Toronto: Hunter, Rose 1898.

Pike, Warburton. *Through the Sub-Arctic Forest*. London: Edward Arnold 1896.

Riggs, Thomas. "Running the Alaska Boundary." *Beaver*, outfit 276 (1945), 40–3.

Schwatka, F. "The Great River of Alaska: Exploring the Upper Yukon," *Century Magazine*, vol. XXX (October 1885), 819–29.

– *Report of a Military Reconnaissance in Alaska Made in 1883*. Washington: Government Printing Office 1885.

– *A Summer in Alaska*. St. Louis: J.W. Henry 1893.

Selous, F.C. *Recent Hunting Trips in British North America*. London: Witherby 1909.

Service, Robert. "The Squaw-Man," in *Rhymes of a Rolling Stone*. Toronto: Ryerson 1929.

Sheldon, Charles. *The Wilderness of the Upper Yukon*. New York: Scribner & Sons 1911.

Simpson, Alexander. *The Life and Travels of Thomas Simpson, the Arctic Discoverer, by His Brother*. Toronto: Baxter Publishing Company 1963.

Sola, A.E.I. *Klondyke Truth and Facts About the New El Dorado*. London: Mining and Geog. Inst. 1897.

Stuck, Hudson. *Voyages on the Yukon and Its Tributaries*. New York: Scribner & Sons 1917.

Swanson, Cecil. *The Days of My Sojourning: A Reminiscence*. Calgary: Glenbow-Alberta Institute 1977.

Taylor, Sarah. "Toot! Toot!," YTA Pamphlet 1926–2.

Tollemache, Stratford. *Reminiscences of the Yukon*. Toronto: W. Briggs 1912.

Turner, J.H. "The Boundary North of Fort Youcon," pt. III of "The Alaska Boundary Survey," *The National Geographic*, vol. 4 (February 1893), 189–97.

United States Government. *Compilation of Narratives of Explorations in Alaska*. Washington: Government Printing Office 1900.

Walden, Arthur. *A Dog Puncher on the Yukon*. Boston: Houghton Mifflin Company 1931.

Wesbrook, Mary E. "A Venture into Ethnohistory: The Journals of Rev. V.C. Sim, Pioneer Missionary on the Yukon." *Polar Notes*, no. 9 (1969), 34–45.

Whittaker, Charles. *Arctic Eskimo: A Record of Fifty Years' Experience and Observation Among the Eskimo*. London: Seeley Service 1937.

Whymper, Frederick. "Russian America or 'Alaska'; The Natives of the Yukon River and Adjacent Country." *Transactions of the Ethnological Society of London*, vol. 7 (1869).

– *Travel and Adventure in the Territory of Alaska*. Ann Arbor: University Microfilms 1966.

Wilson, Amy. *No Man Stands Alone*. Sidney: Gray's Publishing 1965.

Yukon Native Brotherhood. *Together Today for Our Children Tomorrow*. Whitehorse: YNB 1973.

Yukon Territorial Government. *Journals of the Council of the Yukon Territory*, 1903–07.

SECONDARY SOURCES

Abel, K.M. "The Drum and the Cross: An Ethnohistorical Study of Mission Work among the Dene, 1858–1902." PH.D. thesis, Queen's University 1984.

– "The South Nahanni River Region, N.W.T., 1820–1972: Patterns of Socio-Economic Transition in the Canadian North." M.A. thesis, University of Winnipeg 1981.

Acheson, A.W. "Nomads in Town: The Kutchin of Old Crow, Yukon Territory." PH.D. thesis, Cornell University 1977.

Adams, David W. "Schooling the Hopi: Federal Indian Policy Writ Small, 1887–1917." *Pacific Historical Review*, vol. 48, no. 3 (1979), 335–56.

Adams, Howard. *Prison of Grass: Canada from the Native Point of View*. Toronto: New Press 1975.

Albach, P.G. and G.P. Kelly, eds. *Education and Colonialism*. New York: Longman 1978.

Andrews, Isabel. "The Crooked Lake Reserves: A Study of Indian Policy in Practise from the Qu'Appelle Treaty to 1900." M.A. thesis, University of Saskatchewan 1972.

Armstrong, F.B. and A.M. Edwards. "Intracranial Tuberculoma in Native Races of Canada: With Special Reference to Symptomatic Epilepsy and

Neurological Features." *Canadian Medical Association Journal* 89 (1963): 56–65.

Armstrong, Terence. *Russian Settlement in the North*. Cambridge: Cambridge University Press 1965.

Asch, Michael. "Capital and Economic Development: A Critical Appraisal of the Recommendations of the Mackenzie Valley Pipeline Commission." *Culture*, vol. 2, no. 3 (1982), 3–9.

– "The Ecological-Evolutionary Model and the Concept of the Mode of Production," in D. Turner and G. Smith, eds. *Challenging Anthropology*. Toronto: McGraw-Hill Ryerson 1979, 81–99.

– "The Economics of Dene Self-Determination," in D. Turner and G. Smith, eds. *Challenging Anthropology*. Toronto: McGraw-Hill Ryerson 1979, 339–52.

– "Some Effects of the Late Nineteenth Century Modernization of the Fur Trade on the Economy of the Slavey Indians." *Western Canadian Journal of Anthropology*, vol. 6, no. 4 (1976), 7–15.

– "Steps Toward the Analysis of Athapaskan Social Organization." *Arctic Anthropology*, vol. 17, no. 2 (1980), 46–51.

Ashburn, P.M. *The Ranks of Death: A Medical History of the Conquest of America*. New York: Coward-McCann 1947.

Axtell, James. "Ethnohistory: An Historian's Viewpoint." *Ethnohistory* 26/1 (Winter 1979), 1–14.

– "The Ethnohistory of Early America: A Review Essay." *William and Mary Quarterly*. 3rd series, vol. 35, no. 1 (January 1978), 110–44.

– *The European and the Indian: Essays in the Ethnohistory of Colonial North America*. New York: Oxford University Press 1981.

– *The Invasion Within: The Contest of Cultures in Colonial North America*. New York: Oxford University Press 1985.

– "The White Indians of Colonial America." *William and Mary Quarterly*, vol. 32, no. 1 (January 1975), 55–88.

Bailey, Alfred. *The Conflict of European and Eastern Algonkian Cultures, 1504–1970*. 2nd edition. Toronto: University of Toronto Press 1969.

Bales, R.F. "Cultural Differences in Rates of Alcoholism." *Quarterly Journal of Studies on Alcohol*, vol. 6, no. 4 (1946), 480–99.

Balikci, A. *Vunta Kutchin Social Change: A Study of the People of Old Crow, Yukon Territory*. Ottawa: Northern Co-ordination and Research Centre, Department of Northern Affairs and Natural Resources 1963.

Ball, Victoria. "A History of Wildlife Management in British Columbia." M.A. thesis, University of Victoria 1981.

Barman, J., Y. Hebért, and D. McCaskill, eds. *Indian Education in Canada*. 2 vols. Vancouver: University of British Columbia Press 1986–87.

Barron, F.L. "Indian Agents and the North-West Rebellion," in F. Barron and J. Waldram, eds. *1885 and After*. Regina: Canadian Plains Research Centre 1987.

Bennett, Gordon. *Yukon Transportation: A History*. Canadian Historic Sites: Occasional Papers in Archaeology and History, no. 19. Ottawa: National Historic Parks and Sites Branch, Parks Canada 1978.

Berger, Thomas. *Northern Frontier, Northern Homeland: The Report of the Mackenzie Valley Pipeline Inquiry*. 2 vols. Ottawa: Supply and Services 1977.

Berkhofer, Robert, Jr. "The Political Context of a New Indian History." *Pacific Historical Review*, vol. 40 (1971), 357–82.

– "Protestants, Pagans and Sequences Among the North American Indians, 1760–1860." *Ethnohistory*, vol. 10 (1963), 201–32.

– *Salvation and the Savage: An Analysis of Protestant Missions and American Indian Response, 1787–1862*. Lexington: University of Kentucky Press 1965.

– *The White Man's Indian: Images of the American Indian from Columbus to the Present*. New York: Knopf 1978.

Berton, Pierre. *Klondike: The Last Great Gold Rush, 1896–1899*. Revised edition. Toronto: McClelland and Stewart 1972.

Best, C.T. "Biography of Robert McDonald." Unpublished Archives of the Ecclesiastical Province of Newfoundland (PAM), no. 4001, box J.

Betke, Carl. "Pioneers and Police on the Canadian Prairies, 1885–1914." Canadian Historical Association, *Historical Papers*, 1980, 9–32.

Bishop, Charles A. "Archival Sources and the Culture History of the Indians of the Eastern Subarctic." *Canadian Review of Sociology and Anthropology*, vol. 12, no. 3 (1975), 244–51.

– *The Northern Ojibwa and the Fur Trade: An Historical and Ecological Study*. Toronto: Holt, Rinehart and Winston 1974.

– and A.J. Ray. "Ethnohistoric Research in the Central Subarctic: Some Conceptual and Methodological Problems." *Western Canadian Journal of Anthropology*, vol. 6, no. 1 (1976), 116–44.

Bockstoce, John. *Steam Whaling in the Western Arctic*. New Bedford: Old Dartmouth Historical Society 1977.

Bodley, John. *Victims of Progress*, 2nd edition. Don Mills: Benjamin/Cummings 1982.

Boon, T.C.B. *The Anglican Church from the Bay to the Rockies*. Toronto: Ryerson Press 1962.

– "William West Kirkby, First Anglican Missionary to the Loucheux." *Beaver*, outfit 295 (Spring 1965), 36–43.

Borah, W. and S. Cook. *The Aboriginal Population of Central Mexico on the Eve of Spanish Conquest*. Berkeley: University of California Press 1983.

Bovey, John. "The Attitudes and Policies of the Federal Government Towards Canada's Northern Territories, 1870–1930." M.A. thesis, University of British Columbia 1967.

Bowden, Henry. *American Indians and Christian Missions: Studies in Cultural Conflict*. Chicago: University of Chicago Press 1981.

Bowes, R.P. *The Indian: Assimilation, Integration or Separation?* Scarborough: Prentice-Hall 1972.

Boyd, R. "Another Look at the 'Fever and Ague' of Western Oregon." *Ethnohistory*, vol. 22, no. 2 (1975), 135–54.

Breynat, Gabriel. *Flying Bishop: Fifty Years in the Canadian Far North.* London: Burns and Oates 1953.

Brody, Hugh. *Maps and Dreams: Indians and the British Columbia Frontier.* Vancouver: Douglas and McIntyre 1981.

Brown, Jennifer. *Strangers in Blood: Fur Trade Company Families in Indian Country.* Vancouver: University of British Columbia Press 1980.

Bryce, Peter. *The Story of a National Crime: Being an Appeal for Justice to the Indians of Canada.* Ottawa: James Hope 1922.

Buckley, Arthur. "The Alaska Highway." M.Sc. thesis, University of Alabama 1956.

Buikstra, Jane, ed. *Pre-Historic Tuberculosis in the Americas.* Northwestern University Archaeological Program, Science Papers, no. 6. Northwestern University 1981.

Bullen, Edward. "An Historical Study of the Education of the Indians of Teslin, Yukon Territory." M.Ed. thesis, University of Alberta 1968.

Bush, E. "Policing the Border in the Klondike Gold Rush." *Canadian Geographic*, vol. 100, no. 5 (1980), 70–3.

Cairns, H.A.C. *The Clash of Cultures: Early Race Relations in Central Africa.* New York: Praeger 1965.

Cardinal, Harold. *The Rebirth of Canada's Indians.* Edmonton: Hurtig 1976.

– *The Unjust Society: The Tragedy of Canada's Indians.* Edmonton: Hurtig 1969.

Careless, J.M.S. "Limited Identities in Canada." *Canadian Historical Review*, vol. 50, no. 1 (March 1969), 1–10.

– "Limited Identities–Ten Years Later." *Manitoba History*, no. 1 (1981), 3–9.

Carnoy, M. *Education as Cultural Imperialism.* New York: David McKay 1974.

Chamberlain, A.F. "New Religions among the North American Indians." *Journal of Religious Psychology*, vol. 6 (1913), 1–49.

Chamberlin, J.E. *The Harrowing of Eden: White Attitudes Toward Native Americans.* New York: Seabury Press 1975.

Chevigny, Hector. *Russian America: The Great Alaskan Venture, 1741–1867.* New York: Viking Press 1965.

Church of England in Canada. *Chouttla Indian School.* Missionary Society, Indian Residential School Commission, n.d..

Clark, S.D. *The Developing Canadian Community.* Toronto: University of Toronto Press 1962.

Clarke, Ian. "Clifford Sifton in Relation to His Times." Unpublished paper presented to the Canadian Historical Association, Montreal 1980.

Clendinnen, I. "Landscape and World View: The Survival of Yucatec Maya Culture under Spanish Conquest." *Comparative Studies in Society and History*, vol. 22 (1980), 374–93.

Coates, Ken. "The Alaska Highway and the Indians of the Southern Yukon, 1942–50: A Study of Native Adaptation to Northern Development," in Ken Coates, ed., *The Alaska Highway: Papers of the 40th Anniversary Symposium.* Vancouver: University of British Columbia Press 1985.

–, ed. *The Alaska Highway: Papers of the 40th Anniversary Conference.* Vancouver: University of British Columbia Press 1985.

– "Asking for All Sorts of Favour: The Anglican Church and the Indians of the Yukon Territory, 1860 to 1911," in B. Ferguson, ed. *The Anglican Church in Western Canadian History.* Regina: CPRC, forthcoming.

– "Best Left as Indians: The Federal Government and the Indians of the Yukon, 1894–1950." *Canadian Journal of Native Studies,* vol. 4, no. 2 (1984), 179–204.

– "Betwixt and Between: The Anglican Church and the Children of the Carcross (Chouttla) Residential School, 1910–1955." *BC Studies,* no. 64 (Winter 1984–85), 27–47.

– *Canada's Colonies: A History of the Yukon and Northwest Territories.* Toronto: James Lorimer 1985.

– "Controlling the Periphery: A Comparison of the Territorial Administrations of Alaska and the Yukon Territory." *Pacific Northwest Quarterly,* vol. 78, no. 4 (October 1987), 145–51.

– "The Federal Government and the Economic System of the Yukon Territory: Historical and Contemporary Aspects of Northern Development," in K. Coates and W.R. Morrison, eds. *For Purposes of Dominion: Essays in Honour of Morris Zaslow.* Toronto: Captus Press 1989.

– "Furs Along the Yukon: Hudson's Bay Company–Native Trade in the Yukon River Basin, 1840–1893." *BC Studies,* no. 55 (Autumn 1982), 50–78.

– "Furs Along the Yukon: Native-Hudson's Bay Company Trade, 1830–1893." M.A. thesis, University of British Columbia 1980.

– "Mixed Blessings." *Horizons Canada,* 70, 1670–5.

– "Northern Society in Transition: Efforts to Assimilate Canada's Northern Native People." *Englisch-Amerikanische Studien, 1990.*

– *The Northern Yukon: A History.* Manuscript Report no. 209. Winnipeg: Parks Canada 1979.

– "The Northern Yukon: A History." Manuscript Record Series no. 403, Parks Canada 1979.

– "On the Outside in Their Homeland: Native People and the Evolution of the Yukon Economy." *The Northern Review,* no. 1 (Summer 1988), 73–89.

– "Send Only Those Who Rise a Peg: Anglican Clergy in the Yukon, 1858–1932." *Journal of the Canadian Church Historical Society,* vol. 28, no. 1 (1986), 3–18.

– "Sinews of Their Lives: Aboriginal Resource Use and Government Regulation in the Yukon, 1894–1950: in K. Abel and J. Friesen, eds. *Aboriginal Resource Use: Historial and Legal Aspects.* Forthcoming.

– "Upsetting the Rhythms: The Federal Government and Native Communities in the Yukon Territory, 1945 to 1973," in G. Dacks and K. Coates, eds. *Northern Communities: The Prospects for Empowerment*. Edmonton: Boreal Institute for Northern Studies, 1988, 11–22.

– "A Very Imperfect Means of Education: Indian Day Schools in the Yukon," in J. Barman, Y. Hebert, and D. McCaskill, eds. *Indian Education in Canada*, vol. 1. Vancouver: University of British Columbia Press 1986–87, 132–49.

Coates, Ken and Judith Powell. *The Modern North: People, Politics and the Rejection of Colonialism*. Toronto: James Lorimer 1989.

– "Whitehorse and the Building of the Alaska Highway." *Alaska History* (Summer 1989).

Coates, Ken and W.R. Morrison. *The Army of Occupation: Americans in the Canadian Northwest, 1942–1946*. Forthcoming.

–, eds. *Interpreting the Canadian North: Selected Readings*. Toronto: Copp Clark Pitman 1989.

– *Land of the Midnight Sun: A History of the Yukon Territory*. Edmonton: Hurtig 1988.

– "More Than a Matter of Blood: The Government, the Churches and the Mixed Blood People of the Yukon and Mackenzie River Valley, 1870–1950," in F.L. Barron and J. Waldram, eds., *1885 and After*. Regina: CPRC 1986, 253–73.

– "Northern Visions: Recent Historical Writing on the Canadian North." *Manitoba History* 10 (1985): 2–9.

–, eds. *For Purposes of Dominion: Essays in Honour of Morris Zaslow*. Toronto: Captus Press 1989.

– *The Sinking of the Princess Sophia: Taking the North Down with Her*. Toronto: Oxford University Press 1990.

– "Transiency in the Far Northwest after the Gold Rush: The Sinking of the *Princess Sophia*," in K. Coates and W.R. Morrison, eds. *Interpreting the Canadian North: Selected Readings* Toronto: Copp Clark Pitman 1989, 185–98.

– *Treaty Eleven*. Ottawa: Treaties and Historical Research Centre 1987.

– *Treaty Five*. Ottawa: Treaties and Historical Research Centre 1987.

– *Treaty Ten*. Ottawa: Treaties and Historical Research Centre 1987.

– *Working the North: Labour and the Northwest Defence Projects, 1942–1946*. Forthcoming.

Cody, H.A. *An Apostle of the North: Memoirs of the Right Reverend William Carpenter Bompas, D.D.*. New York: E.P. Dutton and Company 1908.

Conkling, Robert. "Legitimacy and Conversion in Social Change: The Case of French Missionaries and the Northeastern Algonkian." *Ethnohistory*, vol. 21/1 (1974), 1–24.

Cooke, Alan and Clive Holland. *The Exploration of Northern Canada, 500 to 1920: A Chronology*. Toronto: Arctic History Press 1978.

Crosby, Alfred. *The Columbian Exchange: Biological and Cultural Consequences of 1492*. Westport: Greenwood Press 1977.

Crosby, Alfred. *Ecological Imperialism: The Biological Expansion of Europe, 900–1900*. New York: Cambridge University Press 1986.

– "Virgin Soil Epidemics as a Factor in the Aboriginal Depopulation: America." *William and Mary Quarterly*, 3rd series, vol. 33 (April 1976), 289–99.

Crowe, Keith. *A History of the Original Peoples of Northern Canada*. Montreal: Arctic Institute of North America, McGill-Queen's University Press 1974.

Cruikshank, Julie. *Athapaskan Women: Lives and Legends*. Mercury Series, Canadian Ethnology Service, Papers no. 57. Ottawa: National Museums of Canada 1979.

– "Becoming a Woman in Athapaskan Society: Changing Traditions on the Upper Yukon River." *Western Canadian Journal of Anthropology*, vol. 5, no. 2 (1975), 1–14.

– *Early Yukon Cultures*. Whitehorse: Yukon Government, Department of Education 1975.

– "Legend and Landscape: Convergence of Oral and Scientific Traditions in the Yukon Territory." *Arctic Anthropology*, vol. 18, no. 2 (1981), 67–94.

– "Matrifocal Families in the Canadian North," in K. Ishawaran, ed. *The Canadian Family*, revised edition. Toronto: Holt, Rinehart and Winston 1976.

– "The Potential of Traditional Societies and of Anthropology, Their Predator." *Anthropologica*, vol. 13, nos. 1–2 (1971), 129–42.

– "The Role of Northern Canadian Indian Women in Social Change." M.A. thesis, University of British Columbia 1969.

– *Their Own Yukon*. Whitehorse 1975.

– *Through the Eyes of Strangers: A Preliminary Survey of Land Use History in the Yukon During the Late Nineteenth Century*. Whitehorse: Yukon Archives 1974.

Cumming, Peter and Neil Mickenburg, eds. *Native Rights in Canada*. Toronto: Indian-Eskimo Association of Canada 1972.

Dacks, G. and K. Coates, eds. *Northern Communities: The Prospects of Empowerment*. Edmonton: Boreal Institute for Northern Studies 1988.

Daily, R.C. "The Role of Alcohol Among North American Indian Tribes as Reported in the Jesuit Relations." *Anthropologica*, vol. 10 (1968), 45–57.

de Laguna, Frederica. *The Prehistory of Northern North America As Seen from the Yukon*. Memoirs of the Society for American Archaeology. Menaska: Society for American Archaeology 1947.

– *Under Mount St. Elias: The History and Culture of the Yakutat Tlingit*, in *Smithsonian Contributions to Anthropology*, vol. 7, pt. 1–3. Washington: Smithsonian Institution Press 1972.

Denevan, W.H., ed. *The Native Population of the Americas in 1492*. Madison: University of Wisconsin Press 1976.

Dickason, Olive. "Europeans and Amerindians: Some Comparative Aspects of Early Contact." Canadian Historical Association, *Historical Papers, 1979*, 182–202.

Diubaldo, Richard. *Stefansson and the Canadian Arctic*. Montreal: McGill-Queen's 1978.

Dobyns, Henry F. "Brief Perspectives on a Scholarly Transformation: Widowing the 'Virgin' Land." *Ethnohistory*, vol. 23/2 (spring 1976), 95–104.

– "Estimating Aboriginal American Population: An Appraisal of Techniques with a New Hemispheric Estimate." *Current Anthropology* 7, no. 4 (1966), 395–416.

– *Native American Historical Demography: A Critical Bibliography*. Bloomington: Indiana University Press 1976.

Dozier, E.P. "Problem Drinking Among American Indians: The Role of Sociocultural Deprivation." *Quarterly Studies on Alcohol*, vol. 27, no. 1 (1966), 72–87.

Dubos, R. and J. Dubos. *The White Plague: Tuberculosis, Man and Society*. Boston: Little, Brown and Co. 1952.

Duerden, Frank. "The Evolution and Nature of Contemporary Settlement Patterns in a Selected Area of the Yukon Territory." Centre for Settlement Studies, series L, Research Report no. 3, University of Manitoba 1971.

Duff, Wilson. *The Indian History of British Columbia*, vol. I: *The Impact of the White Man*. Anthropology in British Columbia Memoir no. 5. Victoria: Provincial Museum of Natural History and Anthropology 1969.

Dunning, R.H. "Some Aspects of Governmental Indian Policy and Administration." *Anthropologica*, vol. 4, no. 1 (1962), 209–32.

Dunning, W. "Ethnic Relations and the Marginal Man in Canada." *Human Organization*, vol. 18, no. 3 (1959), 117–22.

Edgerton, Robert and C. MacAndrew. *Drunken Comportment: A Social Explanation*. Chicago: Aldine Publishing Co. 1969.

Elias, Peter. *The Dakota of the Canadian Northwest: Lessons for Survival*. Winnipeg: University of Manitoba Press 1988.

Elliott, David. "Some Constitutional Aspects of the Government of the Yukon Territory." Unpublished manuscript, Yukon Territorial Government.

Ewers, John. "The Influence of Epidemics on the Indian Populations and Cultures of Texas." *Plains Anthropologist*, vol. 18 (1973), 104–15.

Fallding, Harold. "The Source and Burden of Civilization Illustrated in the Use of Alcohol." *Quarterly Journal of Studies on Alcohol*, vol. 25, no. 4 (1964), 714–24.

Fenna, D., L. Mix, O. Schaefer, and J.A.L. Gilbert. "Ethanol Metabolism in Various Racial Groups." *Canadian Medical Association Journal*, vol. 105 (1971), 472–5.

Field, P. "A New Cross-Cultural Study of Drunkenness," in D. Pittman and C. Snyder, eds. *Society, Culture and Drinking Patterns*. New York: J. Wiley 1962.

Fisher, A.D. "A Colonial Education System: Historical Changes and Schooling in Fort Chipewyan." *Canadian Journal of Anthropology*, vol. 2, no. 1 (spring 1981), 37–44.

Fisher, Robin. *Contact and Conflict: Indian-European Relations in British Columbia, 1774–1890*. Vancouver: University of British Columbia Press 1977.

- "Historical Writing on Native People in Canada." *History and Social Science Teacher*, vol. 17, no. 2 (Winter 1982), 65–72.

- "Impact of European Settlement on the Indigenous Peoples of Australia, New Zealand and British Columbia: Some Comparative Dimensions." *Canadian Ethnic Studies*, vol. 12, no. 1 (1980), 1–14.

Fisher, Robin and K. Coates, eds. *Out of the Background: Readings in Canadian Native History*. Toronto: Copp Clark Pitman 1988.

Foster, John E. "The Metis: The People and the Term." *Prairie Forum*, vol. 3, no. 1 (1978), 79–90.

Francis, Daniel and Toby Morantz. *Partners in Furs: A History of the Fur Trade in Eastern James Bay, 1600–1870*. Montreal: McGill-Queen's University Press 1983.

Friesen, Richard. "The Chilkoot Pass and the Great Gold Rush of 1898." Manuscript Report Series no. 236, Parks Canada 1978.

- "The Chilkoot Pass: A Literature Review." Manuscript Report Series no. 203, Parks Canada 1977.

Fuchs, Estelle and Robert Havinghurst. *To Live on This Earth: American Indian Education*. Garden City: Doubleday 1972.

Fumoleau, Rene. *As Long As This Land Shall Last: A History of Treaty 8 and Treaty 11, 1870–1939*. Toronto: McClelland and Stewart 1973.

Gaffin, Jane. *Cashing In*. Ottawa: J. Gaffin 1982.

Galbraith, John S. *The Hudson's Bay Company as an Imperial Factor, 1821–1869*. Toronto: University of Toronto Press 1957.

Gartrell, G.E. "The Work of the Churches in the Yukon during the Era of the Klondike Gold Rush." M.A. thesis, University of Western Ontario 1970.

Getty, Ian and A.S. Lussier, eds. *As Long as the Sun Shines and Water Flows: A Reader in Canadian Native Studies*. Vaucouver: University of British Columbia Press 1983.

Gibbs, M. "History of Chouttla School." Unpublished manuscript, YTA, Acc. 82/77.

Gibson, James R. "European Dependence Upon American Natives: The Case of Russian America." *Ethnohistory*, vol. 25, no. 4 (1978), 359–85.

- "Smallpox on the Northwest Coast, 1835–1838. *BC Studies*, no. 56 (Winter 1982–83), 61–81.

Graham-Cumming, G. "Health of the Original Canadians, 1867–1967." *Medical Services Journal of Canada*, vol. 23 (1967), 115–66.

Grant, John Webster. *Moon of Wintertime: Missionaries and the Indians of Canada in Encounter since 1534*. Toronto: University of Toronto Press 1984.

Grant, Shelagh. *Sovereignty or Security? Government Policy in the Canadian North, 1936–1950*. Vancouver: University of British Columbia Press 1988.

– "The Story of Canol and the Impact on the Land and People." Unpublished manuscript, YTA, Acc. 79/82.

The Gravel Magnet. Television documentary produced by Northern Native Broadcasting Yukon, February 1988.

Green, Lewis. *The Boundary Hunters.* Vancouver: University of British Columbia Press 1982.

– *The Gold Hustlers.* Anchorage: Alaska Northwest Publishing Co. 1977.

Gresko, J. "White 'Rites' and Indian 'Rites': Indian Education and Native Responses in the West, 1870–1910," in A.W. Rasporich, ed. *Western Canada: Past and Present.* Calgary: McClelland and Stewart West 1975, 163–82.

Grove, Kenneth. *A History of the Original Peoples of Northern Canada.* Montreal: McGill-Queen's University Press 1976.

Guest, Dennis. *The Emergence of Social Security in Canada.* Vancouver: University of British Columbia Press 1980.

Guest, Hal. "Dawson City: San Francisco of the North or Bootown in a Bog." Manuscript Report Series no. 241, Parks Canada 1978.

– "A History of the City of Dawson, Yukon Territory, 1896–1920." Microfiche Report Series no. 7, Parks Canada 1983.

Guillemin, Jeanne. "The Politics of National Integration: A Comparison of United States and Canadian Indian Administrations." *Social Problems,* vol. 25, no. 3 (1978), 319–32.

Hagan, William. "On Writing the History of the American Indian." *Journal of Interdisciplinary History,* vol. 2 (summer 1971), 149–54.

Hall, D.J. "Clifford Sifton and Canadian Indian Administration, 1896–1905." *Prairie Forum,* vol. 2, no. 2 (1977), 127–51.

– *Clifford Sifton.* Vol. 1: *The Young Napoleon, 1861–1900.* Vancouver: University of British Columbia Press 1981–85.

Hall, Edwin. "Speculations on the Late Prehistory of the Kutchin Athapaskans." *Ethnohistory,* vol. 16, no. 4 (1969), 317–33.

Hallowell, A.I. "The Backwash of the Frontier: The Impact of the Indian on American Culture," in Walker Wyman and C. Kroeber, eds. *The Frontier in Perspective.* Madison: University of Wisconsin Press, 1957, 229–58.

Hamelin, Louis-Edmond. *Canadian Nordicity: It's Your North, Too.* Montreal: Harvest House 1978.

Hamer, John and Jack Steinbring, eds. *Alcohol and Native Peoples of the North.* Lanham: University Press of America 1980.

Hammond, Lorne. "Any Ordinary Degree of System: The Columbia Department and the Harvesting of Wildlife, 1825–1849." M.A. thesis, University of Victoria 1988.

Harper, Allan. "Canada's Indian Administration: Basic Concepts and Objectives." *America Indigena,* vol. 5, no. 2 (1945), 119–32.

Harris, Burt. Prostitution in the Yukon Territory during the Klondike Gold Rush. Undergraduate essay, University of Calgary, c. 1988.

Harris, Marvin. *Cultural Materialism: The Struggle for a Science of Culture.* New York: Random House 1979.

Hawthorn, H.B., ed. *A Survey of the Contemporary Indians of Canada: A Report Economic, Political and Education Needs and Policies,* pt. II. Ottawa: Queen's Printer 1966–67.

Heidenreich, Conrad. *Huronia: A History and Geography of the Huron Indians, 1600–1650.* Toronto: McClelland and Stewart 1971.

Helm, June, ed. *Handbook of North American Indians.* Vol. 6 *The Subarctic.* Washington: Smithsonian Institution 1981.

– *The Lynx Point People.* Ottawa: National Museum of Canada, Bulletin no. 176, 1961.

Helm, June, T. Alliband, T. Birk, V. Lawson, S. Reisner, C. Sturtevant, and S. Witkowski. "The Contact History of the Subarctic Athapaskans," in A. McFayden Clark, ed. *Proceedings: Northern Athapaskan Conference, 1971,* Canadian Ethnology Service, Paper no. 27, vol. 1. Ottawa: National Museums of Canada, 1975, 302–49.

Helper, Rose. "The Yukon Gold Rush: A Study in Social Disorganization and Reorganization." M.A. thesis, University of Toronto 1945.

Hendry, Charles, *Beyond Traplines. Does the Church Really Care?* Towards an Assessment of the Work of the Anglican Church of Canada with Canada's Native Peoples. Toronto: Ryerson Press 1969.

Henripin, J. *Trends and Factors of Fertility in Canada.* Ottawa: Statistics Canada 1972.

Hillson, John. "Constitutional Development of the Yukon Territory, 1960–1970." M.A. thesis, University of Saskatchewan 1973.

Hinckley, Ted. *The Americanization of Alaska, 1867–1897.* Palo Alto: Pacific Books 1972.

– "We Are More Truly Heathen Than the Natives: John G. Brady and the Assimilation of Alaska's Tlingit Indians." *Western Historical Quarterly,* vol. 11, no. 1 (1980), 37–55.

"History of the Klondyke Indians." Unpublished manuscript, YTA, Acc. 82/84.

Honigman, J. "On the Alaska Highway." *Dalhousie Review* (January 1944), 401–8.

Honigman, John. *Culture and Ethos of Kaska Society.* New Haven: Yale University Press, Yale University Publications in Anthropology, no. 40, 1949.

– *The Kaska Indians: An Ethnographic Reconstruction.* New Haven: Yale University Press, Yale University Publications in Anthropology, no. 51, 1954.

– and I. Honigman. "Drinking in an Indian-White Community." *Quarterly Journal of Studies on Alcohol,* vol. 5, no. 4 (1945), 575–619.

Horton, D. "The Function of Alcohol in Primitive Societies: A Cross-Cultural Approach." *Quarterly Journal of Studies on Alcohol,* vol. 3 (1943), 119–220.

Hunt, W.R. *North of 53°: The Wild Days of the Alaska-Yukon Mining Frontier, 1870–1914.* New York: Macmillan 1974.

Innis, Harold. *The Fur Trade in Canada: An Introduction to Canadian Economic History.* Revised edition. Toronto: University of Toronto Press 1962.

– *Settlement and the Mining Frontier.* Toronto: Macmillan 1936.

Irving, W. "Recent Early Man Research in the North." *Arctic Anthropology,* vol. 8, no. 2 (1971), 68–82.

– and J. Cinq-Mars. "A Tentative Archaeological Sequence for Old Crow Flats, Yukon Territory." *Arctic Anthropology,* vol. 11 supplement (1974), 65–81.

– and C.R. Harrington. "Upper Pleistocene Radio-carbon Dated Artifacts from the Northern Yukon." *Science,* vol. 179 (1973), 335–40.

Iverson, Katherine. "Civilization and Assimilation in the Colonized Schooling of Native Americans," in P. Altback and G. Kelly, *Education and Colonialism.* New York: Longman 1978, 149–80.

Jacobs, Wilbur R. "The Fatal Confrontation: Early Native-White Relations on the Frontiers of Australia, New Guinea and America–A Comparative Study." *Pacific Historical Review,* vol. 40 (1971) 283–309.

– "The Tip of an Iceberg: Pre-Columbian Indian Demography and Some Implications for Revisionism." *William and Mary Quarterly,* 3rd series, vol. 31 (January 1974), 123–32.

Jaenen, Cornelius. "Amerindian Views of French Culture in the Seventeenth Century." *Canadian Historical Review,* vol. 40 (1974): 261–91.

– *Friend and Foe: Aspects of French-Amerindian Cultural Contact in the 16th and 17th Centuries.* Toronto: McClelland and Stewart 1976.

– "The Meeting of the French and Amerindians in the Seventeenth Century." *Revue de l'Université d'Ottawa,* XLIII (1973), 128–44.

Jarvenpa, Robert. "The Ubiquitous Bushman: Chipewyan-White Trapper Relations of the 1930's," in J.W. Helmer, S. van Dyke, and F.J. Kense, eds. *Problems in the Prehistory of the North American Subarctic: The Athapaskan Question.* Calgary: University of Calgary Press 1977 165–83.

Jennings, Francis. *The Invasion of America: Indians, Colonialism and the Cant of Conquest.* Chapel Hill: University of North Carolina Press 1975.

Jennings, John. "The Mounted Police and Canadian Indian Policy, 1873–1896." ph.d. thesis, University of Toronto 1979.

Johnson, S. "Baron Wrangel and the Russian American Company." ph.d. thesis, University of Manitoba 1978.

Johnson, S.D. *Alaska Commercial Company, 1868–1940.* San Francisco 1940.

Jones, Gareth Stedman. *Outcast London: A Study in the Relationship between Classes in Victorian Society.* Oxford: Clarendon Press 1971.

Jones, Ted. *All the Days of His Life: A Biography of Archdeacon H.A. Cody.* Saint John: New Brunswick Museum 1981.

Jordan, Winthrop. *White Over Black: American Attitudes Toward the Negro, 1550–1812.* Williamsburg: University of North Carolina Press 1968.

Kalbach, Warren and Wayne McVey. *The Demographic Bases of Canadian Society*. Toronto: McGraw-Hill Ryerson 1979.

Karamanski, T. *Fur Trade and Exploration: Opening the Far Northwest, 1821–1852*. Vancouver: University of British Columbia Press 1983.

Katz, M. and P. Mattingly, eds. *Education and Social Change: Themes From Ontario's Past*. New York: New York University Press 1975.

Kay, Jeane. "Indian Responses to a Mining Frontier," in William Savage and S. Thompson, eds. *The Frontier: Comparative Studies*, vol. 2. Norman: University of Oklahoma Press 1979, 193–203.

Kehoe, Alice. *North American Indians: A Comprehensive Account*. Englewood Cliffs: Prentice-Hall 1981.

Kelly, Ian. "The Canol Project: Defense, Politics and Oil." M.A. thesis, Trent University 1977.

Kennicott, Robert. "The Journal of Robert Kennicott," in James G. James, ed. *The First Scientific Exploration of Alaska, and the Purchase of Alaska*. Evanston: Northwestern University Press 1942.

King, A. Richard. *The School at Mopass: A Problem of Identity*. New York: Holt, Rinehart and Winston 1967.

Knight, Rolf. *Indians at Work: Native People in the B.C. Labour Force, 1860–1930*. Vancouver: New Star Books 1978.

Krech, S. "Changing Trapping Patterns in Fort McPherson, N.W.T." Ph.D. thesis, Harvard 1974.

Krech, Shephard, III. "Disease, Starvation and North Athapaskan Social Organization." *American Ethnologist*, vol. 5, no. 4 (1978), 710–32.

– "The Eastern Kutchin and the Fur Trade, 1800–1860." *Ethnohistory*, vol. 23/3 (1976), 213–35.

–, ed. *Indians, Animals and the Fur Trade*. Athens: University of Georgia Press 1981.

– "The Nakotcho Kutchin: A Tenth Aboriginal Kutchin Band?" *Journal of Anthropological Research*, vol. 35, no. 1 (1979), 109–21.

– "On the Aboriginal Population of the Kutchin." *Arctic Anthropology*, vol. 15, no. 1 (1978) 89–104.

– *The Subarctic Fur Trade: Native Social and Economic Adaptations*. Vancouver: University of British Columbia Press 1984.

– "Throwing Bad Medicine: Sorcery, Disease and the Fur Trade Among the Kutchin and Other Northern Athapaskans," in S. Krech III, ed. *Indians, Animals and the Fur Trade*. Athens: University of Georgia 1981, 73–108.

Kroeber, A.L. *Cultural and Natural Areas of Native North America*. Berkeley: University of California Press 1963.

Lain, D.B. "The Fort Yukon Affair, 1869." *Alaska Journal*, vol. 7, no. 1 (1977), 12–17.

Lange, Lynda. "The Changing Structure of Dene Elders, and of Marriage, in the Context of Colonialism: The Experience of Fort Franklin, 1945–1985," in G. Dacks and K. Coates, eds., *Northern Communities: The Prospects for Empowerment*. Edmonton: Boreal Institute 1988, 23–32.

Lantis, M.. ed. *Ethnohistory in Southwestern Alaska and the Southern Yukon*. Lexington: University of Kentucky Press 1970.

Leacock, Eleanor B. and Nancy O. Lurie, eds. *North American Indians in Historical Perspective*. New York: Random House 1971.

Lee, Richard and I. DeVore, eds. *Man the Hunter*. Chicago: Aldine Publishing Company 1968.

Leechman, D. *The Vunta Kutchin*. National Museums of Canada. Bulletin no. 130. Ottawa: Queen's Printer 1954.

Legros, Dominque. "Structure Socio-Culturelle et rapports de domination chez les Tutchone Septentrionaux du Yukon au dix neuvième siècle." ph.d. thesis, University of British Columbia 1981.

Leighton, Douglas. "The Development of Federal Indian Policy in Canada, 1840–1890." ph.d. thesis, University of Western Ontario 1975.

Lemert, E.M. "The Use of Alcohol in Three Salish Indian Tribes." *Quarterly Journal of Studies on Alcohol*, vol. 19, no. 1 (1958), 90–107.

Leslie, John and R. Maguire, eds. *The Historical Development of the Indian Act*. Ottawa: Indian and Northern Affairs Canada, Treaties and Research Centre 1978.

Levy, Jerrold and S. Kunitz. *Indian Drinking: Navaho Practices and Anglo-American Theories*. New York: J. Wiley 1974.

Linton, Ralph, ed. *Acculturation in Seven American Indian Tribes*. New York: Appleton-Century 1940.

Lurie, Nancy. "Ethnohistory: An Ethnological Point of View." *Ethnohistory*, vol. 8/1 (1961), 78–92.

– "The World's Oldest On-Going Protest Demonstration: North American Indian Drinking Patterns." *Pacific Historical Review*, vol. 40 (1971), 311–32.

Lysyk, K., E. Bohmer, and W. Phelps. *Alaska Highway Pipeline Inquiry*. Ottawa: Supply and Services Canada 1977.

McArthur, Norma. *Island Populations of the Pacific*. Canberra: Australian National University Press 1967.

McCandless, R. *Yukon Wildlife: A Social History*. Edmonton: University of Alberta Press 1985.

McCandless, Robert. "Trophies or Meat: Yukon Game Management." Unpublished manuscript, yta.

McClellan, Catharine. "Culture Contacts in the Early Historic Period in Northwestern North America." *Arctic Anthropology*, vol. 2, no. 2 (1964), 3–15.

– "Feuding and Warfare among Northern Athapaskans," in A.M. Clark, ed. *Proceedings: Northern Athapaska Conference, 1971*, vol. 1. Canadian Ethnology Service Paper no. 27. Ottawa: National Museum of Canada 1975, 181–258.

- "Indian Stories about the First Whites in Northwestern America," in M. Lantis, ed. *Ethnohistory in Southwestern Alaska and the Southern Yukon*. Lexington: University of Kentucky Press 1970, 103–33.
- *My Old People Say: An Ethnographic Survey of Southern Yukon Territory*. Ottawa: National Museum of Canada 1975.

McClellan, Catharine et al. *Part of the Land, Part of the Water: A History of the Yukon Indians*. Vancouver: Douglas and McIntyre 1987.

McCullum, H. and K. McCullum. *This Land Is Not for Sale: Canada's Original People and Their Land, a Saga of Neglect, Exploitation, and Conflict*. Toronto: Anglican Book Centre 1975.
- and John Olthius. *Moratorium: Justice, Energy, the North and the Native People*. Toronto: Anglican Book Centre 1977.

MacDonald, Malcolm. *Down North*. Toronto: Oxford University Press 1943.

MacGregor, J.G. *The Klondike Rush Through Edmonton, 1897–1898*. Toronto: McClelland and Stewart 1970.

MacInnes, T.R.L. "History of Indian Administration in Canada." *Canadian Journal of Economics and Political Science*, vol. 12, no. 3 (1946), 387–394.

McLeod, R.C. *The NWMP and Law Enforcement, 1873–1905*. Toronto: University of Toronto Press 1976.

McNeill, William. *Plagues and People*. Garden City: Anchor/Doubleday 1976.

Marchand, J.F. "Tribal Epidemics in the Yukon." *Journal of the American Medical Association*, CXXII (1943), 1019–20.

Martin, Calvin. "Ethnohistory: A Better Way to Write Indian History." *Western Historical Quarterly*, vol. 9 (1978), 41–56.
- "The European Impact on the Culture of a Northeastern Algonquian Tribe: An Ecological Interpretation." *William and Mary Quarterly*, 3rd series, vol. 31 (January 1974), 3–26.
- *Keepers of the Game: Indian-Animal Relationships and the Fur Trade*. Berkeley: University of California Press 1978.
- "The Metaphysics of Writing Indian-White History." *Ethnohistory*, vol. 26/2 (1979), 153–60.

May, Philip. "Arrests, Alcohol and Alcohol Legalization Among An American Indian Tribe." *Plains Anthropologist*, vol. 20, no. 8 (1975), 129–34.

Meek, R.J. "Report on the Yukon Indian Agency." Unpublished report, 1955.

Memmi, Albert. *Dominated Man: Notes toward a Portrait*. New York: Orion Press 1968.

Miller, James. *Skyscrapers Hide the Heavens: A History of Indian-White Relations in Canada*. Toronto: University of Toronto Press 1989.

Miller, Virginia. "The Decline of Nova Scotia Micmac Population, AD 1600–1850." *Culture*, vol. 2, no. 3 (1982), 107–20.

Milloy, J. *The Plains Cree: Trade, Diplomacy and War, 1790 to 1870*. Winnipeg: University of Manitoba Press 1988.

The Mission School Syndrome. Television documentary produced by Northern Native Broadcasting Yukon, 1988.

Monkman, Leslie. *A Native Heritage: Images of the Indian in English-Canadian Literature.* Toronto: University of Toronto Press 1981.

Monnet, Rev. A. "The Oblates and the Yukon." Unpublished essay.

Mooney, James. *The Aboriginal Population of America North of Mexico.* Washington: Smithsonian Institution, Miscellaneous Collection 80, no. 7, 1928.

Moore, P.E. "No Longer Captain: A History of Tuberculosis and Its Control amongst Canadian Indians." *Canadian Medical Association Journal,* vol. 84 (1961), 1012–16.

Morice, Adrian. *History of the Catholic Church in Western Canada.* 2 vols. Toronto: Musson Book Co. 1910.

Morlan, R.E. "The Late Prehistory of the Middle Porcupine Drainage, Yukon Territory." ph.d. thesis, University of Wisconsin, 1971.

Morner, Magnus. *Race Mixture in the History of Latin America.* Boston: Little, Brown 1967.

Morrison, David R. *The Politics of the Yukon Territory, 1898–1909.* Toronto: University of Toronto Press 1968.

Morrison, W.R. "Native Peoples of the Northern Frontier," in Hugh Dempsey, ed. *Men in Scarlet.* Calgary: McClelland and Stewart West 1974, 77–94.

– "The North-West Mounted Police and the Klondike Gold Rush." *Journal of Contemporary History,* vol. 9, no. 2 (1974), 93–106.

– *Showing the Flag: The Mounted Police and Canadian Sovereignty in the North, 1894–1925.* Vancouver: University of British Columbia Press 1985.

Muise, D.A., ed. *Approaches to Native History in Canada* [History Division Paper, no. 25]. Ottawa: National Museums of Canada 1977.

Mulhall, D. *Will to Power: The Missionary Career of Father Morice.* Vancouver: University of British Columbia Press 1986.

Nash, Gary B. *Red, White and Black: The Peoples of Early America.* Englewood Cliffs: Prentice-Hall 1974.

– "Whither Indian History: A Review Essay." *Journal of Ethnic Studies,* vol. 4, no. 3 (1976), 69–76.

Nelson, Richard K. *Hunters of the Northern Forest: Designs for Survival Among the Alaskan Kutchin.* Chicago: University of Chicago Press 1973.

Newell, Diane. "Importance of Information and Misinformation in the Making of the Klondike Gold Rush." *Journal of Canadian Studies,* vol. 21, no. 4 (Winter 1986/87), 95–111.

Nielsen, Erik. *The House Is Not a Home.* Toronto: Macmillan 1989.

Nixon, P.G. "Eskimo Housing Programs, 1954–1965: A Case Study in Representative Bureaucracy." ph.d. thesis, University of Western Ontario 1984.

O'Neill, John. "The Politics of Health in the Fourth World: A Northern Canadian Example," in K. Coates and W.R. Morrison, eds. *Interpreting Canada's North.* Toronto: Copp Clark Pitman 1989.

Orlove, Benjamin. *Alpacas, Sheep and Men: The Wool Export Economy and Regional Society of Southern Peru*. New York: Academic Press 1977.

Osgood, Cornelius. *Contributions to the Ethnography of the Kutchin*. Yale University Publications in Anthropology, no. 7. New Haven: Yale University Press 1936.

– *The Distribution of the Northern Athapaskan Indians*. Yale University Publications in Anthropology, no. 14. New Haven: Yale University Press 1936.

– *The Han Indians*. Yale University Publications in Anthropology, no. 74. New Haven: Yale University Press 1971.

– "Kutchin Tribal Distribution and Synonymy." *American Anthropologist*, vol. 36 (1934), 168–79.

Ostenstat, W. "The Impact of the Fur Trade on the Tlingit." M.A. thesis, University of Manitoba 1976.

Owram, Douglas. *Promise of Eden: The Canadian Expansionist Movement and the Image of the West, 1856–1900*. Toronto: University of Toronto Press 1980.

Pannekoek, Fritz. "Protestant Agricultural Zions for the Western Indian." *Journal of the Canadian Church Historical Society*, vol. 14, no. 3 (1972), 55–66.

Pargellis, S. "The Problem of American Indian History." *Ethnohistory*, vol. 4/2 (1957), 113–24.

Parker, James. "The Fur Trade and the Chipewyan Indian." *Western Canadian Journal of Anthropology*, vol. 3, no. 1 (1972), 43–57.

Patterson, E. Palmer. *The Canadian Indian: A History since 1500*. Don Mills: Collier-Macmillan 1972.

Peake, Frank. *The Anglican Church in British Columbia*. Vancouver: Mitchell Press 1959.

– *The Bishop Who Ate His Boots*. Don Mills: Anglican Church of Canada 1966.

– "Fur Traders and Missionaries: Some Reflections on the Attitudes of the H.B.C. Towards Missionary Work Among the Indians." *Western Canadian Journal of Anthropology*, vol. 3, no. 1 (1972), 72–93.

– "Robert McDonald (1829–1913): The Great Unknown Missionary of the Northwest." *Journal of the Canadian Church Historical Society*, vol. 17, no. 3 (1975), 54–72.

Peterson, Jaqueline and J. Anfinson. "The Indian and the Fur Trade: A Review of Recent Literature." *Manitoba History*, no. 10 (autumn 1985), 10–18.

Philip, Kenneth. "The New Deal and Alaskan Natives, 1936–1945." *Pacific Historical Review*, vol. 50, (1981), 309–27.

Ponting, J.R. and R. Gibbins. *Out of Irrelevance: A Socio-Political Introduction to Indian Affairs in Canada*. Toronto: Butterworths 1980.

Powell, Alan. *Far Country: A Short History of the Northern Territory*. Carlton: Melbourne University Press 1982.

Prentice, Alison. *The School Promoters: Education and Social Class in Mid-Nineteenth Upper Canada*. Toronto: McClelland and Stewart 1977.

Prucha, Francis Paul. *American Indian Policy in Crisis: Christian Reformers and the Indian, 1865–1900*. Norman: University of Oklahoma Press 1975.

– *Americanizing the American Indians: Writings by the "Friends of the Indian," 1880–1900*. Cambridge: Harvard University Press 1973.

– *The Churches and the Indian Schools, 1888–1912*. Lincoln: University of Nebraska Press 1979.

– *Indian Policy in the United States: Historical Essays*. Lincoln: University of Nebraska Press 1981.

Ray, A.J. "Periodic Shortages, Native Welfare and the Hudson's Bay Company, 1670–1930," in S. Krech III, ed. *The Sub-Arctic Fur Trade*. Vancouver: University of British Columbia Press 1984, 1–20.

Ray, Arthur. "Competition and Conservation in the Early Subarctic Fur Trade." *Ethnohistory*, vol. 25, no. 4 (1978), 347–57.

– "Diffusion of Diseases in the Western Interior of Canada, 1830–1850," in S.E.D. Shortt, ed. *Medicine in Canadian Society*. Montreal: McGill-Queen's University Press 1981.

– "Fur Trade History As an Aspect of Native History," in Ian Getty and Donald Smith, eds. *One Century Later: Western Canadian Reserve Indians Since Treaty 7*. Vancouver: University of British Columbia Press 1977.

– "The H.B.C. Account Books As Sources for Comparative Economic Analysis of the Fur Trade: An Examination of Exchange Rate Data." *Western Canadian Journal of Anthropology*, vol. 6 (1976), 30–51.

– *Indians in the Fur Trade*. Toronto: University of Toronto Press 1974.

– "Periodic Shortages," in Shephard Krech, ed. *The Sub-Arctic Fur Trade*. Vancouver: University of British Columbia Press 1984.

– "Reflections on Fur Trade Social History and Metis History in Canada." *American Indian Culture and Research Journal*, vol. 6, no. 1 (1982), 91–107.

– "Some Conservation Schemes of the Hudson's Bay Company, 1821–1850: An Examination of the Problems of Resource Management in the Fur Trade." *Journal of Historical Geography*, vol. 1, no. 1 (1975), 49–68.

– and Donald Freeman. *"Give Us Good Measure": An Economic Analysis of Relations between the Indians and the Hudson's Bay Company before 1763*. Toronto: University of Toronto Press 1978.

Raymond, Charles. "Reconnaissance of the Yukon River," in US Government, *Compilation of Narratives of Explorations in Alaska*. Washington: Government Printing Office 1900.

Rea, Kenneth J. *The Political Economy of the Canadian North*. Toronto: University of Toronto Press 1968.

– *The Political Economy of Northern Development*. Science Council of Canada Background Study no. 36. Ottawa: Science Council of Canada 1976.

Remley, David. *Crooked Road: The Story of the Alaska Highway*. Toronto: McGraw Hill 1976.

Rich, A.R. *The Pathogenisis of Tuberculosis*. 2nd edition. Springfield: C.C. Thomas 1951.

Rich, E.E. *The Fur Trade and the Northwest to 1857*. Toronto: McClelland and Stewart 1967.

– "Trade Habits and Economic Motivation among the Indians of North America." *Canadian Journal of Economics and Political Science*, vol. 26, no. 1 (1960), 35–53.

Riches, David. *Northern Nomadic Hunter-Gatherers: A Humanisitic Approach*. London: Academic Press 1982.

Riggs, T. "Running the Alaska Boundary." *Beaver*, outfit 276 (September 1945), 40–3.

Robbins, Stanley and R. Cotram. *Pathologic Basis of Disease*. Toronto: W.R. Saunders 1979.

Romaniuk, Anatole and Victor Piche. "Natality Estimates for the Canadian Indians by Stable Population Models, 1900–1969." *Canadian Review of Sociology and Anthropology*, vol. 9, no. 1 (1972), 1–20.

Rotstein, Abraham. "The Fur Trade," in A. Rotstein, *The Precarious Homestead*. Toronto: New Press 1973, 135–58.

Rutman, D.B. and A.H. Rutman. "Of Agues and Fevers: Malaria in the Early Chesapeake." *William and Mary Quarterly*, 3rd series, vol. 33 (January 1976), 31–60.

Sahlins, Marshall. "Notes on the Original Affluent Society," in *Stone Age Economics* (Chicago: Aldine-Atherton 1972).

Saum, Lewis. *The Fur Trader and the Indian*. Seattle, University of Washington Press 1965.

Saunders, D.E. "Native People in Areas of Internal National Expansion." *Saskatchewan Law Review*, vol. 38, no. 1 (1974), 63–87.

Scott, Duncan C. "Indian Affairs, 1840–1867," in A. Shortt and A. Doughty, eds. *Canada and Its Provinces*, vol. V. Toronto: Glasgow, Brook 1914, 331–62.

Sealey, Gary. "The History of the Hudson's Bay Company, 1870–1910." M.A. thesis, University of Western Ontario 1967.

Sheehan, B. "Indian-White Relations in Early America: A Review Essay." *William and Mary Quarterly*, 3rd series, vol. 26 (1969), 267–86.

Sheehan, N. et al. *Schools of the West*. Calgary: Detselig 1986.

Slobodin, Richard. "The Dawson Boys: Peel River Indians and the Klondike Gold Rush." *Polar Notes*, vol. 5 (1963), 24–35.

– *Metis of the Mackenzie District*. Ottawa: Canadian Research Centre for Anthropology 1966.

Smith, Glenn. "Education for the Natives of Alaska: The Work of the United States Bureau of Education, 1884–1931." *Journal of the West*, vol. 6, no. 3 (1967), 440–50.

Southwick, L., C. Steele, A. Marlatt, and M. Lindell. "Alcohol-related Expec-
tancies: Defined by Phase of Intoxication and Drinking Experience." *Journal
of Consulting and Clinical Psychology*, vol. 49, no. 5 (1981), 713–21.

Spicer, Edward H. *Cycles of Conquest: The Impact of Spain, Mexico and the United
States on the Indians of the South-West, 1533–1960*. Tucson: University of
Arizona Press 1962.

Stager, John. "Fur Trading Posts in the Mackenzie Region up to 1850." Canadian Association of Geographers, British Columbia Division, *Occasional
Papers in Geography*, vol. 3 (1962), 37–46.

Stanley, G.F.G. "The Indian Background of Canadian History." Canadian Historical Association, *Annual Report, 1952*, 14–21.

Stefansson, V. *The Northward Course of Empire*. New York: Harcourt, Brace 1922.

– *Northwest to Fortune*. London: Allen and Unwin 1958.

Sternsher, Bernard. *Consensus, Conflict and American Historians*. Bloomington:
Indiana University Press 1975.

Stevenson, Alex. "Herschel Haven." *North*, vol. 15, no. 6 (1968), 24–32.

– "Lawless Land." *North*, vol. 16, no. 1 (1969), 22–30.

– "Whaler's Wait." *North*, vol. 15, no. 5 (1968), 24–32.

Stewart, E. "Kutchin Trade Prior to 1840." *Beaver*, outfit 310 (Summer 1979),
54–8.

Stewart, E.G. "Fort McPherson and the Peel River Area." M.A. thesis, Queen's
University 1955.

Stock, Eugene. *The History of the Church Missionary Society*. London: Church
Missionary Society 1899.

Stoddard, N.B. "Some Ethnological Aspects of the Russian Fur Trade," in
Malvina Bolus, ed. *People and Pelts: Selected Papers of the Second North American Fur Trade Conference*. Winnipeg: Peguis 1972, 39–58.

Stone, Thomas. "Flux and Authority in a Subarctic Society: The Yukon Miners in the Nineteenth Century." *Ethnohistory*, Vol. 30/4 (1983), 203–16.

– "The Mounties As Vigilantes: Perceptions of Community and the Transformation of Law in the Yukon, 1885–1897." *Law and Society Review*, vol.
14, no. 1 (1979), 83–114.

– "Whalers and Missionaries at Herschel Island." *Ethnohistory*, vol. 28 (1981),
101–24.

Stuart, Richard. "The Underdevelopment of Yukon, 1840–1960: An Overview." Unpublished paper presented to Canadian Historical Association,
Montreal 1980.

Surtees, Robert. *Canadian Indian Policy: A Critical Bibliography*. Bloomington:
Indiana University Press 1982.

Szasz, Margaret. *Education and the American Indian: The Road to Self-Determination, 1928–1973*. Albuquerque: University of New Mexico Press 1974.

Tanner, Adrian. "The Structure of Fur Trade Relations." M.A. thesis, University of British Columbia, 1966.

− *Trappers, Hunters and Fishermen: Wildlife Utilization in the Yukon Territory.* Ottawa: Department of Northern Affairs and Natural Resources 1966.

Taylor, William B. *Drinking, Homicide, and Rebellion in Colonial Mexican Villages.* Stanford: Stanford University Press 1979.

Tennant, Paul. "Native Indian Political Organization in British Columbia, 1900–1969: A Response to Internal Colonialism." *BC Studies,* no. 55 (Autumn 1982), 3–49.

Thomas, Lewis. *The Struggle for Responsible Government in the Northwest Territories, 1870–97,* 2nd edition. Toronto: University of Toronto Press 1978.

Titley, Brian. "Indian Industrial Schools in Western Canada," in N. Sheehan, J.D. Wilson, and D. Jones, eds. *Schools in the West.* Calgary: Detselig Enterprises 1986.

− *A Narrow Vision: Duncan Campbell Scott and the Administration of Indian Affairs in Canada.* Vancouver: University of British Columbia Press 1986.

Tobias, John. "Protection, Civilization, Assimilation: An Outline History of Canada's Indian Policy." *Western Canadian Journal of Anthropology,* vol. 6, no. 2 (1976), 13–30.

Trigger, Bruce. *Children of the Aataentsic: A History of the Huron People to 1660.* 2 vols. Montreal: McGill-Queen's University Press 1976.

− *Natives and Newcomers.* Montreal: McGill-Queen's University Press 1985.

− "The Historians' Indian: Native Americans in Canadian Historical Writing from Charlevoix to the Present." *Canadian Historical Review* 67, no. 3 (1986), 315–42.

Ugarenko, Susan. "The Distribution of the Kutchin and Their Spatial Patterns of Trade, 1700–1850." M.A. thesis, York University 1979.

Upton, L.F.S. "Contact and Conflict on the Atlantic and Pacific Coasts of Canada." *Acadiensis,* vol. 9, no. 2 (1980), 3–13.

− "The Extermination of the Beotucks of Newfoundland," in Robin Fisher and Ken Coates, eds. *Out of the Background: Readings on Canadian Native History.* Toronto: Copp Clark Pitman 1988, 45–65.

− *Micmacs and Colonists: Indian-White Relations in the Maritimes, 1713–1867.* Vancouver: University of British Columbia Press 1979.

− "The Origins of Canadian Indian Policy." *Journal of Canadian Studies,* vol. 8, no. 4 (1973), 51–61.

Usher, Jean. "Apostles and Aborigines: The Social Theory of the Church Missionary Society." *Histoire sociale/Social History,* vol. 4 (April 1971), 28–52.

− "Duncan of Metlakatla: The Victorian Origins of a Model Indian Community," in W.L. Morton, ed. *The Shield of Achilles: Aspects of Canada in the Victorian Age.* Toronto: McClelland and Stewart 1968, 286–310.

− *William Duncan of Metlakatla: A Victorian Missionary in British Columbia.* Ottawa: National Museums of Canada 1974.

Usher, Peter. "Canadian Western Arctic, a Century of Change." *Anthropologica,* vol. 13, no. 1/2 (1971), 169–83.

– "The Growth and Decay of the Trading and Trapping Frontiers in the Western Canadian Arctic." *Canadian Geographer*, vol. 19, no. 4 (1975), 308–20.

– "The North: Metropolitan Frontier, Native Homeland?" in L.D. McCann, ed. *Heartland and Hinterland: A Geography of Canada*. Scarborough: Prentice-Hall 1982, 410–56.

Van Kirk, Sylvia. *Many Tender Ties: Women in Fur Trade Society in Western Canada, 1670–1870*. Winnipeg: Watson and Dwyer 1980.

VanStone, James. *Athapaskan Adaptations: Hunters and Fishermen of the Subarctic Forests*. Chicago: Aldine 1974.

– *Ingalik Contact Ecology: An Ethnohistory of the Lower-Middle Yukon, 1790–1935*. Anthropological series no. 71. Chicago Field Museum of Natural History 1979.

Waldram, James. *As Long As the Rivers Run: Hydroelectric Development and Native Communities in Western Canada*. Winnipeg: University of Manitoba Press 1988.

Walker, J.W. "The Indian in Canadian Historical Writing." Canadian Historical Association, *Historical Papers*, 1971, 21–51.

– "The Indian in Canadian Historical Writing, 1971–1981," in Ian Getty and A.S. Lussier, eds. *As Long As the Sun Shines and Water Flows*. Vancouver: University of British Columbia Press 1983.

Wallace, A.F.C. "Revitalization Movements." *American Anthropologist*, vol. 58, (1956), 264–81.

Warner, Iris. "Herschel Island." *Alaska Journal*, vol. 3, no. 3 (1973), 130–43.

– "Taylor and Drury Ltd., Yukon Merchants." *Alaska Journal*, vol. 5, no. 2 (1975), 74–80.

Washburn, Wilcomb. "Ethnohistory: History 'In the Round.'" *Ethnohistory* 8 (1961): 31–48.

Washburne, C. *Primitive Drinking: A Study of the Uses and Functions of Alcohol in Pre-Literate Societies*. New York: College and University Press 1961.

Watkins, Mel, ed. *Dene Nation: The Colony Within*. Toronto: University of Toronto Press 1977.

Weaver, Sally. *Making Canadian Indian Policy: The Hidden Agenda, 1968–1970*. Toronto: University of Toronto Press 1981.

Webb, Melody. *The Last Frontier: A History of the Yukon Basin of Canada and Alaska*. Albuquerque: University of New Mexico Press 1985.

Welsh, A. Ancheson. "Nomads in Town: The Kutchin of Old Crow." ph.d. thesis, Cornell University 1977.

Welsh, Ann. "Community Pattern and Settlement Pattern in the Development of Old Crow Village, y.t." *Western Canadian Journal of Anthropology*, vol. 2, no. 1 (1970), 17–30.

Wesbrook, M. "A Venture into Ethnohistory: The Journals of V.C. Sim." *Polar Notes*, no. 9 (May 1969).

Westfall, William. "On the Concept of Region in Canadian History and Literature." *Journal of Canadian Studies*, vol. 15, no. 2 (1980), 3–15.

Wharett, G. *The Miracle of the Empty Beds: A History of Tuberculosis in Canada.* Toronto: University of Toronto Press 1977.

Whitehead, Margaret. "Christianity, a Matter of Choice: The Historic Role of Indian Catechists in Oregon Territory and British Columbia." *Pacific Northwest Quarterly*, vol. 72, no. 3 (1981), 98–106.

– *They Call Me Father: Memoirs of Father Nicolas Coccola.* Vancouver: University of British Columbia Press 1988.

Williams, R.M., M.S. Goldman, and D.L. Williams. "Expectancy and Pharmacological Effects of Alcohol on Human Cognitive and Motor Performance: The Compensation for Alcohol Effect." *Journal of Abnormal Psychology*, vol. 90, no. 3 (1981), 267–70.

Willson, Beckles. *The Life of Lord Strathcona and Mount Royal.* London: Cassels 1915.

Wilson, Clifford. *Campbell of the Yukon.* Toronto: Macmillan of Canada 1970.

Wilson, J. Donald, ed. "Schooling on a Distant Frontier: Yukon's Educational Heritage." Unpublished manuscript, YTA, Acc. 82/526.

Wright, A.A. "The Kluane Area." Unpublished manuscript, YTA.

– *Prelude to Bonanza: The Discovery and Exploration of the Yukon.* Sidney: Gray's 1976.

Yerbury, J.C. "The Nahanny Indians and the Fur Trade, 1800–1840." *Musk-Ox*, No. 28 (1981), 43–57.

– *The Subarctic Indians and the Fur Trade, 1680–1860.* Vancouver: University of British Columbia Press 1986.

Young, T.K. "Changing Patterns of Health and Sickness among the Cree-Ojibwa of N.W. Ontario." *Medical Anthropology*, vol. 3, no. 2 (1979), 191–223.

Zagaskin, L.A. *Lieutenant Zagaskin's Travel in Russian America, 1842–1844.* Toronto: University of Toronto Press 1967.

Zaslow, Morris. *The Northward Expansion of Canada, 1914–1967.* Toronto: McClelland and Stewart 1988.

– *The Opening of the Canadian North, 1870–1914.* Toronto: McClelland and Stewart 1971.

– *Reading the Rocks: The Story of the Geological Survey of Canada, 1842–1972.* Toronto: Macmillan 1975.

Index